The Architecture of Distributed Computer Systems

A Data Engineering Perspective on Information Systems

Richard L. Shuey, David L. Spooner, and Ophir Frieder

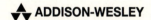 **ADDISON-WESLEY**

An imprint of Addison Wesley Longman, Inc.

Reading, Massachusetts • Harlow, England • Menlo Park, California
Berkeley, California • Don Mills, Ontario • Sydney • Bonn • Amsterdam
Tokyo • Mexico City

Editorial Production Services   Amy Willcutt
Compositor   Michael Wile
Cover Designer   Diana Coe
Technical Artist   George Nichols

Library of Congress Cataloging-in-Publication Data

Shuey, Richard L.
    The architecture of distributed computer systems : a data
engineering perspective on information systems / Richard L. Shuey,
David L. Spooner, and Ophir Frieder.
      p. cm.
    Includes bibliographical references and index.
    ISBN 0-201-55332-5
    1. Electronic data processing--Distributed processing.
2. Computer architecture.   I. Spooner, David L.   II. Frieder,
Ophir.   III. Title.
QA76.9.D5S543 1997   96-46975
004'.36--dc21   CIP

Access the latest information about Addison-Wesley titles from our World Wide Web page: http://www.awl.com/cseng

1 2 3 4 5 6 7 8 9 10-MA-00999897

Preface

As technologies and industries converge, what is emerging is a new "global information industry." The new marketplace will no longer be divided along current sectorial lines. There may not be cable companies or phone companies or computer companies, as such.... There will be information conduits, information providers, information appliances and information consumers.

Al Gore, Vice President of the United States

Distributed computer systems will be of increasing importance in our society. This we take as a key premise in this book. In distributed systems, shared data may be the only thing that binds together different subsystems. Thus the key paradigms and concepts of distributed systems should be associated with data considerations. Designing a distributed system so that the data required by its individual components, applications, and processes will be available when needed in the proper form, and with appropriate security, etc. is a substantial engineering task. Data engineering is the area of activity dedicated to developing the design and implementation discipline required in meeting that task.

Distributed information systems are a combination of distributed applications and supporting distributed computer systems. Architecture in this context considers the overall requirements of an information system and merges hardware and software considerations into a coordinated and integrated view. As shared data provide the basis for coordination and integration, we view distributed computer architecture from a data engineering perspective. Our emphasis is the generic underlying processes, limitations, and tradeoffs implicit in such systems.

If the sharing or exchange of data plays a key role in distributed systems, then both communication and database issues are of great importance. Those issues extend far beyond the classical "transport" perspective of communications engineering and centralized databases in computer science. It becomes impossible to establish a clear line of demarcation between computing (e.g., node database operations and computation) and communications functions (e.g., data transport and associated data manipulation). Rather than viewing these as separate fields, it is far better to integrate the technologies. That integration will be emphasized in this book. There are no separate computer and communications problems. There is a single problem, that of distributed information systems, and our thinking should be based on that principle. We are concerned with the architecture for such systems.

We believe that there is a gap today between the books available on computer architecture and the needs of the information system designer. The computer per se functioning as a single computing engine is well covered in other publications. Research and literature on multiprocessor computers is increasing. There is little that addresses in a comprehensive and fundamental sense the heterogeneous, widely spaced, computer and database systems that make up distributed information systems. It is to be expected that such systems will continue to play an ever-increasing role in our society. That trend is driven by ever-expanding technological capabilities, the desire of computer users to more fully integrate their information systems, the existence of heterogeneous systems that must pragmatically be evolved, not redone, and the certainty that in the foreseeable future users will continue to implement and introduce new systems that are not members of a homogeneous family. The overriding architectural challenge is the development of a structure and framework that will permit heterogeneous systems to work together. An equally important area is the development of automated tools that will make possible design and implementation. The purpose of this book is to address the fundamentals of these areas. Emphasis is given more to the underlying science and engineering as well as the associated issues and tradeoffs than to the details of current practice.

In addressing this broader field we must of necessity cover the relevant parts of both computer and communications technology. Emphasis is given to important relevant areas that are not generally covered in computer science curricula. Unfortunately, our understanding of the technology of distributed information systems is immature. In this book, we cannot present overall solutions or a formal framework in which many of the questions involved in the design of large systems can be answered. The framework does not exist today. Our focus is on those parameters that are important in distributed systems. Our objectives are to present what is known today and to provide insight into the tradeoffs that are an essential part of design. In the process, we believe that we can develop a realistic perspective of the field some insight about what can be done, and an understanding of key issues and research opportunities.

It may be said that in such an approach more issues are raised than there are solutions provided. Distributed information systems are a "leading edge" area of work. As is often the case in exciting new areas of science, understanding the issues and tradeoffs, and incidentally specialized small domain models and systems, will very likely come before the development of a fundamental understanding and satisfactory "closed form" solutions. Furthermore, the design and implementation of state-of-the-art systems will be dependent on an understanding of tradeoffs and a willingness to make design decisions based on those tradeoffs. Tradeoff decisions must often be made in the absence of adequate standards, models, and design discipline. This may be true in application areas where models of the relevant processes exist, but those models do not scale to the magnitude of the real-world problems at hand. Throughout, liberal use is made of examples. The text also includes a discussion of those aspects of social, economic, industrial, business and government environments that appear relevant to, and impact on, the technology and implementation of distributed systems.

If we consider the fine-grain (sub) disciplines of computer science and computer engineering, distributed computer systems are, in that context, a multidisciplinary field. The different aspects of distributed systems share the technology of those fine-grain disciplines. For example, communications switching is relevant to single computers, multiprocessors, electronic chip design, security issues, networks, protocol matters, memory hierarchies, and so forth. As another example, database management is relevant to almost all aspects of distributed computing, including most of those mentioned in the preceding sentence. An overall viewpoint must consider the common features of and interactions between the various fine-grain technologies. Consequently, the reader will find that key core technologies, usually from a different perspective, are discussed at multiple locations and under different topics in the book. To the degree that it is possible, the relevant fine-grain technology will first be discussed in its own right and later in the context of overall distributed systems.

It is our hope that this book will be useful to the practicing computer and information system designer, the communications engineer, and to those responsible for research and academic courses in information science and engineering. Academically, we expect that this volume will fill a role in upper division and graduate education in computer science, computer system engineering, communications engineering, and management. The problems that appear at the end of each chapter include essay type questions requiring analysis and decision processes similar to those demonstrated in quality research and design. Those early in the book are often directed at getting students to think about some of the issues at an early time. In addition, the answers from the class will indicate to the instructor the background level of members of the class. The book is organized into the chapters reviewed below.

Chapter 1: Introduction

The importance of distributed systems is discussed with emphasis on societal systems and from an information system viewpoint. In most cases, the use of the term computer system is synonymous with the term information system. The focus of the book is on heterogeneous distributed computer systems where in general the different components are working on different problems. Such systems are the general case of both free-standing and homogeneous distributed systems. The objective of the book is to address, at a relatively high architectural level, the fundamental issues in distributed computer/information systems.

It is important that one consider the distribution of both computer systems per se and the distributed development of information systems and their applications. This is the environment that must be served. Emphasis is given to the key role of data and the ability to exchange data in making distributed systems possible. In recognition of the key role that data play, the concept of data engineering is introduced.

Because of the importance of distributed information systems and the role of information system architecture, there is discussion of what the term architecture means and what we expect architectural considerations to provide. The discussion emphasizes heterogeneous systems as distinct from multiprocessor systems. Heterogeneous systems are the general case.

The ability to exchange data between components is a core requirement of distributed systems. It follows that communication and database technologies are central technical components of work in distributed systems. Some of the reasons for this are discussed. The material considers primarily those aspects of these technologies that are particularly relevant to distributed computer systems.

The concepts and distinction between data services and data computation are introduced. The issue of performing data services in the network is raised. Emphasis is given to understanding the role of tradeoff considerations. Much of what follows is oriented to developing perspective on tradeoff considerations. The chapter ends with a brief summary of the emphasis and perspective objectives of the book.

Chapter 2: Industrial Technological Trends

The technological trends in the computer and communications sectors are both a driving force and a constraint with respect to the development of distributed systems. Consequently, in Chapter 2, we discuss the relevant business and technological trends in these two key industrial sectors. The specific comments are often in the context of the impact on products and services.

Technology continues to open up many opportunities. At the same time, the environment that impacts on technological trends limits the rate of evolution. For example, the large capital investment in switches and other aspects of the current national communications network, and the investment that would be involved in any wholesale replacement, limit the options open to the common carriers.

In many information system applications, the investment in software and associated operational practices indicate that evolution is more likely than revolution. Existing systems must be modified, adapted, and evolved rather than thrown away for something that in light of today's capabilities might be better. Today's system must be able to operate with yesterday's data. The computer manufacturers, and those associated with supplying operating system and application system software, must provide vehicles that will permit that evolution. This is a considerable constraint on the developers of system hardware and software.

There is a real opportunity to implement significant technological advances, increase dramatically application (user) opportunities, and improve cost and productivity in the information industry. Beyond the economic constraints implied above, there is the challenge of accepting and managing change. It is very difficult for an organization to change its culture, and that in many cases is what is required. Examples of success and failure are provided. The importance is that this may be the limiting factor and the major challenge.

Chapter 3: Physical Technology and Its Implications

The chapter focuses on understanding the opportunities, challenges, and limitations that physical technology presents to the computer architect. We discuss the performance and physical limitations of today's computer systems. Then we overview the trends in semiconductor technology. It is to be expected that improvements in the performance of very large scale integration (VLSI) computational and memory chips will continue. It is also to be expected that CPU capability with respect to speed will continue to outstrip that of memory, and cost considerations will make it necessary to utilize memory hierarchies. As a consequence there is a need for a memory hierarchy that makes memory at any one level appear to be faster than it is. The one-level store concept and its descendants (e.g., caches and virtual memory) are introduced. Next, the importance of propagation time and other communications delays at all levels of distributed systems (e.g., from chip to national) is considered. Lastly, we discuss the need for architectures that lead to more parallelism and more effective use of memory.

Chapter 4: An Information System Viewpoint

The societal impact of computers lies in the information systems that they make possible. A discussion of the necessity of an information systems viewpoint in distributed system design is provided.

We review the overall generic requirements of information systems. By overall we mean our current perspective on requirements and features that in some applications may be very important. Those information system requirements carry over into those that must be met by the computer systems that will be utilized. It is understood in making these observations that cost considerations will always dictate that in a specific application only needed features should be implemented.

The driving forces behind the trend to distributed computing are then discussed. VLSI driven paradigms and other technological trends leading to the distribution of computer systems are briefly reviewed. In many respects, there is no longer an economy of scale in computing. Based on the relative cost of computing and communications, it is to be expected that communications technology will play an increasing role in the design of distributed systems. Unless there is a reason for centralization, computing and data storage will be distributed.

There are many other factors impacting on the move to distributed systems. Information system business, cultural, and operational factors fueling the trend to distributed systems are discussed. The trend for increasing decentralization and the distribution or decentralization of information system development is noted as are the problems that arise from that trend.

There is need for a common overall coherent architecture and minimum set of standards that will permit the interfacing of systems. The requirement for coherence applies to hardware, software, information system developers, and users.

Chapter 5: Categories of Distributed Systems

We discuss the different categories of computer systems and specifically those that might be considered distributed systems. Emphasis is given to the large range of capabilities and application requirements over the spectrum of categories.

We begin with an overview of the development of distributed systems and focus on the motivating factors behind their evolution. Both general purpose and general-purpose with attached processor centralized configurations are discussed. With higher performance demands of users, these centralized systems evolved to supercomputers and multiprocessor systems. The capabilities and limitations of centralized systems over a range of applications are highlighted.

The advances in communications technology and methods of work introduced at diverse workplace environments naturally lead to a greater distribution of information processing. Initially, the majority of distributed systems were homogeneous, and in this context, distributed operating systems are discussed. Currently, many distributed environments are heterogeneous. We believe that distributed systems design must focus on heterogeneous environments, treating homogeneous systems as merely a special case of a heterogeneous world. We highlight key issues in distributed systems design and consider a key question: Where should specific functionality be located within the information infrastructure: at the nodes or within the network itself?

Chapter 6: Communications System Fundamentals

The focus here is on distributed computing in an environment of multimedia services. The objective is a review of that part of communications technology that is particularly relevant to the communication, storage, and retrieval of data and information.

There are brief reviews of discrete probability, data and information concepts, and models of communication, information storage, and information retrieval. A measure of information is defined. Average information or entropy is discussed. The concept of redundancy is applied to the coding, storage, and retrieval of information. There is a brief discussion of security issues in the same context.

The representation of electromagnetic signals in different function spaces is introduced. The concepts of modulation, multiplexing, baseband, and broadband are reviewed. The uncertainty principle of time and frequency is summarized.

The concept of representing a signal by samples is discussed. Generalized Fourier series are introduced and their properties reviewed. The sampling theorems for baseband and broadband signals are summarized. Analog to digital (AD) and digital to analog (DA) converters are examined, as are threshold detection and error rates in additive noise. Systems involving quantization and the regeneration of signals are introduced. The relative merit of amplifiers and repeaters at relay points in communications systems is considered.

The geometric representation of signals in frequency, time, energy and space, including the concepts of dimensions and degrees of freedom is discussed. The Shannon capacity theorem (intuitive justification only) is introduced and the implications with respect to bandwidth versus power tradeoffs discussed.

Chapter 7: Switching

The relative costs in communications systems of switching, transmission, etc., are summarized. The implications of these costs with respect to computer and video services are discussed.

The chapter focuses on definitions in the switching area of CCITT, an important organization that has established international standards. The need to examine alternatives for switching is discussed. The relative sizes of the data needed to control a network and the message data sent over the network are discussed. The desirability of separating control from message information is clearly stated.

Voice channel and switch parameters are discussed. They play a key role in communications practice and standards and impact on coupling computer systems to communications systems. Time slot interchange and bus switch concepts are introduced. Common switch architectures and examples are provided. Generalized switching concepts and theory are introduced. The implications of breaking messages into segments or packets are reviewed. These generalized concepts provide a fundamental framework in which current and future switches can be described. The analysis is in terms of the fundamental concepts discussed in the preceding chapter.

Synchronization considerations, their importance, and the implication to networks are reviewed. This is followed by a review of miscellaneous switching concepts and techniques that are of particular relevance to current work in distributed computers.

Chapter 8: Common Carrier Network Considerations

There is a brief summary of some of the properties of the communications industry. Central offices and the national network hierarchy are discussed. These provide the communications highway system used by most data communications systems. This is followed by a general discussion of the features of the national network that are relevant to distributed computing. The common carrier network hierarchy is important because the common carriers provide the data highway that is utilized by most information systems and added-value communications services. At some level, networked computers must conform to the communications standards of the national network.

Traffic estimates for the national network are discussed. This is followed by a review of studies on the reliability of the national network. The point is made that information system design should assume that both computer and communications systems will fail. There are then a few remarks that campus-like environments are more innovative than the national networks.

The driving forces for, and the history of, the Integrated Services Digital Network (ISDN) development currently being implemented are reviewed. Basic, primary, and broadband service systems are introduced with examples. There is a brief review and assessment of ATM developments. Projected schedules for the wide-scale introduction of ISDN are reviewed. The chapter closes with a few comments on the Internet.

Chapter 9: Database Management Concepts

The basic concepts, definitions, and motivation for database management systems are discussed. The principle structural alternatives are reviewed. The importance of schemas, data integrity, concurrency control, backup and recovery, and access control in information system applications is discussed. Basic techniques of processing queries are presented, and it is shown how query processing can be extended to include the concept of database views. Throughout the chapter, an example of an inventory database is used to illustrate the concepts. As each topic is discussed, its impact on distributed systems and the additional complexity caused by distributed systems are identified.

The chapter also includes a discussion of database design issues, user interface issues, and the handling of change as a database and the application systems that use it evolve over time. These are practical issues that must be addressed if a database system is to be an effective general-purpose tool for managing data. This is followed by a discussion of future trends in database systems, including client server architectures, multimedia databases, and knowledge bases to give the reader an indication of the directions in which the database field is moving.

Chapter 10: Interfacing Systems, Protocols, and Standards

The concept, need for, and definition of protocols are discussed. The goal is effective communications between entities, not just data transport. Consequently protocols and standards involve many more information system issues than those normally associated with data communication.

Layered protocol concepts and the motivation behind them are discussed. The concepts of (N–1) and (N-k) hierarchies are introduced. The OSI conceptual model is presented and the model's strong and weak points reviewed. Alternatives to a layered structure and the tradeoffs associated with those alternatives are considered. Examples are given.

The challenge in distributed heterogeneous information systems is to interface the "foreign" or dissimilar components of the overall system. Examples of data exchange in such systems are discussed. The current state of general purpose data exchange systems is reviewed.

Much of the world's data are in the form of books and publications. Entering text, figures, graphs, pictures, etc., into computers is fairly routine. However, extracting meaningful information once the core data are in computers requires a great deal of knowledge of data and metadata. The mechanization of that extraction is a real challenge. Examples are discussed.

There is a brief review of types of standards and standards organizations that impact on distributed systems.

Chapter 11: Data Classification and Distribution

A satisfactory system for exchanging and controlling data is key to distributed systems. In a large system the complexity of detailed administration and control can become unmanageable. Pragmatically, both data and users must be divided into nonexclusive categories or subsets. To accomplish this, it is necessary to examine the real data requirements of an organization and in that context the alternatives for classification.

Data classification and distribution are extremely important issues in structuring information systems and defining architectures. The impact on the design of overall memory hierarchies with regard to logical levels and spatial location in networks is discussed. Basically at issue is how to decide where data should be located. A methodology is introduced for making such decisions. The need for automated tools to handle the detailed requirements, properties, and restrictions on data, and to support a design methodology is discussed. Typical rules of thumb for data classification and distribution are reviewed.

Chapter 12: Distributed Memory, Memory Hierarchies, Directories, and Data Retrieval

Previous chapters demonstrated the need for memory hierarchies. The purpose of this chapter is to expand that thinking into the area of very large scale distributed databases accessed by spatially distributed computers. In the context of distributed information systems as a whole, new problem areas are introduced.

Distributed computers will need to access databases of hundreds, even thousands, of terabytes. Physical memory will exist at many different levels and locations. Throughout this hierarchy, it is necessary to make the memory at each level and location appear to be faster than it is. Implementation of the one-level store concept throughout the memory hierarchy is essential. In some cases, the dynamic relocation of data or caching is desirable.

Throughout the memory hierarchy, communications capabilities and limitations can be very important. Communications constraints are a major factor in deciding where data should be placed, although there are also other important factors such as security. In a multimedia environment, it is also important to synchronize the data streams from different sources. Communications considerations have a large impact on acceptable architectures and on the location of data.

The efficient retrieval of data and information play a central role in many librarylike systems. The requirements for browsing and locating information are quite different from reading data. For an effective retrieval system, abstracting and cataloging throughout the hierarchy will be a necessity. Today these are tasks performed by humans. For the large databases under consideration, it will be necessary to automate these tasks. This is a fruitful area for research.

Directories to locate data and users play an important role in large memory systems. Various alternatives for directory structures are discussed. Access control also becomes an important issue. It is state-of-the-art practice to put many forms of data into computers—for example, text, pictures, figures, charts, and audio. In that sense, today's data can be put into machine-readable form. However, it may be difficult to build the bridge from raw data to information. Consequently, there is a great deal of raw data that in a pragmatic sense is not machine-readable in any meaningful way. Converting them into useful information may involve a combination of data and metadata. We lack adequate methods of automatically performing the conversion. Unless this problem can be solved, it will be difficult to make full use of today's computing capability.

Chapter 13: Communications Networks as Providers of Data/Information Services

There are two main purposes of this chapter. The first is to summarize the state of the art and practice in the national network with regard to communications transport. The second is a similar review of more general information services that utilize that network, the Internet being the principle example. These considerations are an evolutionary starting point for what might come next.

To take a more general view, a distinction is made between "computing services" and "data services." The latter provide data to enable the former to accomplish the requested tasks. Data services can be provided at nodes internal to a network, at computers attached to external network nodes (ports of the network with a direct gateway to the outside world), or both. Internal nodes generally have broader communications bandwidths than external ports, the propagation delays are different, and the network itself potentially has use of knowledge not available at individual external computers. These are important factors when it comes to providing data services. Cost and performance considerations dictate that some data services are better performed at internal nodes of the network than in computers attached to network ports.

It is also clear that in a high transaction rate situation, it would be desirable to relocate data and data services depending on the applications that are active at a particular time, the location of users, etc. There are communications systems today that reallocate communication transport resources dynamically, and these are an example of the type of functionality that is required. There are also systems that relocate data to different external nodes. A case can be made for selectively relocating and placing data internal to the network.

The issue and challenge are to provide more general data services, and in a way that optimizes the performance of overall information systems. The performance improvement must not be realized, however, at the expense of jeopardizing the possibly mandated control of the service. We badly need a design discipline and tools to make this possible. With this in mind, important design issues and practices are reviewed. Developing the discipline and tools remains an open research area.

Chapter 14: Outstanding Problems and Research Opportunities

Good engineers and scientists recognize what is important and significant. Important factors are the relation of work to societal needs and the impact on filling those needs. The good design engineer knows what the problem really is and works on it. The good scientist recognizes what is really important and works in an area where he or she can obtain significant results. Selectivity is the issue.

This chapter discusses a methodology for being selective in professional technical work. Although the approach is general, the focus is on industrial and academic work. The discussion is in the context of these two environments. As a final example, the methodology is then applied to a small part of the field of distributed computing/information systems.

Acknowledgments

The genesis of this work goes back to the experiences of the three authors. For our professional education we would like to acknowledge the role of the University of California at Berkeley, Pennsylvania State University, and the

University of Michigan. The experience of one of the authors at the General Electric Research Laboratory, and the close association with company operations in the computer, communications, and control fields has also been extremely important. Continuing close contact with research and academic work in computer science and engineering at Stanford, Berkeley, and other major universities has also been very significant.

It goes without saying that the support of the academic and administrative staffs and the graduate students of the universities with which the authors are presently affiliated is acknowledged and appreciated. Two are associated with Rensselaer Polytechnic Institute and one with George Mason University.

The individuals who have influenced the preparation of this book are too numerous to mention. However, we want to especially acknowledge three who were kind enough to read a preliminary outline of the proposed material and give us the benefit of their thoughtful comments: James R. Bell, of Hewlett-Packard; Arthur J. Bernstein, of SUNY Stony Brook; and Gio Wiederhold, of Stanford University. We are also indebted to Jack H. Westbrook for discussions concerning engineering data, and associated metadata relative to the challenge of transferring much of the world's data to computers in a meaningful way.

Lastly, although really first in dedication, the role of Frances F. Shuey, the wife of the senior author, is greatly appreciated. Not only did she cheerfully put up with the disruptions of normal life involved in the preparation of a book, but she proofread all of the material.

Richard L. Shuey
Schenectady, New York

Contents

7   Switching   129

Chapter 1

Introduction

Distributed processing: The term is loosely used to refer to any computers with communications between them. However, in true distributed processing, each computer system is chosen to handle its local workload, and the network has been designed to support the system as a whole.[1]

Electronic Computer Glossary

1.1 Chapter Objectives

The objectives of this chapter are to introduce the reader to the field of distributed computer systems, review the concept of data engineering, and provide a general perspective on this book as a whole. In meeting these objectives, we briefly review many of the concepts that are discussed later in more detail.

In reading this chapter, we suggest that you look for concepts, accept them, and try to understand how those concepts and paradigms fit into the overall picture of distributed computer systems. If you wish, consider them to be just hypotheses. Do not expect complete understanding at this time. We are interested in creating a framework in which we can later establish a sound basis for the components of that framework. In our view, it is desirable to have an overall picture of such a structure as the motivation and justification for later detailed discussion in specific areas. We intend to focus on important fundamental areas and issues. Importance is determined in the context of the overall framework of distributed systems, and in this case overall architecture.

It is said that one can prove something to a person or convince him or her that it is so. As Thomas Kuhn points out, the history of science provides many examples of beliefs that were not so, and models that were not believed, even

---

1. Alan Freedman, *Electronic Computer Glossary,* © 1981–1996 (Point Pleasant, PA: The Computer Language Company, Inc.).

though the evidence and proof were staring people in the face.[2] Believing in a flat earth is an example of the former, and nuclear fission an example of the latter. These two aspects of developing concepts or paradigms, belief and proof, are in many respects iterative. We are suggesting that the reader in this introduction accept the hypotheses, and later let us provide the justification.

This chapter does not repeat the preface in detail but presents those views that are common in a different context. Consequently in some areas a more detailed outline of the material to be covered in the book is contained in the preface rather than in this introduction.

1.2   The Rationale of a Data Engineering Viewpoint

We are an information-oriented society. The industrial revolution relating to our use of energy and material goods (physical) has been overtaken by the information revolution associated with our use of information. During the industrial revolution of the last century, workers improved by an order of magnitude their ability to accomplish physical tasks, profoundly changing their lives and the society in which they lived. The dependence of the urbanization of America on improvements in transportation speeds and cargo carrying capability, including people, is a good example. The intentional isolation of North American Amish communities from the rest of society is due in great part to Amish restrictions on the use of modern transportation and communications. Even a single order of magnitude change in the ability to do something often changes society.[3] Sometimes the changes are good, sometimes they are dangerous, and sometimes they are bad. In the information revolution we face all three possibilities.

During the last 50 years, we have seen unprecedented changes in our ability to process and communicate information. The changes have been many orders of magnitude. What is not necessarily fully understood is that we are just at the beginning of major changes in our ability to process information. It is still early morning in the information age. We have yet to understand and assess the likely impact of the information revolution on our society. We do know that we shall increasingly utilize the massive and rapid exchange of information between computer-based systems and between people and computer systems. Correspondingly, people to people communications will be

2. Thomas S. Kuhn, *The Structure of Scientific Revolutions* (Chicago: University of Chicago Press, 1962).

3. R. W. Hamming, "Intellectual Implications of the Computer Revolution," *American Math. Monthly* 70, no. 1 (January 1963): 4–11.

different as demonstrated by those using electronic mail. The core technologies will be computers and communications. In the long run the biological and social sciences will establish how effective these are, and the likely consequences. A spectrum of good, dangerous, and bad opportunities, as in the industrial revolution, is present. For example, the impact of information technology on education will be very large and could be very good. We would all like that. On the other hand, the same technology could also provide the means of totally controlling society and our individual lives—an outcome few of us would approve of.[4] As a society, it is important that the social, economic, and governmental sectors adapt to the realities of onrushing information technology. These facts are today undisputed. This is a book on information technology, and our focus will be primarily on computer and communication issues. At the same time, we recognize that the technology will force more serious consideration of related social and economic issues and that technically trained people must become involved. The broad technical perspective presented here should foster such involvement.

Clearly the future will involve a great deal of exchanging and sharing of data. A distributed computer system utilizing common or shared data can function only if its components can exchange data. That data may range from static data, in which case the exchange is only necessary occasionally or perhaps once, to rapidly changing dynamic data where propagation delays, concurrency controls, etc., may be important. The availability of data, subject to appropriate controls, is a necessary condition for the components of a distributed system to operate in a cooperative and cost-effective fashion. Data, and the exchange of data, are the lifeblood of a distributed system.[5] Consequently the engineering of data functions and services are a significant part of the design of a distributed system.

Data engineering addresses the availability and control of data in information systems. To the degree possible, we shall try to separate, in our thinking, issues and systems that make data available from those that utilize those data for some task or application. The availability of data is the key issue in distributed computer systems. Data engineering, as a specialty, is the area of activity dedicated to developing the knowledge, and the design and implementation discipline, required to meet the data requirements of information systems.[6]

---

4. Calvin C. Gotlieb, "Computers—A Gift of Fire," *Information Processing* 80 (IFIP 1980): 863.

5. Richard L. Shuey, "Guest Editor's Introduction—Special Issue on Data Engineering," *Computer* 19, no. 1 (January 1986): 14.

6. Richard Shuey and Gio Wiederhold, "Data Engineering and Information Systems," *Computer* 19, no. 1 (January 1986): 18.

With the increasing introduction of shared and distributed data, and in a multimedia data source and data sink environment, data engineering is a key discipline.

1.3 The Role of Information Systems

Information systems have existed since the dawn of organized human society and the elemental need to exchange and process information. What is new is the "mechanization" of information systems. The printing press is an early example of mechanization and as we all know had a profound impact on society. We are of course more used to thinking of mechanization in terms of electrical and electronic equipment. In the remainder of this book when we use the term *information system* we imply mechanization with an emphasis on electronic means. More specifically, we are concerned with information systems that use computer and communication systems to serve the information needs of society—from scientific computing to running businesses to providing entertainment.

Information systems impact on all phases of our society. Our emphasis here will be on systems that are essential to the functioning of society, for example, in business, education, industry, government, and medicine. The users of such systems have no more interest in the computer per se than the average citizen has in the electric motor. In the former case the interest is in the features and performance of the information system being used; in the latter case the concern is air conditioning, home appliances, etc. The use of information systems outside of science and engineering is paramount. We may refer to such systems as societal systems. Emphasis will be given to providing the needs of societal systems, for that is where the long-term impact will be greatest. It should be recognized that the computer-related problems in societal systems are often different than those in systems for scientific and engineering applications.

An overall objective of science and technology is to provide the technical basis for better serving society's needs. In keeping with this, we can identify the specific objectives of information technology and related academic and research programs:

1. Provide a sound basis for more fully realizing the implicit potential of computer and communications technology.

2. Participate in the design, implementation, and operation of information systems serving society.

In a broad sense, information systems are a combination of applications, communications resources, and computer systems. It is necessary to address all three in an integrated and often iterated fashion.

1.4   Information System Architecture

In the context above, architecture considers the overall requirements of an information system and merges hardware and software considerations into a coordinated and integrated view. Architectures are created to support, in a cost-effective manner, the requirements of society for computation and information processing. The term *information* as used encompasses the technical fields of computers, databases, communications, control, etc. The perspective in this book is that of integrated systems involving all of these components.

We shall examine the issues important to generic architecture. The goal is a framework within which it will be possible to expand the potential capabilities of information systems to meet the requirements and expectations of users. To take full advantage of new technology as it becomes available, that framework should permit evolutionary changes that will utilize new technology. In some cases we have a good idea of what will become available in the future. For example, improvements in the performance of semiconductor devices and chips, and the storage density of devices for magnetic mass memory, are predictable for the next ten to twenty years.[7] We should be able to create architectures that can take advantage of such improvements as they become available. On the other hand, our crystal balls will not be very good in other areas, and it will be more difficult to provide architectural structures that can adapt to the use of unanticipated advances in science. For example, we do not have a clear picture of how biological information systems function. When we do, our models of computers may prove to be inadequate in many of the application areas where people perform so well. Will it be possible to evolve our present architectures into areas more like those of biological systems? A major restructuring may be necessary. This in turn may require new models and new approaches in theoretical computer science.

From a long-range design standpoint, we must do the best we can today. Within the limits and reservations discussed above, a generic architecture should be a covering architecture in the sense that it provides certain features:

1. A framework for implementing both today's applications and the applications that we expect to make in the future.

---

7. John L. Hennessy and Norman P. Jouppi, "Computer Technology and Architecture: An Evolving Interaction," *Computer* 24, no. 9 (September 1991): 18.

2. Where possible, an interface with existing systems (this is almost a corollary of point 1 in that many new systems being implemented today must interface with existing systems).

3. Modification, fine tuning, and performance optimization of a system in light of application use experience.

4. A basis for smooth evolution that will take advantage of future technological advances.

5. An analysis of alternatives in the context of requirements, cost performance, and economics.

It should be clearly understood that for cost and performance reasons, what is implemented for a particular application, and at a particular time, should be only that which is necessary. The necessary "hooks" for anticipated evolution, either in the services offered or to take advantage of technological advances, should be provided. Providing those hooks is a nontrivial challenge and general solutions are not understood at the present time. The term "open architecture" implies an ability for arbitrary different systems to interact and there is much work in this area at the present time. Today there are no all-encompassing solutions. This subject will be discussed in more detail in other sections of this book, including those that focus on protocols and standards.

Not only will computing be distributed, but the development of information systems will be distributed. No longer does a central group build the systems for all users. The functional users with their own hardware and software are implementers. This is an important consideration for it alters the design and development environment of information systems. The architecture must be viable in this new environment. This is the environment in which an architecture must serve. There must be sufficient built-in structure—for example, a minimum set of necessary protocols, standards, and practices—that systems and subsystems developed under these conditions will effectively interact. The integration problems that information system users face today are largely due to the lack of adequate standards and discipline.

The coordination and integration of computing components, communication networks, and individual information systems are essential if the end user is to be provided acceptable performance. During the period when centralized computing, programming, and information systems work was the almost universal practice, integration was in principle relatively easy. That method of operation and centralization is no longer viable. At the same time, we would like to maintain in decentralized distributed systems the potential for a level of coherent integration in information system development and use that was possible in centralized systems. We would then like to go beyond that. This coherence applies to hardware, software, the information system developers, and the users.

1.5 Multiprocessor and Distributed Heterogeneous Information Systems

Our focus will be on distributed heterogeneous information systems as distinct from multiprocessor systems. The latter are usually composed of similar processors, and the objective is to get many processors working on one or a small number of well-structured problems. The former often contain dissimilar processors and may involve many different loosely related problems. They appear in a variety of settings:

1. Hospitals and medical systems, where it is desirable to interface a variety of services and equipment types.

2. Industry, where it is necessary to integrate the functions of engineering, manufacturing, marketing, distribution of products, maintenance, etc.

3. Travel businesses, where schedules, hotel accommodations, etc., must be coordinated.

4. Libraries, where mechanized cataloging, information retrieval, and a multitude of different on-line remote databases must be dealt with.

5. The military, where large-scale real-time integration of the assignment of resources and tactical control must occur.

6. Education systems, which form the basis of interactive learning and access to the world's information.

Such a list could be extended almost indefinitely, beginning at home, where access to many external sources of multimedia information is routine. In all cases, the objective is to get a diverse group of systems and users working together in a coordinated fashion to use common resources and data. The users (computer processes or people) are usually working on different problems, but these problems do interact in the data sense. They may have little else in common.

Distributed heterogeneous information systems are often powered by networks of communicating heterogeneous computer systems. We believe that a better understanding of distributed heterogeneous computer systems is central to our future use of computers in the information society. Such systems represent a major evolutionary opportunity of the future. It should be noted that the requirements of what we have called societal systems are quite different from those for most computer systems, which are oriented toward scientific and engineering calculations. One striking difference is that most scientific calculations can be redone if necessary, which is not a viable option in many societal systems. This entirely changes our view toward reliability, availability, loss of data, etc. It is a striking fact that today, in much of government and business, the only records (data) are computer records. Modern organizations cannot operate without their computer systems, and increasingly those systems are distributed in nature. Lost data cannot be tolerated.

From a research, engineering, and educational viewpoint, heterogeneous systems are attractive for another reason. One method of categorizing computers has standard free-standing machines at one extreme and heterogeneous distributed systems at the other extreme. Overall capabilities and operating system requirements vary widely over the different categories between these two extremes. In fact, the applicability of normal operating system concepts to a truly heterogeneous system is an open issue. The importance of this type of computer categorization, however, is that the extreme representing a network composed of distributed heterogeneous computer systems is a superset containing all the other categories. Particularly when large spatial dimensions are included, it is the most general case and the one given most emphasis in this book. The other categories may be viewed as special cases in which pragmatically only a restricted number of the concepts and parameters of the general case are important.

1.6   The Role of Communications, Information, and Database Technology

Selected concepts of communications technology and its extensions into the area of information are useful in understanding computing systems. The concepts and associated design discipline share certain features:

1. They are relevant to the communication and network aspects of distributed computing.

2. They provide a sound basis for the compression of data for either communications or storage.

3. They suggest a framework for information storage and retrieval.

4. They form the base for understanding analog to digital and digital to analog conversion.

5. They are applicable to security issues.

6. They provide a measure of how much information is really present in a given set of data.

There are two reasons that selected concepts from communication technology are important in this book:

1. The paradigms that they represent are applicable to many of the problems that we face in distributed computers, and those paradigms lead us to easy understanding and solutions. If they are unable to give us complete solutions, they often indicate trends and tradeoffs between alternatives.

2. In many areas, they provide a sound theoretical basis for our understanding, and they establish bounds on models and performance. In the process, they suggest meaningful measures of performance.

We are concerned only with those aspects of communications technology that are applicable to the architecture of distributed computer systems. Establishing the key concepts and paradigms will make the task of describing and analyzing distributed computer systems much easier. Our readers will in turn find in their professional lives that those paradigms will make the understanding and solution of complex problems much easier.

We have discussed in an earlier section the importance of data and data engineering. Databases and database management systems play a central role in almost all computer applications. They become even more complex and challenging in the distributed computer area. It is inescapable that we must address those aspects of database technology that are applicable to spatially distributed heterogeneous systems. Specifically, we must consider complex distributed databases where there may be functional relationships between the data at different locations. From an architectural standpoint, we must face up to the issues of where specific data should be located, whether location assignments should be static or dynamic, how data should be partitioned, etc. As in the communications area, emphasis will be given to those areas of database technology that are of particular relevance to the distributed systems that are the subject of this book.

In a very real sense, the major architectural issues of distributed heterogeneous computer systems are not associated with the computing engines per se at the nodes of a network. The central issues are more closely associated with data services and communications resources that are necessary to support those nodes in a coordinated fashion. This is why we must establish the key paradigms in those two areas.

1.7   New Issues

We are accustomed to thinking in terms of nodes and networks. In the classical sense, computers are at the nodes and do the work. The network transports data between nodes. The nodes may of course have dumb terminals connected to them, which in turn communicate to their host node. This is the old paradigm of distributed computers. In this book, we take issue with this model as the general case.

People think in terms of concepts or paradigms. We solve problems in terms of the paradigms that we believe. If one has the correct paradigms, matched to the problem area under consideration, solutions may be easy. If one is working with paradigms that are not a good match to the problem area, the number of steps involved may be very large and the solution complex. A good example is arithmetic. Although one can multiply in either the Roman or Arabic number system, we all recognize the simplicity that results from using the latter. As compiler writers know, it does matter how you describe things and how you think about things.

The authors of this book prefer a model of distributed systems and a paradigm different from the above. We believe that it is far better to think of nodes that do the work and networks that may do far more than just data transport. Both will, as they do today, contain computers. Specifically, we believe that the network can in many cases provide data services that either the nodes cannot do or cannot do as effectively as the network. Thus we prefer to make a distinction between data services and data computation in the workstation sense. It is clear, that in a distributed system of the type we are discussing, the network in principle knows far more about what is going on with respect to data services than the nodes. For example, the network knows what data are being accessed and from where. With regard to data transport, we recognize this today in both data and voice systems. Network internal data are used to route voice and data messages. As a second example, it can be argued that protocol conversion should often be a network function. We shall see that the network is the place to perform many other data service functions as well.

The key issues raised in this book are the merger of computer and communications technology so that they are viewed as one and the paradigm that data services should be provided by facilities at both external nodes and within the communications network. We make a distinction between external nodes that are connected to the network and nodes that may be internal to the network. Where particular data services should be performed will depend on the circumstances. We would like the reader to think in these terms. In utilizing this new viewpoint, we recognize that there are situations in which the boundary between data services and computation may not be clear. However, we feel that such a viewpoint will clarify thinking. Science is full of imperfect models and theories that are a great help—and of course the hope is, with experience, to modify those theories and models so that they become perfect.

1.8   Performance Tradeoff Considerations

The development of a new information system is based on a set of requirements that indicates what the system is expected to do. These may be incomplete and inadequate, and they may also be unattainable. The originators of requirements may well not understand what can and cannot be done. They may also fail to understand the cost of providing some of the features requested. There are two aspects of cost. The first is money. The customer will usually pay only so much for a feature. In addition a feature may come in different values or degrees. It should be possible to provide the customer with the incremental cost of a feature. For example, consider time of response. In a simple system with fixed load, time of response will depend on the size of the computer system, communications resources, etc. These cost money. If the time of response is increased, how much less will the system cost? In other words, what is the tradeoff between time of response and monetary cost? (Of course it may be decided to decrease the time of response, but the same type of analysis would be needed in order to estimate the additional cost.) Such factors are important to both the customer and the system architect.

The second dimension of cost is often of more importance and of more interest to systems people than monetary cost. We pay a performance price for most things that we ask a computer system to do. It may be impossible to provide everything that is desired regardless of system size and cost. Under such circumstances, if the requirements are relaxed, can the new requirements be met? What are the alternatives for relaxing the requirements? For example, we know that there are physical limitations on the time needed to access any type of memory. If a database application requires that a particular small portion of memory be accessed by a very large number of users per unit time and possibly modified, we know that there is a limit to the number of users that can be accommodated. What is the tradeoff between the number of users and the response time? Where is the limit? Are there architectural tradeoffs? For example, would it be possible to distribute the database physically and thus make it possible to attain the required performance?

These are important issues. Throughout our discussion a decisive factor will be tradeoff considerations in optimizing cost and performance. Tradeoff analysis and tradeoff decisions are central to most design and implementation tasks. They are particularly important in considering architectures for the types of distributed systems considered in this book. They will be considered in more detail in later sections.

1.9   Emphasis and Perspective

It is assumed that the reader is familiar with computing engines per se, their general structure, and architecture. Within this context, the book is self-contained and does not assume that the reader is knowledgeable in the various areas discussed. At the same time, the reader may benefit from some understanding of parallel processing and communications. Such an understanding is not essential.

It is our intention to integrate the relevant portions of many disciplines and provide an overall perspective on distributed computer systems. The emphasis is on high-level architecture and the issues therein. To accomplish this objective, our main concern will be the fundamental concepts and issues from those disciplines that are relevant to distributed computing. These are often quite different from bit level details. It could be said that we are more interested in the forest than the trees. The trees that we are interested in, and their properties, are those that are necessary to see what the forest could be like. It is often desirable to understand the objectives of a proposed new forest, and the interrelationships and tradeoffs between plants, before you rush out and start planting trees. We shall focus on the fundamental issues in protocols and standards rather than the details of today's implementations. Our success in the long term will depend more on resolving these fundamental issues than on implementation details.

From an academic standpoint, computer scientists and computer engineers may be extremely competent in their particular specialty, but they are often not well versed in many of the disciplines that are important in distributed information systems. The same is true of many professional people working in the field. Consequently, special attention will be given to important relevant areas not normally covered adequately in computer science and engineering.

Throughout this book, the emphasis will be largely technical and strongly influenced by ever-increasing user requirements. The challenge is for architectural design and implementation practice to catch up with the potential of state of the art hardware and software.

To restate the obvious, distributed heterogeneous computer systems are very complex and the key issues, interactions, and tradeoffs related to them are also. We cannot present solutions to many of these issues because they do not exist. We can however present the issues and some of the tradeoffs involved, we can outline what is known today, and we can suggest approaches to obtaining acceptable solutions. The value, viewpoint, and perspective of such an approach are central to both design and research.

1.10 Problems

1. Write not more than two pages on each of the following: (a) What do you believe are the five most important driving forces related to distributed computing and distributed information systems? (b) What are the five most important factors limiting the speed with which society is moving toward distributed systems?

2. It is generally agreed that distributed computer systems will play an increasing role in our society. Write not more than two pages summarizing what in your opinion are (a) the most important factors that will make this possible; (b) the dangers inherent in this trend to distributed systems; (c) the technical problems that need to be overcome if we are to realize positive outcomes and minimize negative ones; and (d) the incompatibilities between maximizing the positive and minimizing the negative.

3. Write not more than two pages on what you consider to be the role of architecture in distributed systems.

Chapter 2

Industrial Technological Trends

Technology: (a) the application of science, especially to industrial or commercial objectives; (b) the scientific method and material used to achieve a commercial or industrial objective.[1]

The American Heritage Dictionary

2.1   Chapter Objectives

We focus here on a discipline that addresses the design and deployment of leading edge information systems during the next decade—in other words, on the technology of distributed information systems. Information system development is a multidisciplinary activity that is limited by the existing knowledge in key scientific areas. It is important for us to understand these areas so that research can be focused on them. At the same time, our goals will be limited by the products and services available from commercial sectors. Business and industrial trends are a good indication of what resources are likely to be available. In many cases, the unavailability of appropriate products and services will limit our options more than our scientific knowledge. In brief, the trends of applied technology are not simply an indication of the needs and requirements that future information systems should meet; they are also an indication of the capability that is likely to exist for meeting future goals. We do not imply that these are the only indicators, but they are key factors. In some cases, unless extraordinary things happen, they will provide bounds on how fast applications are likely to be implemented or deployed.

An architecture for distributed information systems involves both computer and communications technology. Consequently, understanding the technical and business trends in the computer and communications sectors of our

---

1. *American Heritage Dictionary for Windows* (Novato, Calif.: Wordstar International, 1993).

economy will be important in assessing the alternatives open to us and the tradeoffs between those alternatives. This chapter will clarify the trends of today and their implications with regard to future research, development, and applications in the area of distributed computers. The reasons for these trends as well as their pragmatic consequences and implications will be discussed later in this book.

2.2   Relevant Computer Industry Trends

The performance and production of semiconductor and thin film devices have improved by many orders of magnitude. (The details are discussed in the next chapter.) A companion of this trend has been the use in computer hardware of integrated circuit (IC) and very large scale integration (VLSI) technology.[2] The absolute performance of semiconductor circuits has improved dramatically, the cost has dropped by a significant amount, and the size of components and systems has been greatly reduced. There are reasonably good projections indicating that these trends will continue for the next decade—that they will have a large impact on the computer hardware of the future.

Electronics provides the platform upon which computer hardware is designed and produced. The net result of the above trends is that for almost any elementary hardware function, such improvements carry over. To a large degree, they also carry over to elementary computers, as represented by the microprocessor. Thus, the personal computer and the workstation of today have a performance that exceeds that of the mainframe of a decade ago. (It is difficult for us to differentiate here between workstations and personal computers, and for convenience in the remainder of this book we shall use the terms interchangeably.) It is expected that the performance of both will continue to improve, although, as we shall see in the next chapter, that will depend upon improvements in architecture. Companion improvements in software are essential and will play an important role.

Today large computers are using essentially the same VLSI chips as personal computers. Consequently, the elementary speed per basic logic unit is roughly the same for all computers. Increasingly there is commonality at the next level of logical complexity, including up to the level of the microprocessor. VLSI and microprocessors have provided the means of making large computers that are composed of hundreds or thousands of general purpose and special purpose microprocessors. For example, in the telephone industry, a

2. John L. Hennessy and Norman P. Jouppi, "Computer Technology and Architecture: An Evolving Interaction," *Computer* 24, no. 9 (September 1991): 18.

large central office electronic switch may have thousands of both general purpose microprocessors, often running Unix, and special purpose microprocessors that perform many of the signal processing functions. To realize the potential of a large multiprocessor computer, we must address the issues of memory management and communications internal to that computer. These issues are being addressed today at major research universities and industrial research laboratories. High performance products are available today for certain classes of applications, and it is to be expected that more general purpose products will become available in the future. It remains to be seen how "general purpose" future computers that are constructed from many microprocessors will be. For cost and cost performance reasons, it may well be that interprocessor communications and memory management will be specialized. As we shall see in the next chapter, these issues become more important as the performance of the elementary electronic building blocks improves, and that performance improvement is precisely what is happening.

The preceding paragraph focused on what we shall later call multiprocessor systems that constitute one computer. In this book, we are more concerned with a system of interconnected computer systems. Two current examples are networked workstations in a research or engineering group, and the Internet world-wide complex of interconnected computers when utilized for some of its more complex features. The latter qualification excludes electronic mail and library systems in considering computers that really interact. Computers in library and mail systems exchange information but do not generally process it interactively. Increasingly customer requirements (opportunities) indicate a need for active multilateral interaction between systems.

The above observations and associated challenges, well recognized in the computer industry, can be summarized as follows:

1. *For any function, there has been a continuing increase in performance accompanied by a companion decrease in hardware cost.* Cost performance has thus improved dramatically. This is true for special function electronics, special purpose computing systems, and general purpose computers.

2. *There have been dramatic reductions in the size of the logic and memory portions of computers.* This has not been as true for input/output devices that are other than purely electronic (printers, keyboards, displays, etc.).

3. *Because the costs have gone down, computers are all pervasive in society.* A good party question is to ask people how many electric motors they have in their homes. The correct answer is almost always more than

the person's response (since they usually forget the clocks and the multiple motors in many appliances).

We have already reached the point where many products have one or more internal computers invisible to the user—from telephones, washing machines, clothes dryers, microwave ovens, stoves, automobiles, dishwashers, TV sets, clocks, watches, and VCRs, to home security systems, furnaces, video games, electronic games, and hearing aids. Essentially all new home appliances contain computers, and it is worth noting that the computers are cheaper than the mechanical clocks and control mechanisms that were used in the past. Computers are even being introduced in the base of lightbulbs to control dimming and automatic shut off—which means computing elements must be cheap if they are going into lightbulbs. We have also reached the point where today large numbers of people can afford a personal computer, and in some cases may in the long run wish to interconnect with other systems either locally or externally.

Here are a few more observations that can be made:

1. *Communications are important at all levels of a computer or information system—from the a single processor to the multiprocessor to the computer network.* Computers only exchange data by utilizing a communications network whether that network consists of a bus or the national network.

2. *Memory management is important at all levels of a computer or information system.* This topic is given emphasis in this book as it is of particular importance in work on architecture.

3. *The network and its components, more than the node computers, often define and determine the performance of a distributed system.* We shall discuss this in considerable detail in later chapters of this book.

4. *The "open system" philosophy is widely accepted.* The concept goes back to a Canadian white paper of several decades ago on what was called the "open world" and the work in Japan on computers and communications ("C & C") systems.[3] These efforts stressed the importance of being able to interconnect a variety of data sources, including computers, in a way that would be transparent to the user. They provided motivation for the development of the Open System Interconnection Reference Model, a topic to be discussed in Chapter

3. Koji Kobayashi, *Computers and Communications—A Vision of C & C* (Cambridge: MIT Press, 1986).

10. The desirability of open systems is universally understood today and is being addressed. It is not clear if and when we shall have an entirely satisfactory or general solution. It is also understood that there will never be an "open world" in some domains, given their applications.

5. *The creation of a widely agreed upon set of standards is necessary if the open system concept is to be implemented.* Chapter 10 will present a succinct summary of the role of standards and a realistic appraisal of pragmatic limitations on the development of standards. The consequences of those limitations, including proprietary considerations, are included in the discussion.

6. *The major technical and business investment has shifted to the PC or workstation size machine.* The shift of emphasis applies to both hardware and software. From an information systems standpoint, innovative applications system software is primarily available on small machines. That is where the software development effort is located.

7. *The human component is vital.* That is, the user must be able to interact with the computer in as obvious a way as possible (computer-human interaction and visualization). User friendliness, on the human's terms, is a must.

8. *The realization that the merger of a computer viewpoint with that of a communications perspective is necessary.*[4] It is our thesis in this book that there must be one integrated viewpoint, not two.

2.3   Relevant Trends in the Communications Industry

The technology trends discussed at the start of this chapter, and many of the issues reviewed in Chapter 1, are equally applicable to the communications industry. A few relevant supplemental observations and trends can be added to the points noted earlier. The discussion is in the context of the impact of communication issues on distributed computer systems and the design of the architecture of such systems. A major distinction is that the communications industry is generally related to the common carriers—those businesses that provide communications transport and related services, which makes them

---

4. Forouzan Golshani and Thaddeus Regulinski, "Prologue: On the Synergism of Computers and Communications," Guest Editor's introduction to a special issue, *Communications of the ACM* 33, no. 4 (January 1990): 9.

distinct from the manufacturers of communications equipment. Examples of common carriers in the United States are AT&T, MCI, and Bell South. Communications issues not related to the common carriers are omitted in this section but covered later as necessary.

We can translate the concerns of the communications industry into a list of observations and trends. Any such list should include:

1. *The common carriers have been digitizing the national network for more than twenty years. The driving forces have been economics and cost savings.* It is sometimes said that the push for digitization was a consequence of the need to transmit digital data to and from computers. That in fact had nothing to do with initiating the trend. The driving force was and is cost. Because of the semiconductor trends mentioned at the start of this chapter and discussed in more detail in Chapter 3, applying digital technology to POTS (Plain Old Telephone Service) has a large economic payoff.[5] The use of common carrier facilities to transmit computer data is riding on the back of a system that was digitized to more economically transmit analog information such as sound waves.

2. *The digitization of the national network is well underway.* There are variations among common carriers, but today most switches are digital, long lines transmission is mostly digital, and local loops (e.g., from the central office to individual homes) are largely analog. Although the indicated facilities are largely digital today, in a year or two the national network will in effect be universally digital, except possibly for local loops.

3. *Fiber optic lines are being widely installed for long lines and trunk services.* In some cases, fiber is being installed directly into residential areas.

4. *The common carriers are dedicated to using the network to transmit all types of data.* With the focus turning to the digitization of the network, the common carriers realized that the network could be used to transmit digitally all types of data. Thus the original terminology—IDN (Integrated Digital Network)—rapidly evolved into ISDN (Integrated Services Digital Network). This early shift in emphasis to integrated services is reflected in the business and technical literature of that time and up to the present. The importance of the ISDN

5. R. F. Rey, *Engineering and Operations in the Bell System,* 2nd ed. (Murray Hill, NJ: Bell Laboratories, 1983).

thrust is that it defines a communications system architecture that is accepted worldwide by the common carriers and government-owned communications service organizations. As we shall see, ISDN services are being introduced in the United States, Europe, and Japan. For a variety of reasons, the offerings in the United States lag behind those in parts of Europe and Japan.

5. *Communications costs continue to drop less rapidly than computing costs.* As will be discussed later, fiber optic technology has substantially reduced the cost of the transmission component of communications. However, transmission costs are not the major expense of operating an overall communications network. For example, in the national network, transmission costs are less than the cost of switching. Until the development of very wideband optical switches capable of simultaneously handling thousands of interconnections, switching costs are likely to dominate transmission costs. It is also important to note that switching and other costs are not dropping as fast as the cost of computing.

6. *There is increasing emphasis on mobile communications.* Expanding cellular phone and data service is a major technical and business effort of all common carriers.

7. *Regulatory and legal actions have resulted in confusion and constraints.* Due to recent changes in the United States, there is broadened competition but on uneven terms. The components of the old Bell System, the "Baby Bells," have been at a disadvantage compared to newcomers. They, not the newcomers, had to subsidize service to rural areas. Regulatory actions held up the deployment of cellular phone systems in the United States for at least a decade and placed the United States at a disadvantage with respect to countries where the industry was not fettered by such regulations. Government approval of rates, although required in a monopoly, has held up the deployment of some equipment and services—for example, the deployment of digital switches. Approved rates—i.e., tariffs in the communications industry—determine how much money is available for capital investment. The FCC's Computer Inquiry I of several decades ago concluded that computing and communications businesses should be kept separate. Consequently, the federal government continued to prohibit regulated communications companies from participating in any aspect of the computer industry. Pragmatically, they failed to maintain complete separation between communications and computers because it was not reasonable.

Computer Inquiry II was to restudy what was obviously a failed policy. It was never completed and left many unresolved issues. For example, the current separation of common carrier communications services and cable TV services, as with cellular communications, is holding up progress. The courts and the federal and state regulatory agencies have yet to address information services as one integrated opportunity. Once separate agencies to regulate telephone and cable TV services are put in place, as they were in New York State, it becomes a turf issue between two bureaucracies. Thereafter, it is very difficult for government to take a rational view. Recent regulation and constraints on the communications sector have become a major legislative issue and less subject to the whims of regulatory commissions. Whether this will be good or bad remains to be seen.

8. *Government-supported programs may well be important.* The role and impact of federal and state governments with respect to the support of specific programs such as ARPANet has been significant. Most of this support has been in the computer communications area. There are two potential future dangers: (1) the government may try to invest in and thus in effect force things in a direction that does not make technical sense and (2) the government may enter into areas that would be better left to business and industry. It is interesting that as this book was being edited, the Internet was in the process of going commercial.

9. *The communications industry understands that the future emphasis will be on multimedia systems and services.* Depending upon the environment, it is to be expected that the common carriers will provide the required data transport services. The introduction of voice mail and video on demand are examples. The bridge between voice and text systems is in the laboratories and will with time become a service.

10. *Most of the common carriers would like to play a wider role in the information industry.* They would like to provide information services, not just transport services, more broadly. In the United States, the attempts to date have not been very successful. The reasons involve the nature or culture of the common carriers and regulatory constraints. Since the common carriers are now permitted to do business overseas, beyond the reach of national service constraints, some of them are broadening their activities off shore. Although the off shore business is welcome in its own right, there is also the hope that at some future time it will be possible to apply that experience in the United States.

2.4   Summary and Comments

Many of the trends in the computer and communications sectors are identical or similar. Underlying these similarities is common or shared technology. And yet, because of the differences in the historical development of the two sectors, the perception and application of that technology may be quite different. A good example is the development of network concepts in the two industries.

To put it another way, the cultures of the two industries are quite different. This has been a factor in the difficulty encountered by computer companies trying to enter the communications business and vice versa. There are two major challenges facing the professionals in both industries: (1) the management of technological change within their own sector and (2) a shift of sector culture so that it can adapt to the necessity of merging the viewpoints represented by the two groups. The rapidity with which we are able to implement distributed computer systems will depend in part on the success of meeting these challenges.

2.5   Problems

1. Are there statements in Chapter 2 with which you do not agree? If so, explain what they are and why you do not agree with them. Limit your answer to not more than two pages.

2. Both the communications and computer business sectors are involved with the sale of hardware and software. Consider the equipment manufacturers and the hardware and associated software that go with the hardware (e.g., operating systems) but exclude the service component of both business sectors (e.g., computer services, payments for computer time, monthly telephone charges, applications software). (a) What do you believe are the relative dollar sizes of the restricted communications and computer business sectors as defined above? (b) If you remove the constraint indicated above, what do you believe are the relative sizes?

3. What do you believe are the five most important industrial technological trends that are impacting on the distributed computer field? Explain your choices.

Chapter 3

Physical Technology and Its Implications

As I have explained, the problem is mainly one of programming. Advances in engineering will have to be made too, but it seems unlikely that these will not be adequate for the requirements.[1]

A. M. Turing

3.1   Chapter Objectives

A. M. Turing's reference to engineering was of course to what we would today call hardware, thus distinguishing it from programming, which was viewed more as mathematics (and is today spoken of as software). It took many years before it was recognized that the development of software was basically an engineering problem, requiring a corresponding design discipline. The term software engineering became fashionable and acceptable and software engineering is today taught in many computer science academic programs.[2] We are currently going through a period in which viewing the design of information systems as an engineering discipline in computer science is gaining acceptance.[3]

In the early days of computers the numerical problems being addressed were conceptually simple, of limited scope, and involved relatively small amounts of data. The limitation was the hardware. Since then there have been many orders of magnitude improvement in the hardware. The "advances" in engineering visualized by Turing have exceeded his wildest dreams. In a

---

1. A. M. Turing, "Computing Machinery and Intelligence," *Memo* 59, no. 433 (1950).

2. "Software Engineering" (papers presented at a conference sponsored by the NATO Science Committee, Garmisch, Germany, October 7–11, 1968).

3. Philip M. Lewis, "Information Systems Is an Engineering Discipline," *Communications of the ACM* 32, no. 9 (September 1989): 1045.

sense, hardware is no longer the limitation on what we are able to do. The potential of high performance hardware has created a vast number of challenges in the development of software and architecture. However, it would be a mistake to view our opportunities exclusively as software-related challenges. In some areas—for example, in the fields of knowledge engineering and artificial intelligence—new models of computing and new architectures may be necessary. The attainment of these may require new hardware components.[4] With that caveat, we turn to the utilization of more conventional computers.

The information system problems being addressed by today's computer systems are often conceptually complex and broad in scope, and they involve extremely large amounts of data. The limitations are software and our ability to organize and structure the hardware and software as an overall system (architecture). In brief, the raw performance of state-of-the-art hardware components has provided a potential that we have been unable to fully utilize. This is well recognized today.

In computer science and in the use of computers we are dealing largely with mathematical and logical systems—in more modern terms, with software rather than hardware. This book is about high-level architecture. Such architecture includes hardware and software issues and ideally should provide a framework in which overall system performance can be maximized. In other words, the framework should be such that the combined performance of hardware and software approaches an optimum. In reaching for that objective, architecture must realistically conform to the physical realities of the hardware. It must simultaneously take advantage of the strengths of current and projected hardware while living with and minimizing the effects of hardware shortcomings. In like fashion it must adapt to the realities of logical and mathematical capabilities and limitations as represented by software. To conform to the physical properties of the hardware in our considerations, it is necessary to understand the capabilities, present and projected, of electronic hardware and relevant physical phenomena. These are the topics considered in this chapter.

The state of the art of the physical sciences sets limits on the performance of electronic systems. In the long run, the fundamental limits of physics also set limits on everything we do. In a real sense, electronic information systems must conform to the capabilities and limitations inherent in the physical world, as reflected in the physical sciences. In what follows we do not provide

---

4. Terrence J. Sejnowski, "The Hardware Really Matters," Robert Wilensky, "Why Play the Philosophy Game?" and Lotfi Zadeh, "The Albatross of Classical Logic," in *Speaking Minds— Interviews with Twenty Eminent Cognitive Scientists* (Princeton: Princeton University Press, 1995).

a detailed discussion of the physics involved, the state of the art of electronic circuits, or the propagation delays that are to be expected. The details are to be found in the literature. Our interest and focus here are rather on the implications of physical properties and parameters on distributed systems.

This is not a book on physics; it is a book on architecture. We provide only a conceptual overview of relevant physical parameters and their trends. It is important that those concerned with research, design, or implementation of distributed computers and information systems have an understanding of the options and tradeoffs that are implicit in those trends and are often driven by physical considerations. For example, cycle time and speed of logical operations are important factors in many circumstances. They will determine the number of instructions per unit time that can be executed in a simple machine. The values are basically set by the speed of electronic circuits. For a suitable class of problems, parallel architectures such as pipelining can substantially improve the instruction execution rate. Nevertheless, there are other areas in which performance is limited by the availability of the data that are needed by a particular processor. For a single processor, this limitation was the motivation for the one-level store concept that will be discussed later in this chapter.[5] Caches and virtual memory are examples of that concept. In circumstances where propagation delays are important, the availability of data can be particularly crucial, and system architects may find it desirable to trade off communications network complexity, and multiple memory locations, for overall throughput. We shall see that these factors are of particular concern in spatially distributed information systems.

Our objective here is to examine the underlying capabilities and limitations of physical devices and physical systems that are relevant to distributed computer systems. Such factors influence many architectural requirements and decisions. They also often imply an upper limit on performance. In some cases it is important to realize how far we are from those limits and why. Such knowledge can provide us with a goal to reach for. It is equally important to understand how in other areas we have already reached limits and are constrained. The challenge of architecture is to develop structures that will exploit the potential limits of what is theoretically attainable and concurrently maximize performance within the constraints of the unattainable.

---

5. T. Kilburn, D. Edwards, J. L. Lanigan, and F. H. Sumner, "One-Level Storage System," *IRE Transactions on Electronic Computers* (April 1962): 223.

3.2   Microprocessor and Mainframe CPU Performance

We shall first consider the trends in microprocessor and mainframe CPU performance. Hennessy and Jouppi provide a good summary of these and the limits of the underlying electronic circuitry.[6] The material is also covered in Hennessy and Patterson.[7] A more recent review of the impact of microprocessors on supercomputing is given by Pool.[8] These four references are excellent sources for further details and extensions on some of the material covered in this chapter.

The performance trends for the CPUs of supercomputers, mainframes, minicomputers, and microcomputers are shown in Fig. 3.1. Clearly, the performance growth of the microcomputer is outpacing the other classes of computers. As the density of components increases, more and more of the overall system can be placed on a chip. Factors such as propagation delay are less significant in a microprocessor on a chip than in a larger machine that occupies more physical space. As we shall see, memory management is very important, and the ability to put more on a chip permits on-chip memory management. A cache is an example. Thus the higher density of components makes it possible to improve on-chip architecture and that is probably the reason for the sharp break in the microprocessor performance curve. The break point corresponds to the time that the number of on-chip components reached the point where sophisticated architecture and memory management were possible in microprocessors.

It is clear that the improvement in performance is not just a result of increased circuit speed. The circuit speeds of all classes of processors are roughly the same. In the absence of low-cost, low-temperature electronic components and their potential speed, we can expect circuit speed to increase slowly. That increase will not in itself provide the performance that we would expect. Processor architecture is important and our freedom with regard to microprocessors is largely a function of the number of components that we can get on a chip. It is therefore appropriate to turn to the semiconductor trends that are increasing component density.

6. John L. Hennessy and Norman P. Jouppi, "Computer Technology and Architecture: An Evolving Interaction," *Computer* 24, no. 9 (September 1991): 18.

7. John L. Hennessy and David A. Patterson, *Computer Architecture: A Quantitative Approach* (Morgan Kaufmann, 1991); David A. Patterson and John L. Hennessy, *Computer Organization and Design: The Hardware/Software Interface* (Morgan Kaufmann, 1993).

8. Robert Pool, "Off-the-Shelf Chips Conquer the Heights of Computing," *Science* 269, no. 5229 (September 8, 1955): 1359.

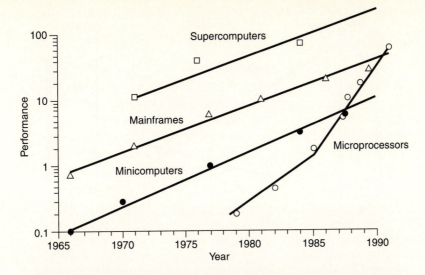

Figure 3.1   Trends in microprocessor and mainframe CPU performance. *Source:* John L. Hennessy and Norman B. Jouppi, "Computer Technology and Architecture: An Evolving Interaction," *Computer* 24, no. 9 (September 1991): 18. Reprinted with permission of IEEE.

3.3   Semiconductor Trends

There are two aspects of the physical dimensions on a chip that are important. The first is the resolution of the imaging system, or lithography, that determines the number of lines or components that are possible in one direction. This is often referred to as feature size. We shall refer to its inverse L_f. In other words, L_f indicates the resolvable lines per unit length and is an indication of the number of components per linear dimension. The second parameter is the size (linear dimension) of the chip, or the length of the die edge, which we shall refer to as L_c. Trends in feature size and chip size are shown in Fig. 3.2. (Note that L_f is proportional to the inverse of the feature size shown on the graph.)

It is significant that the feature size is decreasing much more rapidly than the die edge length is increasing. The number of components that it is possible to get on a chip will be proportional to the square of the length of the edge of the die, and inversely proportional to the square of the feature size. At the same time, logic speed will be approximately inversely proportional to the feature size. The consequences of these trends in lithography are indicated below.

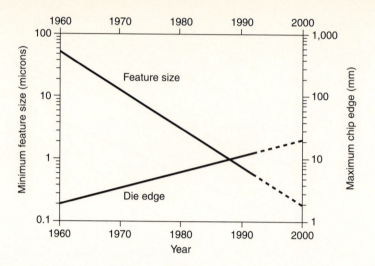

Figure 3.2   Trends in minimum feature size and maximum chip edge. *Source:* John L. Hennessy and Norman B. Jouppi, "Computer Technology and Architecture: An Evolving Interaction," *Computer* 24, no. 9 (September 1991): 18. Reprinted with permission of IEEE.

It is assumed that overall computational capability is bounded by the number of available elements.

Implications of Semiconductor Trends (Computational Impact)

If: L_f = represents resolvable lines per unit length (i.e., inverse of feature size)

            L_c = represents chip size (i.e., linear dimension)

Then: Number of components per unit area ~ $(L_f)^2$

            Circuit Speed ~ (L_f)

            Number of unit areas per chip ~ $[(L_c)^2]$

From which: Potential computational capability per chip due to improvements in lithography:

            ~ $[(L_f)^2][(L_f)][(L_c)^2]$ ~ $[(L_f)^3][(L_c)^2]$

Note that in Fig. 3.2 the improvement in (L_f) is much larger than in (L_c). Thus most of the improvement in on-chip raw computational capability has come from improved lithography, not larger chips. The architectural challenge is to make use of the increased capability resulting from improvements in lithogra-

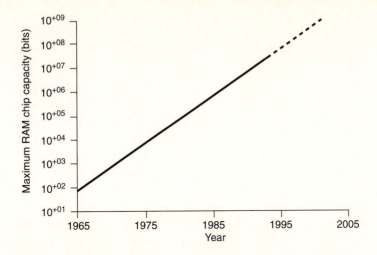

Figure 3.3   Trends in semiconductor RAM density. *Source:* John L. Hennessy and Norman B. Jouppi, "Computer Technology and Architecture: An Evolving Interaction," *Computer* 24, no. 9 (September 1991): 18. Reprinted with permission of IEEE.

phy. It is also clear that x-ray lithography, with its potentially higher resolution, might make a substantial difference in performance, providing the physical properties of thin films of semiconductor materials—for example, the etching of edges—can utilize the improved resolution.

To utilize the raw "in principle" computational capability of a chip discussed in the preceding paragraph, we need structure and data exchange mechanisms that will keep the different sub-micro computing elements busy. There are structures that provide capability along these lines for particular types of calculations—for example, pipelining and simultaneously calculating several possible branches of a calculation. We do not elaborate on such structures, the principle reason being that in our later considerations the single computer (or engine) is a given and our challenge is getting a multitude of computing engines to work together. The interested reader is referred to the previous references given in this chapter, and to Stone[9] and Flynn.[10]

Considering the orders of magnitude improvement in computational capability per chip, have semiconductor memory systems been able to keep up and provide the needed data? The simple answer is no. A more correct answer is that in some cases, due to system architecture advances, they have. Figure 3.3 indicates the trend in the capacity of chips devoted to memory.

9. Harold S. Stone and John Cocke, "Computer Architecture in the 1990s," *Computer* 24, no. 9 (September 1991): 30; Harold S. Stone, *High Performance Computer Architecture* (Reading, MA: Addison-Wesley, 1990).

10. Michael J. Flynn, *Computer Architecture* (Boston: Jones and Bartlett, 1995).

This growth rate is not surprising, for the size of random access memory available on a chip should be proportional to $[(L_f)(L_c)]^2$ and as we have noted there have been substantial improvements in lithography. So on nearby chips, a very substantial amount of memory should be available to a microprocessor. How about the speed of that available memory? Unfortunately, the speed of affordable memory has not kept pace with the speed of computation. For large memories, the number of high-speed, high-performance elements that would be required are not affordable. There is a need to have very high-element densities in memories in order to conserve space and minimize cost, and that limits design options. Figure 3.4 illustrates the trends of cycle times for CPUs and random access memory.

In addition to memory speed limitations, in referencing off chip data, propagation and other delays may be significant. We shall shortly consider how important they are, but for now assume that they can be significant. We can thus summarize the implications of semiconductor trends on memory as follows:

1. Memory size is proportional to $[(L_f)(L_c)]^2$.

2. Memory speeds continue to fall further behind that of logic.

3. Chip-to-chip communication can involve significant delays.

4. The mismatch between computation capability and memory is widening.

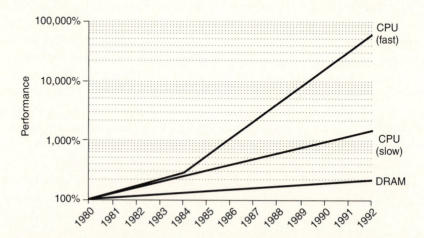

Figure 3.4   Trends in DRAM and processor cycle times. *Source:* John L. Hennessy and Norman B. Jouppi, "Computer Technology and Architecture: An Evolving Interaction," *Computer* 24, no. 9 (September 1991): 18. Reprinted with permission of IEEE.

So far we have limited our discussion to fast semiconductor memory. In later sections of this chapter we further discuss delays and transfer rates with regard to both semiconductor and other types of memory. However, it is clear that in general, purely on the basis of lithography and semiconductor technology, computational capability is surpassing the ability of memory systems to supply data to computation units. The overall trends can be summarized as follows:

1. Chip computational capability is increasing as the third power of dimension (lithographic resolution) improvement.

2. Computational (logic) capability is increasingly becoming the dominating factor. To make full use of it, architectural designs are needed that involve more parallel logic and processing.

3. To take advantage of computational (logic) speeds, memory systems must appear to be faster than they are.

As we pointed out earlier, we do not intend to explore further parallel logic and processing within a single computer. We do intend to discuss the problems associated with distributed computers and in particular the availability of data in such systems. However, before focusing on such factors, we must consider one other physical parameter that impacts on the exchange of data both on and off chips and between computers. This parameter is delay. Delays due to propagation times, switching circuit delays, and the time to execute communications software can be significant.

3.4   Propagation Time and Other Delay Considerations

At some point a system knows that a particular computing logical unit will require data. If the requirement is known prior to the actual need, and the data exist, then it may be possible to prefetch the data. It should be noted that the data may depend on calculations not yet completed, and therefore they may not exist until a later time. If this is the case, then it is impossible to prefetch data unless it is possible to precalculate all the values that the data might take and to select the valid ones when needed. Since our focus here is on inherent delays in the transfer of data, we shall for the time being assume that the data exist and that there is no prior knowledge of specific need—i.e., that it is not known in advance what specific datum will be needed next. The delays fall into several categories, some of which are fundamental limitations and some of which can be minimized.

Delays due to propagation time are perhaps the most fundamental delays and represent a hard limitation on the transfer of data. When the clock rate and corresponding logic execution rate of central processors were slow (compared to today's values), propagation time was not a significant factor in performance. That is no longer true. Propagation time is a consideration on a chip, and a significant factor within a high-performance computer. It can be a major consideration in a system that is widely dispersed geographically. There are other delays that are often more significant than propagation time—for example, software delays are the limiting factor in most packet-switched systems. But propagation delay considerations provide a lower bound on the delay that is attainable. It is therefore of interest to us. Table 3.1 illustrates this point, indicating the delay to be expected between components at different locations. Clock rates of 100 MHz and 500 MHz are assumed. The separation between the communicating devices varies from the distance across a chip to around the world. As we might suspect, the criteria of a good design is reducing the time to transfer a message that is required for a decision by logic or software, not just the inherent delay. A recent analysis summarizes some of the problems with VLSI/ULSI circuit delays and makes some specific on chip

Table 3.1   Propagation Delays for Different Areas

AREA	Dimension in Meters	Delay in Seconds	Delay in Clock Cycles at	
			100 MHz	500 MHz
On chip	1.00E−02	3.33E−11	3.33E−03	1.67E−02
In computer	6.00E−01	2.00E−09	2.00E−01	1.00E+00
Building	1.20E+02	4.00E−07	4.00E+01	2.00E+02
Campus	1.20E+03	4.00E−06	4.00E+02	2.00E+03
Local area	3.00E+04	1.00E−04	1.00E+4	5.00E+04
Wide area	3.00E+06	1.00E−02	1.00E+06	5.00E+06
International	3.00E+07	1.00E−01	1.00E+07	5.00E+07

CONSTANTS

Vel Light (m/s)	3.00E+08	
Clock Rate	1.00E+08	(100 MHz)
	5.00E+08	(500 MHz)

communications network suggestions to minimize them.[11] For example, to minimize the effects of long on-chip interconnections, communication pipelining, repeaters, and other network techniques can be utilized to provide more cost-effective performance. The important thing to realize from a pragmatic standpoint is that there is a communications network problem associated with chips. Furthermore, if there are such problems on a chip, although the significant parameters may be different, they must be present on systems that cover a wider spatial area.

It is perhaps worth noting that if propagation delay is important, satellite systems have their shortcomings because of the long up and down paths involved. It is interesting that this factor alone has made satellites unsatisfactory for high-quality telephone service where delays in response annoy the customers. Our nervous systems operate with millisecond logic; computers operate on a time scale of microseconds or better. It is easy to visualize circumstances in which satellite communication would be unacceptable in a distributed computer system.

In the transfer of data, the time needed to set up a connection and for the first part of a message to transverse the path, and the transfer rate of data once a connection is functioning are all important.[12] The first two processes determine how soon any data are transferred, and the third determines how long it takes to transfer the desired quantity of data after the flow is started. These factors may result in delays that greatly exceed the delay due to propagation time. They vary widely with the type of network, the types of switching used, the proximity of nodes, and so forth. We do not wish to go into details now, for they will be discussed in later chapters, but perhaps a few examples are in order. (New terms will be defined later and in the glossary.)

1. Direct hard-wired connections, such as those found on chips, have zero setup time and a high transfer rate.

2. A shared bus structure may have preassigned time slots, and in that sense zero setup time. On the other hand, a process may have to wait its turn.

3. The conventional common carrier network has a relatively long setup time, as you undoubtedly have noted when you dial a number, but if configured for wideband service can have a relatively high transfer rate.

---

11. D. Audet, Y. Savaria, and N. Arel, "Pipelining Communications in Large VLSI/ULSI Systems," *IEEE Transactions on Very Large Scale Interaction (VLSI) Systems* 2, no. 1 (March 1994): 1.

12. L. Kleinrock, "The Latency/Bandwidth Tradeoff in Gigabit Networks—Gigabit Networks Really Are Different," *IEEE Communications Magazine* 30, no. 4 (April 1992): 36.

4. Packet switching has little setup time but a lot of processing delay as packets progress through the network.

5. Packet switching that utilizes virtual circuits does in effect have a setup time—i.e., setting up the path that will be used by all packets in a particular message—but processing during the flow of packets is greatly reduced.

Delays in categories like those given above can be due to hardware cycle or switching time, delays in associated hardwired logic, or as is usually the case, the time that it takes to execute software. Stored program logic is so pervasive in communications equipment today that software execution time is by far the biggest cause of delay in setting up communications circuits. In some circumstances, it may also be the biggest cause of delay after a circuit is established.

In this section, we have been concerned with the transport of data. If we turn to the post office for an analogy, we have been concerned with transporting an envelope from one place to another. We have not been concerned with what is in the envelope. We have tried to establish some of the physical parameters that may be important in reaching decisions concerning the transport of data and the interconnection of computing engines of all sizes.

3.5   The One-Level Store Concept

We discussed earlier that processor speed is increasing much more rapidly than memory speed. It is imperative that we utilize concepts that will make the speed of memory appear to the processing unit to be faster than it actually is. Data buffering in registers or very fast memory are examples. A cache is another example, and most readers probably have some knowledge of the cache concept from experience with personal computers and workstations.

In addition to confronting the local memory to CPU mismatch in speed, we are faced with obtaining access to very large databases. Taken as a whole, databases may be spread out over a mixture of memory storage devices of various capacities and performance levels. The memory in a computer complex can range from fast on-chip semiconductor memory associated with the CPU to banks of storage elements—for example, magnetic tape cassettes similar to those used in VCRs or optical disks similar to CD-ROMs. The banks of storage elements may be on-line as in a RAID memory system, off line (but when called for automatically loaded by a jukebox arrangement), or a combination of the two approaches. A RAID (Redundant Array of Inexpensive Disks) system is a bank of on-line hard disks connected in a sophisticated way to increase the total storage, transfer rate, and reliability of the overall disk system,

Table 3.2 Typical Memory Costs (as of 1995)

Storage Type	Dollars Per Megabyte	Remarks
Semiconductor RAM	40.	Tens of nanosecond access time; high transfer rates.
Hard disk	0.4	Tens of milliseconds access time;
Hard disk (RAID)	.9	tens of MB/s transfer rates; average RAID values better than above.
Magnetic tape cartridge	0.02	Access time long; transfer rate may
Magnetic tape cartridge plus jukebox	0.1	be high.
CD-ROM raw disk	0.002	Access time hundreds of milliseconds;
CR-ROM disk plus reader	.3	transfer rate hundreds of KB/s; disk
CD-ROM disk plus jukebox reader	.2	loading from jukebox in seconds.
CD-R raw disk (read plus record once)	0.02	For single disk unit.
CD-R disk plus reader/recorder	3.	
CD-ROM jukebox complex including a few optional recordable drives	0.15	Total capacity may reach terabytes.

and, at the same time, to reduce the access time.[13] A jukebox is a mechanical loader that holds a number of individual storage devices and upon demand physically moves a specific storage element (e.g., a magnetic cassette or CD-ROM) to an internal reading station that is in turn connected to a computer. We should not underestimate the applicability of some of these techniques. For example, information from the U.S. Patent Office is stored in a jukebox arrangement that contains 1,600 CDs for a total of 1.04 terabytes of data.[14]

Table 3.2 provides typical approximate cost figures (1995) per megabyte of memory for a few of the alternatives for storage. The important thing to notice is the large range in costs. As far as the future is concerned, there are developments that appear promising and it is to be expected that storage device capacities will continue to increase.[15]

---

13. T. A. Skeie and M. R. Rusnack, "An Overview of RAID Technology," *HP Journal* 46, no. 3 (June 1995): 74.

14. L. G. Paul, "Jukeboxes Can Harmonize Storage in a Net Environment," *PC Week,* December 26, 1994–January 2, 1995, p. 83.

15. Robert F. Service, "Pushing the Data Storage Envelope," *Science* 269 (July 21, 1995); Praveen Asthana and Blair Finkelstein, "Superdense Optical Storage," *IEEE Spectrum* 32, no. 8 (August 1995): 25.

The early work on sophisticated memory management and cachelike systems goes back to the Atlas computer at the University of Manchester in England. A paging system called a one-level storage system[16] was implemented on that computer and ran for several years before the concept was introduced in the United States and referred to by terms like cache and virtual memory. The one-level store concept was, and is, probably the most significant memory management concept that has been invented. It is of major importance in all computers—from personal computers to supercomputers—and it is central to viable architectures for distributed computers. The central concepts are discussed in this chapter for they are needed throughout the book. The applicability of the technique to distributed information systems and data networks is discussed later. We need additional background before embarking on that discussion.

The Atlas had a magnetic core memory of 16 K words and a 96 K word magnetic drum. (In computers, 1 K = 1024.) The objective was to build a system in which, as far as the application programmers were concerned, there was just one large memory, the size of the drum, but with an effective speed approaching that of the core memory. The designers met that objective, obtaining the following results:

1. The effective time to access a memory location approximated the access time of the core memory. This is the result that has had the most significant impact on the performance of modern computers and distributed systems.

2. The applications programmers wrote programs for a random access memory the size of the drum memory. This was also very important. In many applications this may be of less significance today because of the very large memories that are available. However, virtual memories are widely used today, are very important in solving problems with large data sets, and are basically an example of the one-level store concept in action.

The concept of the one-level store is applicable to the multilevel memory hierarchies of today. We have elected to discuss it in terms of that hierarchy rather than a single computer and its CPU. We use the term memory hierarchy to imply different memory systems, coupled together, and ranging from fast on-chip semiconductor memory to banks of cassette magnetic tape drives. The former is the fastest and the most expensive; the latter is the cheapest and the

16. T. Kilburn, D. Edwards, J. L. Lanigan, and F. H. Sumner, "One-Level Storage System," *IRE Transactions on Electronic Computers* (April 1962): 223.

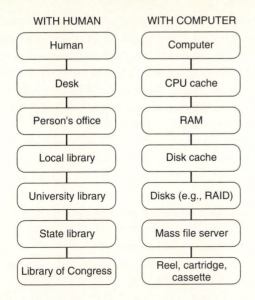

Figure 3.5 How humans and computers handle data

slowest. The goal is for the user to perceive this hierarchy as one memory, with a speed approaching that of the top member of the hierarchy. The details of what data are where in the hierarchy should be transparent to users unless they ask for and are entitled to those details. Figure 3.5 explains the basic concept by showing how humans handle data and how data are processed in a memory hierarchy. The comparison is presented in terms of memory components with both read and write capability although conceptually read-only components (e.g., optical disks) could be added. Furthermore, the prospects are good that in the future read/write optical disks will be available.

Let's look first at the human, a person working without a computer in an office and who consequently must use classical methods of getting information. The human does all of the computing or data processing utilizing his brain, working papers on his desk, and referring to papers and books that for the moment may be on the desk. In brief, the human corresponds to the CPU of the computer, the material on the desk to the cache and the remainder of the chain of data sources are just to provide either human or computer with information. The concept is simple. When the human wants a piece of information (data), he looks first on the desk; if it is not on his desk, he looks in the office. If necessary, he then goes down the library chain—from local to university to state to federal—until he obtains what is needed. In practice he does not have to do all the work of searching catalogs down the chain. Local librarians will usually perform this service—and if they cannot, they will make a request to a university library and so on. The strategy is clear. Keep what you need at the present time where it is easy (fast) to get at. Furthermore, once you get material (information) from a lower source, keep it close (on your desk) until you are finished with it. When you are finished with it, send it back because your desk can hold only so much and the space will be needed for new material. (If you think you might need it again soon, you may keep it in your office or in the local library until you are really finished with it.)

What does the computer system (CPU) do? It follows the same strategy with minor modifications. When the CPU wants data, it looks first in the cache, and if the data are in the cache, it has almost immediate access just as the human does with data on a desk. If the data are not in the cache, the CPU looks in the RAM, and if the data are there, it moves them to the cache, just as the human moves information to the desk. If the data are not in the RAM, the CPU looks in the disk system and so forth.

The differences between human and computer systems can be further summarized:

1. The computer system usually works with copies, not originals. Thus what is in a cache is also in RAM and so forth down the chain. In the age of photocopy machines, this may not be too different for the human.

2. If there are changes made that should be reflected in the source documents, the human must accept responsibility for updating the documents further down the chain. The computer system does this automatically, assuming of course that it does not malfunction. This is not a problem for a CPU and its on-chip cache. It is a serious problem if many users are accessing and making changes in data from a shared file. We shall have much more to say about this later.

We have presented a global picture of one-level stores. We elected to do so because it is the global picture and the associated memory hierarchy that are important in distributed information systems. That is the perspective that is needed in architectural work. To summarize what is taking place:

1. The CPU always looks at the highest memory level of the hierarchy for the data that it needs.

2. If the desired data are not there, the operating system, and the services provided by the distributed system architecture, take care of delivering the data to the CPU.

3. In like fashion, the human looks first on his desk and in his office, and then turns to administrative assistants and librarians to do the rest.

To make the implementation appear more real, we provide two examples, with the understanding that there are many configurations and implementations that differ in detail. The examples are provided in textual form. When used as a course text or reference, details can be covered by the instructor. Those interested in exploring the implementation of one-level stores further will find details in the literature under additional topics such as paging, segmentation, virtual memory, and memory hierarchy.

Utilizing Address Mapping Hardware: A RAM Cache Example

1. The original Atlas implementation partitioned the virtual memory (i.e., the available memory on the drum) into pages. The pages were defined by higher order bits in the address field. Those pages that were active had copies in the high-speed core memory. A fast associative memory, called a page box, was used to map the higher order bits that defined the location of a page on the drum into the actual base address of the copy of that page in the high-speed memory. Thus, if the page was in the high-speed memory, the requested data word was rapidly obtained from high-speed memory.

2. If the word was changed as a result of computation, the change was made by an analogous procedure to the corresponding high-speed memory location and also in the original on the drum.

3. If the page was not in high-speed memory, then there was no match in the associative memory. A copy of the page was then taken from the drum, placed in high-speed memory, and the page box updated to reflect that change. Things then proceeded as described above.

4. Pages cannot be added to high-speed memory without making room for the new pages. The space occupied by recently unused pages is made available for new pages by a procedure called *garbage collection*. *Garbage* refers to pages that contain data no longer referenced. There are various algorithms used for garbage collection—for example, reuse the space of the pages that have gone unused for the longest time.

5. This same basic implementation was used in the IBM 367, the GE 645, and the SDS 940 computers. A similar procedure of mapping addresses is used higher up the memory chain in many of the on-chip caches that can be found in personal computers and work-stations.

Utilizing Address Mapping Software: A Disk Cache Example

1. Disk paging was first introduced in large-scale systems; today, as with many other techniques, it is widely used in PC size machines. Those blocks of data (from the disk) that are in use are kept in a special part of high-speed memory. In IBM compatible PCs, extended memory is usually used. Instead of using a hardware page box, the mapping from virtual memory to high-speed memory is through software that runs in high-speed memory. Although software has replaced hardware, the basic logical concept is the same. Other than the above, the operation is similar to that of the original one-level store on the Atlas.

2. Disk caches can make a significant difference in performance. For example, in working on this book for several hours, it was typical for there to be 200,000 file (disk) requests. More than 95 percent of those requests were usually filled from the disk cache in high speed memory. At an average saving of 40 milliseconds for each request filled from high speed memory—instead of the disk—the saving in time was substantial. The ratio can go much higher. In a single three-hour session, an author working with a genealogy database problem experienced several million disk requests, of which more than 99 percent were filled from the cache. Pragmatically, when a disk cache is used, the disk memory appears to the CPU to be much faster than it is. The 95 percent is typical of experience with caches at a CPU, memory, or disk level.

As noted earlier, there are many different ways that the one-level store concept can be implemented, and there is a wide choice of parameters for such systems. The parameter values can make a big difference in performance and are dependent on the applications that are expected. When a distributed system has many components or is widely dispersed, the number of important parameters and the tradeoffs implicit in selecting parameter values can become very large. These are issues that we shall discuss later.

3.6 Summary and Comments

Physical parameters and state-of-the-art semiconductor electronics set boundary conditions within which architecture must be established. Architecture should provide performance that maximizes inherent hardware capabilities and minimizes the effects of hardware and physical limitations.

Improvements in lithography and its use in the production of semiconductors are rapidly improving on-chip computational capability. It is expected that this will continue in the foreseeable future.

There is a widening gap between CPU speed and that of memory. Add to this the pragmatic fact that for cost reasons it is necessary to use a spectrum of memory in a hierarchy composed of devices of widely varying sizes, access times, and transfer rates. Consequently, architectures must be sought that make memory appear faster than it is. The one-level store (or cache) concept can be effective in accomplishing this.

Architectural designs are needed to provide more concurrent (parallel) processing within a single CPU and within a collection of core computing engines that may make up a larger computer.

Propagation time and other data transport (e.g. transfer) delays are important at all levels of a computational hierarchy. They become even more critical if the overall system is spread over a large geographical area.

Memory management and associated data availability capabilities are probably the key issues in distributed computers and information systems.

3.7 Problems

1. Consider the trends of physical technology discussed in this chapter. Include in your thinking software that is directly associated with the performance of hardware. Write less than two pages in response to the following questions: (a) What do you believe are the five most important trends? Explain your reasoning. (b) What do you believe are the five most important limitations? Explain your reasoning.

2. The amount of RAM available in the computers of today is increasing consistently. Main memory resident systems such as databases are being studied. Given this reality, defend or criticize the following statement: "Given sufficient RAM per computer, one-level store technology is an issue of the past."

Chapter 4

An Information System Viewpoint

In recorded history there have perhaps been three pulses of change powerful enough to alter Man in basic ways. The introduction of agriculture. . . . the Industrial Revolution . . . (and) the revolution in information processing technology of the computer.

Herbert A. Simon[1]

4.1   Chapter Objectives

The essential role that mechanized information systems play in our society was discussed in Chapter 1. The use of computers in such systems is key to the functioning of almost all segments of society—with many businesses unable to operate if their computerized information systems are down. Dependency on computerized systems will become more prevalent in the future. Those countries, and the segments of society within those countries, that make full use of the technology will have a distinct competitive advantage. This will be true in the political, commercial, military, educational, social, and other areas of activity.

The first objective of this chapter is to review the technical requirements that information systems must be prepared to meet. Understanding these needs is extremely important for they provide a basis for specifying many of the requirements that we would like computer systems to meet. In many system-related areas, these may be different and more severe than the requirements for systems to serve science and engineering. The intention is to review those features that might be required in an information system. Similar to the earlier discussion of distributed system architecture, we are looking for a superset of requirements that will encompass those that we are likely to meet in

1. H. A. Simon, "The Impact of the Computer on Management," in Yoneji Masuda, *The Information Society as Post-Industrial Society* (Bethesda, MD: World Future Society, 1981).

a specific application. For a specific application, realistic requirements, attainable performance, and cost performance criteria should determine which of the possible features should be included.

The second objective is to consider the technical and nontechnical driving forces for distributed computing. In the context of this chapter, the driving forces for distributed information systems would be a better description. Technology-based cost performance tradeoffs, organizational issues, and human relations are all important. It may well be, however, that the nontechnical driving forces, those associated with organizations and people, are the most important. The third objective of this chapter is to explore that possibility.

4.2   Information System Requirements

4.2.1   Environmental Considerations

It was noted earlier that computerized information systems are essential to the functioning of modern society. Adapting to these changed circumstances, that is, utilizing the opportunities presented by the computer age, has required a major change in the culture and structure of many organizations.[2] For example, when computerized information systems were introduced in product development, one of the payoffs was the ability to better integrate the functions of advanced development, advanced engineering, manufacturing engineering, manufacturing, distribution, and in some cases marketing. In this process, the managers and administrators of the various functions lost a good deal of their independence of action. It was necessary in many respects to merge the previously almost independent domain of advanced engineering groups with the previously almost independent domain of the manufacturing engineering groups. Such changes were often only grudgingly accepted by, say, a manager of manufacturing engineering who had been running his own independent group for almost two decades. Even today, the precise role, limitations, and implementation problems associated with Integrated Computer Aided Design and Computer Aided Manufacturing (CAD/CAM) are not fully appreciated.[3] A similar and perhaps more severe situation exists in the medical field where many hospitals are basically divided into independent fiefdoms according to specialties such as surgery, radiology, etc. Whether we like to admit it or not,

---

2. Michael S. Scott, Morton, *The Corporation of the 1990s: Information Technology and Organizational Transformation* (New York: Oxford University Press, 1991). This book focuses on the results of a six-year study at MIT's Sloan School of Management.

3. Robert J. Thomas, *What Machines Can't Do—Politics and Technology in the Industrial Enterprise*, Berkeley: University of California Press, 1994. A good discussion of the human side of technological innovation.

the introduction of state-of-the-art computerized societal systems have often been more limited by cultural and organizational questions than by technology or economics.

Why are issues like this important to us? Succinctly, such factors are part of the environment in which we as computer professionals must work. Computer systems people can neither design nor implement an information system without understanding the application, including the culture and people involved.[4] To complicate matters further, the ultimate user generally has little knowledge of the limitations of technology nor the tradeoffs involved in seeking a cost-effective solution to a problem. Somehow these different perspectives must be brought together. The development of requirements for a specific system should be a joint effort of systems people with design responsibility and the user community, which must be and feel a part of the development.

As this is a book largely for technologists, the focus in this section is on bringing to that group the perspective of the ultimate user. The question is, what does the ultimate user need and expect? What do we as technologists have to provide to meet that portion of his perceived needs that can be met economically by state-of-the-art technology? What's in it for the user? What are the performance requirements that must be met? We must address these questions from the viewpoint of the user. Societal interest lies far more in the capabilities and performance of information systems than in the computing and communications engines that go into them. It is a safe assumption that the user will have no real interest in computers or communications per se.

We believe that it is proper to call to the attention of the reader such user-oriented issues. There are too many information systems that have proven to be unsatisfactory because either:

1. The stated requirements did not reflect what was really needed; thus although the requirements were met, the need was not filled.

2. The users would not use the system because they did not feel they were a part of it and were not adequately prepared for it or trained to use it.

The success of a design and implementation must be judged primarily by the ultimate use of the product. Design and implementation should be addressed in that context. With that in mind, let us turn to the alternatives. What requirements might we need to fill?

---

4. Donald C. Gause and Gerald M. Weinberg, *Exploring Requirement—Quality Before Design* (New York: Dorset House, 1989); Karen Holtzblatt and Hugh R. Beyer, "Requirements Gathering: The Human Factor," *Communications of the ACM* 38, no. 5 (May 1995): 30.

4.2.2   Potential Requirements

There are only certain things that information systems do. For example, one function may be to retrieve data. The overall system combines elementary functions to perform what is needed. This is similar to a FORTRAN program combining elementary operations such as divide, multiply, add, etc., to produce an engineering result. For scientific calculations, we reduce requirements to such things as millions of floating-point instructions per second. If vector operations are not needed, they should not be included in a requirements statement. We select from the alternatives those operations that are needed, assign appropriate parameter values, and include them in the requirements statement. In what follows we consider the elementary system operational requirements of information systems. As might be expected, they are oriented to data. Most of the things that, from a requirements standpoint we expect a specific information system to do, should be describable in terms of an appropriate selection of those elementary operations and associated parameter values. Information systems should have the following potential capabilities to be invoked and utilized as required by specific applications:[5]

1. *Data must be promptly captured at its source.* Whether it will be necessary to make the data immediately available to the information system and users as a whole will depend on the application. For example, payroll related information is generally not needed in real time, as payroll processing is scheduled at specific intervals. In contrast, the present status of a machine in a factory is needed for scheduling, the assignment of personnel, and factory control in general. Similarities exist in airline systems where information for ticketing purposes has quite different requirements than that for payroll, scheduled maintenance, etc.

   The immediate capture of data at the source can also provide an immediate check on the consistency of data. Information systems often contain either redundant data or data that should meet some calculable criteria. If either a redundancy check, or a calculable check fails, that failure calls attention to an inconsistency, and either human or machine action, or both, can be taken to correct the situation before the consequences spread. Information systems are often designed with this in mind. If a tray of semiconductor wafers has one less wafer than at the last workstation, there must be a reason. If a part going through a sequence of machining operations that remove metal has suddenly gained weight, something is wrong with

5. Richard L. Shuey, "Industry and Computers," *IEEE Transactions on Manufacturing Technology* MFT–4, no. 2 (December 1975): 37–42.

the instrumentation or human input. If too little material has been removed, perhaps the cutters are worn, etc. The control room at the Three Mile Island nuclear plant at the time of the accident contained lots of inconsistent data. However, at Three Mile Island consistency and other checks, and a program for action, had not been thought out in sufficient detail. If this type of situation had been anticipated, and the control room computers programmed accordingly, the accident could have been avoided. As it was, the operators were presented with hundreds of visual inputs with no real assessment of what they meant taken as a whole. Designing in redundancy, and utilizing it, can improve quality and system control.

In any application area, there is a requirement to capture data. There are situations where the data are not immediately required, and they may even be submitted in paper form by a person later. An example is the submission on paper of expense accounts, or students' grades. But even in these examples there is a tendency to go to direct computer input. In this section we are considering the most severe case in each category of elementary requirements, and the most severe case of data capture is to capture data immediately at the source. As is appropriate, the requirement can be relaxed, but a covering architecture must be able to meet this requirement. This also is true of the requirement categories discussed below, but for brevity this observation will not be repeated.

2. *Where possible, mechanize or automate the capture of data.* The automatic capture of data is important for several reasons. First, human beings are notorious for making errors in inputting data. Where data capture is mechanized, error rates are greatly reduced. Second, there are many circumstances where for time of response or other reasons, capture must be mechanized. Third, it is often the case that even if a human can play a direct role in the capture of data, the cost will be substantially more than mechanized capture. Fourth, if mechanized, the sheer quantity of data that can be captured may increase by orders of magnitude. This can be very important. One has the option of capturing essentially all available data, and later discarding the data that with time are shown to be of no importance. The black boxes in aircraft that are used in investigating the causes of crashes are an example. The same system would be desirable in a nuclear plant: Capture all the data from the thousand or so sensors, discard most of them after a period of normal operation but have them available in the short term if needed to analyze and correct abnormal operations.

3. *Once captured, data accepted by the information system cannot be lost.* This is increasingly a requirement of information systems. For reasons discussed earlier, there is often no paper backup. It is important to understand what is implied when we say that data accepted by an information system cannot be lost. That statement applies to information systems in general, including those containing distributed computers and communications equipment that we must assume will fail. In such circumstances, data cannot be considered as entered into an information system until that system indicates that it has accepted the data. An indication of accepting data implies that data have already been stored in a sufficient number of locations, including perhaps ones spatially removed, that they will not be lost. When the extreme end of this requirement is needed, the consequences on architectural design and performance can be very serious.

   This requirement is often not necessary in engineering calculations. In this case many of the calculations can be redone. Tradeoff considerations may indicate that it will be more cost effective to redo the calculations than to pay the necessary price in performance and dollars if the rigorous requirement not to lose data is imposed. Again, the reader is reminded that we are intentionally taking the view of a superset of requirements.

   The preparation of this textbook is an example of the authors' strong feeling that data should not be lost by a computer system. The text rarely exists in printed form. All the text is in personal computer files. This particular section is being written at 30,000 feet in an airplane over the Midwest. Prior to turning off the laptop being used, a backup disk will be prepared. It is normal practice to keep two sets of backup disks.

   Finally, in some domains within the field of information systems, there can be catastrophic consequences caused by the loss of data. Consider a medical information system containing patient records. If the attributes of the stored data that indicate that a particular patient is allergic to penicillin are corrupted, a doctor may unknowingly prescribe penicillin to that patient, resulting in dire consequences. Information systems in such domains typically are strictly and legally regulated regarding the capture and retention of data.

4. *The database must provide a current consistent view of factual and derived information to all users. Data integrity is essential. Everyone in an organization must be using the same consistent and correct data.* This is again a very tight restriction. The users of a system do not always need current real-time data, as was illustrated by the payroll example. Others do not require precise data. There are requirement tradeoffs that

must be made between adhering to the strict requirement above and, where acceptable, relaxing those conditions for performance and cost reasons. Consequently, when it comes to deciding what features will be provided for a specific application and user, there are design tradeoffs to be made. At the same time, for a variety of reasons including cost performance, we cannot preclude intentionally restricting the views (data visible to a process or person) in some applications, even to the point that those processes or people will be working with inconsistent data. For example, in a reservation system, in order to cover the no-shows, the reserver may be informed that vacancies exist when in fact they do not. In the marketing of products, the field force may be given a different view of products than that available in advanced engineering and manufacturing. For national security reasons, those in high-level intelligence work may be provided with a much more accurate picture of events than others. In addition, from a computer system standpoint, there are situations in which imposing strict concurrency controls will unacceptably degrade performance. In these examples, there may be inconsistencies between the views mentioned.

5. *There must be adequate control of the access to data and information, including solutions to privacy and security requirements.* As information systems become all-pervasive, the sharing of data becomes more common. At the same time, shared data are used for many purposes. Whether or not access should be permitted to data will depend on both the user and the use that the person or process intends to make of the data. This area can be very complex, is usually inadequately addressed, and is very difficult to control. For example, assume that it is appropriate for an individual to have access for statistical purposes only to a financial database. If you are skilled enough and can ask unrestricted statistical questions, you may well be able to obtain specific data. Problems of this type are often referred to as aggregation and inference problems for statistical databases. Security involves many architectural alternatives and tradeoffs. For example, it is often possible to deny access to unauthorized users at the network level prior to reaching a computer system. Access may be a function of the communications node used—for example, a boss may obtain access only by being at the terminal in his or her office and using certain passwords. Considering the tradeoffs, which alternatives should the designer pick?

6. *Many of the multiple users of a system must be able to alter the data contained in the database.* This is the essence of multiple user transaction processing systems—and it is the only way that data can be kept cur-

rent. The degree to which multiple users may simultaneously wish to alter a specific data item has a crucial impact on architecture. The fundamental limitations on attainable response time in such circumstances must also be considered.

7. *Where necessary, the results of computations and data processing must be rapidly and readily available.* The operation of most organizations is dependent upon information. The processing of raw data is essential and necessary if conclusions are to be reached. Deciding a course of action—whether it be in a business setting, factory operation, government agency, or military installation—requires derived information. That derived information must be available in a timely fashion.

8. *The information and control system must be available when needed (i.e., in some cases at all times).* The preceding paragraph implies that when required, the information systems must have rapid responses. Almost as a corollary to that requirement, the systems must be reliable, not subject to operational failure, and available as needed.

9. *The overall information system must be able to meld together various heterogeneous subinformation systems and databases, many of which may have been independently developed.* Pragmatically one cannot do everything over again. An evolutionary path is desired that can utilize systems that exist. It is also true that the issue is not just older systems. Increasingly the information systems within a given organization develop a need to interface with information systems in other organizations. This melding is a formidable problem. The experience of the U.S. Department of Defense in this area is interesting.[6] We shall return to relevant issues on this topic in later chapters of this book.

4.2.3   Tradeoff Considerations

The requirements outlined in Section 4.2.2 are not entirely independent or orthogonal. Many of them strongly interact. For example, the requirement that data not be lost impacts on time of response, cost, and system availability, among other factors. A system that updates and verifies duplicated databases prior to acknowledging receipt of data can be expensive. The user is confronted with a decision: should this course be followed, or are the journal files (logging of transactions) that will permit reconstruction of a database sufficient? The latter will be much less costly. If you are on a mission to the moon and the data involve your flight control, you would prefer the former. If you

6. P. Aiken, A. Muntz, and R. Richards, "DoD Legacy Systems: Reverse Engineering Data Requirements," *Communications of the ACM* 37, no. 5 (May 1994): 26.

are running a factory, you may play the statistics and be willing to shut down the factory for the time that it takes you to reconstruct the database from journal files. Tradeoffs of these types are very real.

Providing the technical features that meet all of the requirements discussed earlier can be expensive. Cost performance considerations will always be important. Furthermore, in some cases, requiring stringent features may make it impossible to attain the required performance. It is not just a question of cost. An appreciation of tradeoffs is a requirement for design. Cost and performance considerations often dictate that only that which is necessary should be implemented. One should include only those features that are really needed and to the degree (parameter values) that they are needed. At the same time, if possible, select an architecture that will support evolution into a system with more stringent requirements.

4.3   Why Distributed Computing?

4.3.1   The Necessity for an Information System Viewpoint

The point has already been made that in our society people are much more involved with the information systems made possible by modern computer and communications technology than with computers per se. They are concerned with what systems involving computers can do for them. These people are the customers of our technology. They indirectly finance and support our work, whether it be in education, research, development, government, or commerce.

The users of computers are active participants in the trend toward distributed information systems. In fact, the attitudes and actions of users have been the driving force. What are the forces behind this movement? Some of those forces are technological. Others are much more related to sociological issues. Let us now focus on the forces in both categories.

4.3.2   Hardware Technical Factors

Chapter 3 discussed the trends of electronic very large scale integration (VLSI) and the computer system implications resulting from those trends. The implications with respect to distributed computing can be summarized by the following paradigms.[7]

---

7. For scientific usage of the term paradigm, see Thomas S. Kuhn, *The Structure of Scientific Revolutions* (Chicago: University of Chicago Press, 1962).

VLSI Driven Paradigms

Paradigm 1: By purchasing items in large quantities, the unit cost is often reduced. Similarly, it used to be that the cost per calculation was much less if performed on a very large computer than if performed in a small computer. This type of thing is referred to as economy of scale. *Except in special cases, an economy of scale in computing no longer exists. This applies to both computing and storage.*

Paradigm 2: The costs associated with computation and storage have decreased at a faster rate than overall communications costs. It is expected that this trend will continue.

Paradigm 3: Unless there is a reason for centralization, computing and data storage will occur where needed.

It is evident from these paradigms, that the location of information system components will be determined by factors other than the cost of raw computing, storage, or communications. What are some of those factors? What are the driving forces? How do we decide whether a system should be distributed? How do we decide where the elements of a distributed system should be? These are issues that will be addressed in the remainder of this book. They are, however, only selectively touched on in the remainder of this chapter. Specifically, we mention several that are related to information system operation.

System Cost Considerations

We are not concerned with the cost of free-standing distributed systems—systems that are not connected by some type of electrical communications network. If a problem, such as writing this book, can be done on free-standing personal computers, economic considerations and other factors favor doing it that way. In this case, three authors were involved and they used different personal computers. However, care was taken to use compatible hardware and common software, and to establish standards and production practices that ensured the easy exchange of data. In a case like this, we are not concerned with system costs, which are essentially those of the computers and software. The system cost considerations we will focus on in this chapter imply the costs associated with establishing and operating a network of electronically interconnected computers. This is increasingly the model for the overall information system of an enterprise and for the interconnection of the information systems of separate enterprises.

The semiconductor-based paradigms discussed above indicate that economy of scale of computing or storage will not be a reason to centralize. However, the location of computing and storage may impact overall system costs, and designers must be aware of this possibility. In fact, experience has shown that system-related costs can be substantial. The reasons for this, some of which were mentioned earlier, will be examined in detail later. Others will be introduced later. Introducing system costs associated with networked computers at this time should not be interpreted as an indication of the desirability of reversing the movement to distributed computing. We do not believe that this should or will occur. The material is included here to provide perspective, indicate tradeoff issues, and focus on areas where advances in technology can reduce system costs. Although not a subject of this book, there is also a need to adjust management and administrative practices to minimize overall system costs.

Recent studies have indicated that a client server network is roughly twice as expensive to support as a mainframe system.[8] The proliferation of portable computers only complicates the problem of system integration, and adds operational expense.[9] It was noted earlier that the implementation of information systems has become distributed. In the absence of common standards, an agreed-upon implementation discipline, and an overall strategic information system plan, the distributed developers too often produce component information systems that do not work together easily. There is no fundamental reason that this should be so. In part, this book is focused on the issues that must be resolved if the system costs of distributed information systems are to be properly controlled. There is no turning back, for the advantages of distributed systems are too great. It is a challenge to take the necessary steps to put things in order.

4.3.3   Technical and Business Factors in the Trend to Distributed Systems

Appropriately designed distributed systems can provide superior low sensitivity to failures of specific computing and communications components compared with what is attainable with a centralized system. This has been a very difficult thing for much of management to take seriously. One must assume that computer and communications systems will fail, or be rendered inoperative for other reasons. In addition to equipment failures, a specific location

8. Ken Miller, "Fighting the High Cost of Client-Server Computing," *Data Communications,* May 21, 1994, p. 29; Michael Meyer, "Rethinking Your Mainframe," *Newsweek,* June 6, 1994, p. 49.

9. Brian Gillooly, "Pulling the Strings—How Can IS Manage Laptop PCs that Are Scattered Far and Wide," *Information Week,* August 28, 1995, p. 47.

may face power outages, earthquakes, strikes, fires, bombs, and sabotage. Several years ago a fire in the Hinsdale, Illinois, central telephone office made it impossible for a substantial number of businesses to operate, upset the air traffic control system at O'Hare airport causing substantial delays, and was a general inconvenience to many area enterprises. For those national and international businesses depending upon centralized computers and databases in the affected area, the result was devastating. Other disasters come to mind: the bombings at the World Trade Center and the Oklahoma City federal building, the failure of AT&T's network in New Jersey, the Los Angeles earthquake. All have captured the attention of managers and administrators, and all provide a strong driving force for distributed systems. An architectural challenge is to provide the required level of availability and, when failures occur, reduced information-processing capability that includes essential services. It is usually better to operate with partial, local, or old data, than none at all. Essential data should be available. A remote centralized computer system that is unavailable may provide none of these. If it is disabled, there is nothing. Perhaps an example is in order.

It has been seriously proposed by major computer manufacturers and the providers of computer services that remote large-scale systems be used to control factories. It would be very foolish to follow this practice. The information system controlling the short-term operation of a factory should be local. It should be independent of the catastrophes mentioned above occurring at a remote location. On the other hand, the long-term control of the factory—e.g., scheduling—may be unavoidably dependent on more global information located at a remote location.

Increasingly, there is a need to interact with the computer systems of customers, suppliers, government agencies, libraries, and other data repositories. Such interactions almost by definition form distributed systems.

Certain organizations, like the military or mobile groups, have distributed operations that are constantly moving. In the case of the military, they must also assume the destruction of fixed installations. These considerations introduce unique problems. It is clear that in many cases, key information systems should be local and go with the organization when it moves.

There are many reasons—psychological, organizational, management, legal, etc.—for distributing computing. Managers like to have things for which they are responsible within reach and under their control. From a technical standpoint, such attitudes may not be entirely rational, but they are real. They are often the determining factor in reaching decisions and cannot be ignored.

Security and privacy have to a large degree been inadequately treated in most information system work. Unfortunately, it is often the case that adequate focus and action are unlikely until serious detectable breaches occur.

Communications security has a strong integrated companion in security issues associated with information storage. The techniques are basically the same, and we shall consider them as one. Their importance permeates national security, crime control, business operations, and perhaps most significantly personal privacy, freedom, and rights. For the time being, two points should be noted: (1) these issues will become more important in the future, and (2) at a certain level, the best practice is to use a local computer, put a well-guarded fence around the installation, and make it impossible for the computer system to communicate with the outside world (other than by human intervention). Those interested in further details are referred to Levy for an overview and to Denning for a technical discussion.[10]

4.4   Summary and Comments

Some important overall observations and guidelines are summarized below.

1. With some limited but significant exceptions, information processing will be done where it is needed and can be properly controlled with respect to access and use.

2. In distributed systems, we would like to restore the level of coherent integration in information systems that was possible in centralized systems. The implied coherence applies to hardware, software, the information system developers, and the users.

3. The coordination and integration of components are essential if the end users are to be provided with an acceptable interface on their own terms. That interface includes both the users and information system developers who to a large degree will be in the organizations of the users.

4. Increasingly, the development of the individual components of an overall information system will be distributed. Unless properly structured and implemented, distributed development can lead to serious system integration problems.

5. Define a minimum set of standards, which if conformed to, will make it possible for the distributed components of the overall system to work together. This must involve the integration of standards in computers, communication, and information systems.

---

10. Steven Levy, "Battle of the Clipper Chip," *New York Times Magazine,* June 12, 1994; Dorothy Denning, *Cryptography and Data Security* (Reading, MA: Addison-Wesley, 1982).

6. Indicate and encourage the adjustments in administrative and management practices necessary to make effective use of distributed systems. The trend to distributed computing, and information system development, cannot, and should not, be stopped.

7. Aim for functional transparency between all applications and the databases that they may share. We do not know if this is attainable in any generic sense, nor if possible, do we know the necessary and sufficient conditions that must be met.

8. There is often a real need to bring together diverse, heterogeneous, subinformation systems in a coherent fashion.

4.5   Problems

1. Consider the potential requirements in Section 4.2.2. (a) Have requirements that you consider important been omitted? If so, what are they? (b) Have requirements that you consider unnecessary been included? If so, which ones?

2. The move to distributed systems is well underway. What do you believe are the five most important business or operational factors that are responsible for the trend to distributed computing?

3. At the present time it is widely believed that the overall hardware, software, and operational costs of a server-oriented system exceed those of a centralized system performing the same functions. What steps do you believe need to be taken to make server-based systems less costly?

Chapter 5

Categories of Distributed Systems

Engineers try to create better artifacts (i.e., artifacts that offer greater utility or functionality in the computational setting, or the same utility for a smaller investment of resources). Because what is better is at root a human judgment, engineering . . . often involves a degree of creativity and insight into how an artifact can be made better.

National Research Council[1]

5.1   Chapter Objectives

Electronically stored information, or what we generically refer to as data, is distributed across a wide geographical area in data repositories, or warehouses, virtually all of which are linked together via the Internet. The type of data stored in such warehouses and their available storage capacity varies dramatically: it can be one individual's storage on a workstation or personal computer, or it can be a medium-sized repository such as the National Institute of Health's Human Genome Database, or it can be as massive and complex an undertaking as NASA's Earth Observing Satellite Data Information System (EOSDIS). Each type of data warehouse is managed by different organizations with different governing regulations, using a wide variety of storage architectures and employing a dichotomy of computer systems. Simply stated, we live in a vastly heterogeneous, distributed information world.

To provide an understanding of engineering practice in the design of distributed information environments, we categorize the components of a distributed system—namely, conventional sequential machines, conventional

1. National Research Council Computer Science and Telecommunications Board, *Academic Careers for Experimental Computer Scientists and Engineers* (Washington, D.C.: National Academy Press, 1994), p. 30.

machines with added special processors or accelerators, multiprocessor systems, and homogeneous and heterogeneous distributed systems.

Our purpose here is to summarize the properties and requirements of each category of distributed systems. It is important to understand how different these categories are. In the context of this chapter, we shall view distributed heterogeneous systems as the framework in which we operate and assume that an environment consisting of only individual components of a homogeneous nature is merely a special case of the more general heterogeneous domain.

5.2   Distributed Systems Overview

In the early days of computing from the mid–1940s to the early 1980s, computers were scarce, expensive, stand-alone components. Users typically executed scientific or commercial business applications by submitting programs and data to their mainframe or minicomputer. Computer CPU time was a more valuable commodity than human efforts. By today's standards, most of the communications networks in use were very slow. There were distributed systems, but they were organized around "host" mainframe computers. Minicomputers were either free-standing or coupled to host computers. To a large degree, communications occurred by means of file transfer for input and output from computers at remote sites to a host computer. Host computers, for the most part, operated independently from one another.[2] Communications at up to 56 Kb/s was the common practice, but there were instances of connecting host computers for file transfer at T1 rates or 1.54 Mb/s. At the same time, dumb terminals (e.g., teletypes and simple keyboards with cathode ray tubes) were introduced that would communicate with a remote computer on a character-by-character or line-by-line basis. Typical systems were used for airline reservations, factory control, financial transactions, etc. Such terminals were also used for more general purpose time sharing, which was becoming popular. However, to a large degree overall information systems were oriented toward immense host computers that did most of the computation, and distributed components whose usual role was input and output for file transfer, transaction processing, or time sharing. If there was a hierarchy of computing engines (e.g., large host, minicomputers in factories, computerized controllers on machine tools) the central focus was still the large host. This scenario typifies the situation of our first category of distributed systems—conventional sequential machines. In this case, the number of large scale computing entities comprising the distributed environment was usually limited to a single node.

2. Richard L. Shuey, "The Industrial Need for Adequate Computer Communications," *IEEE Communications Magazine* 15, no. 4 (July 1977): 16.

A slight modification in the functionality of the architectures represents our second category of distributed components: conventional machines with special processors or accelerators added to the CPU of conventional architectures to enhance performance. The introduction of special purpose components is a foreshadowing of more advanced systems, in which a specialization of functional behavior or performance is assumed for a given set of nodes within a distributed environment. Examples of attached processors include math coprocessors, graphics accelerators, information retrieval filters, and database processors. A database back-end is an example of an attached system.

Our third category consists of multiprocessor or multicomputer systems, predominantly characterized by a tightly coupled set of processors, usually housed within a single chassis or frame, interconnected via some form of a relatively high-speed network and usually designed to work on small sets (possibly one) of problems simultaneously. In cases where the nodes are actually individual computers, the systems are referred to as multicomputer rather than multiprocessor systems. For our intentions here, there are minor differences between multiprocessor and multicomputer systems, and we shall hence use the term multiprocessor to refer to both. A notable feature that clearly distinguishes this third class from the more general distributed system, our fourth category, is that in the typical multiprocessor systems changes to the stored data result from computations that are computed strictly at the multiprocessor. In the distributed system, changes in the locally stored data may be a result of activities or computations that occur at a remote site.

Finally, our fourth category is distributed computer systems, the most general case. These systems can contain many computers that are often separated by significant geographical distances. The individual computers are interconnected by some form of network, typically slower and cheaper than those found in multiprocessor systems. The individual computers often work on different problems but may share common or related data. Changes in common data may not be caused by local processing. Most distributed systems are viewed as loosely coupled systems.

The first distributed systems were homogeneous in nature, predominantly interconnected via a local area network (LAN). This allowed every computer connected to the network to interact through a common operating system that ran on each of the individual computers. Each computer was of the same family of machines. Today, and clearly in the future, the majority of the distributed environments will be heterogeneous. We must thus accept the fact that the heterogeneous distributed environment is the most general category and that all others are but a special case of the heterogeneous environment.

Consider the following notational convention. Let N represent the number of computers in the system, and let M represent the number of different types (families) of computers attached to the network. In the first category, conventional sequential systems, $N = M = 1$. In the case of a conventional system with an attached processor or system, depending on the implementation of the architecture, either $N = 1$ and $M = 2$, if the attached element is connected on the internal bus, or $N = 2$ and $M = 2$ if there is a dedicated back-end machine attached to the host computer. In the multiprocessor system, N varies from a single node (a conventional sequential machine), up to 65,536 nodes in the old Thinking Machines CM2. In most cases, however, $M = 1$. N varying and $M = 1$ is also true in the case of a distributed homogeneous environment. In fact, multiprocessor systems and homogeneous environments are from an architectural point of view very similar, with the possible exception of the communications network connecting the individual components. Finally, if we consider the heterogeneous distributed environment using our notation, N varying and M varying, it is easy to understand why indeed this subcategory is the general case.

In the remainder of this chapter, we provide a general description of each category and an example system where appropriate. In selecting these examples, we have purposely avoided choosing the most commonly known cases. Our goal is to provide an insight into the types of distributed systems that exist, not to educate readers on the many architectures that have been previously designed. Many books that describe past and present computer systems are readily available.

5.2.1 Conventional Sequential Systems

Conventional sequential systems have been around since the mid–1940s and the development of the ENIAC, the first electronic computer.[3] Since that time most of the available conventional sequential computer architectures have been designed and implemented using what is referred to as the von Neumann model. That model describes computer systems as consisting of three main components: the input/output (I/O) devices, the main memory module, and the central processing unit (CPU), all interconnected through an internal bus. Figure 5.1 presents a diagram of the von Neumann model.

Conceptually, von Neumann–based architectures operate as follows. All processing is at the control of the CPU. Data enter (and leave) the system through the various devices. When data are to be processed, the I/O routines take control of the shared internal bus and transfer the data to the main mem-

---

3. A. W. Burks, H. H. Goldstine, and J. von Neumann, *Preliminary Discussion of the Logical Design of an Electronic Computing Instrument* (report prepared for U.S. Army Ordnance Department, 1946).

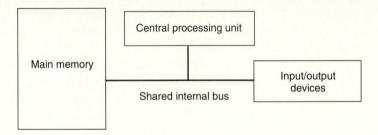

Figure 5.1   The von Neumann Model

ory. When the data transfer stage has been completed, the CPU fetches the operands from main memory, as needed for the execution. Having completed processing, the CPU either transfers or facilitates the transfer of data from main memory back to the appropriate I/O device, and possibly back to the user.

A caution is in order here: The description above is clearly an oversimplification—but for our purposes here in understanding the evolution toward heterogeneous distributed systems, it suffices. For introductory expositions on the fundamentals of computer architectures, the reader is referred to any of the many texts on the subject.[4]

Since the inception of von Neumann–based architectures, implementations have varied greatly. The early stages were fueled by the desire for "bigger, cheaper, and faster" technology, and the kilo (thousands) prefix was used to measure the three key component indicators. That is, CPU speed was measured in thousands of operations per second, main memory was measured in the thousands of bytes, and I/O transfer speeds were listed in terms of thousands of bits per second. Today, component measurements on personal workstations, which cost a mere fraction of what the computer forefathers cost, use the hectomega (hundreds of millions) prefix and soon will use the giga (billions) prefix in their unit descriptors.

Basket and Hennessy noted that a direct contributing factor to the performance improvements over the last two decades has been the increase in the number of transistors per die both in terms of memory and microprocessor technology.[5] Based on a tracking of technology curves, Intel predicts that the

---

4. J. P. Hayes, *Computer Architecture and Organization,* 2nd ed. (New York: McGraw Hill, 1988); G. A. Gibson, *Computer Systems: Concepts and Design* (Englewood Cliffs, NJ: Prentice-Hall, 1991); D. Patterson and J. Hennessy, *Computer Organization and Design: The Hardware/Software Interface* (San Mateo, CA: Morgan Kaufman, 1994); Michael J. Flynn, *Computer Architecture* (Boston: Jones and Bartlett, 1995).

5. F. Baskett and J. Hennessy, "Microprocessors: From Desktops to Supercomputers," *Science* 261 (August 13, 1993): 864–871.

microprocessor in the year 2000 will be comprised of roughly 50 million transistors per chip, a 250 MHz clock rate, 750 million instructions per second (MIPS), and a multimegabyte cache.[6]

In conventional systems, data sharing among geographically dispersed users is quite limited. Most applications that reside on a sequential conventional system rely on the programs and data that are physically housed within the computer itself. For example, banking or reservation scheduling applications rely on the data stored on the I/O devices attached to the processing system. If external data are needed, they are usually sent via magnetic tapes, optically recorded media, or electronic file transfer.

Communication across multiple machines is limited. When it does occur, it typically involves the sending of electronic mail, logging on to remote machines, or, as mentioned previously, electronically transferring remote files. The predominant advantage of systems within this category is security. Having a single isolated machine, possibly placed in a secure environment, results in a lower probability of outside intrusions into the system. Indeed, if security is of primary concern, a single machine separated from the rest of the world is clearly an excellent solution. However, as discussed later, if security is not the main concern, this isolation comes at significant cost.

5.2.2 Conventional Systems with Special Purpose Components

Conventional systems with special purpose components comprise our second category within the distributed computing spectrum. As the field of computer science and engineering matured and the diversity of computer applications increased, it became clear that the conventional sequential architectures belonging to our first category were not sufficiently powerful or economically feasible. To meet the growing demands of users, conventional architectures with attached dedicated processors, or similarly, dedicated special purpose sequential systems were introduced. Some common examples of these systems include math coprocessors and database accelerators.

It is arguable whether architecturally speaking there exists sufficient difference between computer systems in the two categories. A case can be made that the new systems are but a mere extension of the older ones. In fact, for the most part, most of these new machines looked similar in architectural aspect to their conventional counterparts. Nevertheless, we are differentiating the systems because of the nature of their functions. More specifically, the parti-

---

6. L. H. Turcotte, "Cluster Computing," in A. Zomaya, ed., *Handbook of Parallel and Distributed Computing* (New York: McGraw-Hill, 1996).

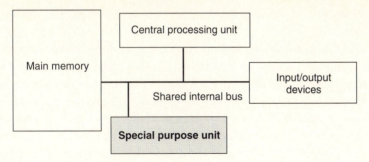

Figure 5.2 A conventional computer system with an attached processor

tioning of functionality or specialization is a foreshadowing of the beginnings of distributed and partitioned computing environments.

Special purpose systems exist in two architectural styles, in both of which the attached processor (or system) acts as a slave to the host CPU (or system). In the first configuration, a special purpose unit is attached to the internal bus of a conventional sequential system, as shown in Fig. 5.2. The second configuration consists of the implementation of a complete additional, or back-end, system, a general purpose host as shown in Fig. 5.3.

Both versions execute as a subordinate to the main CPU or system. In the attached processor option, the special purpose processor monitors the internal data bus. Whenever an instruction with one of the operation codes (opcodes) that are executable by the special purpose processor is placed on the bus, the attached processor, rather than the CPU, executes the given operation. In the case of an attached back-end system, the front-end (host) CPU issues instructions for the back-end system to execute. Once the back-end system completes

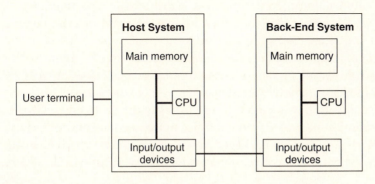

Figure 5.3 A conventional computer system with an attached back-end

its assigned task, it forwards the results to the host system and awaits further instructions.

Remote communications with conventional systems with attached special purpose components rely on approximately the same paradigms as the conventional systems of the first category. Given the better performance delivered by the specialized processor or back-end system, however, it is common for users to specifically look for access to such computers whenever they need to solve a complex or time-consuming problem that can benefit from the use of the special purpose attachment. The functional partitioning of processing based on the type of task is commonly done today in heterogeneous distributed computing environments, as described later in this chapter.

As the case is with conventional sequential architectures, because of the limited supported communications capabilities, the data used or produced by a computation for the most part reside either within the system itself, or within the back-end system.

Case Study: The Intel iDBP 86/440 Database Microprocessor

The Intel iDBP 86/440 microprocessor provides a customized database management subsystem focused predominantly on the relational database arena.[7] The iDBP managed the storage resources and provided its host system with file management facilities. Unlike traditional attached systems, it was not designed with the goal of improving the transaction rates of the host mainframe computer, but instead, focused on supporting transaction coordination, access control, error recovery, and data sharing.

To increase the potential use of the iDBP, Intel designed the processor so that it could manipulate files rather than function as a relational database processor. File manipulation involves positioning and manipulating a cursor within the files, using commands such as START CURSOR, LOOP WHILE <condition>, and FETCH RECORDS. Thus the iDBP directly supported relational database processing but also enabled users to capitalize on the use of the iDBP for hierarchical and network database implementations.

Great attention was paid during the design phase to ensure that the iDBP could easily be integrated into multiple environments. This attention yielded a microprocessor that was packaged in such a way that it could be integrated as an add-on board to a conventional sequential architecture, or as a back-end

---

7. K. Morgan, "The Intel Database Processor" (proceedings of IEEE COMPCON, 1983), pp. 371–373.

stand-alone system attached to a local area network serving the requests of several host systems.

In either configuration, the iDBP was a slave unit, and as such, received its instructions from the CPU of the host computer(s). Given its file cursor manipulation nature, instructions from the host CPU to the iDBP generally were oriented to file instructions rather than "SELECT" or "PROJECT," as would be found for a relational database processor, or to fixed length store and load operations, as would be expected for a conventional CPU. Instead, instructions such as "START CURSOR," "FETCH RECORD," "LOOP WHILE condition," and "STORE variable length and long records" were issued.

Today, the majority of the attached processors are used as accelerators. Conventional sequential machines with attached processors, such as math co-processors or graphics accelerators, are predominantly associated with individual, single-user workstations. These workstations are typically connected to networks and comprise some of the components in a heterogeneous distributed environment, as discussed below.

5.2.3   Multiprocessor Systems

As the range of applications that users were attempting to solve expanded, the conventional systems simply could not meet the computational demands, or they could meet them only at a prohibitive cost. At the same time, technology continued to improve and users quickly noted that the difference in the computational horsepower delivered by mainframe CPUs and microprocessors was not that dramatic. That is, Grosch's Law—which states that quadrupling the computational power of a CPU costs double the original price—could not be applied to microprocessor technology. Simply stated, microprocessors were dramatically cheaper than mainframe CPUs but they were not far less powerful. This generated commercial investigation and research, which led to the process of parallel computing—a system in which microprocessors cooperatively compute portions of a problem in parallel. As with the field of computer architecture, there are many books that focus on this topic both in terms of the algorithms used and the architectures developed.[8] We limit our discussion to a

8. G. S. Almasi and A. Gottlieb, *Highly Parallel Computing,* 2nd ed. (Redwood City, CA: Benjamin-Cummings, 1994); D. P. Bertsekas, *Parallel and Distributed Computation: Numerical Methods* (Englewood Cliffs, NJ: Prentice-Hall, 1989); J. Ja' Ja', *An Introduction to Parallel Algorithms,* (Reading, MA: Addison-Wesley, 1992); V. Kumar, A. Grama, A. Gupta, and G. Karypis, *Introduction to Parallel Computing: Design and Analysis of Algorithms* (Menlo Park, CA: Benjamin-Cummings, 1994); M. J. Quinn, *Parallel Computing: Theory and Practice* (New York: McGraw-Hill, 1994); F. T. Leighton, *Introduction to Parallel Algorithms and Architectures: Arrays, Trees, Hypercubes* (San Mateo, CA: Morgan Kaufmann, 1992).

brief overview and a general discussion of the nature of computing that relies on parallel systems.

In the late sixties, Flynn partitioned high-performance computing engines into two major classes: single instruction multiple data (SIMD) and multiple instruction multiple data (MIMD) architectures.[9] Conceptually, in SIMD systems a single instruction is broadcast to all the processors, and all processors simultaneously perform that instruction on their portion of the data. In MIMD systems, processors act somewhat independently in that they decode and execute their own instructions. Typically, SIMD architectures consist of a significantly larger number of less powerful processors than are found in MIMD architectures. Based on the computational capabilities of the processors and the type of algorithms executed on each machine, SIMD computation is traditionally thought of as "fine-grained" whereas MIMD approaches are viewed as "coarse-grained." Thinking Machine's CM2 is a traditional example of a SIMD architecture, while Intel's iPSC/860 or Paragon is a classic example of a MIMD system. The maximal configuration of a CM2 consists of 65,536 processors while that of the iPSC is limited to 128 nodes. Note that each processor of the iPSC is significantly more powerful than that of the CM2.

The advances in switching and memory technology resulted in a dramatic increase in the diversity of parallel architectures. Given this increase, a finer-grain classification scheme for parallel systems was needed. Early in the development of parallel systems, the classification scheme focused predominantly on the strict physical partitioning of memory to the nodes. In a *shared memory paradigm,* all nodes have access to the same global memory. Simultaneous access to the same memory bank is arbitrated via the switch that connects the processors to the memory. The memory contention leading to the required memory arbitration unit limits the parallel architecture to a maximum number of tens of processors. In the second approach, referred to as the distributed memory paradigm, the physical memory is partitioned across the nodes. Each node is responsible for and can access only its own local memory. Data residing at remote nodes are obtained via the sending of requests (messages) to the node housing the requested data. Once a message is received, the remote node sends the data back via another message. Clearly, the access time for local data is lower than that of remote data.

An extension to the shared versus distributed memory paradigm classification scheme is based on access time to the memory units. This classification scheme consists of three categories: (1) uniform memory access (UMA), (2) nonuniform memory Access (NUMA), and (3) no remote memory access

9. M. J. Flynn, "Very High-Speed Computing Systems" (proceedings of the IEEE, December 1966), pp. 1901–1909.

(NORMA).[10] In UMA-based architectures, all memory is centrally located—that is, all memory is global and it is equidistant in terms of access time to all the processors. Commercial examples of UMA-based architectures include the Encore Multimax and the Sequent Balance.

In NUMA-based architectures, memory is physically partitioned across all nodes. However, all nodes have direct access to all memory locations, but not all memory units are equidistant in terms of access times. Local memory has a lower access time than remote memory. Commercial examples of NUMA-based architectures include the BBN Butterfly and the Mercury RACE.

In NORMA-based architectures, memory is physically partitioned across all nodes. Unlike NUMA-based architectures, however, all nodes do not have direct access to all memory locations. Data from remote memory locations can be obtained only via the sending and receiving of messages. Commercial examples of NORMA-based architectures include the Intel iPSC and Paragon systems.

Case Study: The RACE Parallel Computer System

The Mercury Computer Systems' RACE Parallel Computer architecture is based on a low-latency, high-bandwidth reconfigurable interconnection network.[11] Introduced in May 1993, the RACE architecture has been deployed in systems ranging from 4 to more than 700 nodes.[12] The RACE architecture's domain target is real-time applications, particularly in the signal processing arena. Currently, the RACE system is based on the i860 microprocessor, but Mercury Computer Systems has announced that future products will be based on the Power PC microprocessor.

A key architectural component of the RACE system is its 160 MB/sec, 1 ms application-to-application network latency crossbar chip. The RACE crossbar chip executes at 40 MHz and has 6 input/output channels of 40 bits each (32 data, 8 control and clocking). Routing using the chip is based on *source-path*. That is, at the source node, the message route is provided and each node along the path parses its portion of the route. To improve route contention, an adaptive routing feature is available.

---

10. M. Singhal and N. G. Shivaratri, *Advanced Concepts in Operating Systems: Distributed, Database, and Multiprocessor Operating Systems* (New York: McGraw-Hill, 1994); A. S. Tanenbaum, *Modern Operating Systems* (Englewood Cliffs, NJ: Prentice-Hall, 1992).

11. RACE is a trademark of Mercury Computer Systems.

12. B. S. Isenstein, B. C. Kuszmaul, and B. Blau, "Overview of the RACE Hardware and Software Architecture" IEEE Rapid Prototyping and Application Specific Signal Processors, August 1994; B. C. Kuszmaul, "The RACE Network Architecture," International Parallel Processing Symposium (Santa Barbara, CA: April 1995).

The RACE interconnection network, RACEway, can be configured into a variety of networks, the most common one being the fat-tree. However, Mercury has developed both mesh and Clos-network topology based systems. Note, however, that the interconnection topology is static, with no reconfiguration currently supported. The configuration network topology is decided by the customer of the system prior to delivery.

Each computing environment (or node) consists of a processor, memory unit, crossbar interface, and various support circuitry units (DMA, performance monitoring unit, etc.). The RACE architecture is a NUMA system. To support the direct access to remote memory locations, the remote DMA support unit can route data stored within its local memory directly through the network to the requesting node without interfering with the activities of its CPU.

Finally, realizing the difficulty in software integration, particularly in parallel environments, an easy to integrate Multicomputer Software Backplane was developed. In terms of system operation, particular emphasis was placed on the configuration and launch interface for controlling the nodes. That is, the system developers placed a premium on providing users with the ability to easily install and initialize the machine. System monitoring and debugging tools along with an applications programming interface are provided.

In terms of use, like the previous two categories of distributed computing environments, the majority of multiprocessor systems rely on and produce data locally. Simultaneous users of multiprocessor systems are usually few in number. Such users generally submit compute intensive or I/O intensive applications to the multiprocessor either directly from the local front-end host system of the multiprocessor, or by logging onto the front-end system from a remote site and then submitting their task. Interaction and data sharing among users is often quite limited. Today, multiprocessors are widely found in academic communities and in institutions that support industrial research. The U.S. government is also a strong supporter of parallel computation and, in fact, has set up several parallel processing research centers across the country where users can request computer use time for the available facilities.

5.2.4   Distributed Computer Systems

With the decline in cost of computer technology and the advancement of user-friendly software systems, the number of individuals using computers dramatically increased as did the number of individual computers. Given the stability and availability of local communications technology—namely, local area networks (LANs)—the era of distributed computing emerged. However, it is seldom the case that technology fuels use; instead, it is almost always the case that interest fuels technology. The technology does not explain the emergence and widespread development of distributed systems. To understand the interest, the advantages of distributed systems over centralized computing facilities (our first three categories) must be explored.

As discussed in detail in Chapter 11, the major driving motivation of distributed systems is data locality. Users are physically distributed. Thus it only makes sense that the data itself, generated by these users, be physically distributed. The matter of pragmatics alone leads to distribution.

Another motivating factor is the potential for incremental growth and scalability, both at relatively lower hardware costs when compared to mainframe systems. While still being cheaper, 100 microprocessors computing in parallel yield a greater number of MIPS than a mainframe CPU. This is a bit of a simplification but is essentially accurate. If the computational resources delivered by 100 microprocessors are not sufficient, then add some more. It is economically feasible to scale the computational resources incrementally as one's needs increase. Note that in the case of distributed systems, reduced hardware cost, as compared to stand-alone systems, also provides flexibility in terms of incremental growth as well as greater computational resources. In contrast to multiprocessor systems, growth in distributed environments is typically less constrained. For example, growth is not bound to the doubling of the number of nodes, as it is in hypercube-based systems. That is, increasing the size of a 64-node system does not require adding an additional 64 nodes. Ten nodes, for example, can be added to create a 74-node distributed system. Furthermore, chassis and I/O infrastructure costs of multiprocessor engines tend to be significant.

Collaborative efforts or data sharing is greatly diminished in a stand-alone computer environment. Given the complication of transferring data among remote users, distributed multiindividual collaboration is all but eliminated. In distributed systems, data sharing is emphasized.

In stand-alone systems all functionality must reside within the single machine; thus relatively little specialization is possible. That is, most conventional systems are general purpose in nature and thus are not optimized for a particular task. An exception to this statement are the machines in our second category—conventional systems with added special processors or accelerators. But even in this case, the specialization is typically limited to one or two functions. Clearly, it is much easier to support a dedicated machine per function if there are many machines available. Consequently, in distributed systems, the user is provided with the ability to choose a special purpose machine, and hence benefit from its functionality, for a far greater number of applications than in a stand-alone world.

Finally, but no less important, fault tolerance is increased in a distributed environment. Since not all the data and functionality reside at one computer, a fault at a single site does not disable all processing. If there are multiple sites available (distributed systems) for the computation, and there happens to be a fault in one of these sites, then it is still possible to continue executing at any of the remaining operational sites provided that the needed data are accessible by the alternate execution sites. In a single computer system, a fault typically disables all processing.

For balance, however, the disadvantages of distributed systems as compared to stand-alone systems must be presented. One such disadvantage has already been stated—security. It is easier to safeguard stand-alone systems against intruders. In distributed systems, data sharing and remote user access is emphasized, clearly reducing the isolation, and hence security, of the system.

One possible solution to lessen the security concern is to compartmentalize the data and to store the highly sensitive data on a separate stand-alone configuration. All the remaining non- or less-sensitive information is maintained on the distributed environment. This, of course, attempts to sidestep the concern; however, it is an option that is satisfactory in some limited domains.

For example, in a university domain, highly sensitive information such as grades can be maintained on a dedicated system in the registrar's office. No access is provided to the grade data from outside the registrar's office. Changes can, therefore, be made on the dedicated system only by authorized people in that office. Information that the academic staff needs can periodically be transferred to a system that is accessible to others. In these circumstances, it is very difficult for a clever student to change his grade in the important computer. Non- and less-sensitive information such as schedules for university sporting events can always reside on the distributed environment.

Another disadvantage, and possibly, the most significant issue, is the fabric itself. Distributed systems promote communication and data sharing. Supporting such an environment requires software and hardware not previously needed. These additional resources introduce additional complexity and another source of potential faults from the communications network itself. A brief overview of network fault tolerance and a short discussion on some of the distributed file systems proposed to promote data sharing are provided in Section 5.3.

Homogeneous Systems

Homogeneous and heterogeneous distributed systems share common benefits, concerns, and obstacles. The old adage "One needs to crawl before one walks," is appropriate here. Because many of the distributed systems issues are simplified, and some even eliminated, much attention has focused on homogeneous environments. For example, load balancing and other scheduling issues are simplified if all systems have similar characteristics. Different families of architectures represent data in differing ways—e.g., there are a multitude of data representation standards. Data exchange or sharing across architectures belonging to differing families requires data representation interchange. This is an example of an issue that is eliminated in the case of information systems that are homogeneous at all levels, including the applications level. In this section, we briefly address those issues simplified by homogeneity since, in the case of homogeneous systems, some solutions for these problems already exist. In the case of heterogeneous systems, most of these issues are still in the research phase, although in the case of specific applications information system designers have found solutions.

Users of a homogeneous distributed system typically view the system as comprising only a single node—namely, their own workstation. A workstation user does not wish to be cognizant of where the data are physically located. Instead, users view all data as local and access the data as such. Thus in the design of homogeneous distributed systems a cardinal principle that provides the user with such an illusion is transparency. Transparency in distributed systems refers to the hiding of the physical computer boundaries from the user's point of view. That is, as far as the user is concerned, all data reside on and all processing takes place on a single central machine. In fact, data and processing may be distributed. Among other requirements, a central requirement for this transparency is name transparency in which all objects are accessed via a physical location independent name. (See the DUNIX case study below.)

Similar to multiprocessor systems, an unbalanced load across the network of computers results in a poor global system throughput. However, in a distributed system, unlike in a multiprocessor environment, multiple concurrent applications are often active. Given normal user load fluctuations and the diversity of active applications, the load across machines is nonuniform. Without load balancing, some sites might become overloaded, while others may remain idle. Overloaded workstations (machines) provide users relying on these machines (either local or remote) with poor response times. To improve response times, load balancing techniques are commonly employed. A treatment of load balancing techniques is beyond the scope of this chapter. Various load-balancing algorithms are described in a number of sources.[13]

Another issue often considered in distributed systems is process migration. Process migration is the determination of whether or not to move a process from one machine to another, and if so, which process to move, when to move

13. D. L. Eager, E. D. Lazowska, and J. Zahorjan, "Adaptive Load Sharing in Homogeneous Distributed Systems," *IEEE Transactions on Software Engineering* 12, no. 5 (May 1986): 662–675; C. G. Rommel, "The Probability of Load Balancing Success in a Homogeneous Network," *IEEE Transactions on Software Engineering* 17, no. 9 (September 1991); N. G. Shivaratri, P. Krueger, and M. Singhal, "Load Distributing in Locally Distributed Systems," *IEEE Computer* 25, no. 12 (December 1992): 33–44.

it, and to where to move it. Obviously, the location of the data that the process depends on also plays a role in the decision of which process to move where. Many studies have focused on these issues, and there does not exist a panacea for all applications and system loads. What is clear is that to provide users with acceptable performance under a diverse set of system loads, process migration is typically needed. For a good overview of process migration, see Goscinski.[14] There is further discussion of this issue in Chapters 9, 12, and 13 of this book.

Finally, homogeneity provides for the ability to increase reliability. Since ideally all sites within the network can access all the data and since all the processing sites are identical, all execution sites should be interchangeable. This is clearly an oversimplification. For example, although execution sites in the computation sense may be interchangeable, the loss of data that are located at a single site may be a disaster. Nevertheless, given solutions to the above issues and the appropriate additional hardware and software support, a fault at a processing site or within the network can be masked by a diversity of mechanisms. A brief discussion of network fault tolerance is provided in Section 5.3.

We conclude our discussion on homogeneous distributed systems with an example of a system that supported each of the above issues.

Case Study: The DUNIX Distributed Operating System

The DUNIX distributed operating system was developed at Bellcore during the mid- to late 1980s.[15] A UNIX derivative, DUNIX was a complete, operational distributed operating system. Like other distributed systems of that era—e.g., MOS and LOCUS—DUNIX hid the individual computer boundaries.[16] Users were provided with the illusion that the distributed system was comprised of only a single machine when in fact multiple machines were online.

Following Dijkstra's concept of software levels, DUNIX was composed of levels of abstractions, with each level relying only on lower levels.[17] Modules interacted with other modules only through their calling interface. Such an ar-

---

14. A. Goscinski, "Distributed Operating Systems: The Logical Design" (Reading, MA: Addison-Wesley, 1991).

15. A. Litman, "The DUNIX Distributed Operating System," *Operating Systems Review* 22, no. 1 (January 1988).

16. A. S. Tanenbaum and R. Van Renesse, "Distributed Operating Systems," *ACM Computing Surveys* 17, no. 4 (December 1985): 419–470; A. Barak and A. Litman, "MOS: A Multicomputer Distributed Operating System," *SP&E* 15, no. 8 (August 1985): 725–737; B. Walker et al., "The LOCUS Distributed Operating System" (proceedings of the Ninth Symposium on Operating System Principles, 1983).

17. E. W. Dijkstra, "The Structures of THE Multiprogramming System," CACM 11, no. 3 (March 1968): 341–346.

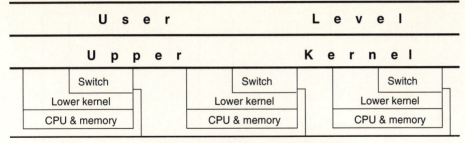

Packet-Switching Network

Figure 5.4   The structure of the DUNIX system. *Source:* O. Frieder, A. Litman, and M. E. Segal, "DUNIX: Distributed Operating Systems Education Via Experimentation," *Microprocessing and Microprogramming* 27, no. 5 (September 1989): 811–818. Reprinted with permission from Elsevier Science Publishing, Amsterdam, The Netherlands.

chitectural organization allowed modification of modules without fear of side effects.

The structure of DUNIX is shown in Fig. 5.4. The kernel was composed of three main components: (1) the lower kernel, (2) the upper kernel, and (3) the switch. The lower kernel maintained the local objects and provided abstractions of these objects for integration. The upper kernel maintained the context and current bindings of the lower-level objects. Finally, the switch was the only module that was cognizant of the network traffic and was responsible for binding the upper-level kernel of one computer with the lower-level objects of a remote computer.

One proposed use of DUNIX was for educational purposes. Thus in contrast with other operational operating systems—e.g., Berkeley 4.x UNIX—the kernel of DUNIX had to be modular, lower in complexity, and substantially smaller in size. For example, a modestly configured kernel (device drivers, RS232 line, but no TCP/IP software) consisted of roughly 17,400 lines of source code. (Source code line count includes roughly 5,200 lines of white space and comments, but only counts lines in include files once.)

In DUNIX, all objects resided at exactly one computer. All system-wide objects—objects residing at one computer but having potential interest to processes in other computers—had a global name across the system, and that name was never reused. All object location and access information were maintained by the system. Accessing the objects was via procedure calls as the system was procedure call oriented. That is, processes did not invoke a server to access or modify the object. Instead, a procedure call was invoked with the target computer being that computer where the object was located.

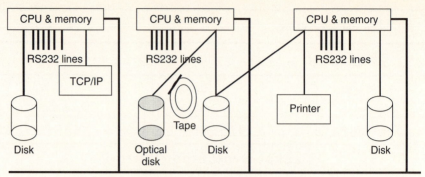

Packet-Switching Network

Figure 5.5   The DUNIX hardware base. *Source:* O. Frieder, A. Litman, and M. E. Segal, "DUNIX: Distributed Operating Systems Education Via Experimentation," *Microprocessing and Microprogramming* 27, no. 5 (September 1989): 811–818. Reprinted with permission from Elsevier Science Publishing, Amsterdam, The Netherlands.

Individual computers were fully configured, and they were all interconnected via a packet-switching network, as shown in Fig. 5.5. Every disk was dual port but physically connected to only a single machine. In the case of a fault to the computer to which the disk was attached, the physical connection was switched and the disk would then be on-line and available.

Each individual computer was autonomous, had its own complete copy of the kernel, and operated in an identical manner. In fact, to the user, it was transparent whether the processes were local or remote and on one or more computers. There was no distinction made regarding the locality of an operation.

Heterogeneous Systems

We live in a heterogeneous distributed systems world, where data are produced and processed in a distributed manner on a wide range of data processing systems. Only a portion of these systems can be considered conventional computer systems. For example, in the medical imaging domain, data sources for three-dimensional imaging include computed tomography, ultrasound tomography, magnetic resonance imaging (or nuclear magnetic resonance), positron emission tomography, and single photon emission computed tomography scanners.[18] These systems are routinely integrated into daily data collection

18. M. R. Stytz and O. Frieder, "Three-Dimensional Medical Imaging Modalities: An Overview," *Critical Reviews in Biomedical Engineering* 18, no. 1 (1990).

and presentation at a majority of our hospitals. Clearly a distributed environment for medical processing must deal not only with the conventional patient data commonly stored in relational databases but also with the wide variety of available data modalities and the vast amount of data that they produce. The average size of one radiological image is approximately 10 MB but can be as large as 50 MB for a 2048 by 2048 display.[19]

Besides medicine, there are many other applications and domains within a heterogeneous distributed processing community that are being irrevocably altered by the advances in high-speed digital communication, computing, and recording technologies. Based on current trends, by the end of this decade, the following developments can safely be predicted:

1. NASA's Earth Observing System (EOS) will deliver over a terabyte of new data every day. Researchers worldwide will query the database that houses these data.

2. The FBI and other law enforcement agencies will rely on an international data network and databases containing hundreds of millions of records to detect drug traffic and to enforce laws against fraud and extortion conducted through the digital network.

3. Billions of financial transactions worldwide will be carried out daily with digital money.

These applications require and manipulate data from multiple sources. Heterogeneity within these applications exists at multiple levels. That is, the applications will run on a plethora of computer architectures that rely on a dichotomy of operating systems. Both the machines and the operating systems will vary over time and organizations. Finally, a multitude of networks will be used to connect this communicating body of users.

Heterogeneity complicates all design issues. For example, it is commonly believed that heterogeneity is the greatest hindrance in the efficient use of resources within the network. That is, load partitioning, scheduling, and balancing algorithms must take into account the existing differences between the execution sites both in terms of hardware and software and the differences in the ability to access the data. The development of a user model is complicated. In homogeneous distributed systems, transparency is the generally accepted

---

19. L. Allen and O. Frieder, "Exploiting Database Technology in the Medical Arena: A Critical Assessment of Integrated Systems for Picture Archiving and Communications," *IEEE Engineering in Medicine and Biology* 11, no. 1 (March 1992).

model. In heterogeneous systems, the appropriateness of a location independent system—i.e., a transparent environment—has been questioned.[20] In fact, the entire underlying operating system model differs. For heterogeneous distributed systems, a network operating system is the more appropriate model.[21] That is, the data-sharing environment, and hence the associated protocols, differ. In homogeneous distributed systems, users view the system as one node. Hence, the assumed granule of data being accessed and shared is relatively small compared to heterogeneous systems, where data sharing is limited to designated sharable data. Furthermore, in homogeneous systems, transparency in object location is stressed, whereas in heterogeneous systems, the users explicitly "hunt around" to find the appropriate data.

Case Study: The World Wide Web

The World Wide Web (WWW) was initiated by the European Center for Nuclear Research (CERN) to study approaches for building distributed hypermedia systems.[22] Access to the WWW is accomplished via the use of *browsers*.[23] Browsers, either line or graphics oriented, access the various storage and processing sites across the Internet. One popular browser is Mosaic, a graphics-oriented system developed at the National Center for Supercomputing Applications (NCSA) at the University of Illinois.[24]

Originally an X Windows application, Mosaic now runs on Macintosh and on IBM and IBM-compatible personal computers. Mosaic is a wide-area distributed hypermedia information discovery and retrieval system. Mosaic documents are written in either the Standard Generalized Markup Language (SGML) or in HTML (Hyper-Text Markup Language). Support tools exist to assist users in creating their own HTML documents. By "clicking" on hyperlinks, users can retrieve cross-referenced documents without explicitly requesting them. As noted by Vetter, Spell, and Ward, according to the sheer volume of bytes transmitted, the WWW is currently the eighth most popular service on the Internet.

20. L. Svobodoba, "Workshop on Operating Systems in Computer Networks: Workshop Summary," *Operating Systems Review* 19, no. 2 (1985).

21. A. Goscinski, *Distributed Operating Systems: The Logical Design* (Reading, MA: Addison-Wesley, 1991).

22. E. Krol, *The Whole Internet: User's Guide and Catalog* (Sebastopol, CA: O'Reilly and Associates, 1992).

23. R. J. Vetter, C. Spell, and C. Ward, "Mosaic and the World-Wide Web," *IEEE Computer* 27, no. 10 (October 1994): 49–57.

24. B. Schatz and J. B. Hardin, "NCSA Mosaic and the World Wide Web: Global Hypermedia Protocols of the Internet," *Science* 265, no. 5174 (August 12, 1994): 895. This is from a special issue entitled *Computers '94 Networks and Modeling.*

Navigating the WWW is accomplished via the use of uniform resource locators (URLs), which are basically a naming convention used by the WWW to locate files. The format used is *scheme://host.domain[:port]/path/filename*. Scheme refers to the type of access method used. Currently, the following methods are supported: FTP, HTTP, WAIS, Telnet, Gopher, and News. The naming component after the colon designates the machine host name followed by an optional port name followed by the complete filename, including path. If an optional port name is given, a colon is used to separate the port name from the host name.

Figure 5.6 illustrates a sample window interface using Mosaic. This is the home page image for George Mason University. As shown, the document URL is listed along with various command options (the buttons on top).

The limitations of Mosaic that are commonly cited include the difficulties associated with too many hypermedia links, the problem of remembering how one reached a destination in terms of traversing a set of links, and the support for change detection. That is, it is quite difficult to know what entities actually exist on the Internet, and given a particular entity, when the last changes to this entity transpired. Attention is focused with the hope of alleviating these

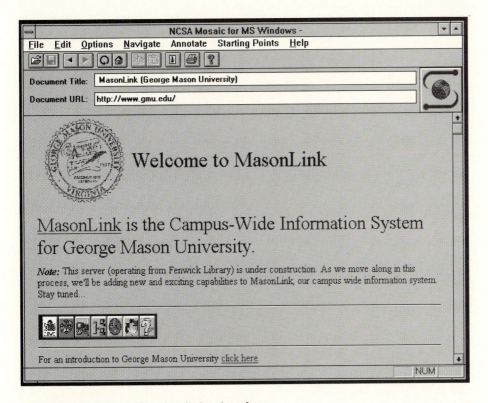

Figure 5.6   A Mosaic window interface

concerns. For example, electronic navigational logs are being developed, and public Internet facility libraries are cropping up across the Internet.[25]

Finally, the amount of network traffic linked to the WWW between January and August of 1993 multiplied by a factor of 414.[26] Also recorded was the usage of the server at CERN, which is doubling every four months, roughly twice the growth rate of the Internet.

Many of the issues regarding the design of heterogeneous distributed systems are still in their infancy in terms of general practice. In the remainder of this book, we provide the tools needed to approach the design of heterogeneous systems.

5.3   A Perspective on Distributed Environments

Our discussion of distributed environments cannot be complete without commenting on the mechanisms associated with the design of distributed systems. In Section 5.2.4, we noted the inherent disadvantages of distributed systems when compared with centralized systems—namely, security, software complexity to provide the desired user model, and the potential network failures. We saw that security is a harder problem for distributed systems because of their need for communications security and the required coordination of security systems at the nodes of a distributed system. To provide data consistency across users and to enable data sharing, sophisticated file systems must be developed. These file systems reduce the complexity of the distributed systems software and serve as one means of trying to alleviate the concern of distributed systems increasing the software complexity. To reduce the number of faults introduced into the data processing environment by the network itself, network fault-tolerance strategies are implemented. We conclude this chapter with a discussion of four classical distributed file systems: (1) the Apollo DOMAIN Distributed File System, (2) the Network File System, (3) the Andrew File System, and (4) the Coda File System. Each file system represents a different driving goal in the design. We also provide a brief overview of the issues and elementary nomenclature associated with the design of fault tolerant networks.

---

25. "The WWW Virtual Library," page on the World Wide Web with address http://info.cern.ch/hypertext/Data-Sources/bySubject/Overview.html, June 1994.

26. Vetter et al., "Mosaic and the World-Wide Web," 56.

5.3.1   A Commentary on Selected Distributed File Systems

We now present an overview of four distributed file systems. Each was designed with a unique goal in mind—namely, data sharing, system independence, scalability, and support for mobility.

The primary goal of the Apollo DOMAIN Distributed File System was to provide a mechanism for the efficient sharing of information by coworkers.[27] Files were stored using a *single-level store* (recall the discussion in Chapter 3). To access files, a hint manager was developed. The hint manager decoded the unique identifier (UID) and demand paged the needed information. The UID consisted of a node address component and a time stamp indicating the creation time of the file. Based on user file usage, recently used files were cached into the local memory.

The Network File System (NFS) was developed by Sun Microsystems in 1985 originally for Unix systems.[28] Currently, a DOS version of NFS exists as well. The motivating goal of NFS was to create a system independent file system. NFS is remote procedure call-oriented and supports the existence of multiple simultaneous virtual file systems. A virtual file system is similar to a database view. Users are given the illusion that their portion or representation of the file system is the actual physical layout of the file system. Each user has his or her own, and possibly different, view of the system.

Filename look-up is done by components. That is, each component of the complete filename is routed from server to server. Each server decodes its portion of the name and routes the rest of the filename to the next server for further processing. This name decoding mechanism is flexible but slow, since it suffers from the vast amount of traffic caused by sending each filename from server to server.

NFS uses stateless servers. That is, no information is maintained by the server regarding the state of a file. Client requests provide all the information needed to complete a task. If a server does not respond, the client resends its request. Server recovery (from a fault) is relatively simple since no restoration of state is needed. On the other hand, caching in stateless servers is complicated due to the lack of file status information. Furthermore, messages are larger (higher traffic volume) since file requests from the clients must contain all file-related information.

27. P. H. Levine, "The Apollo DOMAIN Distributed File System" (proceedings of the NATO Advanced Study Institute on Distributed Operating Systems: Theory and Practice, August 1986).

28. R. Sandberg et al., "Design and Implementation of the Sun Network File System (proceedings of the Summer Usenix Conference, 1985).

The Andrew File System (AFS), developed at Carnegie Mellon University, is named after the benefactors of the university: Andrew Carnegie and Andrew Mellon.[29] The primary design goal of AFS was scalability in terms of the number of machines. AFS is intended to support roughly 5,000–10,000 computers.

Because of the intended degree of scale, an underlying assumption in the design was that users must do as much local processing as possible and should engage the software backplane as little as possible. Therefore in AFS caching is at a file (or near complete file if the file is exceptionally large) level.

Architecturally, AFS clusters machines where each cluster contains on the order of dozens of machines. AFS is a client-server based architecture. Clients execute standard UNIX applications, various editors, and window manager routines. The servers support the VICE and VENUS routines. VICE handles file requests and VENUS is predominantly a cache manager and an interface between client requests and VICE.

Finally, given the large number of users, security in AFS is a problem. To reduce risk, the servers do not trust the clients. Thus all communications between clients and servers are encrypted.

The Coda File System, an extension of the AFS, was designed with the primary goal of supporting mobile computing systems.[30] The growth in popularity of laptop computers and other mobile computing units fueled the need for a file system that enabled users to gracefully connect and disconnect from the network servers. Transparency of the connection status of the mobile computing unit was stressed. Several observations were made about mobile computer systems:

- They are resource poor compared with their static counterparts.

- They are more prone to damage.

- They must operate under a greater diversity of network conditions.

A key requirement of mobile computers is data transparency. That is, regardless of the state of the system, whether connected or not to the network, critical data elements must be accessible. This necessity implies a level of caching, a requirement for consistency and reconnect primitives. Precaching strategies were developed to allow continuous operation in the case of network discon-

29. J. H. Howard et al., "Scale and Performance in a Distributed File System," *ACM Transactions on Computer Systems* 6, no. 1 (February 1988): 51–81.

30. M. Satyanarayanan, "Mobile Computing," *IEEE Computer* 26, no. 9 (September 1993): 81–82; J. J. Kistelr and M. Satyanarayanan, "Disconnected Operation in the Coda File System," *ACM Transactions on Computer Systems* 10, no. 1 (February 1992): 3–25.

nect. Later versions of Coda support a background mode of file consistency checking upon reconnection.

The needs of future applications, particularly multimedia-based applications, are likely to reduce the possibility of near-complete transparency since the volume of data that must be precached will be prohibitive. The possibility of using some form of compressed video instead of full video, for example, in the detached mode is being considered.

5.3.2   A Commentary on Fault-Tolerant Networks

Fault-tolerant networks can be characterized by the type of redundancy employed and consistency maintained. *Static redundancy* (also referred to as masking) introduces permanent, redundant components that mask out possible failures. Consider, for example, a network attachment component that is replicated threefold (triple modular redundancy). If a majority vote among the three units is taken prior to initiating any action, then a fault present at any one of the three units would not affect the behavior of the system. That is, a single fault is masked.

Dynamic redundancy involves the replacement (or cutover) of a faulty component by a "spare" component available within the system configuration. The U.S. public telecommunications network employs dynamic redundancy to remove faulty switches and lines from the network.[31] When a switch fails, the system "cuts over" to a spare switch without the need for human intervention.

Either strong or weak consistency can be maintained. Strong consistency demands a rigid, lockstep, synchronized execution. Every site within the distributed system that performs the same function maintains the same value during each step of the computation. Weak consistency allows for each site to maintain a copy of the data that may be temporarily outdated. Primary copy and various voting algorithms can be used to guarantee eventual consistency.[32] That is, at specified points in the computation, all executing sites will have identical values.

Several traditional approaches exist for eliminating or preventing faults caused by the network. Firewalls, stopgap measures used to isolate network problems, prevent the spread of faults across an entire network. By creating a barrier (border) between neighboring LANs and controlling the flow of traffic through the border, problems within a LAN cannot spread to neighboring

31. R. F. Rey, ed., *Engineering and Operations in the Bell System,* 2nd ed. (Murray Hill, NJ: AT&T Bell Laboratories, 1986).

32. S. Hariri, A. Choudhary, and B. Sarikaya, "Architectural Support for Designing Fault-Tolerant Open Distributed Systems," *IEEE Computer* 25, no. 6 (June 1992): 50–62; S. Mullender, *Distributed Systems* (Reading, MA: Addison-Wesley, 1989).

LANs. One popular use of firewalls is in the prevention of network overload. In multi-LAN networks that communicate using the TCP/IP protocol suite, firewalls are used to prevent the spread of a surge in network traffic (called a *broadcast storm*) to neighboring LANs. Containment is possible only if LANs are connected by routers.

A second common approach is the use of redundancy. Faults are eliminated by either masking them out through an overruling consensus of non-faulty units or via actual replacement, as stated earlier.

A network is termed *self-stabilizing* if it reconfigures itself without human intervention within a "reasonable" amount of time, so as to return to its specified behavior after the occurrence of a fault. In contrast to network redundancy, self-stabilizing networks do not necessarily operate properly in the presence of faults. However, in a self-stabilizing network, repair merely involves the removal of the faulty agent. The network automatically reconfigures itself, and downtime is minimized. A study of network outage in the telecommunications domain demonstrated that significant network downtime is caused by human error during the maintenance process.[33] Thus simplifying the repair process can significantly enhance network availability.

A primary advantage of self-stabilizing networks is their inherent security against sabotage.[34] To corrupt a self-stabilizing network intentionally, malicious messages must be transmitted repetitively and frequently since an "error state" immediately results in the network "correcting" itself. Non–self-stabilizing networks, however, can be corrupted by only a single malicious action. For greater details on fault tolerance in distributed systems, the reader is referred to Cristian and to Jalote.[35]

5.4   Summary and Comments

Throughout this chapter, we developed a taxonomy of computer systems. Four major categories were identified: (1) conventional sequential machines, (2) conventional machines with added special processors or accelerators, (3) multiprocessor systems, and (4) homogeneous and heterogeneous distributed systems.

33. S. R. Ali, "Analysis of Total Outage Data for Stored Program Control Switching Systems," *IEEE Journal on Selected Areas in Communications* 4, no. 7 (1986).

34. R. Perlman, "Interconnections: Bridges and Routers" (Reading, MA: Addison-Wesley, 1992).

35. F. Cristian, "Understanding Fault-Tolerant Distributed Systems," *Communications of the ACM* 34, no. 2 (February 1991): 56–78; P. Jalote, *Fault Tolerance in Distributed Systems* (Englewood Cliffs, NJ: Prentice-Hall, 1994).

We saw that a primary distinction across the types of architectures is the means by which the data are accessed and generated. In all but the last category, the data primarily reside locally. Remote data are usually obtained prior to the start of the computation. Communication with remote sites containing the data is typically explicitly invoked by the user. Traditionally, the users of these types of systems are directly connected to the host machine. That is, the users either reside at the same site as does the processing system or communicate with the host system via remote log-in mechanisms. The main limitation of these systems is the matter of data pragmatics. The authors believe that today, and even more so in the near future, the data needed for commonly used applications (computations) are generated and reside in a distributed manner. Centrally locating the computation unnecessarily constrains the operating environments of the users.

In distributed processing environments, on the other hand, data are generated, stored, and manipulated across often geographically dispersed processing sites. Providing a suitable working environment for users that supports efficient yet easy-to-use paradigms is the challenge for data engineers. In a homogeneous environment, many of the challenging design issues are simplified, and hence, many solutions, both research prototypes and commercial products, have been developed.

Today's data-processing world, however, is heterogeneous in nature. For heterogeneous environments, many of the key design issues are yet unsolved. Even for the most fundamental of questions—such as "what should be the user's view of the system?"—there are no definitive answers. The lack of a definitive user model complicates the design of satisfactory research solutions, particularly to problems such as data security, load balancing, storage hierarchies, performance metrics, and the design of appropriate debugging and performance assessment tools. Given the current state of the art in heterogeneous distributed systems and the dynamics of our topic of focus, information systems, it is clear why so many related research topics are still wide open. In Chapter 14, we outline an approach for the selection of "key" research topics. It is our hope that by the time you finish that chapter, we will have provided you with a sufficient understanding to tackle at least some of these research avenues.

5.5   Problems

1. Centralized systems are generally considered more secure. Describe several means to handle the security issue in heterogeneous distributed systems. Are there simplifications to be made in homogeneous environments?

2. The IBM SP2 is a multicomputer system based on the NOW (Network of Workstations) model. In which category does this system fit? Justify your answer.

3. Propose a load-balancing algorithm for heterogeneous distributed systems. Demonstrate the simplifications that can be made in the case of a homogeneous environment.

4. "Transparency is the appropriate model for a heterogeneous environment." Defend or argue against this belief.

5. Obtain access to Mosaic and find several documents related to heterogeneous distributed systems. What are the key points discussed in each of these documents?

6. Consider an application that consists of three independent computations of varying complexity. A result from this application is obtained only after all three of the computations have been performed. Based on a dollar per millions of instructions per second (MIPS) argument, defend or criticize the following claim "A heterogeneous distributed system is the preferred computational platform for this problem."

Chapter 6

Communications System Fundamentals

The fundamental problem of communications is that of reproducing at one point either exactly or approximately a message selected at another point.

C. E. Shannon[1]

6.1 Chapter Objectives

It is clear that communications technology plays a key role in distributed computer systems. To interact, individual computers must communicate with each other. Furthermore, even within a single simple computer, communication plays a significant role in making possible the interconnection of the CPU, memory, mass storage, etc. If the individual computer is a multiprocessor computer containing hundreds of microprocessor or special purpose computers, it may involve a substantial internal communications network. The role of communications per se is self-evident. What is not as well understood is that the underlying concepts and technology extend beyond that limited area into things such as storage in computer systems, data retrieval, compression, presentation, analog to digital (AD) and digital to analog (DA) conversion, cryptography, transmission of data in noise, and security.

We extend the original concept of communications theory and take more of a theoretical information approach. At the same time, we restrict the breadth of the discussion to those parts of the overall field that are most relevant to distributed computers. Only that part of communications technology that we need in studying information systems is considered. Those interested

1. C. E. Shannon, "A Mathematical Theory of Communications," *BSTJ* 27 (July, October 1948): 379–423, 623–656 (Bell Telephone System Monograph B–1598, p. 1).

in additional details are referred to books on electrical engineering.[2] In general, computer scientists are not familiar with the field of communications technology or the fundamental concepts and issues involved. As we shall see, some of those fundamental concepts provide in a simplified form a sound basis for analyzing and solving many problems in distributed systems. Underlying the discussion are the following assumptions:

1. We must be concerned with communications for a distributed computer and information system environment that includes multimedia systems.

2. The design and architectural issues will be more concerned with data and information than with pure voice. Voice and video are just special cases of data.

3. Our interests in communications are far broader than just data transport.

4. Those concepts of communication and information technology that are relevant to such things as information storage and retrieval, the architecture of memory systems, data compression, redundancy in data, and system security and availability, should be covered.

The objectives of this chapter are as follows:

1. To introduce, without detailed proof, the core concepts of communications technology, including those concepts of associated information technology that are relevant to distributed computer systems. The objective is to establish the key paradigms.

2. To provide an understanding of the communications industry. The relevance is that at a minimum the communications "data (transport) highway" infrastructure will in all likelihood continue to be provided by the communications sector of society. For example, as this book is being written, although Internet services are being transferred to the commercial sector, it still uses the common carrier communications highway. How much the communications industry will be able to move into the more general information system area depends on many factors, some of which are government regulatory in nature.

---

2. Edward C. Jordan, *Reference Data for Engineers: Radio, Electronics, Computer and Communications*, 7th ed. (Indianapolis: Howard Sams, 1985).

3. To provide a basis for further discussion of the data service issues that are key to much of what is done in distributed systems.

6.2 Theoretical Fundamentals

6.2.1 Data or Information

The following definitions are from Alan Freedman's glossary:[3]

> Data: Technically, raw facts and figures, such as orders and payments, which are processed into information, such as balance due and quantity on hand. However, in common usage, both data and information are used synonymously.

> Information: Summarization of data. Technically, data are raw facts and figures that are processed into information, such as summaries and totals. But since information can also be raw data for the next job or person, the two terms cannot be precisely defined. Both terms are used synonymously and interchangeably.

As the above excerpts indicate, there are no satisfactory definitions for data and information. Although they are often used interchangeably, we want to distinguish between data and information. We also want to avoid the more exotic definitions of information that are better left to the artificial intelligence community. We shall take *data* to imply raw facts, numbers, text, etc. Examples might be:

> You are a college student, and you are over one year old.

> The score was Michigan 14 and Ohio State 13, and Michigan defeated Ohio State.

We shall take *information* to imply a higher level of abstraction than data and specifically relate it to uncertainty. A formal definition will be provided shortly.

Information theory provides simple solutions to many computer science problems involving data compression, data storage, sorting, information retrieval, security, error correction, etc. Before we consider information theoretic concepts, however, it is desirable to review probability, which is the basis for much of the theory.

---

3. Alan Freedman, *Electronic Computer Glossary*, © 1981–1996 (Point Pleasant, PA: The Computer Language Company, Inc.).

6.2.2   Discrete Probability

There are precise definitions for probability concepts, but we do not need them for our purposes.[4] Instead, we shall define probability in terms of the frequency of events. We assume for the time being that the events are random and independent, like flipping a coin or throwing dice.

Given a set of events $\{M_i\}$, the probability of a specific event M_i is

$$p(i) \;=\; Lim_{n_T \to \infty}\left(\frac{n_i}{n_T}\right), \tag{6.1}$$

where n_i = the number of occurrences of M_i in a random sequence of events chosen from the set $\{M_i\}$, and n_T = the total number of events in the random sequence of events chosen from $\{M_i\}$.

It follows that

$$\Sigma_i p(i) = Lim_{n_T \to \infty} \Sigma_i\left(\frac{n_i}{n_T}\right) = 1. \tag{6.2}$$

We are concerned with very large numbers of possible events—for example, the number of messages that might be transmitted by a communications system or the combinations of symbols that might be stored in a computer memory. The notation M_i is in keeping with the origin of communications theory where the concern was sending messages. It should be noted that the number of possible messages in the set $\{M_i\}$ may be very large. For example, the number of possible messages of length N made up from the 26 letters of the alphabet (forgetting about capital letters, spaces, punctuation, etc.) is $(26)^N$. Fortunately, as we shall see, only a very small percentage of these messages are English, and that fact is the basis upon which English text can be compressed for either communications or storage in a computer. For a binary string, Equation (6.2) becomes

$$p(0) + p(1) = 1, \text{ from which} \tag{6.3}$$

$$p(1) = 1 - p(0) \quad \text{and} \quad p(0) = 1 - p(1). \tag{6.4}$$

It should be noted that in this case the probability of a 1 occurring can be obtained by subtracting from one the probability that it does not occur (in this case the probability that a 0 occurs). It is often easier to calculate the probability that an event occurs by this indirect method. In other words, calculate the probability that it does not occur and subtract it from 1. For example, assume

---

4. For example, see Harald Cramer, *Mathematical Methods of Statistics* (Princeton: Princeton University Press, 1951).

that four players each throw a single die. Try to calculate the probability that two or more produce the same number by both the direct and indirect method. The answer is (13/18).

Given a function $F(x_i)$ associated with the set of events $\{x_i\}$, where $i = 1, 2, 3, \ldots\ldots$, the average, or expected value of $F(x_i)$, is

$$\text{Expected value of } F(x_i) = Lim_{n_T \to \infty}\Sigma_i[n_iF(x_i)]/n_T = \Sigma_i[p(i)F(x_i)]. \quad (6.5)$$

If the events in a sequence of events do not depend upon each other, then they are said to be independent. This is not always the case. The probability of one event in a sequence may depend on the preceding events. The probability of the event under the condition that the preceding events have occurred is called the conditional probability. Examples are the letters in a word, the digits in a number, the cards that have been previously dealt, etc. The concept can be generalized so that it extends beyond a sequence of events. For example, the probability of rain during the next ten minutes if the sky is entirely clear is quite different than the probability of rain if the sky is full of thunderhead clouds. We need to consider conditional probability because so many of the statistics that we deal with in information processing depend on the conditions and what has previously occurred.

Continuing with the probability of discrete events, consider events i and j. Let

$$p_j(i) = \text{the probability of event } i \text{ if event } j \text{ is known} \quad (6.6)$$

$$p(j,i) = \text{the probability of } j \text{ followed by } i$$

$$= [p(j)][p_j(i)]. \quad (6.7)$$

This is an extremely important theorem sometimes referred to as Bayes' theorem. If j and i are independent events, then

$$p(j,i) = p(i,j) = [p(i)][p(j)] = [p(j)][p(i)]. \quad (6.8)$$

6.2.3   Communication and Information Theory Concepts

The concept of information is very important in understanding communication, data storage, and information retrieval. The basic model is applicable in all three areas. We use the term *information* somewhat differently than did Shannon.[5] He restricted his theory to a precise mathematical description of secrecy systems and communications systems. His concern was messages and

---

5. C. E. Shannon, "Communication Theory of Secrecy Systems," *BSTJ* 28 (October 1949): 659–715; C. E. Shannon, "A Mathematical Theory of Communications," *BSTJ* 27 (July, October 1948): 379–423, 623–656.

message sets. It is interesting that although the papers referenced were published in the reverse order, Shannon's work on secrecy systems done during World War II actually preceded that on the general theory of communications.

Our definition of information is due to P. M. Woodward and has its motivation more from radar and signal processing.[6] Woodward's approach is intuitively neat, compatible with, and in many cases equivalent to Shannon's more mathematical approach. For our purposes, Woodward's viewpoint is more directly applicable to computer-related issues than is Shannon's. The problem with Woodward's approach is that the quantity of information received depends on who or what is receiving it. In this respect it is no longer universally additive taken over a set of receivers. As Shannon assumes equivalent statistics or knowledge at the transmitter and all receivers, this is not a problem. However, as we shall see, this is not a realistic situation with many computer and database systems. For example, because they may have different backgrounds and knowledge, the search patterns of different people exploring the same topic in a library may be quite different. What is new information for one individual may be of no interest to another who already knows it. Each would like a search pattern and retrieval system that is matched to his or her knowledge, and optimizing the library structure for both is a difficult problem for the librarian.

For the time being, assume the following:

1. We are given a message set $\{M_i\}$.

2. Information is to be measured as some function of uncertainty or probability.

3. The messages are independent of each other.

4. The information sent in messages is to be additive. In other words, if a message is sent as two submessages, the sum of the information in the two submessages will be the same as if the information was sent in one message.

These assumptions are framed in the context of a model of communications, Fig. 6.1(a), but they are equally applicable to data storage and information retrieval, Figs. 6.1(b) and 6.1(c).

It follows that information should be defined by some function of $p(i)$, where $p(i)$ is the probability of message M_i:

$$I[i] = \text{information in message } M_i = I[p(i)]. \tag{6.9}$$

---

6. P. M. Woodward, *Probability and Information Theory, with Applications to Radar* (New York: McGraw Hill and Pergamon Press, 1953, 1955, and 1964).

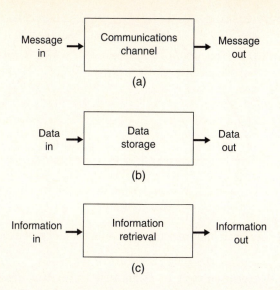

Figure 6.1   Generic model for communications, data, and information

We require messages to be additive, and they are assumed to be independent:

$$I[p(i)] + I[p(j)] = I\{[p(i)][p(j)]\} = I[p(i,j)]. \qquad (6.10)$$

Under these conditions, it can be shown that the function $I[p(i)] = I[M_i]$ must have the form

$$I[M_i] = I[i] = I[p(i)] = A \; x \; Log_B[p(i)], \qquad (6.11)$$

where A and B are constants.

If the log is to the base 2 (i.e., $B = 2$) and $A = -1$, the information is in bits. This is the normal convention. Unless we specify otherwise, when we use the function Log( ) in this book, we mean the logarithm is taken to the base 2.

A logical extension, which we have never seen used, would be to let B = 256 as a definition of information in bytes. This might be convenient in computer work. A definition where B = 10 was once used in the communications field.

As the number of messages approaches infinity, the average information per message is the following, where H is Shannon's notation for entropy:

$$\text{Average information per message} = H = -\Sigma_i p(i) \times Log_2[p(i)]. \qquad (6.12)$$

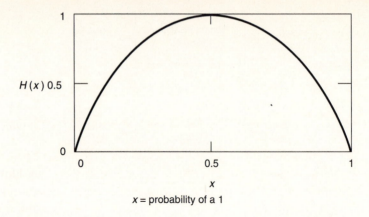

Figure 6.2   Average information (*H*) as a function of probability

Shannon used the term entropy or *H* because of the functional similarity to thermodynamic entropy. Like its thermodynamic equivalent, *H* is a maximum when the $p(i)$ are equal. This implies that to maximize the information obtainable from a message or a question, the messages or the answers to the questions should be equally likely. Figure 6.2 is a plot of *H* for the binary case where there are only two possible symbols, which we take to be a 0 and a 1. It is worth noting that the maximum is fairly flat.

Maximizing information is an excellent way to do the following:

1. Ask questions of another person or a computer system (database). This is the information retrieval problem.

2. Decide on a sorting strategy. You would like, on the average, to get the maximum information possible from each sort.

3. Decide where and how to store data in a memory hierarchy.

4. Code to reduce bandwidth or storage (memory) requirements (e.g., compression).

5. Design encryption and secrecy systems.

A Chessboard Example

Perhaps these ideas are best illustrated by an example or two. The first involves an 8 × 8 chessboard with a single man located on a randomly selected square. How much information do you acquire when you learn which square the man is on? The man is equally likely to be on any one square. Therefore the probability of his being on a specific square is (1/64). Consequently, the information required to locate him, or the information obtained when you have located him, is

$$-Log_2(1/64) = Log_2(64) = 6 \text{ bits.}$$

If you play this game many times, what is the minimum of the average number of yes or no questions that you can ask to locate the man?

Clearly, you might try asking if he is on a specific square and he might be, in which case you would have found his location in one question. However, following this strategy will on the average require 32 questions. You might try to calculate the average information obtained with each question, the first, the second, etc. if you follow this strategy. That will convince you that we need to consider conditional probability.

If you can ask yes or no questions where the answers are equally likely (equal probability), then you would obtain 1 bit of information per question. It would appear that six such questions should be sufficient. Can you code your questions properly? You can of course do so in a series of steps:

1. Divide the 64 squares into two equal groups—a horizontal line dividing it into an upper and a lower part for example. Then ask if the man in the upper (or lower) part. The answer now tells you which half he is in.

2. Divide the remaining 4×8 rectangle in two 2×8 groups.

3. Divide the remaining rectangle into two 1×8 groups.

4. Divide the remaining rectangle into two 1×4 groups.

5. Divide the remaining rectangle into two 1×2 groups.

6. Divide the remaining rectangle into two 1×1 groups.

So after six questions you have located the man, and you know from information theory that on the average that is the best that you can do.

However, a piece in chess, say a king, is not equally likely to be at any position. It is a function of how far the game is along. The probability is conditional on what you know about the position of other pieces, the number of pieces your opponent has left, etc. This changes both the questions you should ask and the minimum average number of questions. Such considerations complicate the problem, and you must use conditional probability. There is also the further complication that you may more often ask where the opposing queen is than a pawn.

Any similarity that this problem has with locating data in a computer memory system is intentional and will be considered in more detail later.

An English Example

As the second example, we consider the English language. This has real applicability to computer work and will utilize conditional probabilities. The example is taken from the work of Shannon.[7]

Consider 26 letters and a space as being allowable symbols. The maximum information transfer using these symbols will be when the symbols are equally likely and independent. The maximum value of H, or the maximum value of the average bits per symbol, is given by Eq. 6.13:

$$H = -\Sigma_i [p(i)][Log_2 p(i)] = \Sigma_{i=1 \rightarrow 27}[1/27][Log_2(27)] = 4.76 \text{ bits/symbol.} \quad (6.13)$$

Of course, a sequence of randomly selected independent letters does not constitute English. Only a small number of the possible sequences are meaningful in that language. The letters in English have a statistical dependency on each other, and consequently the information per symbol in English text will be less. The actual average information per symbol in English text, when compared to the maximum value calculated above, will indicate the redundancy and provide an upper bound for compression schemes. Shannon has estimated the actual information in English text.

In a string of N symbols, such as English, the intersymbol influence can be taken care of by considering the information in the last symbol of the string if the previous $N - 1$ symbols are known. This is of course calculated from the probability distribution of that last symbol if the previous symbols of the string are known. The longer that we make the string, the better the estimate that we shall get. There is another approach that considers the very long strings as the messages and calculates the average information in those messages. This involves a large number of possible messages. The basis of these approaches is shown in Fig. 6.3.

Consider the upper part of Fig. 6.3 and strings of length N. Let G_N equal the average information per symbol in blocks N symbols long. In effect, we are considering a very large set $\{B_i\}$ of possible messages of length N. Clearly from our previous formulas the value of G_N can be calculated from Eq. 6.14:

$$G_N = -[1/N] \times \Sigma_{B_i}[p(B_i)] \times Log_2[p(B_i)]. \quad (6.14)$$

---

7. C. E. Shannon, "Prediction and Entropy of Printed English," *BSTJ* 30 (January 1951): 50–64.

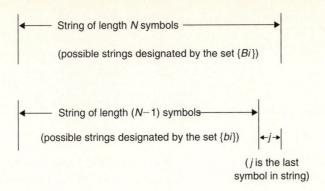

Figure 6.3   The analysis of a string of text

In like fashion, shifting to the lower part of the figure, let F_N equal the average information in the Nth symbol if the previous $(N - 1)$ symbols are known. The information in the Nth symbol, if the previous $(N - 1)$ symbols are known, is $-\log[p_{bi}(j)]$, and F_N is just the expectation of that:

$$F_N = - \Sigma_{bi} \Sigma_j[p(bi,j)] \times Log[p_{bi}(j)]. \qquad (6.15)$$

Because F_N focuses knowledge of all of the preceding symbols on reducing the uncertainty of the Nth symbol, and G_N is an average over all possible sequences, we would expect that for a given value of N,

$$F_N \leq G_N. \qquad (6.16)$$

By using Eq. 6.7 this can be shown to be true and is left as an exercise for the reader.

Estimates of the information content of English can be made from known statistics. However, multidimensional (or parameter) probability distributions for English, or N grams, at the time of Shannon's work were known only out to a few places. With modern computers, they are undoubtedly better known today, but even so the table of N grams will grow exponentially and soon become intractable. Even with our limit of 27 symbols, the number of possible messages or N grams is $(27)^N$ and with a full ASCII set it would be $(128)^N$.

The results from Shannon are given in Table 6.1. He made the estimates using N gram statistics for both letters and words. F_0 in the table is the entropy if the letters are independent and random. As per Eq. 6.16, F_1 considers that letters are random with the probability distribution of English, F_2 is based on the conditional probability if the preceding letter is known, etc. F_{word} is based upon the frequency of words.

Table 6.1   Information Content of English per Symbol

	F_0	F_1	F_2	F_3	F_{word}
26 Letters	4.7	4.14	3.56	3.3	2.62
27 Letters	4.76	4.03	3.32	3.1	2.14

The estimates in Table 6.1 are based on statistical dependencies that extend over only a few letters or words. Even so, the average information per symbol drops from 4.7 bits per symbol to around 2.5 bits per symbol.

It is well known that people, in interpreting text or restoring text containing errors, take advantage of intersymbol influence that extends far beyond a few symbols. Some words have many meanings, and the meaning that is intended may depend on the context of the sentence, paragraph, paper, book, etc. It is difficult to see how it will ever be possible to estimate long-range statistical effects of this type using the above approach. What is needed is statistical filtering that takes advantage of the knowledge possessed by human beings. Shannon cleverly decided to do just that. He made a better estimate using the prediction capability of humans, as shown in Fig. 6.4.

The method is to use human prediction and send the number of guesses. The assumption is that there is an identical twin (an inverse predictor) at the receiver. The human was given N letters of text and would guess the next letter. In a real communications system, the number of guesses (n) required to pick the correct letter would be sent. Knowing the number of guesses, the inverse predictor merely would ask himself what his nth guess would be. Actually, this is not a bad model for compressing data for either communications or data storage. Whatever the initial prediction algorithm is, if you can build the inverse, the system will work.

Going back to the information content in English, the statistics of the human predictor's guesses were used to calculate the entropy (H). Upper and lower bounds were calculated. The results are shown in bits per symbol in Table 6.2.

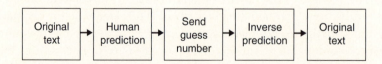

Figure 6.4   Procedure for determining information content of English text

Table 6.2 Estimates of Bits per Symbol in English

Number of letters (N)	15	100
Upper bound (bits)	2.1	1.3
Lower bound (bits)	1.2	0.6

We build communication and storage systems that handle all possible messages. Statistically only a small number of these messages ever appear. We need to build systems that are designed to handle only those messages that are going to occur.

We came to certain conclusions in our English example:

In a string of symbols N long, there are roughly $2^{4.76N}$ possible messages. Our systems are usually designed to handle all of these.

If the actual average information is .5 bits/symbol, then in the limit of long messages only $2^{.5N}$ of these ever occur.

The ratio of the number of messages that are likely to occur to the number of possible messages is $(2^{.5N})/(2^{4.76N}) = (2^{-4.26N})$. For a large value of N, $(2^{-4.26N})$ is a very small number.

The challenge is to find coding methods that will eliminate the redundancy in speech, TV, computer files, etc. There is a good deal of progress today in this area, but putting estimated numbers into an information theory based analysis indicates how far we have to go.

Estimates have been made of the maximum rate at which humans can receive information. For example, put in the numbers from the above for a very fast reader. You can estimate how many words per second a person can read, convert that to letters per second, and then substitute a value for the average information per letter in English. It is believed that the most a human can accept into medium-term memory is about 100 bits/sec. This rate is rather intriguing in light of the wideband visual presentations that are popular today. The implication is that there is a significant mismatch between the information that communications channels and computers present to people for things like speech, or video, and what they can accept. We should not jump to the conclusion that all of that mismatch is wasted. The challenge is to determine how much we can eliminate without altering perceived performance, and what we must retain.

Humans do a lot of scanning of text, pictures, etc. It is not clear, when a picture is presented, what part of it they will look at and what information they will take from the part that they look at. Therefore, unless we a priori know their intent, we must present them with much more information than they can accept. In many situations there are also multiple viewers or listeners who may be focusing on different parts of the data (e.g., music, pictures, text).

At the same time, there is a great deal of inherent statistical redundancy. The English example illustrates this point, as does television. Almost all of the possible pictures in television look like colored snowstorms and never occur. And yet, we have designed systems that can send all of those possible pictures. Medical imaging (e.g., x-ray tomography, MRI) is another example. By removing redundancy, the computer storage required to store medical images would be greatly reduced. In principle we should be able to remove statistical redundancy with no loss of information. There has been a great deal of work on compression, and if anything, because of potentially very large computerized databases, it is increasing.[8]

We have based much of the above discussion on information theory. The pragmatic weakness of that theory is that it applies in the limit of infinite length messages or an infinite number of trials. It has nevertheless proved useful in certain areas:

1. Developing a conceptual rigorous theoretical framework for information system storage, data storage, communications, data and information retrieval, security and coding, and many data manipulation problems.

2. Setting bounds on what we might be able to do and consequently giving us insight as to how well we are doing.

3. Suggesting simple solutions to some problems.

6.3 Representation of Electromagnetic Signals

6.3.1 Baseband Representations

First we consider signals around the origin—that is, signals similar to the audio signals that we hear, going from say zero to 15,000 cycles per second (15,000 Hz or 15 KHz). Although we hear sound waves, the signal driving the

---

8. N. Hubing, "Speech and Image Coding," Guest Editorial, Special Issue of IEEE Journal on Selected Areas in Communications, *IEEE SAC* 10, no. 5 (June 1992): 793; T. C. Bell, J. G. Cleary, and I. H. Written, *Text Compression* (Englewood Cliffs, NJ: Prentice-Hall, 1990); R. M. Gray, M. Cohn, L. W. Craver, A. Gersho, T. Lookabaugh, F. Pollars, and M. Vetteri, "Non-U.S. Data Compression and Coding Research," A FASAC Technical Assessment Report (McLean, VA: Science Applications International Corp., November 1993); Didier Le Gall, "MPEG: A Video Compression Standard for Multimedia Applications," *Communications of the ACM* 34, no. 4 (April 1991): 45–58; S.-U. Chang and D. G. Messerschmitt, "Manipulation and Compositing of MC-DCT Compressed Video," *IEEE SAC* 13, no. 1 (January 1955): 1; Roger Clark, *Digital Compression of Still Images and Video* (San Diego: Academic Press).

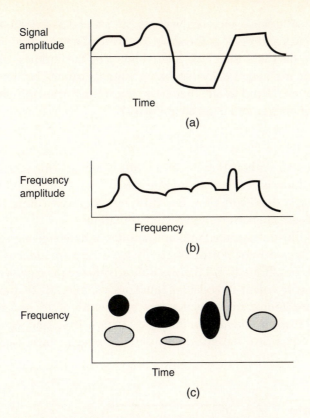

Figure 6.5   Representations of electromagnetic signals

speaker of a radio is electrical and of the same frequency as the sound waves. (Actually, if you can hear signals in the entire range of 0–15 KHz, your hearing is very good.) The electrical signals driving the picture tube in your TV set are another example, although in that case they roughly cover a band from 0 to 5 million Hz (5 MHz).

Electromagnetic signals can be described in terms of frequency, time, and amplitude. Common representations are shown in Fig. 6.5. Part (a) represents a signal by showing its amplitude as a function of time. Any signal can be represented as a function of time $F(t)$. A signal can alternatively be represented as a function of frequency $G(f)$. $F(t)$ and $G(f)$ are related by Fourier transforms or Fourier series. Part (b) shows a signal described as amplitude as a function of frequency, where we hasten to add there has been no attempt to make it a Fourier transformation of the top figure. We have no real use for the mathematics of these common Fourier transformations and will not go into them further. The reader who wishes to explore the subject is referred to books on mathematical analysis. In Section 6.4.1 we examine a particular type of Fourier transform that is particularly important in communications and computer work.

In a pragmatic sense, electrical signals can also be described as a function of both frequency and time, as shown in Fig. 6.5(c). The amplitude of the signal is shown on a third axis, the z axis, and is shown by the darkness of an area.

Strictly (or mathematically) speaking, signals cannot be limited in both time and frequency. And in fact there is an uncertainty principle similar to that in physics that applies and is given in Eq. 6.17:

$$(\Delta f) \times (\Delta t) \sim 1 \qquad (6.17)$$

Thus, in terms of mathematics, a continuous sine wave for which the uncertainty in frequency is zero has an infinite duration and undefined time. A very short impulse, a delta function, has little uncertainty in time but much in bandwidth. These are both well-known observations.

Figure 6.6 illustrates some familiar examples of baseband signals. Electrical baseband signals do not normally go down to zero frequency. The circuits would be too complicated, and there is little advantage to be gained.

It will be convenient to consider functions of time $F(t)$ that are baseband signals and are limited in frequency to a bandwidth of W. In actual fact, for mathematical reasons that are not important to us, a baseband signal has negative image frequencies, the imaginary parts of which cancel each other out.

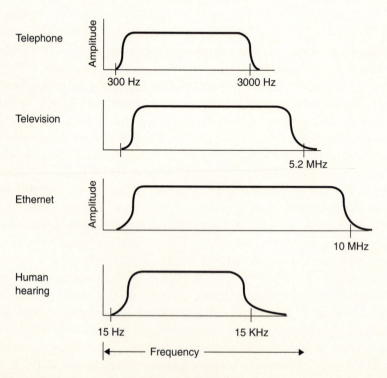

Figure 6.6   Examples of baseband signals

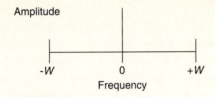

Figure 6.7   A baseband signal

Thus, if a function $F(t)$ is a baseband signal limited around the origin to a bandwidth W, its frequency components lie in the region shown in Fig. 6.7. We use W in keeping with common notation established by Shannon.

6.3.2   Broadband Signals (Heterodyned)

The broadband signals of concern to us will usually be baseband signals that have been moved to a higher frequency by a modulation method. For example, if a signal we are interested in, $F_s(t)$, is multiplied by a "carrier" sinewave at frequency W_c, it is moved up in frequency, as shown in Fig. 6.8. The actual function after it is moved up is given by Eq. 6.18.

To the electrical engineer such signals would be known as carrier-based or heterodyned signals. The term *broadband*, introduced by the computing community, is the term we shall use in this book. However, it should be noted that it is not a very good term. You can move both signals of narrow frequency bandwidth, or signals of broad (wide) frequency bandwidth up in frequency without changing the bandwidth. However, to many computer specialists, once signals have moved up in frequency, they are referred to as broadband signals.

The above is the normal process used for AM radio where a given station is assigned a carrier frequency and must keep its transmission within the corresponding channel, and unused guard bands are left between the channels for individual stations to prevent interference. As the reader probably knows, there are other methods of modulation such as FM, noise carrier, and FSK, and some of these do incidentally widen the frequency band occupied. Particular

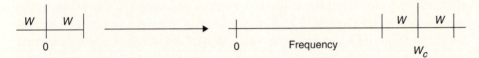

Figure 6.8   Moving a signal from baseband to broadband

$$F(t) = F_s(t) \times Sin(W_c t) \qquad\qquad (6.18)$$

methods of modulation are not of great concern to us at the present time. However, the concept of "Carrier" systems, or moving message carrying signals up to higher frequencies or bands is essential to communications. It is only through the use of carrier systems that we can communicate any distance and achieve high transfer rates over a distance. They are convenient in other circumstances. Once we get outside of a single computer, we are likely to encounter carrier systems, and certainly when we communicate beyond a local campuslike area, it will be by carrier-based communications. For example, on the Rensselaer Polytechnic Institute campus telephone conversations are distributed via carrier systems to subdistribution points (e.g., in a resident halls complex). Fiber optic systems are carrier based and once off campus everything is by carrier. Television signals from either a local station or a cable company are transmitted by carrier systems.

For the time being, we shall be concerned with baseband signals—the signals that carry the data or information. They are moved up in frequency as described above to transport from place to place, but put back down to baseband before they are used. We shall later review some of the relevant properties of broadband systems in the context of networks and system architecture.

6.4   Signal Representation by Its Sample Points

It is often convenient, and it simplifies our thinking, if we represent signals by samples of the associated waveform. Analog to digital (AD) conversion is sampling plus quantization (because we are representing the value of a continuous and therefore infinite set of possibilities at a sample point by a finite number system). Signals can be represented as vectors where the samples are the coordinates (or dimensions) and the sample values are the coordinate values. Can we justify such an approach?

It is reasonable to assume that we can substitute for an analog signal, such as a voice signal, the values of the function at a number of sample points. For example, a correspondence theorem argument would indicate that an infinite number of sample values would in fact represent the function. However, such an approach does not answer some practical questions. How many sample points per second are really needed to represent a signal such as voice? Certainly it does not require an infinite number of samples. If the values at the sample points are described as binary numbers, how many bits per second would be required to transmit the voice signal? As we shall see, it is normal practice to sample voice at 8 KHz and convert it to a 64 kilobit per second (kb/s) digital signal for switching and transmission. Can we convert from analog voice to digital voice and then when necessary back to analog voice? As we have remarked earlier, the national network in switching and transmission is largely digitized today. A normal computer modem used in homes converts the computer digital signal to analog, the central office switch at its input converts it back to digital, etc. Television signals sent over the national network are in digital form, and yet, by the time you see them on your set they are analog. So, apparently this type of thing is done all of the time.

An understanding of the theoretical basis for sampling, and its associated tradeoffs, is based on sampling theory. We shall briefly go through what is known as the sampling theorem. This one theorem is the foundation upon which analog to digital and digital to analog conversions are built as well as being an important concept in understanding much of information theory. We shall consider the sampling theorem conceptually and from the viewpoint of orthogonal representations and generalized Fourier series. The concepts and paradigms are not complicated and once accepted simplify understanding.

6.4.1   Generalized Fourier Series

An orthogonal coordinate system is a convenient way of describing or locating a point in space. There are many simple examples. We can locate a point on a plane by its x and y coordinates. The x and y coordinates are orthogonal[9] in that they are at right angles and the values of x and y can be changed independent of each other. The location on the plane could also be described by polar coordinates—i.e., angle and distance from the origin—and again polar coordinates are orthogonal. Clearly we can extend these concepts into three dimensions and the determination of the location of a fly in a room. In fact, the concepts can be extended into n dimensional space, which we shall see later is a convenient thing to do. In brief, we want to represent a function of time $F(t)$ by its sample values $F(t_n)$ at the times t_n. The values of $F(t_n)$ can then be considered the coordinate values in n dimensional Cartesian coordinate space. The point defined by those values can then be considered as a vector that describes the function. First, however, we must consider how to select the sample points so that this will be a valid representation.

There is a parallel to Cartesian geometry in that a function can be described by an expansion in terms of an orthonormal set.[10] Again, there are many examples of orthonormal sets, but we shall be interested in only one. In selecting either a coordinate system, or an orthonormal set, the application

9. Glenn James and Robert C. James, *The Mathematics Dictionary—Multilingual Edition* (New York: Van Nostrand, 1959).

10. Ruel V. Churchill and J. W. Brown, *Fourier Series and Boundary Value Problems*, 4th ed. (New York: McGraw Hill, 1979); see chapters 3, 4, and 5 on orthogonal sets and generalized Fourier series.

must be considered and the best one picked for that application. In a practical sense, the time functions that we consider here will be limited in bandwidth, as was illustrated in Fig. 6.7. Our goal is to represent a time function that is band limited by its sample points and to reconstruct the original time function from its sample points. One function, the sinc(x), or [sin(x)]/[x] function, is particularly suitable in meeting those objectives. The family of sinc(x) functions forms an orthonormal set. But before going into the details of that function, let us briefly review generalized Fourier series. We do so in the belief that the perspective and concepts of the general case are no more difficult to understand than a specific case, and that once understood many specific cases fall into place. What follows is applicable to normal sinusoidal Fourier series, LeGendre polynomials, etc.

Let $\{G_n(x)\}$ be a set of orthonormal functions in the interval a to b, and let $F(x)$ be an arbitrary function that we want to represent by an expansion in terms of an infinite series of orthonormal functions $G_n(x)$. For the members of the set to be orthogonal,

$$\int_a^b G_m(x) \times G_n(x)dx = 0 \text{ if } m \neq n$$
$$= 1 \text{ if } m = n. \tag{6.19}$$

It is also important that the sets be closed and complete, which we shall assume is the case. These conditions ensure that the functions can represent all of the desired function space. What these conditions imply pragmatically will become clear later. We can then represent $F(x)$ as

$$F(x) = \sum_{n=-\infty}^{n=+\infty} C_n \times G_n(x), \tag{6.20}$$

where the C_n are constants. The approximation of the series to $F(x)$ is in the mean, and (a) the integral of the square of the difference of $F(x)$ and the series representation approaches zero, and (b) at a point of discontinuity the series converges to the mean value of $F(x)$.

Multiplying both sides of Eq. 6.20 by $G_m(x)$ and integrating, we see that

$$\int_{-\infty}^{+\infty} G_m(x) \times F(x)dx = \int \sum_n C_n \times G_m(x) \times G_n(x)dx. \tag{6.21}$$

And from Eq. 6.19,

$$C_m = \int_{-\infty}^{+\infty} [F(x) \times G_m(x)]dx. \tag{6.22}$$

For the reader familiar with normal Fourier series, this is precisely the formula used to evaluate the coefficients in that series. It applies to all generalized Fourier series, including the sinc function. However, it involves integration, and integration is not always easy. We shall see that because of the properties of the [Sin(x)/x] function, the C_m are equal to the values of the function $F(t)$ at properly selected sample points, t_n. Consequently, integration is not necessary. In this case, values of the constants in Equation (6.20) are equal to the value of the function at the sample points, and that is the reason that communications engineers are so fond of the sinc(x) function.

The condition for closure and the meaning of convergence in the mean previously discussed can be written in equation form:

$$Lim_{n\to\infty} \int_{-\infty}^{+\infty} [F(x) - \Sigma C_n G_n(x)]^2 dx = 0. \tag{6.23}$$

Expanding Eq. 6.23 and from Eqs. 6.19 and 6.22, we obtain

$$\int_{-\infty}^{+\infty} \{[F(x)]^2 - \Sigma 2C_n[F(x) \times G_n(x)] + [C_n G_n(x)]^2\} dx = 0 \tag{6.24}$$
$$\qquad\qquad\qquad\quad | \qquad\qquad\qquad\qquad |$$
$$\qquad\qquad\quad (6.22) \qquad\qquad\qquad (6.19)$$
$$\qquad\qquad\qquad\quad | \qquad\qquad\qquad\qquad |$$
$$\qquad\qquad\quad 2[C_n]^2 \qquad\qquad\quad [C_n]^2$$

And from Eq. 6.24 we see that,

$$\int [F(x)]^2 dx = \Sigma [C_n]^2. \tag{6.25}$$

It is important to note that the above relationships apply to all generalized Fourier series. Our concern is with functions of time. The energy of a function of time is given by the integral of the square of its amplitude. Consequently, from Eq. 6.25, the energy in a waveform will equivalently be equal to the sum of the squares of the values of the waveform at the sample points.

6.4.2   The Sampling Theorem for Baseband Signals

We want to consider functions that (a) are limited to a bandwidth W around the origin, and (b) extend from $-T$ to $+T$ as T goes to infinity. The functions $Sinc(x)$ form an orthonormal set over this domain where

$$Sinc_n(t) = \{Sin2\pi W[t - n/(2W)]\}/\{2\pi W[t - n/(2W)]\}. \tag{6.26}$$

It will be convenient for us to assign a specific notation t_n to the values of $n/(2W)$, as in Eq. 6.27, and, as we shall see, these are the times at which a waveform should be sampled if the sample values are to be equal to the Fourier coefficients:

$$t_n = [n/(2W)]. \tag{6.27}$$

As the $\{Sinc_n(t)\}$ form an orthonormal set and are a particular functional form of generalized Fourier series, any time function that is band limited to W, can be represented by

$$F(t) = \sum_{n=-\infty}^{n=+\infty} C_n Sin2\pi W[t - n/(2W)]/2\pi W[t - n/(2W)]. \qquad (6.28)$$

We could use Eq. 6.22 to evaluate the coefficients C_n, but that would involve multiplication and integration. This is what is done with normal Fourier series and most generalized Fourier series. However, we can also note that at the points at which $t = n/(2W) = t_n$ all terms but one in the series are zero (i.e., as the sine is 0 and only the $[\sin(0)/0]$ term has the nonzero value of 1). Consequently,

$$F(t) = \sum_{n=-\infty}^{n=+\infty} F(t_n) Sin2\pi W(t - t_n)/2\pi W(t - t_n), \qquad (6.29)$$

where $t_n = [n/(2W)]$.

Equation 6.29 is the sampling theorem. It states in brief that a time function, $F(t)$, limited in frequency around the origin to a bandwidth of W:

1. It can be represented by the series expansion (Eq. 6.29).

2. The constants $\{F(t_n)\}$ are the values of the function $F(t)$ at the times t_n.

3. Equation 6.29 converges to the actual function in the mean.

Theoretically the above is true for bandlimited functions of infinite time duration. Pragmatically, in practice we have functions that are neither band limited nor of infinite duration. If the real world does not meet that ideal, how close does it come? Is it close enough that the formalism is useful? The answer is that with a proper selection of sampling rate it comes close enough and is very useful. We shall want to understand the tradeoffs involved in picking parameter values and the margins or safety factors, like the guard bands in the assignment of radio channels. These will be considered in later examples.

6.4.3   An Example of the Sampling Theorem

We shall consider the Sinc function, and expansions in terms of it, in more detail. The main reason is to provide the reader with experience and understanding of such expansions and the relevant guard bands, precautions, and tradeoffs involved. We want to talk of signals of bandwidth W and time duration T. Realistically, in the practical world, signals are both band limited and

$t = -40, -39.9..40$

$$A(t) = \frac{\sin (t)}{t}$$

$$B(t) = \frac{-\sin (t - 10)}{2 (t - 10)}$$

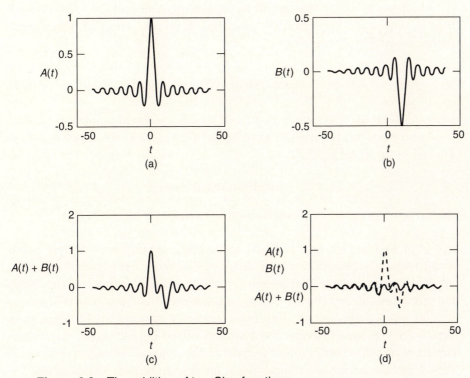

Figure 6.9   The addition of two Sinc functions

time limited and such signals have $2TW$ dimensions. Understanding of communications, switching, and some aspects of computers is based on the above concept.

Figure 6.9(a) is a $\sin(x)/x$ function plotted around the origin. Figure 6.9(b) is a similar function, half the height, negative, and displaced 10 units of time. Figure 6.9(c) is the sum of the functions in Figs. 6.9(a) and 6.9(b). This illustrates how two members of the $\sin(x)/x$ family can be added to form a new function. When using the sampling theorem as in the next example, we shall use a large number of terms, not just two. Figure 6.9(d) plots the previous three figures on the same curve. These plots should give the reader some feel for the $\mathrm{Sin}(x)/x$ or $\mathrm{Sinc}(x)$ function.

It is often necessary to decide how often to sample a class of functions. We may know that they are band limited (as with telephone signals), or we may know some of their time function properties (as with some control signals). In any event, it may be desirable to review an example of reconstructing a typical signal to get a feel for what sampling rate is needed and to illustrate what happens at a discontinuity, as indicated in the discussion of Eq. 6.23.

As above, it will be convenient to measure time in units of $1/2W$. Time is then in units more appropriately described in terms associated with sample points. Equation 6.29 becomes

$$F(t) = \sum_{n=-\infty}^{n=+\infty} F(n) \times [Sin(\pi \times (t-n))]/[\pi \times (t-n)], \qquad (6.30)$$

where n designates the sample point, and time is measured in units of $1/2W$.

As an example, we wish to sample and then recreate the function $G(t)$ of Eq. 6.31 by applying Eq. 6.30:

$$G(t) = t \text{ if absolute value of } t \leqslant 1$$
$$= 0 \text{ if absolute value of } t > 1. \qquad (6.31)$$

$G(t)$ is plotted in Figs. 6.10 and 6.11 for a different number of sample points along with its expansion and the difference between the expansion and the original function. (Note that because of the way we have normalized things the numeric scales for the two figures are different.) The points of discontinuity and rapid change result from high frequency components in the original signal. Because the expansion has assumed a band-limited signal and will reconstruct only the band-limited portion of the original waveform, we would expect that the largest error would be at the discontinuities. This is indeed the case. It is also true that if we examine the functions in more detail than is possible in these figures, the reconstruction does converge to the mean value at points of discontinuity. Readers having access to MathCad, Maple, or a similar software package, should experiment with expansions like the above. It will provide more of a feel for the tradeoffs.

6.4.4   AD and DA Conversions

By sampling a signal $F(t)$ along the lines discussed above, we obtain a set of numerical values as shown in Fig. 6.12. We can convert those numerical values to the nearest binary numbers (within the available word lengths) and in the process create a digitized approximation of the original signal. In the example we have rounded the original values to the nearest integer. In the terminology

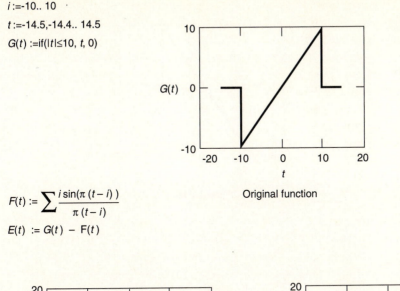

$i := -10.. 10$

$t := -14.5, -14.4.. 14.5$

$G(t) := \text{if}(|t| \le 10, t, 0)$

Original function

$$F(t) := \sum \frac{i \sin(\pi (t - i))}{\pi (t - i)}$$

$E(t) := G(t) - F(t)$

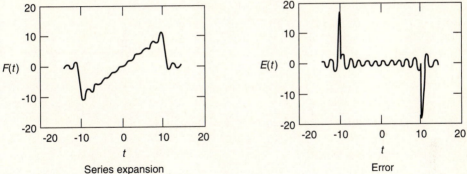

Series expansion   Error

Figure 6.10   Sampling theorem—21 sample points

of the communications engineer, this is quantizing the original sample points to the nearest integers, or more generally, to the nearest values from a preselected finite set. Quantization, in this sense, is a very important concept in communications. The round-off errors introduced are referred to as quantizing noise in communications. Because of this noise, introduced in the process of quantizing the original signal, we must select levels of quantization and associated binary word lengths that will provide the necessary precision. By necessary precision, we imply an acceptable difference between the original analog values and their binary approximations. Analog signals are usually no better than one part in a hundred, and therefore a word length of 8 or 9 bits should be satisfactory. For speech it is common practice to use 8 bits.

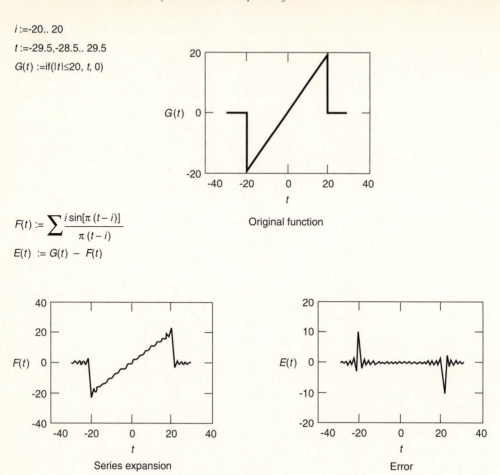

$i := -20..\ 20$

$t := -29.5, -28.5..\ 29.5$

$G(t) := \text{if}(|t| \leq 20,\ t,\ 0)$

$$F(t) := \sum \frac{i\,\sin[\pi\,(t-i)]}{\pi\,(t-i)}$$

$E(t) := G(t) - F(t)$

Original function

Series expansion

Error

Figure 6.11   Sampling theorem—41 sample points

Examples of signals that are usually in analog form include speech, television, scanned photographs, radar, sonar, music, medical imaging, much of the nontext data in books, etc. Communications systems often are mixed analog and digital, which means that AD conversion is a very important requirement. Many of the detectors, actuators and display devices attached to computers are also analog.

If AD conversion is important, then DA conversion must also be important. In computers we deal with binary signals, and we therefore need to reconstruct the sample values from the binary words that represent the sample values. There are various ways of doing so, which we shall not go into in detail. Basically, we know the amplitude that should be attached to each binary symbol that is present in a word, and it is merely a problem of adding up

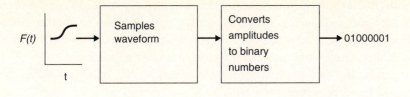

Sample time	Sample value	Rounded value	Binary value
1	7.7	8	01000
2	6.3	6	00110
3	6.8	7	00111
4	3	3	00011

Figure 6.12   Analog to digital conversion

those values to obtain the analog value of a sample point (within the limits of quantizing noise or round-off error). Having the sample values, however, we must then construct the series in Eq. 6.29 or its equivalent. It turns out that an impulse (i.e., a spike or delta function) put into a perfect low pass filter (i.e., a filter similar in frequency to Fig. 6.7) will produce a $\sin(x)/x$ function at the output. Thus impulses with amplitudes of the relevant sample points put into such a filter at appropriate times will produce the original function. The process of DA conversion is shown in Fig. 6.13.

6.4.5   The Sampling Theorem for Broadband Signals

It was noted earlier that carrier systems are very important. It is common practice in such systems to move many baseband signals up in frequency and place them in adjacent frequency bands, just as the FCC does in assigning radio channels. With fiber optics, there are even more channels at very high frequencies. How do you sample the data carrying waveforms and separate out

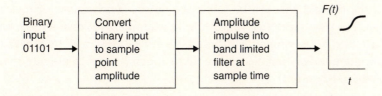

Figure 6.13   Digital to analog (DA) conversion

the individual signals? You certainly do not sample a voice, TV, or data stream signal at light frequencies. This is one of the real problems facing the common carriers today. Most transmission, except on local loops, is by high frequency or optical systems. Most switching is done basically at baseband.

It can be shown that an arbitrary real function, $F(t)$, band limited as shown in Fig. 6.14, can be represented as

$$F(t) = I(t) \times Sin(W_0 t) + Q(t) \times Cos(W_0 t), \tag{6.32}$$

where W_0 is the center frequency and $I(t)$ and $Q(t)$ are band limited to W around the origin. This is a solid mathematical result that you might try proving by invoking odd and even functions. $I(t)$ and $Q(t)$ are often referred to as *quadrature components*. The use of the term quadrature probably has its origin in the fact that one can consider that $I(t)$ and $Q(t)$ are modulated on sine and cosine carriers that are orthogonal to each other. There is also a relationship to real and imaginary numbers.

1. In normal circumstances, W_0 is the carrier frequency.

2. We now have twice as many sample points or degrees of freedom as for a baseband signal of equal bandwidth. $I(t)$ and $Q(t)$ each have sample points at intervals of $1/(2W)$. The reason that there are twice as many degrees of freedom is that the symmetry relationship between the plus and minus frequencies of a signal band limited around the origin is no longer applicable. This means that we can get twice the information in a given bandwidth.

3. However, remember that the functions $I(t)$ and $Q(t)$ are band limited around the origin and there is no way we can really lay our hands upon meaningful sample points as long as they are at high frequency.

4. If we want simple operations, or do much with the original waveform, we should synchronously demodulate or detect the signal before sampling. In other words we must first move it to baseband.

In brief, the $I(t)$ and $Q(t)$ can be separated out by synchronous or quadrature detection. The procedure that follows is an example. We consider $I(t)$, and the procedure for $Q(t)$ is similar. Multiply both sides of Eq. 6.32 by $Sin(W_0 t)$ and integrate. Remember that W_0 is usually a much higher frequency than any component in $I(t)$ or $Q(t)$.

$$\int [Sin(W_0 t) \times F(t)]dt = [I(t) \times (Sin(W_0 t))^2 + Q(t) \times Cos(W_0 t) \times Sin(W_0 t)]dt. \tag{6.33}$$

The term containing the product of the cosine and the sine will drop out. The term with the sine squared will remain, in effect leaving $I(t)$ times a constant. (It is not really a constant, but the normal decay "time constant" of a detector circuit will make it pragmatically a constant.) Multiplying by $\text{Cos}(W_0 t)$ and following the same procedure will yield $Q(t)$. We can then work with $I(t)$ and $Q(t)$ as normal baseband limited functions. They can be sampled, digitized, switched, etc. $I(t)$ and $Q(t)$ can later be reconstructed by DA conversion. The waveform can be restored to a band centered around W_0, or any other desired center frequency, by multiplying the $I(t)$ and $Q(t)$ by synchronized carrier sine and cosine functions respectively and adding. The "any other desired center frequency" is important. The signal may have arrived at a switching center at one carrier frequency and been extracted and processed. When sent on to the next switching center, it may be necessary to utilize a different center frequency. There will be more discussion of this later.

Synchronous detection has been mentioned, but is it often not used. Instead detection that extracts the square root of the sum of the squares of $I(t)$ and $Q(t)$ may be used, thus utilizing only half of the potential information-carrying capacity. Synchronous, or as it is sometimes called quadrature, detection is used in such things as single sideband communications. Whereas in normal communications, the signal occupies a bandwidth W, both above and below the carrier frequency W_0 (see Fig. 6.14), in a single sideband system the signal is present in only one of the two. You may also encounter synchronous detection in working with computer networks. You should be aware of synchronous carrier techniques and quadrature components as discussed above. They are a basic concept in broadband signals and are used extensively in parts of the telephone system. Details can be found in books on communications. We have spoken primarily of detection, but there are similar techniques, either synchronous or nonsynchronous, to create broadband signals.

The important thing is that it is not pragmatically possible to sample the waveform $F(t)$ of Eq. 6.32 directly. Whether quadrature or nonsynchronous detection (demodulation) is used, the step of demodulation and extraction of the data carrying components is essential. If W_0 is close to the origin, there are

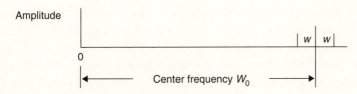

Figure 6.14   A band-limited broadband signal

shortcuts that can be taken to accomplish this, and those shortcuts are sometimes taken in work on circuits for automatic control and robotics. However, the shortcuts will not work at high carrier frequencies. The fundamentals are as described above. As we get more into broadband local area networks and fiber optic systems, they are very relevant to distributed computers.

In this section we have used the term synchronous in the context of carrier frequencies. There is another meaning to the term in both computers and networks that is associated with time of arrival or clocking logical operations. The environments are sufficiently different that there should be little confusion.

6.5   Transmission with Noise

The discussion to date has been limited to communications in the absence of noise. The reason is that in general noise in data communication systems is not a serious problem. This was true prior to the large-scale introduction of fiber optics and is even more true with the very low noise and interference present in fiber optic systems. Fiber optics made a substantial impact on the communications systems used between computers in the control field (e.g., power stations, steel mills, aircraft, machine shops) where prior to their introduction, it was necessary to take very costly steps to ensure adequate data communications. Power circuits and high current switching can create a great deal of electrical noise. Fiber has also reduced costs in common carrier systems.

The information theory and communications system concepts reviewed so far can be extended into the area of noisy communications channels. In making this extension, probability reaches into the area of continuous functions, and the summations used in the discrete case are replaced with integrals. Additive noise is included in the model of transmission channels. We shall not go into those extensions in detail and instead give only a few results that appear to be pertinent.

6.5.1   Error Rates as a Function of S/N Ratio

It is important to understand the role of signal to noise ratio in determining how accurately signals can be communicated. It is the basis for implementations that are responsible for the extremely low error rates in digital systems. For cost reasons, this has been a significant factor in the digitization of the national telephone network that transports voice, video, data, etc. We should understand why certain things are done in designing communications systems. It is also important to realize that with the increased use of portable radio based data communications systems, noise considerations and error rates again may become very important in certain areas of computer use.

The experience with voice circuits will serve as an example. When transmitting an analog voice signal over a long distance, noise is added to the signal in the transmission medium and circuits. Prior to transmission, the signal can be amplified to a level at which the noise is small compared to the signal, but generally speaking the noise is a constant uncontrollable quantity that is added. With distance, the signal is attenuated but the noise continues to be added to it. Thus, with distance, the signal to noise (S/N) ratio decreases. Prior to this becoming a serious problem, the signal must be amplified again so that the signal is large with respect to the inherent unavoidable noise that will be added in the next stage of the transmission system. Unfortunately, the noise component existing prior to amplification is also amplified and consequently amplification does not improve an existing S/N ratio to which more noise is added in the next stage. In brief, noise is continuously added with distance. Signal levels must be maintained that are very large with respect to the accumulated noise. To provide the required S/N ratio is a technical challenge both with respect to equipment and the distance between relay or amplification points.

6.5.2   Threshold Effects with Additive Noise

It has been established that a waveform can be represented by its sample points. The amplitude at a sample point can be converted to a sequence of digital words. For our purposes here, consider the individual bits in those words. Furthermore, assume that a bit is represented by a 0 or a 1. If a bit is sent, noise will be added to it. At a minimum, it will be thermodynamic noise, but it may be much more. In the discussion that follows, we assume random white or Gaussian noise that follows a normal distribution. This is a reasonable assumption that corresponds to the noise created by most physical environments. We make the assumption with the realization that in some circumstances impulse noise, or jamming signals, may be important.

How does the receiver decide what has been sent? Figure 6.15 illustrates the situation. We assume that, in the absence of noise, if a "0" is sent, 0 volts will be received at the receiver. In like fashion, if a "1" is sent, 5 volts will be received. In both cases, noise will be added and the probability distributions for the received signals are shown as $p(x)$ and $g(x)$ respectively. Detection, and this is almost universal in concept, is achieved by setting a threshold, which in our example is at 2.5 volts. If the received signal is below the threshold, the receiver decides that a 0 was sent. If the signal is above the threshold, the decision is for a 1. It is of course possible that when 0 is sent, the additive noise

$x := -5, -4.9..\ 10$

$p(x) := \dfrac{1}{\sqrt{2\,\pi}}\ e^{-.5x^2}$ = probability distribution at receiver for "0" sent

$p(x) := \dfrac{1}{\sqrt{2\,\pi}}\ e^{-.5\,(x-5)^2}$ = probability distribution at receiver for "1" sent

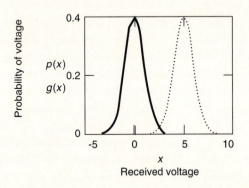

Voltage sent for a "0" = 0 volts

Voltage sent for a "1" = 5 volts

Threshold set at 2.5 volts

Probability of error for a "0" sent
= integrated area of curve $p(x)$
above threshold of 2 1/2 volts

Figure 6.15   An example of threshold detection

will make the received signal above the threshold and an error will be made. How likely is it that such an error will occur? If a zero is sent, the probability of an error is equal to the area under the tail of the distribution curve for a zero that is above the threshold. If the signal to noise ratio is large enough, that area is very small and consequently making an error is very unlikely. The error rate drops off exponentially with an increase in S/N ratio, which means that small increases in S/N have a tremendous effect on the error rate. The probability of error can be made essentially zero.

Figure 6.16 shows the probability distribution to be expected. On the left is a curve that plots the probability of error; on the right is a table that shows how rapidly the probability of error decreases as the threshold level is increased. In this example, moving the threshold from 2.5 to 5 reduces the probability of error from 6×10^{-3} to 2.9×10^{-7}. If the voltage used in sending a 1 in Fig. 6.15 is increased a small amount and the value of the threshold is moved up accordingly, the probability of error will be greatly reduced. For large values of x, the area under the tail actually drops off as $[e^{-x}]/x$. Because of this nonlinearity, transmission powers can be selected that will make the probability of error essentially zero.

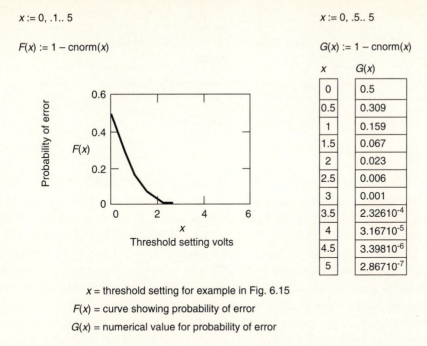

$x := 0, .1.. 5$

$F(x) := 1 - cnorm(x)$

$x := 0, .5.. 5$

$G(x) := 1 - cnorm(x)$

x	$G(x)$
0	0.5
0.5	0.309
1	0.159
1.5	0.067
2	0.023
2.5	0.006
3	0.001
3.5	$2.326 \cdot 10^{-4}$
4	$3.167 \cdot 10^{-5}$
4.5	$3.398 \cdot 10^{-6}$
5	$2.867 \cdot 10^{-7}$

x = threshold setting for example in Fig. 6.15

$F(x)$ = curve showing probability of error

$G(x)$ = numerical value for probability of error

Figure 6.16   Probability of error as a function of signal to noise ratio

The above, however, does not mean that there is no problem if amplifiers are used at relay points. The noise still keeps accumulating, and the signal to noise ratio at the receiving end of a long path with multiple relay points is degraded.

6.5.3   Quantization and Regeneration of Signals, or Amplifiers Versus Repeaters

The binary example of Fig. 6.15 can be extended to a multilevel system. It would be possible to send signals of say 0, 1, 2, ... 7. The receiver would then select as the received message the digit that was closest to the received signal. At the transmitter, a sample point would be taken and compared to the eight allowed signal levels, and the closest value from that set would be sent. Of course, there would be differences between what was sent and the value of the actual sample point, and this would be referred to as quantization noise. As previously noted, quantization noise would be introduced at the sender and corresponds to the round-off error if the value of the sample point is digitized. A multilevel system (as distinct from a two-level or digital system) is an acceptable system with one drawback. Because the noise is independent and fixed for purposes of this discussion, the required signal power will increase

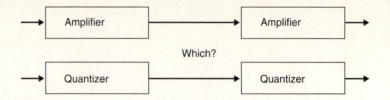

Figure 6.17   Relay station alternatives

with the number of levels. In effect, the separation of levels is determined by the noise and acceptable error rates. At the same time, the power required to send a signal is a function of the number of levels. Thus in the example of Fig. 6.15, voltage levels of 0, 5, 10, 15, 20, 25, 30, and 35 would be required.

The main advantage of a quantized system is that it provides an alternative to amplifiers at the relay stations. Specifically, in the quantized system, only certain levels are allowed, and the received signal can be reset to the correct value before retransmission. In other words, the signal is regenerated. If this is done, then the noise does not accumulate from relay link to relay link. This is a tremendous advantage. One now needs to design only so that there is an extremely low error rate over each link. The alternatives are shown in Fig. 6.17. In fact an examination of tradeoffs indicates that there is really only one choice. The quantized system is far superior. Quantization noise is no real problem, for the original signal source will have some noise or round-off errors and the quantization noise can be made small with respect to those. Upon further examination, it also becomes clear that a two-level or binary system is superior to the multilevel system. The power required is less, the circuits are simpler and easier to design and build, and the tolerances are wider in every area.

It was indicated earlier that the common carriers moved to digital communications systems for economic reasons not associated with computer requirements. The first factor was switching, which we shall consider in the next chapter; the second was transmission, as described above.

6.6   Geometric Representation of Functions

Consider a binary sequence of 3 bits. There are $2^3 = 8$ possible such sequences. Each of these sequences can be represented as a point in three-dimensional space, as illustrated in Fig. 6.18, with the sequences of 000 and 111 indicated. In effect the values at the sample points of a particular sequence have been used to define the coordinate values. We can also say that the message 111 is defined by the vector 111. The concept is extendible to higher dimensions.

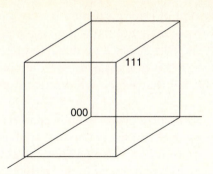

Figure 6.18   Geometric representation of signals 000 and 111

Consider the point or message 111. If one of the bits is in error, it will be modified as shown in Fig. 6.19 with the new possible locations in parentheses.

Correspondingly, the locations resulting from a single error in the message 000 are shown in brackets. It is clear that only one error in a sequence does not move its representation to a point that could be occupied as a result of one error in the other sequence. Consequently, the selection of a message from the message set {000, 111} with two allowable messages, instead of the eight possible messages, has resulted in a one error correcting code. Any one error can be corrected. Forgetting about error correction, how will this configuration work with regard to detecting errors? From the geometry, it is evident that one or two errors in a sequence will always be detected, for such errors cannot move the point to that assigned to the other sequence. In other words, if a message is received at any point other than {000} or {111}, the only two messages that the transmitter is allowed to send, it must be the result of one or two errors in one of those allowable messages.

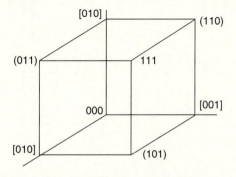

Figure 6.19   An example of a single error correcting code

The geometric concept of error correction is very simple. If the errors (or noise) that are likely to occur cannot move a message point into a region that might be occupied by another message point subject to errors or noise, then it is possible to correct the received message. This is a more general case of coding and regeneration than that which we discussed in the previous three-dimensional case.

Figures 6.18 and 6.19 involve binary signals. However, the same argument can be applied to the values that are obtained by applying the sampling theorem to an arbitrary waveform $F(t)$. There will now be $2TW$ dimensions and coordinate values. The values will be equal to the set $\{F(t_n)\}$. A three-dimensional case is shown in Fig. 6.20. From generalized Fourier series and the sampling theorem, we know that the sum of the squares of the coordinate values is equal to the energy in $F(t)$, and from the geometry we know that the length of the vector representing $F(t)$ is equal to the square root of that sum. Added noise, incidentally, can be represented by a vector added to the vector representing $F(t)$, and as the noise is random we know only that it will be confined to a radius around the end of $F(t)$, where the radius is determined by the noise energy. These remarks clearly apply to long messages, not to the three-dimensional case, but n dimensional space is difficult to draw and the reader will have to visualize the more general case. We are presenting this material because we want to apply the concepts in later chapters, for example, in Chapters 7 and 8.

Consider that in Fig. 6.20 information is sent by changing or assigning an amplitude to $F(t)$ while the direction of $F(t)$ is held constant. In other words, the amplitude of $F(t)$ carries the information; it represents one degree of freedom. That information could be represented by the value at a single sample point. We have, however, elected to represent it by three related sample points. If $F(t)$ is assigned a different value, to hold its direction fixed $F(t_1)$, $F(t_2)$ and

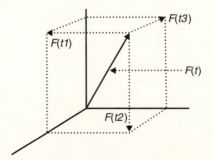

Figure 6.20 $F(t)$ represented as a vector (three dimensions)

$F(t_3)$ must be changed proportionally. The concept is that the modulation method or carrier system being used multiplies the dimensions (or degrees of freedom) in the original message, each of which is represented by an information carrying amplitude, by a factor of n. (In the example, n equals 3.) As the number of sample points have been increased from one (the number necessary to send sample point) to three, we know that we have also multiplied the required bandwidth (remember the $1/2W$ spacing of sample points) by three. Conceptually, this is the basis for the spread spectrum systems that are starting to be used in many radio systems that provide service to portable computers.[11] This will be discussed again later.

The geometric approach described can be extended and used as a basis for deriving Shannon's capacity theorem, which is given in Eq. 6.34. We do not wish to go into a derivation in that it is not sufficiently relevant to the subject of this book. However, the reader should be aware of the theorem. It is clear from the equation that increasing channel capacity by increasing signal power is not the thing to do when compared with increasing bandwidth. Our earlier conclusion that binary systems were a better alternative than multilevel quantized systems is consistent with this. FM, spread spectrum techniques, and asynchronous multiplexed systems in general take advantage of the broader bandwidth. There are cases in data communications where asynchronous systems are almost a necessity. We shall discuss this in later chapters.

The Channel Capacity Theorem (C. E. Shannon)

1. Given a baseband signal of bandwidth W, signal power S, and a noise (white or Gaussian) power of N in the band W, then in the limit of long messages it is possible to transmit at a rate of C bits/second where

$$C = W \times Log_2[1 + (S/N)]. \qquad (6.34)$$

2. Furthermore, it is not possible to transmit at a higher rate. C is often referred to as the channel capacity.

There are advantages to wide bandwidth systems such as FM and other spread spectrum systems. The disadvantage is that they take up scarce radio frequency spectrum and interfere with each other. If fiber optics can be used, wide bandwidth is available and interference may not be a problem.

---

11. Andrew J. Viterbi, *CDMA: Principles of Spread Spectrum Communications* (Reading, MA: Addison-Wesley, 1995); R. Kohno, R. Meidan, and L. B. Milstein, "Spread Spectrum Access Methods for Wireless Communications," *IEEE Communications* 33, no. 1 (January 1995): 58.

We can ask the question, what would be the worst case if there is interference with other signals or channels? The worst case would be a malicious person or organization that is trying to jam and deny you communications. Assume that the jamming energy is large with respect to pure noise energy, which we shall ignore, and that your adversary has been able to synchronize jamming energy with your signal energy. Equation 6.34 then becomes Eq. 6.35,

$$C = W \times Log_2[(S/J)], \tag{6.35}$$

where J is the power of the jamming signal. This result can be obtained by working with the geometry in n dimensional space. Considering the correspondence principle as a check, the answer appears to be reasonable. Given an equal amount of energy and synchronization, your opponent would be able to send a signal that would cancel out yours. In other words, he or she would push your message vector back to zero, or at least to where natural noise makes detection impossible.

6.7   Summary and Comments

In this chapter we have reviewed those core concepts of communications technology that are particularly applicable to distributed information systems. Later chapters will build upon these concepts. The justification for providing the core paradigms and perspective at this time is that they greatly simplify that which follows.

We make a distinction between data and information. Data are raw detailed facts; information that is important to us is derived from data. The importance is that from a perspective of information, and in that context, we can greatly simplify the communications, storage, and retrieval of data and information. In addition, we can remove the redundancy that is usually present in data, or in computer terminology we can compress the data.

Discrete probability was introduced in terms of the frequency of events. Probability is the area of mathematical science upon which the concepts of information theory are based. Except for brief discussion of the effects of noise, continuous probability is not considered. The reason is that, given the low error rates in modern communications and computer equipment, continuous probability is not central to most of the current issues in distributed systems. However, the applicability in areas like artificial intelligence is acknowledged.

The model of a communications channel introduced is equally applicable to information storage and information retrieval. By intuitive definition, the information contained in a message—i.e., symbol string, word, etc.—is required to be a function of uncertainty (i.e., probability). For information to be additive, this is equivalent to a definition in terms of the logarithm of probability. If the logarithm is to the base 2 then information is in bits. The resulting paradigms are applicable to issues in storing, retrieving, and compressing information, as well as to secrecy systems.

Computers operate on and communicate utilizing electromagnetic signals. The signals of interest are usually around the origin in frequency. However, for communication purposes, they are almost universally shifted to higher frequencies and are centered around carrier frequencies. Signals around the origin in frequency are referred to as *baseband signals*. Those that have been shifted to a higher frequency are called *broadband signals*. As far as information processing is concerned, people and computers operate almost exclusively on baseband signals. Thus shifting from baseband to broadband signals and the reverse are important.

If a continuous baseband function of time, or analog signal, is limited in bandwidth—and pragmatically it always is—it can be represented by appropriately selected sample values. If W is the bandwidth, samples should be taken at intervals of $1/2W$. The "sampling theorem" establishes the mathematical basis for sampling the function of time and a procedure to be followed in reconstructing the original function. The values of the sample points can be digitized (A/D conversion) within the limits of round-off error and put into a computer. After processing in the computer, the computer output can be put into analog form (D/A conversion), if that is appropriate. These procedures provide a mechanism for coupling the digital world of computers to the largely analog environment of the world at large. The sampling theorem has wider implications with respect to information theory, switching, and communications technologies. Much of information theory can be derived from viewing a signal as a vector in N dimensional space, where N equals the number of sample points.

State-of-the-art communications channels have very low error rates. This is largely the result of digitizing waveforms and regenerating the digital values at relay points. In regeneration each received bit, that has inevitably had a small amount of noise added to it, is reset to its bit value. Thus noise does not accumulate. This system is far superior to amplifying signals at relay points.

It is far more effective to increase the capacity of a communications channel by widening the bandwidth occupied by the signal than to increase power. This fact, and the application of regeneration technology at relay points, have been principal reasons for the digitization of transmission in the national network.

6.8 Problems

1. Using indirect methods to calculate probabilities—for example, calculating the probability that something will not happen as a step toward calculating the probability that it will—can often greatly simplify calculations. To demonstrate, try solving the following problem both ways.

Assume that you work as a member of a group of 20 people, all of whom were born between 1970 and 1971. Assume further that it is equally likely that a given member of the group was born on any day during those two years.

(a) What is the probability that two or more members of the group will have the same birthday during the year 1994? (b) What is the functional relationship between the number of people in the group, n, and that probability? (c) Calculate and plot the probability for groups from 1 to 35 members. (d) How much more complicated would the problem be if you included leap years?

2. The fact that the entropy of information theory, H, is a maximum when the probabilities are equal is of great importance in communications and computer technology. How sharp the maximum is can be important. (a) Why is the shape of the maximum important? (b) Would you expect that the general shape in the binary case would carry over into higher dimensions? (c) What are the implications with respect to the coding and compression of data? (d) What are the implications with respect to information retrieval?

3. The per symbol average information content in a string of symbols can be estimated using the equations for F_N and G_N. Calculating the relationship between these two functions is an exercise in the use of conditional probabilities. (a) Determine the relationship between F_N and G_N. (b) Prove that F_N is equal to or smaller than G_N for all values of N.

4. Many of our information-processing systems are designed to handle all possible situations when in fact only a limited number of situations are allowable in many cases. The actual information contained in computer displays, or speech over a telephone, are examples. Assume the following:

The maximum number of allowed symbol positions on a page of text is 66 in the horizontal direction and 55 in the vertical direction or 66×55.

A symbol can be represented by 8 binary digits, and the possible symbol set therefore contains 2^8 members.

English text contains on the average 1 bit per symbol.

(a) How many possible arrangements of symbols are there on a page? What is the number of bits required to store (or transmit) an arbitrary random arrangement? (b) What is the average number of bits required to store a completely full page of English text? How many possible arrangements of symbols does this represent? (c) Make a rough estimate of the number of bits required to store this page of text. For a page this full, how many possible arrangements of symbols does this represent? (d) Think about how long it should take to send a page of English text over 2,400, 9,600, and 64,000 bit per second communications lines. (c) If you want a more difficult problem, try to answer the above questions for a picture on the monitor of a computerized mechanical CAD system. You may be surprised.

5. Figures 6.10 and 6.11 provide an example of expanding a function in terms of a series of Sinc functions. The function selected is extreme in that it has sharp discontinuities. It illustrates the effects of the high frequencies inherent in discontinuities and also the convergence of the series to mean values. The following

problem is a much better behaved function and is in many respects more typical of what you could encounter in practice. There are discontinuities in slope, but not in the function itself.

Consider the function $G(t)$, where

$$G(t) = [k - |t|] \text{ if } |t| \leq k$$
$$= 0 \text{ if } |t| > k.$$

$G(t)$ is defined in terms of the constant k to make it convenient for you to use the normalized time interval $1/2W$ as in the text.

The calculations that you are asked to make are similar to those discussed in the chapter. You should note that in solving for values of $F(t)$ you should avoid values of $t = 0$ (where the sine would be equal to 0). This will simplify your calculations. Let $F(t)$ be the Sinc expansion of the function $G(t)$ and let $E(t)$ be the difference of $F(t)$ and $G(t)$, or the error.

a. Plot for 3, 11, 21, and 41 sample points $G(t)$, $F(t)$, and $E(t)$.

b. Calculate for the above cases:

The integral of $[G(t)]^2$

The sum of the squares of the coefficients of the series expansion

6. Many retrieval and indexing systems approximate a binary search. Thus an analysis of retrieval by yes and no questions is relevant. Such an analysis does not tell you how to "code" the questions with real-world probabilities, but it does set a bound.

Consider a very large set of objects that you may wish to locate. For example, these may be files or records that you have stored in a computer system. Assume the following:

Your requests to locate objects are independent of each other.

Each object is a member of one and only one category. For example, the categories may be people that you know in different areas, different subjects for library books, etc.

Within a given category, it is equally likely that you will wish to locate any member of that category.

The frequency of your requests to the different categories may be quite different.

With regard to the different categories, assume the data shown below.

Category	Number of objects	Relative frequency of requests by category
A	10^2	1000
B	10^4	100
C	10^6	10
D	10^8	1

(a) In the limit of an infinite number of queries, what is the lower bound of the average number of yes and no questions (binary questions) needed to locate an object? (b) If you are equally likely to want to locate any object in the combined set of A, B, C, and D, what is the lower bound of the average number of yes and no questions to locate an object?

Note that in actual practice, it would be unlikely to have equal probabilities within a category (a flat distribution), and it is very unlikely that the queries would be independent. If the different categories correspond to different levels in a memory hierarchy, then it is very likely that the cost (in time) for a query will vary with level. Any real optimization should consider that fact.

7. There is a widening gap between the speed of logic and memory (i.e., between CPU and memory). We know that we can make small associative memories (e.g., page boxes and hardware caches), but we wonder what the payoff is. In this problem we consider a case where the memory accesses are randomly distributed over a large memory. How much would we speed up things if that memory were associative? (Caches are in a sense associate memories.)

Assume that there is a large memory with N locations and that the requests are random and independent (neither assumption is likely to be true in the real world). The problem is to retrieve data at a virtual address of unknown physical location. (This is equivalent, for example, to finding a person by last name alone.)

We wish to compare two cases:

> *Case A:* We can ask binary questions. This will correspond to good search or indexing methods.

> *Case B:* We can ask K state questions. This will correspond to an associate memory of K words.

Assume that the time taken to respond to either case will be equivalent. This is unlikely to be completely true, and the circuitry for Case B will be more complex and expensive than that for Case A. However, such an analysis will let us set a bound on average performance in cycles.

Calculate the average minimum speed up in cycles of (b) compared to (a). This is the speed up you would get if you could optimally code the questions in the binary case.

These calculations should convince you of the following:

> A very large associative memory may not be worth the cost.

> Software solutions to large associate memories may be cost effective.

> The associative feature may dynamically solve the indexing, coding, cataloging, or search problem. This may be important.

> Perhaps the most important advantage of a caching system is getting the much-used references into faster memory. This is a function of the probability of accesses, including the conditional probabilities.

To do an analysis of the above type with real probabilities would be very complicated, even if the probabilities were known. This may be the reason so much of the work in the performance of memory hierarchies is done by simulation.

Chapter 7

Switching

The establishment, on demand, of an individual connection from a desired inlet to a desired outlet within a set of inlets and outlets for as long as is required for the transfer of information.

From CCITT, as expressed by J. C. McDonald[1]

7.1 Chapter Objectives

This chapter will provide the reader with a reasonable knowledge of switching techniques and their role and importance to distributed systems, tradeoff considerations, and the alternatives. Our focus will be on present techniques as well as those expected five to ten years in the future. As in earlier chapters, our emphasis will be on those issues that are important to distributed information systems. We offer readers a caution here: What at first glance may appear to be irrelevant to computers may in fact turn out to be relevant indeed. A good example is added-value services, such as those provided by Internet. Because such services utilize and must conform to the core services provided by the national network, it is important that we understand that network. Another example involves ISDN (Integrated Services Digital Network)-like services, which when they become widespread can be expected to have a profound impact on the users of computers. Practical examples of these points will come later in the chapter.

7.2 Introduction

In a communications system, connections are established between the various users of the system. In concept it makes little difference if the users are people, animals, computers, equipment, etc. The connections can be one to one, one to many, or many to many. Connecting all users to each other by direct wire is

1. J. C. McDonald, ed., *Fundamentals of Digital Switching*, 2nd ed. (New York: Plenum Press, 1990).

not a practical solution. Devices are needed that will make only those connections necessary at any one time—and switching is the technology used to establish these connections.

In the communications field, switching is an old technology that has gone through a long period of evolution. The best technical book on the history of switching is probably that by A. E. Joel.[2] For a more current overview, John C. McDonald's book is recommended.[3] Developments in the computer field have introduced new concepts, but many of the old concepts are still applicable. Unfortunately, many of the old concepts are not well known in the computer science sector of society. In addition some of the important concepts that are new from the perspective of the computer community are old from the viewpoint of the communications sector. At the same time, the computer area has contributed new concepts such as Ethernet. Both groups have much to contribute to a common problem, and it is important that the technologies of these two communities be brought together. Both groups will benefit from such a merger. An overview of communications needs in a data-driven (data engineering) world is provided in Frieder and Shuey.[4]

Digital switching and electronic digital switches are the heart of modern communications networks. There are some analog switches still in use in the national telephone network, and there are PBXs being sold today that are analog, but these are irrelevant to computer systems except that they must be circumvented or adapted to. We shall focus our discussion on digital switching techniques. The technology discussed will probably be stable up to the development and deployment of optical electronic switches. Optical switches would provide very broad bandwidths and are likely to provide the next significant quantum jump in performance. Concurrently, it is to be expected that they will profoundly change the tradeoffs in communications networks—for example, the tradeoffs between the design of transmission systems and switching. Today there exist only small optical switches in the laboratory, and it is likely that the deployment of large optical switches is at best at least a decade off.[5]

It is important that those developing distributed information systems realize both the importance and the cost of switching. The importance is that switching systems are what interconnect people, computers, and people to

2. A. E. Joel Jr., *A History of Engineering and Science in the Bell System—Switching Technology (1925–1975)* (Bell Telephone Laboratories, 1982).

3. John C. McDonald, *Fundamentals of Digital Switching,* 2nd ed. (New York: Plenum Press, 1990).

4. O. Frieder and R. L. Shuey, "Communications Needs in a Data Engineering World," *Computer Networks and ISDN* 25 (August 1992): 259.

5. J. E. Midwinter and P. W. Smith, guest eds. *Special Issue on Photonic Switching, IEEE Selected Areas in Communications* 6, no. 7 (August 1988): 1003; H. Scott Hinton, "Photonic Switching Fabrics," *IEEE Communications Magazine* 28, no. 4 (April 1990): 71.

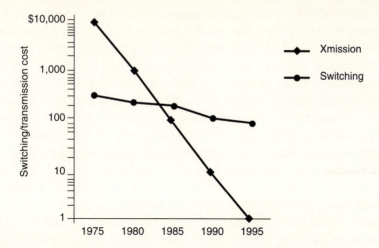

Figure 7.1 Trends in transmission and switching costs. *Source:*
Patrick E. White, "The Changing Role of Switching Systems in the
Network," *IEEE Communications Magazine* 31, no. 1 (January
1993): 12–13. Reprinted with permission of IEEE.

computers. Figure 7.1, indicates that the cost of transmission is dropping
much more rapidly than the cost of switching. Many computer people believe
that advances in transmission, such as the introduction of fiber optics, will
make the cost of communications negligible. That is unlikely. The tradeoffs between switching and transmission are changing and will impact how networks are configured.[6] Those configuration changes may reduce overall
switching costs, but switching costs will still be a major factor. A second factor
is the magnitude of the traffic that the national network and the switches must
support. Estimates of the traffic to be expected in the national network vary
widely and one of the more thoughtful estimates is given in the next chapter
in Table 8.2. The uncertainty in traffic estimates is due to considerations such
as the role of local storage, actual needs, and cost tradeoffs. For example, the
technical ability exists to put on line massive databases—such as all of the
world's literature. However, for static data, in many applications optical discs
or magnetic tape in a memory hierarchy are likely to prove much more attractive and economic. Deciding what it makes sense to do where is important in
the design of information systems, and there will be much discussion of that
issue later. The relevance here is that the tradeoffs involved can have a substantial impact on the real requirements for future communications networks.

6. S. L. Moondra, "Impact of Emerging Switching-Transmission Cost Tradeoffs on Future
Telecommunication Network Architectures," *Selected Areas in Communications* 7, no. 8 (October
1988): 1207.

Switching will be discussed in terms of the following topics: (1) We review what are essentially the relevant definitions of CCITT, an international body that will be discussed briefly with standard setting groups in Chapter 10. (2) We discuss the standard for digitizing voice. The relevance is that switching and transmission equipment in the common carriers is designed around these standards. Wideband circuits are made by combining circuits designed for voice. As digital networks at some level utilize the common carrier communications highway system, they must at that point conform to those standards. (3) We discuss time division multiplexing, a concept important to both switching and transmission. (4) We introduce two particular types of switching widely used by common carriers. (5) We present examples of utilizing these techniques in PABXs, which are private switching systems. This will give the reader a feeling for what switches do. (6) We provide a general overall model of switching based upon some of the concepts introduced in Chapter 6. (7) We discuss some of the switching techniques that are commonly used in the computer area. The reader may already have some knowledge of those techniques, but we would like to review the concepts in the context of the field as a whole. Although the discussion of networks is largely in later chapters of this book, because of the relationships and interactions between switching and network transmission, it will be necessary to introduce relevant network considerations at this time.

7.3   CCITT Definitions: A Perspective on Switching

We shall use definitions, taken from the glossary in J. C. McDonald's book,[7] that are essentially equivalent to those of CCITT, the Committee Consultif International Telephonique et Telegraphique. The reader should understand that historically CCITT has dealt primarily with standards for voice and telegraph systems. Consequently, the definitions given below were developed primarily for an environment of voice service. The definition of switching is fundamental enough that it is repeated here to provide a relatively self-consistent set of definitions.

> *Switching:* The establishment, on demand, of an individual connection from a desired inlet to a desired outlet within a set of inlets and outlets for as long as is required for the transfer of information.

7. J. C. McDonald, ed., *Fundamentals of Digital Switching,* 2nd ed. (New York: Plenum Press, 1990).

Digital switching: A process in which connections are established by operations on digital signals without converting them to analog signals (usually in combination with time division multiplexing and digital memories).

PABX PBX (private automatic branch exchange): A private switching system with a unique dialing plan which can access private stations, the public network or private trunks.

Circuit: A means of both-ways communication between two points, comprising associated "go" and "return channels."

Circuit switching: The switching of circuits for the exclusive use of the connection for the duration of the call.

Packet switching: A switching technique where a message is broken into small segments known as packets and the destination address is added to each packet.

Some examples of switching methods are given below. Many will be familiar to the reader and where they are particularly applicable in computer systems will be discussed later. These examples are not always independent of each other—i.e., some of them have utilized common techniques. The terms, or names, may be confusing in some respects, but they are used.

Direct connection

Plug in

Crossbar switching

Direct connection circuit switching

Polling

Time division multiplex

Frequency division multiplex

Packet switching

Bus switching

Token switching

7.4   Voice Digitization for Switching and Transmission

Telephone circuits and equipment are designed to transmit voice waveforms that lie in the region from 0 to 3000 cycles per second. In other words, a voice telephone signal is band limited to 3000 Hz or 3 KHz. This might suggest that to digitize voice it should be sampled at (2)(3 KHz) or 6 KHz. However, in the practical world, as discussed in Chapter 6, it is best to oversample. The pragmatic standard is to sample voice at 8 KHz. A sampling rate of 8 KHz is equivalent to taking one sample every (1/8000) of a second, or every 125 microseconds.

The next question that arises is how many levels should one quantize to. From Chapter 6 this is equivalent to asking in a binary situation how long a binary word should be used to represent a sample point. The quantizing noise (error) will be from a computer viewpoint the round-off error in the word. The accepted standard is 8 bits per sample point. As $2^8 = 256$, if all the bits were used to measure the amplitude, the accuracy would be one part in 256. However, if we worry about plus and minus amplitudes and use 1 bit for sign, the amplitude measurement is 1 part in 128. One part in 128 is of course a greater accuracy than is present in most analog signals and certainly more than is present in the output of the normal analog telephone. This is why the standard was picked.

Presumably the binary string representing the sample points will be sent over a band-limited channel. The channel bit rate will be,

$$\text{Bit rate in channel} = (\text{bits per sample})(\text{sampling rate}) \qquad (7.1)$$

$$= (8)(8,000) = 64 \text{ Kb/s}$$

The significance of this number, 64 Kb/s, is that most equipment in the common carrier system, or national network, is designed and programmed to handle signals that are multiples of this. Succinctly, that part of the telephone system that is digitized is based on channels of 64 Kb/s. This applies to switches, transmission facilities, synchronizing methods, etc. As we have noted, most of the common carrier system is digitized today. The one area that is still largely analog is the "local loop" (e.g., wiring from the central office to individual homes). There are also some very small PBXs and key systems that are analog, but these are considered to be station equipment (i.e., on the customer's site) and often owned by the customer. Thus, for example, although a customer may have an analog telephone at home, in all likelihood when a transmission reaches the central office it is immediately digitized and switched as a 64 Kb/s channel.

Table 7.1 U.S. Digital Network Common Carrier Multiplex Levels

Name	Channels (64Kb/s)	Line rate (Mb/s)
DS1	24	1.54
DS1C	48	3.152
DS2	96	6.312
DS3	672	44.736
DS3C	1344	90.254
DS4E	2016	139.264
DS4	4032	274.176
DS432	6048	432.00

The discussion above does not preclude very broad channels in transmission facilities or switches. The standard channels used throughout the world are pragmatically fixed multiples of 64 Kb/s, plus additional bits for synchronization and control. These are called multiplex levels similar to the multiplexing of frequency channels discussed earlier. The U. S. standard transmission channels are shown in Table 7.1. The European standards are somewhat different but still based on 64 Kb/s. As noted, the numbers in the table are for transmission channels. Thus, if the implementers of a distributed information system lease a DS 1 channel (often called a T1 channel), they are in effect leasing 24 stacked voice channels that can be used as 24 voice channels, one wider channel for, say, conference TV, multiple data channels, or any combination thereof for which they can provide interfacing equipment.

Most switches used for voice are programmed to switch only 64 Kb/s or 128 Kb/s channels. As we shall see, the 128 Kb/s switch was created to provide concurrently a digitized voice 64 Kb/s channel and a 64 Kb/s data channel. Quite a few systems that utilize digitized telephones have a RS232 jack on the back of the phone that provides an independent 64 Kb/s data channel. In a fashion similar to the above multiplex level table, existing switches that switch 64 Kb/s channels can be programmed to handle much broader bandwidths when appropriate line cards are installed. For example, the InteCom PBX has that capability and can be configured to provide what appears to the user to be a megabit per second Ethernet port.[8] However, at the present time we are discussing voice systems and will later come to some of the more widely used

8. "Intercom Takes Wraps Off PBX/LAN Switch," *Telecommunications* (October 1992): 10.

data features of switches and circuits. Today, as far as the common carriers are concerned, most truly wideband wide area data communications utilize non–switched-leased lines. The leasee, as in the case of Internet, may provide its own data switches. As we shall see in the next chapter, common carriers are also introducing switched data services of various types.

The concepts introduced above and their implications will become clearer when illustrated by examples of current practice in the communications industry.

7.5   Time Division Multiplexing

The definitions that follow, again taken from McDonald and CCITT, are similar to what is used in the computer area. The use of the term *digit* may be confusing and usually is synonymous in usage with *bit*.

> Time slot: Any cyclic time interval that can be recognized and uniquely defined.

> Field: In a record, a specified area used for a particular category of data.

> Frame: A set of consecutive digit time slots in which the position of each digit time slot can be identified by reference to a frame alignment signal.

Synchronization is important and limits what can be done more than often realized. Synchronization is clearly important in transmission. It is also important at a switch. We must know what is where in the input string. The roles of synchronization (i.e., timing) at the receiver include the following:

1. Determining in a clear message the correct position of a symbol or digit. The term *clear* implies an absence of interference.

2. Ensuring that the energy from a symbol, digit, message, or channel does not get in the time position of another symbol, digit, message or channel.

3. If (1) cannot be met, it must be possible to self-synchronize and still detect the message.

Figure 7.2 illustrates an example of a digitized input sequence. It is similar to a sequence representing a DS 1 channel that contains within it 24 digitized voice channels. For convenience, 0.1 microsecond time slots have been used. The discussion will be in terms of voice channels although clearly we could just as well be concerned with binary words. The digitized input sequence shown represents and contains the voice channels A(t), B(t), C(t), ... The

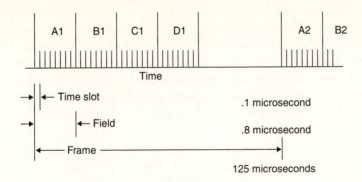

Figure 7.2   A time division multiplexed channel

digitized sequence taken as a whole represents a broader channel similar to a DS 1 channel. In practice, many such channels would be combined into a higher member of the DS family that sends thousands of voice channels between cities or overseas utilizing fiber optics.

The first occurrence of field A, A1, represents the first sample point of voice signal A. The eight time slots within that field contain the binary word that describes the amplitude of that sample point. The second occurrence of field A, A2, contains the second sample point and so forth. In like fashion the sequence $\{B_n\}$ represents voice channel B, $\{C_n\}$ voice channel C, etc. When 0.8 microseconds is divided into 125 microseconds, it becomes apparent that we could send roughly 150 voice channels, with extra time slots being used for synchronization and control. This general method of time division multiplexing many channels into one super channel is commonly used in voice, video, and data communications. In fact, it would appear that once the signal is digitized the communications system should not be concerned with the source. That is largely true, but in some respects it is not. The acceptable error rate may be dependent on the application or source of the data. An occasional error in a voice signal is acceptable, but errors in some computer data circuits are unacceptable. Fortunately, communications systems can be designed so that they are essentially error free. This is the reason that this book spends little time on noisy channels and error rates.

In Chapter 6 it was pointed out that the communications model being used is applicable to data storage systems. Consequently, the discussion above is applicable widely, not just to communications. When applied to the storing of analog data in digital form, there is one word of caution, however. If the storage media degrades with time, errors may be introduced. An analog signal usually degrades gracefully—i.e. the result is a small change in amplitude. A digital system may degrade catastrophically—i.e., an error in a high-order bit may result in a large change in amplitude. Magnetic media do degrade with time, and in the long run digital data should periodically be regenerated. The reasons are similar to those discussed in the previous chapter concerning relay points in a communications system. Computer people often do not realize that under some circumstances analog storage may be a better choice than digital storage. With the rise of optical storage media, errors in long-term storage may no longer be a problem.

There is an interesting twist to this situation. Music is often digitized for many reasons, including higher quality. However, for the reason outlined above, long-term—for example, for 10 to 20 years—storage on magnetic media may be superior if left in analog form. Errors in higher order bits can lead to very undesirable sounds.

Figure 7.3 indicates a method of converting several digital input channels into the time division multiplexed signal shown in Fig. 7.2. We postulate that the incoming phone signals are already digitized. The time gates shown in the figure are nothing more than devices to sample (i.e., look at) the incoming signal at times specified by the gate and timing control memory. It is assumed

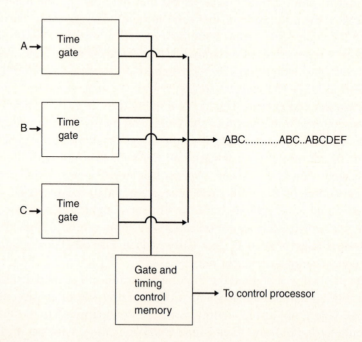

Figure 7.3   From digitized input phone lines time division multiplexed signals

that if buffers are needed for synchronization, they are included. The outputs of the time gates are then added (catenated) to form the time division multiplexed output signal. Of course there must be a mechanism that decides what output time slots are to be assigned to specific input signals. The control processor provides the required information to the gate and timing memory. It is very important to note that once set up, until it is necessary to change the assignment of time slots, the timing control memory has constant values and the control of the time gates is fixed. The reason this is important is that in general the information necessary to control a multiplexing or switching system is very small when compared to the data that is sent once the connections are established. Also, once set up, no further time or resources are wasted establishing or maintaining the channel. A good example is setting up a phone call. Once the number is dialed and the connection is made, nothing is changed in the network until you hang up the phone.

Implicit in Fig. 7.3 is the assumption that if an input represents voice, which by its very nature is an analog signal at its source, the necessary analog to digital conversion has already taken place. If the phone is digital, the conversion will be done in the phone. If it is not digital, the conversion will take place either in the network or just prior to the input of Fig. 7.3. If the input consists of data from a normal home computer modem, it will be treated as analog voice. Lastly, if it is data from a digital phone (which may well have an RS 232 jack on the back), or a computer, it will already be digitized.

The technique above converts a number of parallel signals into a sequential set of signals. It is apparent that the inverse will convert a sequential set of signals into a parallel set of signals. In the sequential output, the channels for A, B, C, etc., are defined by the field positions for the corresponding fields. It is obvious that synchronization is essential. Our switching problem will be one of putting the fields corresponding to the input of source A into the proper time positions in a bit stream going to its destination, and at the destination identifying the fields containing source A and directing them to the appropriate output.

7.6   Time Slot Interchange Switching and Conventional PBXs

How can we switch signals like those in the A, B, C, . . . channels discussed above? In general the signals must be switched to transmission facilities and lines that will take them to different locations. In this section, we discuss the switching mechanisms most commonly used today by the common carriers. Time slot interchange is the mechanism used in most voice switches and its

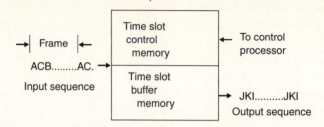

Figure 7.4   Time slot interchange switching architecture

use is also prevalent in small voice, data, and voice data systems. (As we shall see later, bus switching is coming into wider use. Conceptually, bus switching is a time division multiplexed switching method. It provides the basis for many of today's hub and noncontention data switches, including those for Ethernet.)

Figure 7.4 shows the basic objective and architecture for a switch. The purpose is to take the data in the input fields A, B, C, . . . and to transpose those data to specific fields in the output sequence J, K, L, ... This is accomplished by sampling the input sequence at appropriate times, storing the values in a temporary memory, and at the required time taking the values from memory and placing them in the proper frames of the output sequence. With thousands of input fields, and thousands of output fields, the bookkeeping required to set up the appropriate schedule for using the available fields, or time slots, is very large. As in the previous discussion of time multiplexed systems, once established for a call, the schedule for that call is fixed until the call is terminated. The control computer is busy setting up and tearing down calls. The problem is somewhat similar to the bookkeeping problem for memory in a computer storage system. Tracking the time slots in the switch and output channels that are no longer needed corresponds to garbage collection in a memory system. As with memory locations, unused time slots need to be reassigned and utilized for new calls.

A more specific and detailed example of time slot interchange is given in Fig. 7.5. The results are as follows:

A is transferred or connected to J.

C is transferred or connected to I.

B is transferred or connected to K.

The delay of the signal is small (i.e., one frame).

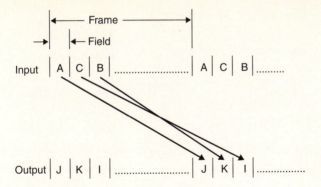

Figure 7.5   A time slot interchange example

Once set up for a specific connection (or call), the control memory does not change. The pattern of interchanging time slots does not change. However, the time to set up a connection, the "setup time" may be important.

With 0.1 microsecond time slots, we can take care of around 150 one-way conversations. A switch of that size is of little interest to the telephone companies or to users of large PBXs. The number of lines that can be handled is much too small. The technique, however, is directly applicable to "key systems" (e.g., the old systems with punch buttons), and most modern so-called key systems utilize "micro" PBXs along the above lines. The technique is also applicable to very small PBXs. It is apparent that the operations required can be performed by high-performance microprocessors, and they are used. For a very small switch—for example, serving a business with 10 to 25 phones and data ports—one microprocessor would be sufficient. This can be seen from the conservative numbers discussed above that indicated 150 one-way channels of voice. A high-performance microprocessor could perform the necessary time slot interchange and have ample resources left over for control and management functions.

For larger systems, switches with only one level of time slot interchange are not feasible. The solution is to cascade or combine a number of time slot interchange "planes" in a hierarchical structure as shown in Fig. 7.6. In the computer area we would call this a tree structure. In switching equipment, it is usually accomplished with a combination of "time division" and "space division" planes. Space division implies that the switching is to physically different paths or wires, as will be illustrated in the next section. For a variety of

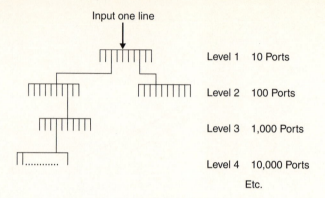

Figure 7.6   An example of a switching hierarchy. Such a hierarchy can provide a very high level of connectivity. A central office switch may interconnect 200,000 telephone lines.

reasons, many existing telephone switches do not utilize as many as 150 channels per plane. For illustrative purposes we have used 10 in the example shown in the figure.

Such a hierarchy can provide a very high level of connectivity. A central office switch may interconnect 200,000 telephone lines.

Telephone switches are generally made with a combination of time division and space division planes. Thus you may see a notation that a switch has TST planes.

Most telephone switches cannot interconnect everyone at once. To simplify the switches, they are designed to interconnect a given percentage—say 20 percent—of the lines at any one time. If that percentage is exceeded, the switch will refuse to accept an additional request usually by indicating a busy signal. This is called blocking and, if this is possible, the switch is referred to as a *blocking switch.* One of the properties of computer networks is that they have distinctly different use statistics than voice networks. Thus a blocking level that is satisfactory for voice may be inadequate for computer data. Because of this, nonblocking switches are now being introduced.

Figure 7.7 depicts the utilization of both time and space division planes. Each time and space gate in the figure has three different physical output lines that comprise the space diversity part as well as the time slots, as in the earlier discussion. A time slot on an input line can be switched to any of the three output lines and to an arbitrary time slot on that line. Although we have combined the T (time) and S (space) functions in the figure, there can be and often are separate time and space planes.

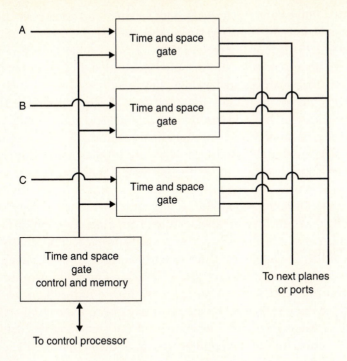

Figure 7.7 Example of time and space division planes

We have discussed two switching mechanisms commonly used in the communications industry: time slot interchange and time shared space division. For reasons that we shall not go into here, most central office and private branch exchange switches utilize a combination of the above. If there are four levels of switching (planes), they might be specified as T/S/T/S. These individual mechanisms (i.e., a single switching plane) Have limited capacity. However, as discussed earlier planes can be cascaded to give a capacity that is a function of the product of the capacity of the individual planes. Switch capacities can be very large. A central office may have 100,000 to 200,000 lines. A PBX—for example at a medium-sized university—may have 10,000 to 20,000 lines. For very large PBXs, modified central office switches are used, as has been done at Stanford, UCLA, and MIT.

Computer people tend to think of telephone switches as narrow bandwidth devices. This is not true. They are generally configured and programmed to switch 64 Kb/s channels. However, the total bandwidth or throughput of a switch may be very high. For example, the throughput of a 10,000 line nonblocking digital PBX is (10,000)(64 Kb/s) = 640 Mb/s. The PBX at Rensselaer Polytechnic Institute is nonblocking, and each port has two 64 Kb/s channels, one for digitized voice and one for data. Hence, the switch bandwidth is 1.28 gigabits per second (1.28 Gb/s). A central office switch with 100,000 voice lines, if nonblocking, would have a total throughput of 6.4 Gb/s. Most central office switches are blocking, however.

Modern switches are usually designed for 128 Kb/S per port. The intention is to provide a 64 kb/s digitized voice channel and concurrently a 64 kb/s data channel plus some control or signaling information. In the communications industry the widely used term *signaling* implies control. Increasingly, switches are being designed to be nonblocking. Computer data communications requirements are driving this. With digital switches, it is much less costly to provide a nonblocking switch than it was with the old technology.

We shall look at the overall architecture of a typical common carrier switch from the perspective of PBXs. Switching mechanisms will be time slot interchange including space planes. Later we shall consider bus switching and hybrid systems that use both technologies. These are important because many of the new data transport services being planned or introduced are based upon one or both of these switching methods. In any event, the overall architecture of a switch is usually no more dependent on the switching mechanism than the overall architecture of a computer system is dependent on the particular CPU being used.

You can view central office switches as very big PBXs that are configured to provide different services and features. "Features" in the telephone industry are customer services or applications that are provided by a switch. Examples are: make the call when the number called is no longer busy, forward my calls to, redial the last number called, the number calling is, conference calls, voice mail, etc. The discussion will be largely in terms of PBXs for several reasons.

PBXs are used in a campus environment. That environment has more flexibility than the national network.

PBXs are simpler (i.e., they do not have some of the telephone features that are of little interest to us).

PBXs often provide more data features than a central office switch.

PBXs are leading central offices in new technology.

In the computer field, most of the innovation is taking place in the area of small machines, which is where the hardware and software effort is going. In like fashion, most of the innovation in communications switching is taking place in small switches. Those innovations are being introduced in the larger switches. In some respects, the communications industry may differ from the

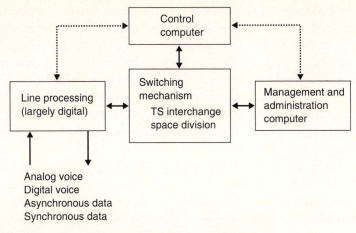

Figure 7.8   A typical PBX (private branch exchange)

computer industry. A communications network almost by definition must be well coordinated and integrated. There is also an economy of scale in a network and associated switching centers that is not evident in computing.

Figure 7.8 shows the logical architecture of a typical PBX. The unit performing the line processing provides an interface to the incoming and outgoing lines, matching the conventions on those lines, and doing the analog to digital and digital to analog conversions if necessary. Increasingly, there is a tendency to include programmable logic or microcomputers in the line processing. The dotted line to the control computer is included so that in a dynamic environment the control computer can provide instructions to the line processors. Again, as in switching, once the conditions for a call are established, the processing is local and the control processor can do other tasks.

The control computer is what does the bookkeeping for the switching mechanism, perhaps sends instructions to the line processing cards, and provides the switching mechanism with instructions for allocation of time slots, etc. It is analogous to the part of an operating system that does memory allocation and the scheduling of other resources. It might be said that the control computer is associated with the real-time internal operation of the switch.

There are management and administrative functions associated with a communications facility, and that is the reason for the management and administrative computer. Logging of calls, call statistics, telephone book files, etc., are some of the functions. For example, if you move your office to a new room, and thus a new line, the only change necessary is a modification in a table in the switch. If your use of the telephone is restricted—for example, if you cannot make off-site calls or have no access to certain computers—those restrictions are just table entries. In the present environment of multiple long distance carriers, PBXs often are programmed to pick the cheapest path for an off-site call. One important function from a computer security standpoint included in some systems is a *call back feature*. From your home PC you call in to access a computer. The switch knows your home number, and calls your computer back to complete the connection. A person with your password at a different location cannot get access. We shall discuss services more generally in later sections.

Figure 7.8 is a functional diagram. For a very small PBX, as previously noted, all the functions shown can be performed in one microprocessor included in the switch. At the other extreme are central office switches that may have thousands of microprocessors or programmable signal processors. For a large central office switch, the required software is in size and complexity comparable to the operating system for a large computer. For example, AT&T's large central office switch 5ESS has 7 to 14 million lines of code.

Table 7.2 shows in one case how program size and running time in a PBX are divided by function. Although most of the software is related to administrative features, most of the CPU time is devoted to call processing.

Up to this point, we have implicitly discussed switching systems in which the wires connected to a given port, be it phone or data, are brought back to a central point for switching. In such a system, if you are talking by phone to a person across the hall, or across the street, the individual twisted-pair wires go back to the central office or the PBX. This is hardly necessary and depending

Table 7.2 Example of PBX Program Size and Running Time

Category	Program Size (KW)	Real Time (Percent)
Execution control	3	11.2
Call processing		
Input	9	28.4
Output	5	14.3
Internal	84	46.0
Administration and fault processing and diagnostics	256	.1

Source: From "Proceedings of the Third International Conference on Software Engineering to Telecommunications Switching Systems," Helsinki, June 1978, pp. 27–29.

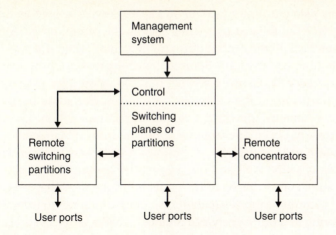

Figure 7.9   Two methods of distributing switches

on distances can be wasteful. Figure 7.9 shows two common methods of circumventing this.

When remote concentrators are used, the channels at the user ports are multiplexed (i.e., combined) into one of the common carrier multiplexed levels shown in Table 7.1. For example, 24 phone lines might be multiplexed into a DS1 or T1 line. Standard multiplexors and demultiplexors are available from the communications industry. In this case, the combined individual voice channels go back to the switch in a fashion more economic than if over individual lines.

The remote switching partition is a different matter. The switching mechanism is partitioned and part of it moved to the remote site. Switching is performed at the remote site by that partition, and for local calls the individual lines do not go back to the central office or the main part of the PBX. The control and management computers are left at the central switch. Since the control information is very small, one channel to the remote site is used for control information. For example, if there is a remote switching partition in your building, you dial the office across the hall, and that request goes to the central switch which then issues orders to the remote switching partition in your building to set up the circuit. Your conversation is switched on the premises—it never leaves the building. There are PBXs and central office switches that use both techniques shown in Fig. 7.9. In the case of the central office switch, because the remote switching partition, or the remote concentrator, can be at an unattended site, it has permitted the elimination of many small town telephone offices.

You may also encounter a common carrier service known as *Centrex*. Old Centrex service ran twisted-pair wires back to the central office. All local traffic was taken back to the central office for switching, even if it was just to talk to the person across the hall. Remote concentrators are now used in some cases. More recently, Centrex service may be offered by placing a remote switching partition on the customer's premises. For some businesses, and campus environments, this can provide an attractive solution. The modernization of Centrex has been due largely to pressure from PBXs. Centrex is the preferred solution of the telephone companies for obvious reasons. They would like to do away with LANs and bring computer communications to your desk via ISDN and Centrex. ISDN, to be discussed in the next chapter, can provide substantial communications capability in many different environments and is already serving as a bridge between remote LANs at some locations.

7.7   Bus Switches and Servers

The communications buses in a computer are really little electronic switches. We consider them here more broadly in the context of communications with the focus on PBXs, which can be for voice or data, or for both. Bus switches in many circumstances are more attractive than the switching methods discussed above, particularly for certain types of data traffic. As such, they can be added to conventional switches forming a hybrid switch. They are also the basis for many innovative switches, many of them data switches. They are expected to play a key role in the next generation of switching centers. For illustrative purposes, the discussion that follows is based on early Northern Telecom switches of this type. For our purposes here, we assume that a bus is very short and that propagation delays are not significant (i.e., we assume that they are zero).

Figure 7.10 shows a bus-switched PBX similar to early switches developed at Northern Telecom and BNR (Bell Northern Research).[9] There are separate control and data buses. In the actual product, buses are duplicated for reliability. Two user ports and a server are shown. Servers can be external or internal to the switch. Examples of servers are voice mail boxes, file servers, security checking, etc. One advantage of internal servers is that they are attached to the internal high-speed bus and are not just at a port of more limited bandwidth at some other location.

For a particular channel to be established, or a message transported between two ports, it is necessary to reach an agreement between controllers as to the assignment of time slots. This usually implies a master controller, but

9. Ned Asam and Bill Williams, "The Meridian DV–1: System Architecture," *Telesis* 12, no. 3 (1985): 13.

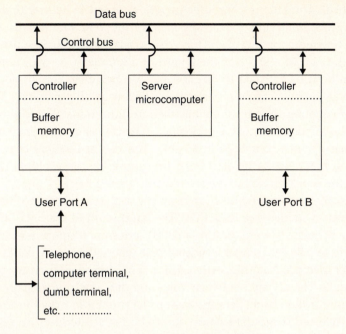

Figure 7.10   Example of a bus switch and servers

usually one whose role can be taken up by another controller if necessary. The sending port must know which time slots to send in, and the receiver must know which time slots to look in for the message. It is the responsibility of the microcomputer serving as the master controller to make those assignments. Unlike classical Ethernet, which will be briefly discussed in Section 7.10.2, the signals on the bus do not contend or conflict with each other. Inputs to the bus are buffered until the time slots to be used by them have been assigned and are available. For voice circuit switching, once the time slot assignment has been made, it is fixed until the call is terminated. For data that are sent in packets, the assignment is made on a per-packet basis.

Analog voice circuits occupy a frequency band of roughly 3 KHz. The local loop twisted-pair wiring plant going to most residential areas was designed primarily for such voice signals. The term *twisted pair*, which may be unfamiliar to the computer scientist, is commonly used in the telephone industry. It refers to a pair of relatively small insulated wires that are twisted around each other. There may be hundreds of twisted pairs in a cable and the twisting minimizes inductive effects and interference with other pairs of wires. The length of the wire runs in a local loop are relatively long (e.g., from your house to the central office). Thus many computer people were led to believe that twisted-pair wiring was good only for narrow band or low data rate signals. For short runs, the common carriers have for years used twisted-pair wiring for T1 channels (i.e., 1.5 Mb/s). Over the length of a kilometer or two, twisted-pair wiring can be used for data at megabit per second rates. For shorter lengths, the rates can be even higher.[10] Telephone wiring is all pervasive. When installing a telephone system, if one has the foresight to install additional wires for data, the incremental cost is very small. The cost is in dragging cables, not the number of wires contained in a cable. The rise of Ethernet over twisted-pair wiring has been associated with the properties of a telephone wiring plant and the type of switches we are now discussing.[11]

The Northern Telecom DV–1, an example of the architecture illustrated in Fig. 7.10, was a small voice data PBX. The bandwidth of the data bus was 40 Mb/s. The processors were Motorola 68000 series microcomputers. The input could be up to 2.56 Mb/s over a twisted pair where the source could be up to a 600-meter distance from the switch. Some time slots were used for voice and some for data. The division between voice and data was dynamically adjusted as a function of the traffic. Servers were programmed to provide direct interfaces into selected computing equipment. The LAN interfaces appeared normal. For example, the Ethernet users would think that they were connected to a normal cable Ethernet when in fact they were connected via a twisted pair of telephone wire to the switch. Because of the time slot assignment role of the controller, the system was not a contention system and the utilization of the bus bandwidth could be very high.

Versions of the DV–1 were used successfully in practice. For a variety of mostly nontechnical reasons, it was not an outstanding commercial success. It was an important step, however, and the concepts are being applied to products ranging from hub LANs to central office switches. There will be more of this later when we discuss additional switching methods in Section 7.10.

As mentioned earlier, the mismatch between voice and data requirements has led to hybrid systems. Figure 7.11 illustrates what a hybrid switch might look like. In fact, with the data additions in some central offices, they look very much like this today. For example, the DMS–100 central office switch, with an adjunct DMS–100 Super Node, is very similar in concept to the figure.[12] In a

---

10. Stephen Saunders, "Premises Wiring Gets the Standard Treatment," *Data Communications* (November 1992): 105; Ernest Eugster, "100 Mbps to the Desktop via FDDI Over Copper," *Telecommunications,* Internet Supplement (October 1992): 51.

11. Stephen Saunders, "Ethernet Gears Up for 100 Mbits/s," *Data Communications* (January 21, 1993): 35.

12. John Perry, "DMS SuperNode—Technology Overview," *Telesis* 25, no. 2 (1988).

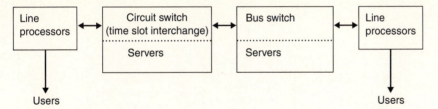

Figure 7.11   An example of a hybrid switch. Some feel that t/s interchange is still most economic for voice. This will probably change. The bus switches can be added to current equipment.

sense hybrid systems are an evolutionary step. However, it is not at all clear that there is one type of switch that is optimum for all types of traffic. The multi-switching mechanism switching center may be here to stay. This issue becomes even more important in a multimedia world.

Consider the following. A very large computer file must be sent between two points. You estimate that it will take one hour with the largest bandwidth available, it would appear that the thing to do would be to establish a fixed channel (i.e., circuit switching) for that duration. The set-up time of that channel is relatively unimportant. On the other hand, if from a dumb terminal you are occasionally sending one line of data, this is probably not what you want to do. The set-up time will be very important, and packet switching is attractive. The core issue is whether there is a common switching mechanism that on the average will result in a satisfactory, cost-effective network throughput. If there is, a standard switch may make sense. If there is not, integrated hybrids may be a better solution. In making that judgment both performance and cost should be considered.

There will be more discussion of these issues later. The reader may wonder why such questions are raised in a section on switching. One reason relates back to Fig. 7.1 and the relative cost of switching and transmission. From a data transport viewpoint, architecture will be based on cost-effective switching, and transmission will conform to that. To the degree that the network will perform data services, those data services may be provided by computers associated with switches.

Figure 7.12 depicts what some analysts feel might be a next generation PBX. It is worth noting the spectrum of services that might be performed by the switch. It should also be noted that such systems have run in the labora-

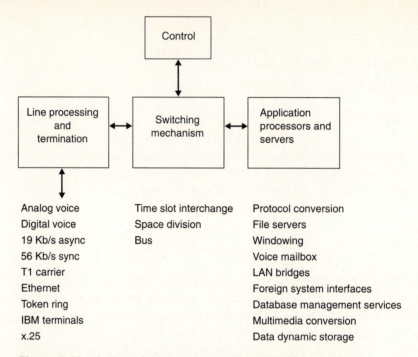

Line processing and termination	Switching mechanism	Application processors and servers
Analog voice	Time slot interchange	Protocol conversion
Digital voice	Space division	File servers
19 Kb/s async	Bus	Windowing
56 Kb/s sync		Voice mailbox
T1 carrier		LAN bridges
Ethernet		Foreign system interfaces
Token ring		Database management services
IBM terminals		Multimedia conversion
x.25		Data dynamic storage

Figure 7.12   A view of the next generation PBX. This picture is likely to change as ATM (Asynchronous Transfer Mode) switches are introduced.

tory and some of the features are available in commercial switches. One can well ask whether common services such as protocol conversion are not better performed within switches and the network rather than in computers attached to network ports. We believe that both options should exist and that the option selected should depend on the data service and the application.

Consider voice mail, in which a caller leaves you a verbal message in what amounts to a mailbox. Many readers undoubtedly have voice recorders on their home phone. They may also have that function served by their personal computer. Most people would agree that these "servers" are at a node of the network.

On the other hand, there is voice mail service available from many central office switches. There are PBXs available that include voice mail service. Lastly, there are micro PBX systems, and in many cases the supplier of a micro

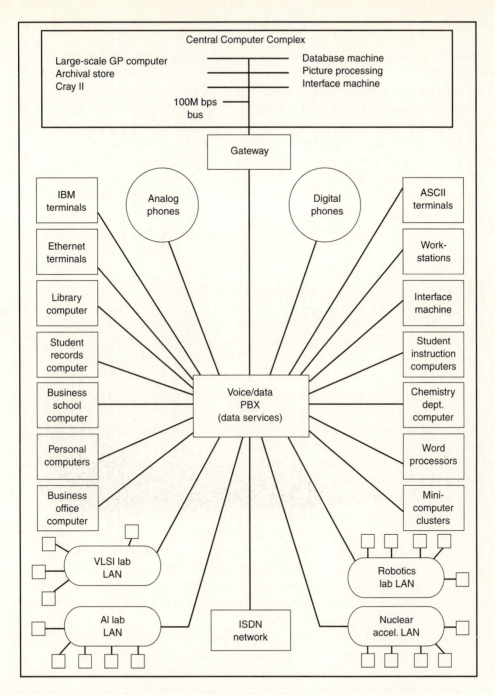

Figure 7.13 Campus computer system hierarchy. *Source:* Richard L. Shuey and Gio Wiederhold, "Data Engineering and Information Systems," *Computer* 19, no. 1 (January 1986): 18. Reprinted with permission of IEEE.

PBX will offer an option that consists of a dedicated personal computer connected to the PBX and serving as a group of voice mail boxes. In these cases it is likely that the voice mail servers would be considered part of the communications network.

So far we have discussed switching from what is primarily the perspective of the communications industry or the common carriers. We shall come to more of a computer industry viewpoint later in the chapter. Figure 7.13 illustrates a campus environment utilizing the techniques discussed to date where interfaces to LAN systems are included. Most computer scientists are familiar with LAN systems, which will be focused on later. The purpose of Fig. 7.13 is to make the reader aware of communications industry capabilities and the relevance of those capabilities to the evolution of more computer-oriented networks.

7.8   Generalized Switching Concepts and Theory

In Chapter 6, we discussed the sampling theorem and the fact that $2TW$ sample points will completely define a band-limited function of time. (Remember that T corresponds to time and W to bandwidth.) Thus there are only $2TW$ independent values (amplitudes) that can be assigned to that function—in other words there are $2TW$ degrees of freedom. These concepts can be applied to switching. Figure 7.14 is a conceptual representation of a switch.

Let us assume that each of the ports is band limited around the origin. The input port i, of bandwidth W_i over a time T_i can put in $2T_iW_i$ amplitudes or sample points. In like fashion, the jth output port can accept not more than $2T_jW_j$ amplitudes. Clearly, the function of the switch is to transfer input sample points to the correct output ports and at the correct time. This is the essence of switching. We are concerned with digital switches and consequently will assume that the amplitudes are limited to 0's and 1's. The switch for its part must be able to transfer the summed sample points from all of the input ports, and this requirement sets the bandwidth requirements of the switch. If it is a blocking switch, it cannot transfer all possible input samples. *It is desirable that the reader become accustomed to thinking of switches as devices that transfer sample points, or if you prefer time slots.*

In one respect, the model illustrated in Fig. 7.14 is inadequate. We have omitted switching to different frequency bands, or in computer terminology, broadband signals in different frequency regions. The added complication is that now at each port there may be a multitude of frequencies. The reasoning above would still apply, but now the degrees of freedom would have to be

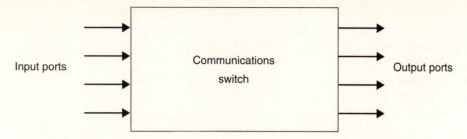

Figure 7.14   Conceptual representation of a switch. For simplicity and clarity, it has been assumed that there are separate input and output ports. In practice ports may be bilateral and a single port serves as both input and output.

summed over all broadband regions. So there is the possibility of time division, space division, and frequency division switching. It is significant that some of the laboratory work on optical switches is in the area of frequency division switching. It would not be unreasonable to expect T/S/F switches in the future.

Figure 7.15 shows a model of a switch in which the possibility of frequency division switching is included. For simplicity, we have indicated one input port and two output ports. The main blocks of sample points have been kept intact and just shifted to different frequency locations and times in the output. It would of course be possible to break up those blocks.

Certain points now become clear:

Synchronization issues are very important.

Buffering of some sort is required to keep things synchronized. There will be different time delays in the input signals coming from different points, and it is necessary to compensate for these offsets.

Figure 7.15 depicts a situation in which the central control of the switch is allocating resources so that those assigned to different channels do not interfere (i.e., it is allocating a clear channel). At the same time, the control tries to optimize the use of available resources.

Figure 7.15 essentially presents a model in which the input sample points are accepted and stored, and they are later put on the output lines at an appropri-

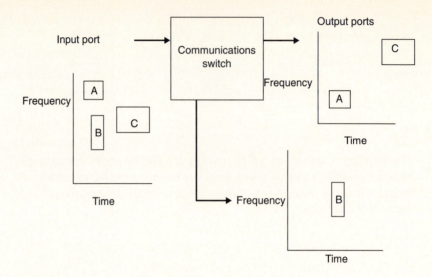

Figure 7.15   A conceptual representation of a switch

ate time. In other words, there is a delay between the input and the output. In that respect the switch can be viewed as a propagation media where the delay corresponds to the propagation time. In the case of the time slot interchange systems discussed earlier, that delay, or *propagation time,* is under the control of the switch. The time that sample point values should be left in intermediate memory is calculable and can be set. If the media are physical media, that is not the case. For example, in the cases of a bus where propagation time is important (i.e., of the same order or larger than 1/2W), as would occur in a cable system or a radio system, it is not possible to control the delay. The implications of this will be discussed in more detail later, but it is best to first recognize this fact in the context of Figs. 7.14 and 7.15.

In the discussion of the time slot interchange method in Section 7.6, it was implied that once the pattern of interchange is set up it is fixed for the duration of the call. This "call duration" assignment of resources can be applied to the concepts expressed in Fig. 7.15. It is also possible to dynamically change resource assignments. This was done many years ago with undersea cables when international bandwidth was expensive. During the relatively long periods of silence (no sample points) in a verbal discussion, the associated voice channel (or circuit) that would have been used for the unused sample points was used for (i.e., switched to) other conversations. In other words, if you were speaking, you were assigned a voice channel; when you were silent, you were not allocated a channel. This was done with special equipment at the ends of the undersea cables.

We have not made a distinction between data to be switched to some point and data for control purposes (signaling to the communications engineer). In other words, some of the time slots will be devoted to data and some to control. The control time slots may be intermingled with the data time slots (in band signaling), or cleanly separated (out-of-band signaling). In Fig. 7.10, a separate bus switch is dedicated to control, and in the national network there are separate communications channels to carry the control information. Remember, in general the control information is small. It is an open question as to whether control information should be intermingled with message information. The answer is very likely a function of the application.

Clearly, if locating time slots is important, synchronization within a network must be important, just as it is in a computer. All switches and ports must be in effect using the same clock, recognizing of course differences due to time delays. Synchronization is a serious problem in a large network and has been a major challenge in the national network. However, in the national network it is under control due to a great deal of effort. In general, synchronization can be a serious problem, and in some situations can rule out a significant number of architectural alternatives.

7.9   Circuit Switching Versus Packet Switching

At this point we would like to repeat some definitions from Section 7.3. The reason is that many of the key issues and much of the confusion associated with alternatives for state-of-the-art and next-generation switching systems centers on breaking up long messages into short messages. Because these issues are closely associated with the previous section on the fundamentals of switching, we introduce them at this time. We do so with the realization that many of the key issues straddle switching and more general network concepts. Network concepts are emphasized in Chapters 8 and 13, but discussion is also necessary at this time.

> *Switching:* The establishment, on demand, of an individual connection from a desired inlet to a desired outlet within a set of inlets and outlets for as long as is required for the transfer of information.

> *Circuit switching:* The switching of circuits for the exclusive use of the connection for the duration of the call.

Packet switching: A switching technique where a message is broken into small segments known as packets and the destination address is added to each packet.

Think about what is meant by the following terms: "for as long as required for the transfer of information," "the duration of a call," and "a message is broken into small segments known as packets." Was the system discussed earlier, that assigned a voice channel during a silent period to another user, a packet-switched system? Is the time that you spend thinking at a computer terminal part of the duration of a call? Is it necessary that the address be added to each packet? In the context of today's networks, there are some things missing in the above concepts.

The concept of circuit switching is simple. A channel or path, with given static properties, is set up and left in place for as long as it is needed. This is a commitment of communications resources for the duration of the call. The resources assigned are sufficient for the users peak dynamic requirements. The problem is, that in many cases, the users requirements vary widely over the interval of interest and consequently resources are wasted.

The original concept of packet switching was that messages to and from the user would be broken up into small segments usually of a fixed size. Thus the user requirements were reflected in the number of segments that were to be sent or received over a given period of time. In addition, it was decided that each segment, or packet, would have an address attached to it. Furthermore, the individual packets would be submitted to the transport network one at a time and the transport network would route them on an individual packet basis. In pragmatic terms, each switch that the packet passed through would have to solve the control and routing problem on a per-packet basis. The problem is that under some circumstances the overhead in switching and routing individual packets can be very large. In effect, there is a set-up time associated with each packet and each switching point in the network.

The large potential overhead of the packet-switched system described above led to what is known as *virtual packet switching*. The original concept of a virtual packet network, or switch, was that the path and assignment of resources would be made once for the duration of a message or session. Consequently, there would be only one set-up time, and delays in the network, once set up, would be minimized. It would no longer be necessary to solve the control and routing problems on a per-packet basis. However, virtual paths share resources and there is a potential problem. As temporal use of the paths that are sharing resources change, the resources may be over- or undercommitted. For example, there may be buffering or contention problems. This implies that perhaps the assignment of paths and resources should be dynamically reinitiated. Reinitiation could be complex and time consuming. Asynchronous transfer mode (ATM) switching is an example of virtual packet switching.

The applicability of the switching techniques implied above are dependent upon two factors:

1. *The applications that are to be served.* It has been pointed out that circuit switching is attractive for the transfer of very large files and unsatisfactory for keyboard or workstation activity.

2. *The state of technology and availability of equipment at any one time.* If an economic, broadband, optical switch were available, with a 1 microsecond set-up time, it would make obsolete many other switching methods.

Underlying the above considerations are the tradeoffs between switching and networks. Fiber optics are making the transfer of information between two points inexpensive. In a sense, transmission bandwidth is not that important. It is to be expected that users will be willing to tradeoff larger transmission bandwidth requirements for simplicity in switching and network control. Fiber optics have already been partially responsible for the increased concentration of switching centers in the national network. Furthermore, in some circumstances, broadband transmission capability may introduce new systems in which the switching is done in the propagation media.

7.10 Additional Switching Concepts and Techniques

This section focuses on switching concepts that are particularly applicable to computer systems but have not yet been covered. Switching is the technology that arranges to get a message between the nodes of a network. Many switching concepts depend on specific properties of communications networks, so relevant network considerations must be understood. We have tried to include only those network issues that are inseparable from core switching issues. The major discussion of networks follows in later chapters.

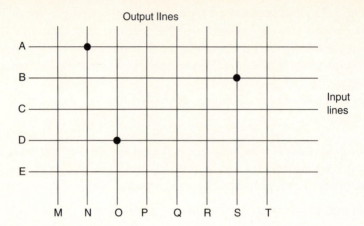

Figure 7.16   Crossbar switch

7.10.1 Crossbar Switching

The original automatic switches used in the telephone industry utilized stepping switches or relays to connect specific input and output lines.[13] In brief, as seen in Fig. 7.16, a mechanical connection was established between given input and output lines. The figure illustrates a mechanical connection between lines A and N, D and O, and B and S. In crossbar switches, bistable reed relays were placed at each crossover point and elaborate mechanical systems used to position a electromagnetic magnet over the cross point of interest. The magnet would then be energized to flip the switch. This minimized the number of magnets required. Clearly, the set-up time to establish a connection was relatively long. To service a large number of channels, mechanisms like the above were arranged in a hierarchy along the lines discussed earlier in this chapter.

In the age of solid state electronics, mechanical switches are of little interest. Our interest is that the crossbar concept is being implemented utilizing solid state electronics. To be specific, a semiconductor switching element is placed at each cross point and the necessary electronics added to activate the switches that are necessary to establish a connection. The set-up time can be quite small.[14] The limiting factors with current technology are cost, and the fact

13. R. F. Rey, ed., *Engineering and Operations in the Bell System* (Murray Hill, NJ: Bell Telephone Laboratories, 1988).

14. Hyun J. Shin and David A. Hodges, "A 250-Mbit/s CMOS Crosspoint Switch," *IEEE Journal of Solid State Circuits* 24, no. 2 (April 1989): 478; John Bond, "Crossbar Switch, Unique Packaging Drive Performance of DEC 9000," *Computer Design* 28, no. 23 (December 1, 1989): 18.

that the size of the switching matrix is usually quite small and not suitable for use in the national network. There are two points that should be emphasized:

1. Even if relatively expensive, small switching matrices with a wide bandwidth and a short set-up time can be useful in computer systems. In fact, more are being introduced today.[15]

2. Whether a crossbar switch makes sense is very much a function of the cost, the set-up time, the bandwidth once set up, and the size of the matrix (i.e., the number of channels that can be handled), etc. All of these parameters are changing as technology advances.

In evaluating switching alternatives, we should consider all alternatives, for the tradeoffs are changing with time. An inexpensive, large, short set-up time, broadband, crossbar switch would be attractive in many applications. Depending upon the application, it does not even have to be inexpensive. A good example is the DEC switch.[16] It is a 100 Mb/s crossbar switch capable of 6.25 million connections per second with 36 ports. Given the short set-up time and broad bandwidth, it is being used to switch packets.

7.10.2 Bus and Cable Switches

Figure 7.17 shows a bus similar to those widely used in computers. It is implied that A is communicating with B and C with D. Buses often are composed of parallel conductors permitting the transfer of entire words in one cycle time. There are various algorithms for controlling the assignment of time slots.

Some algorithms preschedule time slots, others control the assignment dynamically. Still others permit any port to access the bus; if there is interference, they revert to a prearranged algorithm that makes the assignment. The token passing algorithm gives the port with the token sole use of the bus until such a time as that port passes the token on to another port. There are various algorithms for deciding when a port must pass the token. What is a reasonable strategy for control depends very much on the applications and their associated traffic. It is clear from Fig. 7.10 that it is possible to have a communications channel devoted to control information that is separate from the channel that is used to carry message data.

Provided that the messages are long with respect to the propagation delay from one end of the bus to the other, the overhead of clearing the bus between messages can be small. Most of the potentially available time slots can be used.

15. Aaron Boxer, "Where Buses Cannot Go," *IEEE Spectrum* 32, no. 2 (February 1995): 41.

16. R. J. Souza et al., "GIGAswitch Systems: A High-performance Packet-switching Platform," *Digital Technical Journal* 6, no. 1 (winter 1994): 9–22.

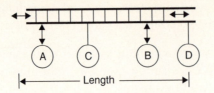

Can be multiple conductor.

Propagation times important.

A second channel cannot be assigned until the bus is cleared.

Figure 7.17   A bus switch

If the bus is very long, it becomes a cable system and the delays become important. If the ends of the cable are connected to each other, it becomes a ring.

Figure 7.18 shows a cable structure and a ring structure. When a cable or a ring is used for switching, it also provides the physical transport mechanism and may pragmatically constitute the network (i.e., an isolated Ethernet). The original Ethernet concept was to segment or divide the material to be sent (e.g., data) into packets. Each segment or packet would have added to it a header that would contain the destination or the recipient's address (i.e., control information). When a packet was ready to be sent, the sending station would put it on the cable. All potential recipients were connected to the cable. A receiving station would look only at packets with its address (i.e., accept and process). If two packets from different stations arrived at the same time,

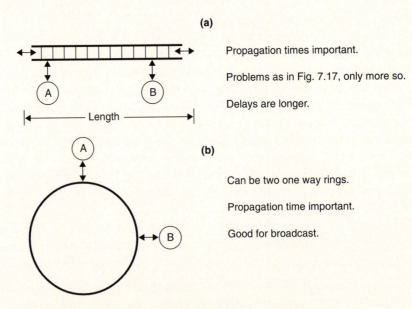

(a)

Propagation times important.

Problems as in Fig. 7.17, only more so.

Delays are longer.

(b)

Can be two one way rings.

Propagation time important.

Good for broadcast.

Figure 7.18   (a) A cable structure and (b) a ring structure.

this would be apparent but, because of the interference, it would not be possible to interpret the received signal. By common agreement, the signals would then be resent. In order to accomplish this with a low probability of interference on the second try, the stations would follow a local assignment rule to determine when to resend a packet. The objective of the rule would be to minimize the likelihood of another conflict. For example, each station would pick a random resend time from a probability distribution. Clearly, as the traffic increased, the probability of conflicts increased, and it became necessary to resend more messages. In practice, cable channel utilization could reach only about 30 percent.

The token approach discussed briefly above was first applied to cable systems. You may recall that the single token is at any one time assigned to one unique station. The station with the token is the only one that is permitted to transmit, and it keeps the token until, following a prearranged algorithm, it passes it to another station. This procedure clearly resolves transmission conflicts. However, to ensure that the users get adequate access to the cable, strict rules must be applied as to how long a given node can keep the token before passing it on to another node. The token passing routine represents control overhead.

7.11 Synchronization and Hub Switch Considerations

Let us now consider functions that are band limited around the origin and occupy the same frequency region. There are two reasons that time synchronization is important:

1. It is important in a communications system to know where a particular data element is in time and what it is associated with. (For purposes of this discussion, we may consider a data element to be the value of a sample point.) This is essential, for example, in the multiplexed levels described in Table 7.1 and in switching.

2. Synchronization is important to prevent energy that belongs to one data element from corrupting the energy that belongs to another data element. The original Ethernet, as described earlier, is a nonsynchronized switching (and transmission) system, and it is subject to contention, interference, and corruption.

A star or hub network configuration makes it possible to meet both of these requirements. Figure 7.19 shows a simple star network. Most common carrier systems are based upon a star network and the interconnection of star networks into a hierarchy. It is the basic structure of the common carrier national

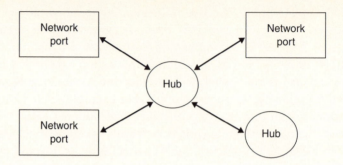

Figure 7.19   A star network

network. Although overall network issues will be discussed in Chapters 8 and 13, it is important that we here review switching related network consideration.

Perhaps the principal advantage of the star network is that its components can be synchronized in time and the two conditions mentioned above can be met. This is associated with the one-to-one physical relationship between hub ports and network ports. There is a single delay between a specific network port and the hub, which is the basis for establishing where in time specific data are. In addition, because there is a single physical path, there is no possibility of energy from two network ports simultaneously arriving at a given hub port. The hub contains a switch which requires uncorrupted input signals and needs to know the location in time of data elements. Then the switch can selectively receive energy from a specific port and separate out its components. The switch can take the data components from all ports, reassemble them appropriately, and send them to the desired ports for transmission to the designated nodes. Buffering is available at the input and output of the hub to permit synchronization with respect to both transmission and switching.

With respect to meeting the switching requirement for synchronization, a star network has an advantage over networks that utilize distributed switching based on buses, cables, or radio. In general, the second condition above can be met in the latter three cases only by invoking guard bands in time, and in the latter two cases those guard bands might be excessive. Figure 7.20 illustrates network ports that are connected to a common media that is utilized for both transmission and switching. The figure shows two dimensions and a media that is confined to one plane. We of course live in a three-dimensional world, but the reasoning that follows carries over into three dimensions.

Computing devices are connected directly to the network nodes that in turn are directly connected to the network ports. The network ports are connected to the common media shared by all (i.e., all network ports receive the

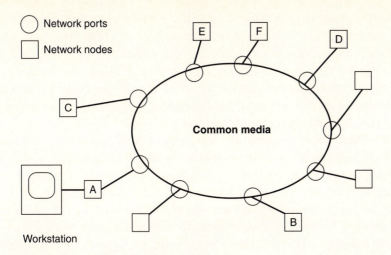

Figure 7.20   Common media switching

energy from a signal). Presumably, arbitrary combinations of network nodes should be able to communicate without interference—for example, A to B, E to F and D, etc. In principle it would be possible to provide identical clocks at all network nodes or ports and to schedule the desired transmissions so that they would not interfere. This, however, assumes control logic of some sort. In addition, if propagation delays are a factor, with any reasonable number of network nodes, a little thought indicates that the guard bands would have to be excessive and consequently channel utilization very low. It should be noted that this deficiency in one way or another is common to most LANs because they use a common media. This, and the low cost of twisted-pair wiring, accounts for the popularity of T-based Ethernet systems that for some time have been out-selling cable systems. As noted earlier, a network node in such a T-based Ethernet system is connected by twisted pair to a hub that in all likelihood contains a noncontention switch.

7.12 Remarks

We have spoken largely of physical configurations in which networks consist of nodes and edges. There is of course the option of channels that just pass through a node in a tied-down manner (e.g., a physically leased line or part of one). In general, however, there will be switching at the nodes. The point has been made earlier that at one extreme detailed specific switching arrangements (e.g., time slot assignments) can be made during a set-up period and left in place for the duration of a call. Often in this case the control information is sent by a separate path. This is generally referred to as circuit switching. At the other extreme, and this is common in packet-switching systems, "in band" destination information is included with the packet and the individual nodes decide on the details of switching and routing. In between these extremes there are a large number of alternatives. For example, the routing can be established prior to the first packet thus establishing a "virtual" circuit that will remain in place for the duration of the session.

For certain classes of computer applications involving many computing elements, it is important that the computer working on a specific element of a computation be able to communicate with its neighbors. For example, in calculating the stresses in a mechanical structure (i.e., stress analysis), it is necessary to exchange the results calculated for one element (i.e., at one location) with results associated with geometrically adjacent elements. This introduces the need for networks with architectures based on hypercubes (*n* dimensional cubes) and polygrids where the computers or nodes are at the vertices of the geometric configuration. Switching is performed at the vertices.

More than two decades ago, technical managers in the communications industry realized that their work was largely in software. More recently they have realized that most delays in switching and networks are due to software. Dynamic decisions at nodes are made by executing software, and this takes time. The relevance here is related to the two extremes discussed earlier. In circuit switching there may be relatively long set-up times, although in some cases this is down to milliseconds. Once set up, however, there are few delays at the switching nodes. In the case of in band signaling and dynamic decisions at each node, the delays can be substantial and today are almost entirely due to software. The dependence of the technology on software should be clearly understood by the reader. Reducing switching and network delay is to a large degree a software problem.

There is one area of switching that we have not discussed. Just as there are asynchronous communications systems, there are companion asynchronous switching systems. These take a message and modulate it by a method that spreads it out over a very wide bandwidth. For this reason, such systems are often referred to as *spread spectrum systems.*[17] Most of them are also common media switching systems, as discussed earlier. Consequently, the technology is potentially applicable to radio data systems serving a distributed computer system.

Assume that in a spread spectrum system the original message, M_K, occupies a bandwidth of W. We would say that message had $2TW$ degrees of freedom in that a value could be assigned to each sample point. Let us further

17. Andrew J. Viterbi, *CDMA, Principles of Spread Spectrum Communications* (Reading, Mass.: Addison-Wesley, 1955).

assume that after modulation it occupies a bandwidth NW. In the notation of Chapter 6, the original $2TW$ degrees of freedom have been spread out over $2TWN$ dimensions. Now consider a second message, M_L, of identical frequency W and time T. If the message is treated in like fashion, it will also have $2TWN$ dimensions, which may be placed in the same media (e.g., cable or radio) and time frequency space as the message M_K. How will the signals interfere?

We have earlier noted that in situations like the above it is the direction of the transmitted signal (i.e., the vector) that determines the channel, and that the amplitude carries the information. Consequently, the only parts of the transmitted signal associated with M_L that will interfere with the signal associated with M_K are components that are in the same direction as M_K. In other words, the interference will be determined by the dot product of the vectors M_K and M_L. If it is a synchronized communications system, and we know how to select the (M_i), it can be made zero, as long as we do not try and assign more channels than there are dimensions.

In an asynchronous system, if the modulation system is properly selected (e.g., random or pseudorandom noise carriers), statistically the dot product of M_K and M_L can be made small. Specifically, if the components of M_L are statistically random, then statistically we can expect that the dot product of M_L and M_N will be proportional to $1/N$. In other words, the transmission associated with M_L will appear as interference (noise) added to the detected message at the receiver for M_K. However, that interference will be reduced by the factor $1/N$.

If N is large, communications will still be satisfactory. Unfortunately, as the number, n, of simultaneous messages in the system approaches the value of N, the interference to signal ratio approaches n/N and performance will become unsatisfactory. Consequently, the attainable channel utilization of the bandwidth NW will be low. In this last statement the use of the term channel implies the total bandwidth NW.

There are applications in which spread spectrum systems are attractive—in some military situations or where multipath is a problem for radio transmission in the middle of a city or infrared in a large room.[18] It is also possible that with fiber optics and the inexpensive bandwidth associated with fiber optics, spread spectrum systems will find utility in fiber optic LANs. Imagine a fiber optic Ethernet system in which contention was not a problem because n/N was small. The impact on circuits, software, and delays could be substantial. Considering such systems in detail would involve more signal processing and communications technology than would be appropriate to include in this book. You should, however, be aware of the potential of such systems. References to spread spectrum communications systems can be found in any

18. R. Kohno, R. Meidan, and L. B. Milstein, "Spread Spectrum Access Methods for Wireless Communications," *IEEE Communications* 33, no. 1 (January 1995): 58.

good book on communications systems, and the extension to switching along the above lines is obvious.

There is one switching technique that is becoming important in the computer field and may well become the most significant one in the multimedia era. As this material is being written, manufacturers are producing what they call small asynchronous transfer mode (ATM) switches. Some common carriers are announcing ATM service. ATM is a packet-based switching and transport mechanism where the control of the network and switches is based upon out-of-band signaling.[19] Its objective is to support broadband ISDN and a multimedia environment. However, one should realize that all the standards have not yet been agreed on. There is also an open question as to whether one switching method will prove to be satisfactory in all application areas. An early study of Department of Defense networks suggested that packet switching might be satisfactory for all DOD traffic.[20] That conclusion was controversial and many parameters have changed since that time. There will be more discussion of some of these issues and of ATM later.

7.13 Summary and Comments

In a distributed system the ability to send or transport messages between the different components of the overall system is essential. Switching is the technology that provides that capability. Switching is important within a computer, where the switch may be simply a bus connecting the CPU to IO devices or to worldwide networks composed of heterogeneous computers. Switching is a major cost in a communications system. This book considers only digital switches with one exception. High-speed electronic crossbar switches are appropriate in some circumstances and, depending upon advances in semiconductor and optical technology, may become more broadly applicable in the future. If so, they will be used to switch digital signals.

It is significant that in the national network switching costs are dropping less rapidly than transmission costs. That observation is applicable to many less global computer networks. The importance is that the relative cost of

---

19. William Stallings, *Data and Computer Communications,* 3rd ed. (New York: Macmillan, 1991); H. Rudin, "The ATM—Asynchronous Transfer Mode," *Special Issue, Computer Networks and ISDN Systems* 24 and 25 (1992): 277–346; Ellen Witte Zegura, "Architectures for ATM Switching Systems," *IEEE Communications Magazine* 31, no. 2 (February 1993): 28; R. Rooholamini, V. Cherkassky, and M. Garver, "Finding the Right ATM Switch for the Market," *Computer Magazine* 27, no. 4 (April 1994): 16.

20. Network Analysis Corporation, "Economic Analysis of Integrated DOD Voice Data Networks," Final Report, ARPA order no. 12286 (September 1978).

switching and transmission may have a large impact on the tradeoffs that must be considered in selecting an architecture.

It is convenient to consider switching, and communications more broadly, in terms of the mapping or transporting a set of digitized sample points between a source of data and its destination(s). We imply that a set of data points can consist of a single binary digit, a field of digits (e.g., a byte), a frame, a packet, a message, etc. It is common practice in the telephone industry to organize both switching and transmission facilities around atoms of data that consist of 8 bit fields that correspond to the digitized sample points of a voice signal. Furthermore, the practice is to sample at a rate of 8 Kb/s, which results in 64 Kb/s voice channels. In general, the industry provides services that are multiples of 64 Kb/s. It should be noted, however, that the multiplication factor can be large and the service in hundreds of Mb/s.

The most common large telephone industry switches (e.g., a few hundreds of thousands of 64 Kb/s channels) primarily utilize time slot interchange switching. This technique is also used in very small PBXs. In the computer area, bus switches are in common use, and they are also being added as adjuncts to large telephone switches to switch data. Thus at a switching center voice may be switched by a time slot interchange component and packetized data by a bus switch.

It is important to recognize that in most cases the information necessary to control a switch, or as a matter of fact a network, is very small with respect to user information that is sent over the network. It is often convenient and cost effective to utilize separate communications facilities for control information (signaling), as distinct from the facilities used to transmit the user's data. One aspect of separating control and user data is the ability to maintain control at a central point and distribute the actual physical switching of user data to remote locations. If communication is largely between local sources, which is often the case, this can be important.

There are a great many management and operational issues associated with a large network. These are in significant part performed by the switches that are part of the network. In addition, there is a tendency to introduce user services as functions performed by the switches. In computer terminology, servers can be made a part of the switch.

Time synchronization is important in both switches and network transmission facilities. First, there is the necessity of knowing what message, and what part of that message, a specific time sample point—i.e., a time slot—is associated with. Second, there is the necessity of ensuring that energy from one message or channel does not distort the energy in another message or channel. In both areas, a hub or star configuration can almost uniquely meet the requirements.

There are asynchronous switching methods that are applicable and widely used in local area networks and wireless communications, but they are not expected to have a major impact on the national network. In the terminology that we are using, ATM (asynchronous transfer mode) systems are synchronized. In ATM the word asynchronous refers to asynchronous data at the source—e.g., keyboard input and digitized voice with silent periods. Ethernet, and noise carrier systems, are asynchronous systems in our terminology.

There are many switching mechanisms discussed throughout this chapter. Switches based upon those techniques have different strong and weak points. At the same time, the traffic over a network, and the environment served, can vary to a significant degree: for example, the traffic may have widely varying properties, such as keyboard activity compared to file transfer; or the users may be located in a single building, or scattered over the world. It is often the case that a particular switching mechanism is well matched to a particular type of traffic and environment, and poorly matched to other circumstances. This is a consideration that has led to hybrid switches—i.e., switches that utilize several mechanisms, and separate out traffic and send it to a mechanism to which the traffic is believed to be well matched. One of the current unresolved issues is the degree to which one switching mechanism can serve all forms of traffic, and all environments, in a performance and cost effective fashion.

7.14 Problems

1. Consider the bus switch as shown in Fig. 7.21. Assume the following:

    K = the number of stations, of which only two are shown in the figure

    M = the length of the individual messages that are sent

    W = the bandwidth of the bus

    V = the velocity of propagation along the bus

    T = the time between accesses that is guaranteed each station

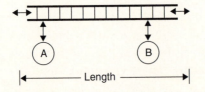

* Single conductor
* Binary signals
* Assume that a second message cannot be put on the bus until the bus has been cleared

Figure 7.21   A bus switch

(a) What is an expression for the maximum possible utilization of the bus? (b) What is an expression for the maximum number of stations that can be placed on the bus? (c) Assume: $M = 16$, $T = 125$ microseconds, $V = .75$ of the velocity of light in air, $L = 1$ meter and $W = 50$ MHz. What is the maximum number of stations that can be supported? If the bus is used as the switching mechanism for a voice data PBX, this should provide an indication of the number of channels that it can support. It is assumed that each channel has both a voice and a data component. (d) What are the answers to (c) if the bus length is .1, 10, 100, and 1,000 meters?

2. There are architectural and performance differences in what one can expect from switches with controllable delays, and switches that use a common media for switching and in which the delays are inherent in the media. Time slot interchange switching is an example of the former and bus switching an example of the latter.

   (a) Prepare in not more than three pages a summary of the strong and weak points of time slot interchange and bus switching. (b) Include in your summary a comparison of the strong and weak points of the two systems. Such comparisons are useful in selecting switches and defining architectures. In other words, having considered the properties of the individual systems in (a), compare the two alternatives in a form that would be useful in designing an overall distributed information system.

3. In problem 1 a common media switching example is considered. The concepts are extendible into radio communications systems. This extension is particularly significant in light of the expanded use of portable computers. An implication of portability and radio communications is that, unlike the bus system, the location of the node may be unknown.

   There are two cases to be considered here:

   Case A: Represented by a bus or a cable; the position of the various nodes is in principle known. This would also apply to a radio or infrared system in which the position of the nodes is fixed and known.

   Case B: Uses radio communications or infrared; the nodes may be mobile, and the positions may not be known. In addition, in situations such as certain tactical military situations, one wishes to communicate only when necessary, which means that tracking or self-synchronization is not possible.

   (a) Prepare in not more than five pages a summary of your perspective on how much more complicated Case B is than Case A. What are the advantages and disadvantages of each case? In preparing your answers give serious consideration to possible interference between channels.

4. You have been asked to design a micro PBX to serve not more that 20 ports. The intended use is in a small motel or a group of summer cottages. Assume that digital phones will be used and that each port is to provide 64 Kb/s digitized voice and a 64 Kb/s data channel. You are to incorporate in the design a high performance microcomputer.

   (a) What switching mechanism would you propose to use and why? (b) Systems like this are often used to do such things as keep track of vacant rooms, track when a room is cleaned up, and indicate when an employee is working on the room. The staff members involved just punch in code numbers on the phone where they happen to be. Such features have been available for years. It would almost appear as if you could either include servers (or server functions) in the switch or modify a more conventional PC class machine to do the switching. Which approach would you favor and why? What features, services, or applications would you propose to provide?

Chapter 8

Common Carrier
Network Considerations

The charter does not have to be narrow or constricting to be effective. For example, the improvement of electrical communications as an objective is sufficiently definite to inspire a research laboratory and delineate the fields of science to be cultivated, but it leaves enormous scope and challenge to initiative.

Ralph Bown[1]
Vice-President, Research, Bell Telephone Laboratories

8.1   Chapter Objectives

The common carrier networks provide the data highway system that is used by almost all data networks and added-value services. This is likely to continue into the future. Consequently, it will be necessary for distributed computer and information systems to continue to interface with national and international common carrier networks. It is therefore important that we understand the present state of those networks and their projected evolution. The objective of this chapter is to provide the reader with that perspective.

8.2   Communications Industry

Generally, when we speak of the communications industry we are thinking of the telecommunications industry and specifically the telephone industry. The telephone industry is a mature industry, but it remains on the frontiers of technology. It is based on sound mathematical principles and state-of-the-art physical science and engineering. It has been an industry driven by technology, and

1. Ralph Bown, "Vitality of a Research Institution and How to Maintain It," Bell Telephone System Monograph 2207 (proceedings of the Sixth Annual Conference on the Administration of Research, Georgia Institute of Technology, September 8–10, 1952), p. 1.

much of that technology forms the foundation of the computer industry. Until recently, the communications industry was prohibited from entering the computer and information processing business. Given permission to enter some segments of the computer business, it has had difficulty adjusting its "culture" to the environment of the computer industry, and competing in that industry. With respect to the subject of this book, the communications network remains the largest distributed computer system in the world.

The following are examples of technological innovation in the telephone industry that are directly applicable to the computer industry:

Logical design and switching theory

The mathematics of encryption

Pioneering work in computer-aided design

First software engineering methods and tools

First industry-wide standard for a design and implementation language for system software

The transistor

Fiber optic technology and fiber system concepts

Large-scale switching systems

Some of the first computers

First really large-scale transaction processing systems

First "algebraic" computer language

Early efforts in making highly reliable computer systems

Transportable operating systems

Large networks

Redundancy measurements and compression of speech and pictures

How big is the communications industry and what is the role of the telephone industry in that context? The U.S. Department of Commerce lumps businesses into various categories. The size of the telephone industry is substantially larger than other industries that might be considered to be in communications, as is illustrated in Table 8.1.

The telephone companies do have categories of business other than the three we have listed—for example, directory services. This is the reason that the numbers in the three categories listed in the table do not add up to the to-

Table 8.1   The Communications Industry (in billions of dollars)

Area	1978	1990	1991
Telephone (total)	52	156	160
Local		39	40
Long distance		66	67
Cellular		29	29
Cellular independent		6	8
Postal service	16	39	43
Newspapers	13	35	34
Television and radio	13	22	23
Periodicals	6	20	20
Books	4.8	15	17
Cable and paid TV	1.4	22	23

Source: Statistical Abstract of the United States: 1993 (Washington: Government Printing Office). The 1978 figures are taken from an older issue.

tal. Beyond the financial figures, the size of the U.S. telephone industry is demonstrated by the fact that in 1991 there were 143 million access lines. The number of phones is much larger. Your home may have one access line and four phones. A small business may have 5 access lines and 30 phones, and so forth. Although major companies have most of the business, there are over 1,300 telephone companies in the United States.

Capital investment is another important parameter. In 1985 plant investment in the telephone industry was roughly $210 billion. In 1990 and 1991 it was $251 and $257 billion, respectively. That does not include station equipment, which is on the customer's site and often owned by the customer. A PBX is an example of station equipment. Incidentally, switching facilities are roughly 20 to 30 percent of the capital investment. It should be recognized that with investments of the size indicated, it is for all practical purposes impossible to change the communications plant rapidly. This has in many cases limited the speed with which it has been possible to introduce new technology and facilities.

The startling thing about Table 8.1 and the associated capital investment figures is the realization that we cannot consider the communications industry without considering the telephone industry. The telephone industry is roughly as big as the rest of the communications industry combined. Roughly speaking, telephone business is equally divided between local and toll (long distance) services. If legal and regulatory circumstances permit, it is likely that the telephone industry will capture a significant portion of the cable TV and home communications businesses. There is an economy of scale in networks. The industry's role in the more general information services area is in doubt for both legal and business (cultural) reasons.

It is interesting to speculate on how the sizes of the telephone and the computer industries compare—a difficult task because in many respects they are so different. Computers are all pervasive, yet much of the work in software and applications is done outside of the domain of computer equipment manufacturers. Should the use of computers in home appliances and automobiles be counted? Should all of the work in software, including Microsoft, be counted? In many cases, should the work and products be placed under computers or communications? How should the activities of Novell be categorized? Perhaps we should just consider all of computer activity to be part of the information industry. Unquestionably, in that context, the activity in the information sector would be far greater than what is usually considered to be either the communications industry, the computer industry, or the two combined.

There is, however, one set of figures, again derived from the *Statistical Abstracts,* that the reader might find of interest. The figures are for 1991 and for details one would have to go to that publication and Department of Commerce reports. Shipments of computer and office equipment totaled $58.8 billion dollars. Shipments of communications equipment totaled $37.9 billion. The total for electronics was $197.8 billion.[2]

8.3   Central Offices and Network Hierarchy

The structure of the national network, shown in Fig. 8.1, is based primarily on AT&T prior to its breakup. It is admittedly more complicated today because of the number of national common carriers involved and the interconnections between those entities. However, as far as the core concepts and structure are concerned, as well as the numbers and scale, this figure remains a good model and can be said to represent the communications highway core that is used by almost all communications services.

---

2. U.S. Bureau of the Census, *Statistical Abstracts of the United States: 1991* (Washington: Government Printing Office).

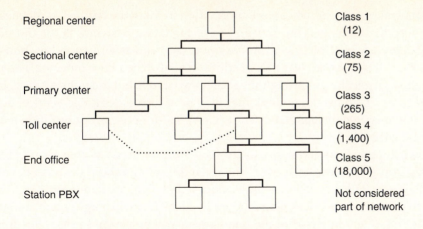

Regional center		Class 1 (12)
Sectional center		Class 2 (75)
Primary center		Class 3 (265)
Toll center		Class 4 (1,400)
End office		Class 5 (18,000)
Station PBX		Not considered part of network

·········· Cross connections are put in place as justified
by traffic loads, or to permit reconfiguration of
the network in the face of breakdowns. Unfortunately
there are fewer than there used to be.

Parameters of typical voice systems:

10% of residential lines are in use at any one time.
20% of business lines are in use during working hours.
1% of lines are dialing at any one time.

Computer traffic is quite different.

Holding time, e.g. how long do you talk or leave your computer on-line?
Automatic dialers
Short interactions in many cases

Figure 8.1   National network structure

The figure depicts central office and higher-level switches, with the number of switches at any one level shown on the right. The larger switches have various mixes of the properties that were discussed in Chapter 7. The control of the network and individual calls utilizes an "out-of-band" signaling system. For example, when you dial a number, as far as the network is concerned, the pulses or tones that represent the called number utilize the voice transmission path only as far as the network port—i.e., the central office to which you are connected. There is a separate communications system that carries network control information and sets up the channel that you use. Signaling in the communications industry refers to control information. The older "in-band" signaling systems sent the control information in the same channel as the message information (e.g., your voice). Today Signaling System 7 is the out-of-band network control system in common use, and it will soon be almost universal.[3] It should be clear that in addition to switched lines there are leased lines that physically go through the switching centers but are not switched. In other cases, customers may think that they have leased dedicated service, but they will be given virtual dedicated service that for network optimization reasons is switched.

Switching centers (offices) usually have dual switches so that if one fails the backup switch can take over. The reliability of switches is excellent. The number of installed switches is large enough that there are good statistics. The statistical downtime is less than 2 hours in 40 years. Switching centers are fail soft in that often only part of the lines served will go down. In cases like this the downtime is based on the fraction of the lines that are down (i.e., if 10 percent of the lines are down for an hour, it counts as the switch being down for 0.1 hour). The problems associated with failures are equally attributable to hardware, software, and operating staff.

The American and Canadian networks had five levels of switches before the breakup of AT&T. They have roughly the equivalent now. The major long-distance common carriers (e.g., MCI and Sprint) have their own switching centers and long lines to major points. Local lines are usually operated by regional operating companies, although there is some competition today. The success of the smaller companies probably depends on regulatory and legal restrictions.

Added-value common carriers (e.g., Telenet) rent dedicated lines from the common carriers and have their own data switches. Corporate, government and similar networks come in several varieties:

Virtual networks, leased from common carriers, in which all the equipment is owned by the common carriers.

Leased switches on their own or common carrier sites.

Owned switches, leased lines, and in selected cases, owned lines, or satellites.

Computer traffic is often quite different from that carrying voice. Most telephone conversations are relatively short, a matter of minutes. In contrast, many computer connections are left active for long periods of time. You may leave your PC connected all day. This interval is referred to as holding time,

---

3. Travis Russell, *Signaling System 7* (New York: McGraw Hill, 1995).

and in a circuit switch, it is very important. Computers are also introducing automatic dialers that can dial many numbers in sequence rapidly. This also adds to the load on the switching centers. Lastly, although a computer may stay connected to a communications port for a long time, the actual traffic may consist of many short messages issued only when a carriage return has been hit. As was indicated in Chapter 7, the properties of computer traffic may be quite different from voice. Modifications will be necessary in a network designed for voice and, as we shall see, modifications are being made.

What does the network look like to the users? Figure 8.2 shows a user's view of the network and the terminal equipment involved. Generally speaking, there are four ways that the user can connect to the network:

1. The terminal equipment can connect to a PBX from a LAN or directly to a PBX. The PBX might also serve as a bridge between LANs.

2. The terminal equipment can connect directly to the network, as a home telephone would.

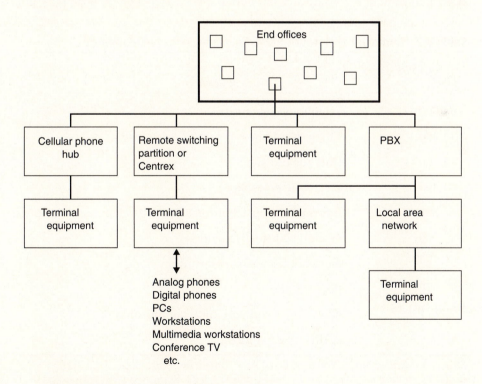

Figure 8.2   A user's view of the network

3. The terminal equipment can connect to a remote switching partition that may be part of Centrex service.

4. The terminal equipment can connect to a cellular radio hub or to some other radio service. Radio access to the network for voice services is well established. It is to be expected that data and computer access will increase.

All of the above alternatives provide access to the national and international networks—and thus to worldwide connectivity.

8.4   Traffic Estimates

What traffic can we expect on the network? As has been pointed out, this is a difficult thing to judge and there are widely varying opinions. A. Michael Noll has made one of the more thoughtful estimates, and his results are summarized in Table 8.2. Noll's assumptions were that 10 percent of the telephone calls are video or picture phone calls; all workers spend all day at terminals accessing information; periodicals and newspapers are created on terminals and

Table 8.2   Summary of Network Traffic Estimates in the United States

Yearly Traffic (bits × 10^{15})	Type of Service
14,000	Telephone conversations
1,400	Video telephones
1,200	Data file transfers
1,000	Electronic newspaper
300	Information age labor force
200	Motion picture distribution
47	Network television distribution
7	People data
1	Newspaper and periodical composition
0.3	Airline reservations

Source: A. Michael Noll, "Voice vs. Data: An Estimate of Future Broadband Traffic," *IEEE Communications Magazine* 29, no. 6 (June 1991): 22. Reprinted with permission of IEEE.

are then sent electronically to printing locations; television programs are distributed to local stations and CATV distributors electronically; and people generate data such as E-mail. We can of course question Noll's assumptions, but on the whole the results are probably valid for the national network. They do not address the local distribution of cable TV and potentially other real-time multimedia material to homes or in a campuslike environment. There are other ways to meet those needs.

We saw in Chapter 6 how redundant written language is. Clearly, speech is also very redundant, and in fact there are methods of compressing speech to the 100 Hz region. This results in intelligible speech (when decompressed), but the trouble is that it does not sound exactly like the original speaker and is considered unsatisfactory for telephone grade service. We can argue that from a theoretical standpoint the missing part cannot represent much information, and that is true. But pragmatically, we just do not know how to extract that missing part and code it. The importance here is that until we are able to remove the redundancy from voice signals, and maintain the required level of fidelity, it is likely that voice traffic will predominate on the national network.

There is a second issue to consider. In Chapter 6 the point was made that pictures are also very redundant, maybe even more redundant than voice. We thus have to think about the following question: If we learn to remove the redundancy from both voice and pictures, will the ratio of these two elements of traffic remain the same? The answer could be very important in the multimedia world.

There are major uncertainties as to what the actual network traffic will be. Some estimates greatly exceed those given above. The uncertainties lie at the heart of the issues considered in this book. Where should data be stored? When will things like optical discs be more cost effective than connecting to central databases, etc.? There is a tremendous amount of material available on CD-ROMs today, and it would be unrealistic to assume that most of that will become network traffic. Accessing dictionaries and encyclopedias over the network is unlikely to be cost-effective compared to local storage. Lawyers are today buying CD-ROMs with that part of the legal database that they use most as a more cost-effective solution than accessing the central service. For something outside of their primary work area they access the network. However, almost all their accesses are to local systems.

Most readers of this book are very likely aware of the Internet and use it at least for electronic mail.[4] We shall discuss it in more detail later in this chapter and in Chapter 13. CompuServe, MCI Mail, and Prodigy are somewhat similar to Internet and provide services in the commercial area. In communications

---

4. Harley Hahn and Rick Stout, *The Internet Complete Reference* (New York: Osborne McGraw-Hill, 1994).

terminology, all of these would be described as added-value carriers or services. The implication is that they provide services in addition to the raw transport of information over the national network. Almost universally the transport facilities of the common carriers provide the data highway system that is used by those providing added-value services.

There are many real-time broadband experimental services offered over the Internet today. However, the use and experience of the research community and implied traffic in this area may not be an accurate precursor to the use of such systems in society as a whole. The point has not yet been reached where the actual needs of society, the alternatives for information services, the costs, and cost tradeoffs can be accurately evaluated. Thus, as far as network traffic is concerned, there is still a large uncertainty as to what the requirements will be. One should not assume that what can be done in the laboratory will necessarily be done on a large-scale over the network. The airline ticket agent does not need a high resolution, wide bandwidth real-time terminal. The airlines will not pay for it.

8.5   Network Reliability Issues

We might be inclined to believe that with the increased reliability of state-of-the-art electronics the national network would become more and more reliable. As documented in recent reports, this does not appear to be the case.[5] There are many reasons for this, some of them given below.

> With the breakup of the Bell System, it became much more difficult to establish and impose strict standards on the network. If a network is to operate in an integrated fashion, a set of common or compatible equipment and standards is required. Bell Communications Research (Bellcore), which is supported by the common carriers, was created in large measure to help alleviate this problem and provide leadership in standardization.

> In the new more competitive environment, the costs associated with establishing highly reliable and fail-soft systems might be unacceptable. If building redundancy into a network to provide alternate paths in case of emergency makes a corporation noncompetitive, it will not be done.

5. National Research Council, *Growing Vulnerability of the Public Switched Networks: Implications for National Security Emergency Preparedness* (Washington, D.C.: National Academy Press, 1989); J. C. McDonald, "Public Network Integrity—Avoiding a Crisis in Trust," Special Issue of IEEE SAC, Invited Introductory Paper, *IEEE Journal of SAC* 12, no. 1 (January 1994): 5. (Other relevant articles in this issue are not referenced in this book.)

The extremely high bandwidth of fiber optic cable means that there are fewer cables required. Consequently, an accident that disables a cable can have more serious consequences.

Technological developments have resulted in switching centers that can handle more lines. Fiber optics have reduced the cost of transmission between centers. Consequently, there is a tendency to go to a smaller number of centers, each serving more lines. Under these conditions, a disaster at one center can have more serious consequences than heretofore.

The network is becoming more and more dependent on software. Despite the fact that the communications industry has probably put more effort into producing reliable software than the computer industry as a whole, there is still increased risk.

The consensus of the National Research Council study group, which prepared the report mentioned earlier, was that the national network was becoming more vulnerable. J. C. McDonald was the chairman of the study group and testified before Congress. This is a serious matter in a society that is becoming more dependent on computer driven information systems. It is a premise of this book that distributed computer or information systems must be viable in the presence of communications failures—i.e., that they must be fail soft, which means that part of the facilities are still usable and capable of filling the most urgent needs of the user. Failures will occur in the communications system, some of which will be due to natural disasters such as earthquakes. In a similar fashion, the design should be such that the system is viable in the presence of computer failures. The requirement that the overall system must work despite the failure of components should be a major architectural consideration in designing distributed systems. The implications of these issues will be considered in more detail later.

8.6   Campus Versus National Network Considerations

A *campus* can be defined as a local environment such as a research laboratory, a factory, a large business office, or even an academic campus. Because it is local, a campus can introduce innovative communications facilities that are not part of and do not necessarily have to conform to the national network and its standards. Thus Ethernet was introduced in the laboratory of Xerox Parc. Data PBXs and voice/data PBXs were used first in campuslike environments. LANs in general have been used extensively on campuses. A campus community has more flexibility than a wide area or national system. Innovation will probably continue to come first to the campus communities.

The downside to this situation is that when two different campus communities wish to interconnect their local communications systems they often must do so utilizing the national network. The synchronization, "multiplex levels," and signaling (control) standards may be quite different on the campus than in the national network. For example, one PBX manufacturer utilizes synchronization and multiplex standards between the PBX and its remote concentrators that are different from those in Table 7.1. That makes it extremely difficult to connect an off-campus remote concentrator to the PBX over a T1 leased line. There are similar problems in interconnecting LANs to the national network, although interfaces are now becoming available. It would be much simpler if there were common standards for the two environments. The introduction of ATM in these two environments may go a long way toward mitigating this problem.

8.7   The Basic Concepts of ISDN

In Chapter 2 it was noted that the digitization of the communications network was initiated for purely economic reasons. The first international workshop discussing the Integrated Digital Network (IDN) in the context of voice systems was held in 1976. The conviction then grew that a digitized network could be used for all communications services, and the name of later workshops was changed to ISDN (Integrated Services Digital Network).[6] Since then, the ISDN workshops held every two to three years have been the key broad-based technical meetings on the subject. The meetings have grown in size from small workshops to major conferences.

The general objectives of ISDN include the following:

To provide a general purpose, all pervasive, communications "highway" system that will carry, in digitized form, voice, data, FAX, conference TV, commercial TV, and other types of data. An implication is that all of the data associated with multimedia services can be sent over a single common communications system.

To serve as the data "transport" mechanism for users and providers of information services. This is similar to the present use of common carrier facilities by radio and TV networks, Internet, governmental networks, airlines, banks, businesses, multicampus universities, etc.

6. NEC Research & Development, *Special Issue on ISDN* (1987), ISSN 0547–051X; Gerald L. Hopkins, *The ISDN Literacy Book* (Reading, MA: Addison-Wesley, 1995); "Introduction to ISDN," *Special Issue of Electrical Communications* (Alcatel) 64, no. 1 (1990): 2; William Stallings, *Advances in ISDN and Broadband ISDN* (Los Alamitos, CA: IEEE Computer Society Press, 1992). Reprinted with permission of IEEE.

To provide appropriate data and information services in the network. In this area there are serious legal and regulatory constraints in the United States.

Professional groups working on ISDN have produced a set of international telecommunications standards and an associated communications system architecture for transmitting voice, video, and data over digital communications lines. ISDN uses out of band signaling (Signaling System 7), which provides a separate channel for control information. Initial ISDN service comes in two forms: BRI, a basic rate interface (or port) to the user; and, PRI, a primary rate interface. The standards for BRI and PRI are well established and service is available at many locations in the world. Ultimately, very broadband ISDN (B-ISDN) will be available. Services in the United States include the following:

BRI provides a 144 kilobits per second service, which includes two 64 Kb/s "B" channels for voice, data, or video, and one 16 Kb/s "D" channel for control information.

PRI provides a 1.54 megabits per second service (Mb/s), which includes 23 64Kb/s "B" channels and one 64Kb/s "D" channel.

B-ISDN initial specifications call for a series of H_N channels that go up to 140 Mb/s.

ISDN is the architecture that the communications industry, private and government, has agreed to on an international basis. It is in all likelihood the communications architecture of the future.

8.7.1   ISDN Basic Rate

In the initial studies for ISDN it was assumed that the basic rate should be available at locations served by local loops which at that time were almost entirely twisted-pair wiring. Succinctly, the constraint was that it be possible to provide basic service to most homes, businesses, etc. Studies of the local loop plant indicated that a data rate of around 150 Kb/s could be supported. Therefore, the decision was to make available at the interface to the user—e.g., at the interface to the user's house—a service that would consist of the following:

$$\text{Service at user interface} = \text{Basic rate} = 2B + D, \tag{8.1}$$

where B = 64 kb/s and D = 16 kb/s.

It was assumed that the B channels would be used for digitized voice or data, although in principle that would be up to the user (e.g., the user could elect two voice or two data channels, etc.). The D channel was intended for control (signaling). It was once intended that it also be used for slow speed data, but this may be dropped.

Expressed in concrete terms, where there is basic ISDN service today, users may have a digitized phone with an RS232 jack on the back. They can use the phone and plug a personal computer into the jack. The voice phone uses one of the B channels and the personal computer has access to the other channel at 64 kb/s. The phone and the data jack can be independently operated and switched. (e.g., they do not have to be connected to the same destination.)

ISDN's basic rate provides a big boost for PC and workstation communications. Commercial ISDN interface boards are available for PCs. ISDN service will operate over most of the local loop wiring plant. It does not provide an alternative for interconnecting LANs transmitting data in the megabit per second range, however.

8.7.2   ISDN Primary Rate

As noted earlier, the bandwidth that a twisted pair of wire can support is very much a function of the length of the wire. For example, a decade ago, instead of the coaxial cable recommended by IBM, the GE Research and Development Center connected IBM 2700 series terminals to the mainframe computer over twisted pair wiring that was installed as part of the wiring plant for the telephone system. Since the computer community discovered that twisted pairs can carry broadband signals, twisted pair Ethernet utilizing hub switches (many somewhat like the DV–1 discussed earlier) have become popular. The line-runs in most business districts are short. What is known as the ISDN primary rate was created for environments where the distances are expected to be relatively short. Equation 8.2 summarizes ISDN primary service.

$$\text{Service at user interface} = \text{Primary Rate} = 23B + D \text{ in U.S.} \qquad (8.2)$$

$$= 30B + D \text{ in Europe}$$

where B = 64 kb/s and D = 64 kb/s.

Again, let us put this in concrete terms. If your office is in a downtown area where the local loop runs are small, or on a campus where the distances are small, and ISDN primary rate service is available, you can potentially connect your personal computer or workstation to a roughly 1.5 Mb/s channel. In addition, it is possible to bridge LANs at this rate over the common carriers. Figure 8.3 illustrates this latter capability utilizing products available from the Develcon Corporation in 1993. Clearly LAN 1 and LAN 2 in the figure can be at different locations that are only interconnected by the common carriers.

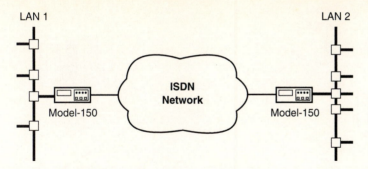

Figure 8.3   Products from Develcon Electronics

8.7.3   Broadband ISDN

At the time this book was written, the specifications for broadband ISDN (B-ISDN) had not been finalized. However, Table 8.3 summarizes tentative channels. It can be seen that very broadband service is intended.

There have been field trials of B-ISDN, often in the medical field, that provide an indication of what the future may hold.[7] Figures 8.4 and 8.5 are examples of such field trials.

Clearly the intent of medical communications systems is to make data, imaging (e.g., x-ray, NMR, acoustic) and other medical information stored at a centralized database, readily available globally. The medical field is particularly interesting because of the high resolution required in medical imaging. Providing imaging information to various workstations in a hospital complex and remotely to physicians' offices could improve the efficiency of medical

---

7. T. P. McGarty, G. J. Baine, and M. Goldberg, "Medical Communications," guest editorial, *Special Issue of IEEE Journal on Selected Areas in Communications* 10, no. 7 (September 1992): 1105.

Table 8.3   ISDN Broadband Channels (Tentative)

Channel	*North America (Mb/s)*	*International (CCITT) (Mb/s)*
B	.064	.064
H0	0.384	0.384
H1	1.920	1.536
H2	32.176	about 44.000
H4	132.032–138.240	132.032–138.240

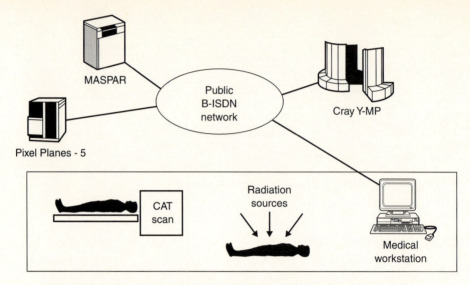

Figure 8.4   Dynamic radiation therapy planning. *Source:* K. Chipman et al., "Medical Applications in B-ISDN Field Trial," *Special Issue of IEEE Journal on Selected Areas in Communications* 10, no. 7 (September 1992): 1173. Reprinted with permission of IEEE.

practice and have a large payoff with respect to time. Thus if a person has a serious accident away from home, medical information including imaging could be provided to medical personnel at a remote site.

8.7.4   ISDN Switch and Network Realities

The primary goal of ISDN is to provide the data transport for all types of services and a framework within which those services can be integrated. Getting from here to there must be an evolutionary process, both from the user's viewpoint and that of the common and added-value carriers. The starting point for that evolution was, and to a very large degree remains, a system designed primarily for voice. In creating an integrated system for voice and other services, switching is probably the key resource.

As discussed earlier, it is not at all clear that there is one switching mechanism that is satisfactory over the entire spectrum of message types, features, and services. By message types we imply the spectrum of message statistics that are encountered in the real world. For example, transaction processing systems may have many very short messages that occur almost at random and

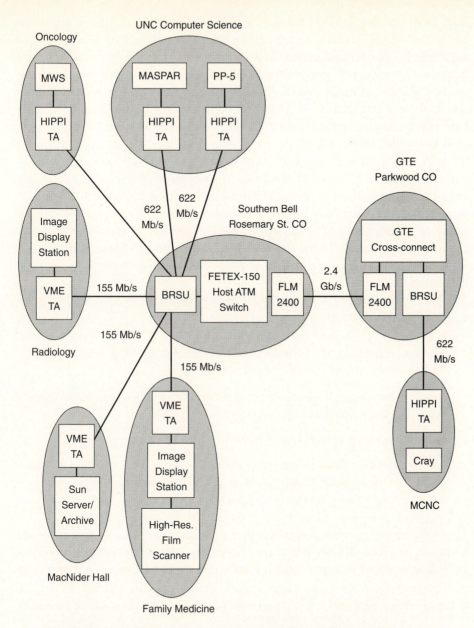

Figure 8.5   B-ISDN field trial network architecture. *Source:* K. Chipman et al., "Medical Applications in B-ISDN Field Trial," *Special Issue of IEEE Journal on Selected Areas in Communications* 10, no. 7 (September 1992): 1173. Reprinted with permission of IEEE.

with large inactive periods between messages. Packet switching is attractive under such circumstances. At the other extreme, the signals on lines leased to networks to connect real-time activity between TV stations are used for very long messages and for long periods of time. Clearly, there is not one switching method that is optimum over the spectrum. The question is whether there is one switching mechanism, or a few mechanisms, that on the average will be both cost effective and satisfactory. The hope is that ATM switches and associated network facilities will meet these criteria, but it remains to be seen whether that hope is realized. It is perhaps worth noting that the ATM program was initiated as part of the ISDN development of the communications industry. As mentioned earlier, ATM is a specific fixed packet size system although more recently there has been discussion of several packet sizes. From a network standpoint, ATM systems establish virtual channels or circuits. Details are to be found in the references.[8] Many of the key issues surrounding ATM involve network services and applications. Some of these issues will be addressed in Chapter 13.

The key concepts of ATM are based on the belief that there is a packet size with certain characteristics:

For long messages, the packets are large enough that the address and control information is small compared with the data sent.

For short messages, the packets are short enough that there is not too much wasted and unused space in the packets.

Buffering and the assembling of packets will make the above true.

Because virtual channels are established, the setup time to establish those channels will be acceptable. (There is of course network control information required to establish those channels.)

The basic long-term question is whether a system that does all things for all classes of service will have adequate performance and be acceptable economically. The layers of protocols and control could be very complicated and time

---

8. Ronald J. Vetter and David C. Du, "Issues and Challenges in ATM Networks," *Special Issue of Comm. ACM* 38, no. 2 (February 1995) (individual articles not referenced in this book); ATM Forum, *ATM User-Network Interface Specifications, Version 3.0* (Englewood Cliffs, NJ: Prentice-Hall, 1993); H. Rudin, "The ATM—Asynchronous Transfer Mode," Special Issue, *Computer Networks and ISDN Systems* 24 (1992): 277; Anthony S. Acampora, *An Introduction to Broad-band Networks: LANS, MANs, ATM, B-ISDN, and Optical Networks for Integrated Multimedia Telecommunications* (New York Plenum Press, 1994); Wolfgang E. Denzel, "High Speed ATM Switching," Special Issue on High Speed ATM, *IEEE Communications Magazine* 31, no. 2 (February 1993): 26; Ann Steffora, "ATM: The Year of the Trial," *Computer Magazine* 27, no. 4 (April 1994): 8; R. Handel, M. N. Huber, and S. Schroder, *ATM Networks: Concepts, Protocols, Applications*, 2nd ed. (Reading, MA: Addison-Wesley, 1994).

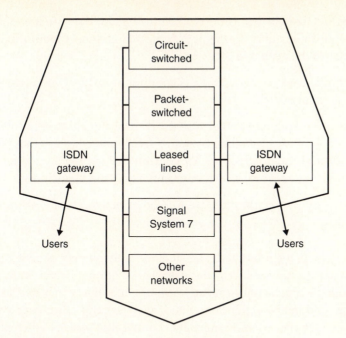

Figure 8.6   Current ISDN network implementation

consuming. The short-term question is whether switching center configurations will be cost effective today.

The national network has a great many installed switches that have been primarily configured and programmed for voice traffic. In the large, it has not been cost effective to make major changes in those switches to meet the new requirements for data transmission. Instead it has been more cost effective to add to existing switches hardware and software to handle the data traffic. For example, the voice portion of a basic ISDN line may be sent to a time slot interchange switching component, and the data portion sent to different hardware and software, perhaps a bus or ATM switch add-on. None of the details of this internal processing of messages and switching need to be apparent to the user. Under the following typical conditions, the network of today looks like Fig. 8.6:

The circuit-switched portion handles voice and other relatively long sessions where the traffic utilizes a substantial part of the channel. The setup time, and information required to set up the circuit, are relatively unimportant (i.e., they do not consume or waste many resources).

The packet-switched portion is likely to handle data streams that are far from continuous and if assigned dedicated channels would make inefficient use of the available capacity.

If the traffic between two points is continuous or heavy enough, dedicated leased lines are used.

It has been mentioned earlier that the control signals are sent over a separate data network. Signaling System 7 (SS7)[9] is the system that is compatible with and intended for ISDN control. SS7 is flexible enough that the control of a good many information services could be included.

Lastly, it is necessary to interface into other networks—for example, AT&T to MCI.

To a large degree, the internal details, including the variety of switching mechanisms used, are not visible to the user. For example, if you were fortunate enough to have a personal computer at home that was connected to an ISDN phone, it would not be apparent to you if at the central office your voice channel was circuit-switched and your data channel was packet-switched. In some campus environments, they might both be circuit-switched. As we noted early, whether hybrid switching prevails in the long run remains to be seen.

8.7.5   ISDN Basic and Primary Service Implementation Considerations

The deployment of basic and primary service ISDN has taken many years and is far from complete. The service is available in many locations, but those locations are not fully interconnected. It is likely to take until the late 1990s for even the basic and primary rate services to become all pervasive.[10] There are many reasons for this long period to implement only the basic and primary services.

The complete digitization of the network is required. As has been pointed out, except for the local loops this has now been pretty much accomplished. However, there is a lot of terminal equipment out there that will require changing (e.g., analog phones to digital phones).

9. E. Cambre and M. Smouts, "CCITT No. 7 Network as the Basis for Advanced Public Network Services," *Electrical Communications (Alcatel)* 63, no. 4 (1989): 1133.

10. J. Srinivasan, "A Comparative Study of National ISDN versus International ISDN Installations and Traffic," *IEEE Network* 9, no. 3 (May/June 1995): 22.

Until mass produced VLSI chips were available for implementing interfacing and terminal equipment, it would have been very expensive to implement the ISDN services (e.g., digital phones require cheap analog to digital and digital to analog converter chips). The required chips are now available in volume.

Because of the large capital investment required for changes, changes take time.

The normal practice of regulatory agencies in the United States is to require that new services pay for themselves during implementation. A parallel situation would be to try to finance a railroad from earnings while it is being built. Who would be willing to buy a ticket on a railroad before that railroad goes everywhere? ISDN will become more attractive when it is completed.

The switches although digital, may not have hardware and software that can easily handle the spectrum of services implied by potential ISDN capabilities and multimedia computer system experience. As implied in the preceding paragraph, it may well be necessary to put hybrid systems in place.

The upside of the ISDN story is that we are on the verge of nationwide implementation and integration of basic and primary service. Today, such service is available in many locations and being used with considerable success. In some areas primary service is already being used to send medical images to remote sites. Computer boards and other interfacing equipment are available. If basic ISDN were available everywhere, many PC owners would be buying the boards. It may well be that ISDN is on the verge of taking off in the service and business sense. At the same time, it must be admitted that all pervasive broadband ISDN will lag basic and primary service by a significant time. The final standards for broadband ISDN remain to be decided and its implementation schedule is uncertain.[11]

8.8   The Internet

Most of the readers of this book will have some familiarity with the Internet. Our purpose here is to briefly summarize, within the context of distributed computing and the objectives of this text, Internet experience, which can provide a picture of the potential use of future distributed multimedia systems.

---

11. T. F. La Porta et al., "B-ISDN: A Technological Discontinuity," *IEEE Communications* 32, no. 10 (October 1994): 84.

The Internet grew out of work on Arpanet, a system originally sponsored by the Advanced Research Projects Agency.[12] In effect, the Internet resulted from the merger of several government-supported data networks similar to Arpanet. In fact, the Internet, as the name implies, can be viewed as a combination of other networks. More recent support has been primarily from the National Science Foundation. Our use of the term Internet in what follows includes all of the systems mentioned above. As implied in our earlier discussion, the Internet utilizes the data highway system provided by the common carriers. The lines utilized are usually leased and the Internet provides its own packet switches.

In addition to coverage in the United States, Internet access is now worldwide. In some cases direct access has been made available to educational institutions or laboratories, in others cases government or private telephone companies are involved and provide interfaces to their own networks. In addition, there are many commercial firms running worldwide added-value data networks that interface with the Internet core. The evolution is similar to that of the telephone industry, in which national services evolved into what appears to the user as an international network.

There are commercial added-value networks that provide services somewhat similar to the Internet and usually interconnect with it. The impact of the Internet compared with those services occurs in several areas:

Arpanet/Internet provided the first widely used transport services for interactive computer data. We exclude from this statement the earlier use of leased lines to transfer data between large computing centers, teletype systems, and conventional store and forward message systems. The contribution was the interactive access from an arbitrary computer node (or a terminal on that node) to another computer node.

Initial use was primarily for electronic mail and file transfer as well as researchers interacting with remote computers.

Internet use fell primarily in the research and education communities. As a result of this, many of the new concepts concerning networks and their use have grown out of experience with the Internet.

There are many other networks that have some of the features of the Internet. However, the Internet has developed into a hub or common interconnection point thus providing access to many other networks. For example, if you have made appropriate business arrangements or are a skilled

12. Peter J. Denning, "The Arpanet after Twenty Years," *American Scientist* 77 (November–December 1989): 530.

"hacker," you can have access through the Internet to many of the on-line databases that are available today.[13]

Largely because of its research orientation and support from the government, the Internet has become the laboratory for data searches, information searches, and multimedia work that involve distributed computers at different locations.

We do not propose to go into the details of the Internet or the services it offers. Suffice it to point out that there are many data search capabilities that span a great number of databases and computers, many of them involving multimedia facilities. Internet capabilities have recently been reviewed in ten articles in a special issue of the *Communications of the ACM*.[14] A particularly interesting addition is MBone, covered in that issue as well as in an article in *Computer Magazine*.[15] Experience with the Internet and ISDN suggests that in the future there will be the potential to do things quite differently than we do today. Interactive multimedia communications between computer systems on a global basis is possible. Regardless of the level of traffic that materializes, the impact on society will be substantial.[16] These types of systems are much more than just communications systems, and they are more appropriately addressed in Chapter 13. They are, however, based upon the availability of adequate data communications services.

When this book was written, there were various administrative movements underway to commercialize the Internet. Most people believe that in the long run commercialization will take place. As a matter of fact, the first steps to commercialization have already taken place. There is no question of the value of the type of services the Internet provides to the scientific, research, and education communities. There is also no question that similar services will find limited application in the commercial community. However, it is not so clear how often those services will be applicable to society as a whole. Economic tradeoffs and other factors will become significant at some point. Perhaps conference TV and picture phones are an example. The technical capability has been there for years, but use is not widespread. We shall just have to wait and see.

13. Clifford Stoll, *The Cuckoo's Egg* (New York: Doubleday, 1989).

14. Barry M. Leiner, "Internet Technology—Guest Editor's Introduction to Special Issue of the Communications of the ACM," *Communications of the ACM* 37, no. 8 (August 1994): 32.

15. Michael R. Macedonia and Donald P. Brutzman, "MBone Provides Audio and Video Across the Internet," *Computer Magazine* 27, no. 4 (April 1994): 30.

16. D. J. Wright et al., "B-ISDN Applications and Economics," special issue, *IEEE Journal on Selected Areas in Communications* 10, no. 9 (December 1992): 1365; M. Mitchell Waldrop, "Culture Shock on the Networks," *Science* 265, no. 5174 (August 12, 1994): 879.

In conclusion, it should be realized that the communications ability to transport data, except for the cost involved, is unlikely to limit the development and use of the Internet. The development of applications, and an information infrastructure to support those applications, will be more important factors. Economics and overall system limitations as discussed in the latter parts of this book will have a major impact on that evolution and its scope.

8.9   Summary and Comments

The communications industry is a mature, technically driven, innovative industry. Its largest component is the telephone industry, which is in fact roughly equal in magnitude to the other components combined. We cannot consider communications without focusing on the telephone industry. For example, the common carriers of the telephone industry provide the data highway transport system that is used by almost all data communication offerings and services.

The national telephone network is a hierarchical structure containing tens of thousands of large electronic switches. Both switching and transmission are largely digital. In other words, the switches are digital switches, and the transmission between sites utilizes bit streams. Consequently, as far as the national network is concerned, analog source information such as voice or video is digitized prior to being transported in the network. The source traffic is largely voice. Although the traffic devoted to computer data is increasing rapidly, it is likely that voice will remain the predominant factor. Admittedly, there are large uncertainties in traffic estimates and any prediction along these lines may prove to be false.

A campuslike environment is quite different from the national network. The traffic patterns to be expected are quite different, and the communication options available less restrictive. It is to be expected that in many respects more innovation will take place in campuslike environments than in the national network.

The national network was digitized for economic reasons. Very early in that evolution it was realized that once digitized the network could be used to carry all forms of source information. The Integrated Services Digital Network (ISDN) development has that specific objective. It represents an architecture for the telephone industry that has worldwide acceptance. When fully implemented, it will provide high-speed data communications over the national network.

The Internet provides a worldwide data communication system for computers and related multimedia information. From the user's viewpoint, it is a prototype of what we might expect in the future. From a business perspective, it is to be expected that it will be commercialized and evolve along the lines of the international telephone network. A big difference will be that the range of added-value services that might be made available over the network exceeds by far our experience in the voice world.

8.10 Problems

1. Consider the following three cases of networks with N nodes:

   A cable system with N nodes

   A ring system with N nodes

   A hub system with N nodes and one hub, with the N nodes connected only to the hub

   Further assume that each node or hub, when it receives a message, processes it and then forwards it. (Unless of course it is the final destination.) Consequently, a message passing through a node or a hub will experience some delay. Therefore, the number of nodes or hubs passed through—i.e., the number of hops—can be significant.

   For each of the above cases, derive an expression for the average number of hops between stations. You may assume that the stations are equally active and can communicate randomly to other stations.

2. One of the problems of the systems considered in problems 1–3 in Chapter 7 is that the signals from several nodes can arrive at another node at the same time, thus causing interference. There is a solution to that problem.

   Consider a star system with one hub and N nodes attached to that hub. The hub will use frequency band W_R for receiving signals and frequency band W_T for transmitting signals. The nodes will all use W_R for transmitting and W_T for receiving. Assume further that the positions and consequently the propagation delays are known. (There is an alternative of a self-tracking synchronization scheme that will measure the delays.)

   Under the above conditions, a control computer at the hub can allocate time slots to the various nodes for communications with it. The thought is that all messages will go through the hub for forwarding to the appropriate receiving node or nodes. The hub serves no other purpose.

   (a) Prepare in not more than four pages your analysis of the merits of the above system. Include an assessment of its weak points. (b) Do you believe that your analysis had anything to do with picking a star network hierarchy for the national network? Would you change it today and if so why?

Chapter 9

Database Management Concepts

The history of database system research is one of exceptional productivity and startling economic impact. Barely 20 years old as a basic science research field, database research has fueled an information services industry estimated at $10 billion per year in the U.S. alone. Achievements in database research underpin fundamental advances in communications systems, transportation and logistics, financial management, knowledge-based systems, accessibility to scientific literature, and a host of other civilian and defense applications. They also serve as the foundation for considerable progress in basic science in various fields ranging from computing to biology.

Avi Silberschatz, Michael Stonebraker, and Jeff Ullman[1]

9.1   Chapter Objectives

The heart of nearly any computer system is its data. In the case of business systems, the data may describe current inventory levels in a warehouse, accounts receivable for customers of a company, or current payroll and employee records. In the case of manufacturing systems, the data may describe the design of a product or the instructions for controlling the machines that make the product. In the case of a real-time system such as a computer system controlling the launch of a rocket into earth orbit, the data may describe acceptable ranges for various sensors and instructions for controlling the firing of the rocket to achieve orbit. For most companies, data are key assets that allow them to make profits and stay in business. Without those data and the ability to effectively access them, companies will lose their competitive advan-

1. A. Silberschatz, M. Stonebraker, and J. Ullman, "Database Systems: Achievements and Opportunities," *Communications of the ACM* 34, no. 10 (October 1991): 111. © 1991 Association for Computing Machinery. Reprinted by permission.

tage. Hence, efficient and reliable management of data is a critical requirement in nearly all computer systems today, distributed or not.

As the trend toward distributed computer systems gathers momentum, the requirement for efficient and reliable management of data must expand to include distributed networks of computers. Data may be shared by multiple systems and users across a network of widely varying hardware and software systems. For example, in a large sales organization, inventory data may be shared by a warehouse computer system that monitors quantities and locations of all items in warehouses, sales computer systems in stores that sell the items in the warehouses, and order-entry systems in the headquarters of the organization that are responsible for refreshing inventories in the warehouses when quantities become low. The warehouses, stores, and company headquarters may be geographically distributed, but all three must be able to access the shared inventory data simultaneously. If the data become unavailable because of a failure of some kind, or if the data become corrupted because two different stores sell the same warehouse item simultaneously, the operation of the company is significantly hampered. Effective management of data in distributed computer systems has all the problems of managing data in a centralized computer system, plus the problems of synchronizing the concurrent operation of multiple systems sharing data in unpredictable ways over unreliable networks.

The goals of this chapter are to provide the basic concepts of database management systems and to illustrate the state of the art for such systems. Entire books have been written about database management systems (for example, see Elmasri and Navathe[2]). Our goal here is not to reproduce this material but instead to provide the background necessary to understand the role that database management systems play in the architecture of large distributed computer systems.

9.2   What Is a Database?

A *database management system* (DBMS) is a software system designed to efficiently manage large quantities of structured data in secondary storage, retrieve that data on demand, and control how the data are accessed and shared by possibly many concurrently executing user processes. The data that are managed by a DBMS are collectively called a *database*, a word often used more broadly to mean any collection of data values, whether they are

2. R. Elmasri and S. B. Navathe, *Fundamentals of Database Systems,* 2nd ed. (Redwood City, CA: Benjamin-Cummings, 1994).

in a file, in the data structures of a user process, or even on paper. In this chapter, we will use the word more specifically to mean the data managed by a DBMS.

There are many important concepts hidden within the informal definition of a DBMS above. First, a DBMS today is usually a *software system* that operates on conventional computer hardware utilizing secondary storage technologies. While special-purpose database machines do exist, they have not achieved a significant share of the commercial market.[3]

Another important concept in the definition above is that most DBMSs are designed to handle *large quantities* of *structured data* as opposed to freeform text. This means that the data managed by a DBMS are composed of individual data values such as numbers or fixed length strings (and other data needed to describe this data, as we shall see later). These data values are organized into a small number of fixed-format data structures (e.g., records). Links between instances of these data structures representing relationships may also be present. A database, then, consists of many instances of a few fixed-format data structures, rather than a large number of different data structures, each with only a few instances. It is not uncommon today for a database to reach the size of gigabytes of data or larger. Users accessing a database typically need only a small fraction of its data at any one time.

The next important concept in the definition of a DBMS is that of efficient *retrieval* of data. As a user process executes, it must have the ability to retrieve and modify the data values in one or more databases. While not all databases can be modified by users (e.g., a database of reference information), many can, and a general-purpose DBMS must be able to handle modifications made by users to the data it retrieves. The DBMS that manages such a database must provide convenient ways for the user processes to request the particular subsets of the databases that they require. The DBMS must also provide efficient mechanisms to retrieve and modify those subsets once they have been identified. A major component in most commercial DBMSs today is a query processor and optimizer that is responsible for providing this functionality.

Another important concept in the definition above is *sharing* of data. Most large databases have many uses. For example, the inventory database in our example is used by many user processes that run the warehouse, control sales, and do ordering of new inventory. As a result, most commercial DBMSs are designed to allow many user processes to access and manipulate a database concurrently. However, this creates a number of problems in managing the

---

3. Teradata Corp., *DBC/1012 Data Base Computer: Concepts and Facilities* (Los Angeles: Teradata Corporation, 1983).

database, and leads directly to a final important concept in the definition above.

This is the concept of *controlling the access* to data. Since it is often the case that many different users and application systems use a database, the DBMS that manages this database must carefully control how these users and application systems access and manipulate the data, to make sure that the integrity of the data in the database is maintained. One form of control is *concurrency control*, as mentioned above. The goal of concurrency control is to maintain the consistency and accuracy of the data when multiple user processes attempt to access and update a datum simultaneously. A second form of control is *enforcement of data security policies* so that user processes access only those parts of a database that have been authorized for their use. A third form of control is *integrity rule checking* to catch erroneous updates to the database that would violate the semantic correctness of the database (e.g., a negative age for a person or a person without a name).

9.2.1   An Example Database

Throughout this chapter, we will use as a sample database to demonstrate new ideas the inventory database introduced above. This database is shown in Fig. 9.1. In the figure, the inventory database is shown as a *relational database*. There are several types of DBMSs in use today, as discussed below; however, the relational DBMS is probably the most widely used today. In a relational DBMS, data are organized into tables called *relations*. Each relation has a fixed set of columns called *attributes*. Each row of data in a relation is called a *tuple*. The value stored in each attribute of each tuple must be an atomic value (e.g., a single number or a single character string).

In the case of the inventory database, there are four relations. The first contains data about each of the items in the warehouse. For each item, it lists the name of the item, its unique item number, the quantity of the item in the warehouse, and the location of the item in the warehouse. The second relation contains sales data. For each sale, it lists the name of the salesperson, the item number of the item sold, and the price at which it was sold. The third relation contains information about the suppliers of the items in the warehouse. This includes a unique supplier number for each supplier, the city where the supplier is located, and the telephone number used to order more of an item. The fourth relation contains information about which supplier supplies which items. Each tuple contains an item number and a supplier number, indicating

Relation ITEM

Item#	ItemName	Quantity	Location
123	pump	25	A23.2
235	saw	42	B3.9
589	hose	110	A23.5
601	ladder	12	B14.6
. . .	. . .	. . .	. . .

Relation SUPPLIES

Item#	Supplier#
123	23
235	23
589	99
601	6
. . .	. . .

Relation SALES

Item#	Salesperson	Price
601	Sam	169.95
123	Sam	99.95
589	Mary	24.98
601	John	169.95
123	Mary	99.95
601	Mary	169.95
235	John	25.49
. . .	. . .	. . .

Relation SUPPLIER

Supplier#	City	Phone
6	Albany	518-555-1234
23	Troy	518-555-4321
48	Schenectady	518-555-6789
99	New York	201-555-9876
. . .	. . .	. . .

Figure 9.1   The inventory relational database

that the supplier with the given supplier number can supply the item with the given item number.

Note that the Item# attribute in the ITEM relation is the same as the Item# attribute in the SALES relation. Using the same attribute in two different relations is the way to establish a link, or relationship, between two relations. Given a tuple from the SALES relation, you can use the Item# value in the tuple to consult the ITEM relation to determine what item was sold. For example, the Item# in the first SALES tuple in Fig. 9.1 is 601. Looking in the ITEM relation, we can easily see that this is a ladder. There is a similar relationship between the ITEM and SUPPLIES relations that uses the Item# attribute in both relations. The inventory database also contains a relationship between the SUPPLIES relation and the SUPPLIERS relation that is implemented with the shared Supplier# attribute.

9.2.2   The Importance of a Schema

If a DBMS is to provide services such as optimized query processing and control of database access and manipulation for multiple shared databases, then it must know something about the content and structure of the databases it manages. For example, a user of the inventory database might want to query the database for all items in the warehouse with a quantity of three or less. To handle a query such as this, the DBMS must know that ITEM is a relation and that Quantity is an attribute of the ITEM relation. It must also know that the value of the Quantity attribute is an integer number. Describing the content and structure of the data in a database is the job of the database schema.

A *schema* (sometimes called a *data dictionary*) is a description of the structure of a database. It includes all of the names used in the database and a description of what each of these names means. A typical schema in a relational DBMS includes for each database the names of all the relations in the database, the names of the attributes in each relation, the data type (e.g., integer, real, string) for each attribute, the address in secondary storage where the relation is stored, what indexes exist to help process queries against the relation, various statistics such as the number of tuples in each relation that the query optimizer can use to determine the most efficient way to process a query, and authorization rules listing which users have access to the data in each relation. It should be noted, and it is particularly important in distributed systems, that location may be in terms of a virtual address in a memory hierarchy rather than a physical location in secondary store.

To a large extent, the schema is the key concept in database management. Without it, a DBMS would know nothing about the data in its databases and would be forced to treat each database as nothing more than a set of files with records. In other words, the concept of schemas is what distinguishes a DBMS from an ordinary file system that is part of most operating systems, and it is what allows the DBMS to provide all the functionality outlined above.

The schema concept also leads directly to another important advantage of a DBMS over an ordinary file system—namely, data independence. *Data independence* is the separation of the physical implementation of a data structure in a DBMS (e.g., a relation) from the logical view of the data structure as seen by user processes. For example, in the inventory database, a user process should not need to know where the ITEM relation is stored in secondary storage or how the data are formatted into records. A user process should see only tuples with four attributes, and it should be able to retrieve those tuples using a high-level query language. This independence of the user view of the relation from the physical storage of the relation in secondary storage is made possible by the schema, which contains the details necessary to map between the user process view and the physical implementation. The concept of data independence is particularly important in distributed systems because it means that a user process should not need to know where in the distributed system a particular data item is stored. The DBMS is responsible for recording the virtual address of a particular data item in a distributed system and for communicating with that other component of the distributed system to retrieve that data item when a user process requests it. The relationships between virtual addresses, the physical location of hardware and physical addresses in that hardware are matters for the one-level store system or virtual memory system to handle for the distributed system as a whole.

An added advantage of data independence is isolation of changes to the physical implementation of a database from user processes. When the physical implementation of a database changes—for example, to improve performance or to take advantage of new hardware—the schema is also changed to redefine the mapping between the user process view of the database and its new physical implementation. The user processes then continue to use the database, unaware that the physical implementation of the database has changed. Since most databases evolve over time as requirements and expectations change, this can be a big advantage and is one of the major selling points for a commercial DBMS today.

9.2.3   The Architecture of a Typical DBMS

It is convenient to think of a DBMS conceptually as composed of three layers and the mappings between them, as shown in Fig. 9.2. At the top level are external schemas defining the views of a database as seen by the user processes that use the data. At the middle level is the conceptual schema that defines the content and structure of the entire database. At the bottom level is the internal schema that defines how the database, as defined by the conceptual schema, is stored in secondary storage.

Two levels of mappings are also needed. The top level defines how the external schemas are derived from the conceptual schema. For example, a particular external schema may omit many of the relations defined in the conceptual schema if they are irrelevant to the user processes that will use the external schema. An external schema may also omit attributes from relations when those attributes are irrelevant to the user processes using the external schema. The bottom level of mappings defines how the conceptual schema is mapped to the internal schema. In other words, the bottom level of mappings implements much of the data independence functionality discussed above.

While not all database systems are implemented in three levels such as this, conceptually, this organization can be used to describe most commercial DBMSs today.

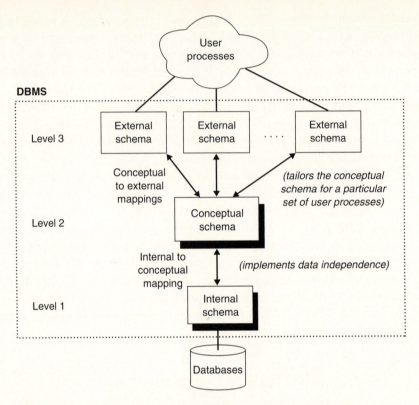

Figure 9.2   The three levels in a DBMS. *Source:* D. Tsichritzis and A. Klug, eds., *The ANSI/X3/SPARC DBMS Framework* (Montvale, NJ: AFIPS Press, 1978).

9.3   Types of Database Systems

All DBMSs allow data that conform to a specified schema to be stored persistently in secondary storage and retrieved on demand by user processes. However, DBMSs differ in two important ways. The first and most significant way involves the specific data structures that a system supports. For example, as we have already seen, a relational DBMS supports a data structure that is much like a two-dimensional table. Other types of DBMSs support data structures that are either similar to a hierarchical tree or to a network with nodes connected by edges.

The second way that DBMSs differ is in the types of services they provide. For example, some systems support high-level query languages that user processes use to describe the data to be retrieved. Other systems provide a set of programming primitives that allow a user to write a program to locate and retrieve data from the database. Some DBMSs provide functionality for things like data integrity and security enforcement, while others do not. Even among those systems that do provide this functionality, they do not all provide it in the same way.

In this section, we concentrate on the different types of data structures supported by database systems. In the sections that follow, we address differences in the services provided. Keep in mind, however, that it is not always possible to separate services from data structures, so the division between the sections is at times blurred.

9.3.1   Linear Files

The earliest type of DBMS and the simplest is one that represents a database as a single linear file of records with a fixed format. The obvious advantage of this system is its simplicity. As a result, this type of DBMS is most often found today on small personal computers. Nevertheless, there are many applications for which the required database is easily represented as a single file, and this type of DBMS is simple and efficient to use. Examples include a database for managing a private collection of audio CDs or the mailing list for a small company. A commercial example of a DBMS of this type is FileMaker Pro for Windows and Apple Macintosh computers.

The most significant limitation of this type of DBMS is the restriction of a database to a single file. For example, the inventory database in Fig. 9.1 cannot easily be represented in a single file. It is more naturally represented as four files: (1) items, (2) sales data, (3) supplier data, and (4) suppliers and the items they supply. This, however, would be four separate databases. Since a DBMS of this type does not usually allow a user process to use more that one database at a time, applications that require more than one database (file) will find this type of DBMS awkward to use. As a result, many of the commercially available DBMSs of this type have been augmented with relational features to make them easier to use. Thus systems like FileMaker Pro are no longer strictly linear file systems.

Let us consider an example of using a strictly linear file system. Suppose that you want to find the names of the items sold by a particular salesperson in our inventory database. The sales database must be opened and the appropriate records accessed for the relevant salesperson to get the item numbers of the items sold. The sales database must then be closed and the items database opened. Each item number retrieved from the sales database must then be used to access its record in the items database and the name of the item retrieved. As we shall see, other types of DBMSs allow this type of processing to be done with a single query to a combined database.

The reason for emphasizing this limitation for a DBMS based on linear files is that it has important consequences for distributed systems. A database that is distributed across the nodes of a network by necessity must consist of multiple files—at least one per node of the network that contains part of the database. Because of the restriction in the paragraph above, we can easily see that a DBMS based on linear files will make processing this distributed database difficult.

Like all DBMSs, this type usually includes a simple query language that allows a user process to specify a Boolean predicate describing characteristics of the records to be retrieved from a database file. The Boolean predicate is composed of clauses of the form

<record field name> <relational operator> <value>.

These clauses are combined using logical AND and OR operators to produce complex query predicates. For example, a predicate to retrieve all the sales records for Mary where the price of the item sold is greater than $100 is the following:

Salesperson = 'Mary' AND Price > 100

To process a query, the DBMS does a linear search of the records in the database (file) evaluating the Boolean predicate for each record one by one. When a record is found that satisfies the query, it is included in the result of the query. All the records in this result are then returned to the user process. To improve the performance of query processing, a DBMS may use an index for one or more fields of the records in a file. If the Boolean predicate in a query includes a field for which an index exists, this index can be used to limit the search to only those records that have the correct value in that field. This can greatly reduce the time required to process a query. The tradeoffs, of course, are the extra space needed to store the index and the time needed to create and maintain the index as the records in the file are updated.

9.3.2   Hierarchical Structure

Hierarchical DBMSs were one of the first commercial types of DBMS to truly integrate data from multiple types of records into a single database, thus overcoming the major limitation of DBMSs based on linear files. As the name implies, a hierarchical DBMS organizes the types of records in a database into a hierarchy or treelike data structure. In our inventory database we have four types of records: (1) ITEM records, (2) SALES records, (3) SUPPLIER records,

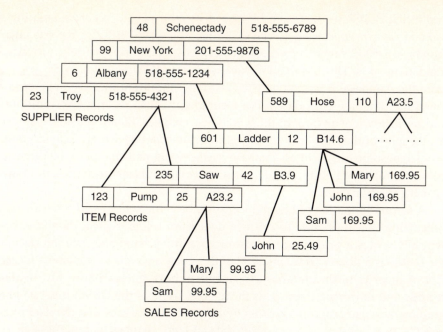

Figure 9.3 A hierarchical inventory database

and (4) SUPPLIES records. We might organize records from three of these four types into hierarchies with SUPPLIER records at the top and SALES records at the bottom, as shown in Fig. 9.3. Each SUPPLIER record is linked to zero or more ITEM records indicating that the supplier supplies those items. Similarly, each ITEM record is linked to zero or more SALES records indicating sales for that item. The result is a hierarchy composed of the three record types. Note that the SUPPLIES records have been eliminated. Their purpose in the relational database of Fig. 9.1 was to link ITEM records to SUPPLIER records. This is accomplished automatically by the hierarchy in this case.

A hierarchical data structure is good for representing *one-to-many relationships* between record types, where a single record of one type is linked to one or more records of another type. For example, in our inventory database, there are multiple sales for each item. This is a one-to-many relationship between ITEM records and SALES records. Now consider the relationship between items and suppliers. In Fig. 9.3 we see that supplier number 23 supplies both pumps and saws. This seems to imply that there is a one-to-many relationship between SUPPLIER records and ITEM records. In many situations, however, one would expect that an item can also be supplied by many different suppliers. In this case, an ITEM record must be linked to many SUPPLIER records and a SUPPLIER record must be linked to many ITEM records, creating a *many-to-many relationship* between ITEM records and SUPPLIER records. A hierarchical DBMS cannot represent this type of relationship without duplicating data records. This has the obvious disadvantage of requiring extra space to store the database. A less obvious but equally important disadvantage occurs when the database is updated. For example, if ITEM records are duplicated and the location of an item in the warehouse changes, then it must be changed in all copies of the ITEM record to keep the database consistent. To avoid these problems, some hierarchical database systems augment the basic hierarchical data structure with additional features that make it easier to represent many-to-many relationships.

A second limitation of hierarchical systems is the *navigational style* of query processing that they use. To retrieve data from a hierarchical database, one typically writes a program in a host programming language. The interface to the DBMS is a library of functions that this program calls to traverse a hierarchy of records in the database from top to bottom, searching for desired records and retrieving them. This means that users of the DBMS must be programmers or use programs written by others. It also means that the user must be fully aware of the structure of the data and any changes that might be made to it as the database evolves. In other words, data independence is limited.

The navigational style of query processing also has important implications for distributed systems that might include a hierarchical DBMS at one or more of the nodes in the network. In such a case, when the distributed system requires data from the hierarchical DBMS, it must generate a program to traverse the database to locate and retrieve the data. Generating code is often much more difficult than generating a query in a high-level query language; it also makes optimization of query processing more difficult.

For many years, hierarchical DBMSs were the most widely used type of DBMS; however, they are rapidly being replaced by other types of systems. Today there are few hierarchical systems commercially available for the reasons discussed above. Probably the most widely used hierarchical DBMS is IMS, a product of IBM for IBM mainframe computers. IMS has many features added to it that partially overcome the limitations of the hierarchical DBMS discussed above.

9.3.3   Network Structure

A network DBMS is similar to a hierarchical DBMS with one important difference. Rather than representing the data using a hierarchical data structure, it represents the database as a network of interconnected records. This allows efficient representation of both one-to-many and many-to-many relationships between records, overcoming one of the major weaknesses of the hierarchical DBMS.

A database in a network DBMS consists of *record types* and *set types*. Conceptually, a set type is a one-to-many link between two record types. It can also be viewed as a circularly linked list with a record of one type forming the header for the list and many records of the other type linked together to form the list. Many-to-many relationships are represented efficiently with two set types (circularly linked lists) and a small link record type, resulting in minimal duplication of data and its disadvantages. For example, suppose that we extend the hierarchical version of our inventory database to allow a many-to-many relationship between ITEM records and SUPPLIER records (i.e., items can be supplied by more than one supplier). To represent this many-to-many relationship, we introduce a new record type that we will call SUPPLIES. We will not be concerned with the contents of this record type. Next we define a set type that creates a one-to-many relationship between ITEM records and SUPPLIES records, so that one ITEM record can be linked in a circularly linked list to many SUPPLIES records. We then define a second set type that creates a one-to-many relationship between SUPPLIER records and SUPPLIES records, so that one SUPPLIER record is linked in a circularly linked list to many SUP-PLIES records. Figure 9.4 illustrates an example.

Each SUPPLIES record now represents a relationship between one item and one supplier. The first set type (linked list type) that we introduced allows an ITEM record to be linked to many of these SUPPLIES records. The second set type (linked list type) allows a SUPPLIER record also to be linked to many of these SUPPLIES records. Together, these two set types and the SUPPLIES records establish a many-to-many relationship between ITEM records and SUPPLIER records. For example, Fig. 9.4 shows both supplier number 6 and

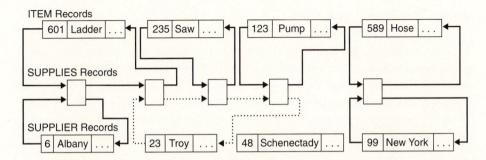

Figure 9.4 A network database with many-to-many relationships. One instance of a set type (linked list) is illustrated with dashed lines.

supplier number 23 as suppliers of ladders and it shows that supplier number 23 supplies ladders, saws, and pumps.

A few words about the graphical representation of set types in Fig. 9.4 are in order. A set type has an *owner record type* (the header of the linked list) and a *member record type* (the members of the linked list). The owner record type is the single record that is linked to possibly many records of the member record type. Hence, in Fig. 9.4, the ITEM record type is the owner of one set type and the SUPPLIER record type is the owner of the other set type. In both set types, the SUPPLIES records are the members. It is traditional in diagrams representing network databases to represent an occurrence of a set type as a circularly linked list of records of the member type with the owner record type serving as the header for this linked list.

While a network DBMS overcomes one of the limitations of the hierarchical DBMS, it does not overcome them all. In particular, a network DBMS, like a hierarchical DBMS, uses a navigational style of query processing. A user writes a program in some programming language that calls database functions to traverse the network of records and sets in a database. Typical functions include operations to FIND the FIRST member of a set, FIND the NEXT member of a set, and FIND the OWNER of a member record in a particular set. It is possible to develop interactive interfaces that translate user queries into sequences of these calls to compute the answer, but it is difficult to do this efficiently and for the general case, although there are examples where it was done successfully.

A few commercial DBMSs based on the network model are available today—for example, IDMS. Most of these systems are based on a report published in 1971 by the CODASYL (Conference on Data Systems Languages) Database Task Group which defined many of the concepts outlined above.[4] As a result, network systems are often called CODASYL or DBTG systems.

9.3.4   Relational Structure

We saw in Fig. 9.1 that a relational database is a collection of tables called relations. Some subset of the columns in each relation forms what is called the *primary key* for the relation. Collectively, the values in the primary key columns uniquely identify each tuple so that no two tuples have the same set of values in the primary key columns. For example, the Item# column of the ITEM relation contains a unique value for each tuple and forms the primary key for the

---

4. Report of the CODASYL Data Base Task Group, ACM, April 1971.

ITEM relation. Similarly, the Supplier# column is the primary key for the SUP-PLIER relation. The SUPPLIES relation has only two columns, neither of which contains unique values across all tuples. However, the two columns taken together are unique, assuming that the fact that a particular supplier supplies a particular item is recorded in the relation only once. Hence the primary key for the SUPPLIES relation consists of the two columns Item# and Supplier# together. What is the primary key of the SALES relation? No single column is unique across all tuples. In fact, all the columns together may not be unique if the same salesperson sells the same type of item for the same price more than once. Hence, the SALES relation as shown in Fig. 9.1 does not have a primary key. While this violates the technical definition of a relation, which demands that all relations have a primary key, many commercial relational DBMSs allow relations without primary keys.

The primary key for a relation is important for several reasons. First, it adds a degree of semantic integrity to the database by allowing the DBMS to check that all tuples have unique primary key values. Second, the primary key can be used to help efficiently locate a specific tuple stored in secondary storage. For example, an index can be created, such as a B-tree index, that allows efficient retrieval of a tuple given its primary key.[5] Third, primary keys help represent relationships between the tuples in two or more relations. Consider the SUPPLIES relation in the inventory database in Fig. 9.1 once again. In particular, note that the Item# column in the SUPPLIES relation is the same as the primary key of the ITEM relation and that the Supplier# column in the SUP-PLIES relation is the same as the primary key of the SUPPLIER relation. When a primary key of one relation is used in another relation, it is called a *foreign key* in the other relation. Hence both the Item# and Supplier# columns in the SUPPLIES relation are foreign keys. This is important because relationships between tuples in a relational database are represented using foreign keys. The use of the Item# and Supplier# foreign keys in the SUPPLIES relation establishes a relationship between ITEM tuples and SUPPLIER tuples. This relationship may be one-to-many, if one or the other of the two columns in the SUPPLIES relation contains unique values, or it may be many-to-many, if neither column contains unique values.

Thus a relational database has great flexibility in representing relationships, giving it an advantage over hierarchical and network databases. Relational databases have another important advantage over these other types of databases as well—namely, the use of high-level, nonprocedural query languages. Most relational database systems today support a query language

5. D. Comer, "The Ubiquitous B-Tree," *Computing Surveys* 11, no. 2 (June 1979): 121–138.

known as SQL (structured query language), which is an international standard.[6] SQL queries have the following form:

> SELECT <list of column names>
>
> FROM <list of relation names>
>
> WHERE <predicate>

A query is processed by identifying all combinations of tuples from the named relations that make the predicate true, and then extracting the specified columns from these tuples as the result of the query. For example, to ask for the names of all items supplied by a supplier located in Troy in our inventory database, we can use the SQL query:

> SELECT ItemName
>
> FROM ITEM, SUPPLIES, SUPPLIER
>
> WHERE   SUPPLIER.City = "Troy" AND
>
>   SUPPLIER.Supplier# = SUPPLIES.Supplier# AND
>
>   SUPPLIES.Item# = ITEM.Item#

The relational DBMS, given this query, must determine how to most efficiently compute its answer. Query optimization techniques in relational DBMSs today have progressed to the point where they are able to determine the optimal or a near-optimal execution plan for most queries, taking advantage of any indexes and other storage structures that might exist to improve the performance of query processing.[7] Further details of query processing are discussed later in this chapter.

Most relational DBMSs also support a programming language interface so that application programs written in some programming language can interact with a relational database. This interface is often designed so that the application program includes the text of SQL queries in its source code. When the queries are executed at run-time, the result, as specified in the SELECT clause of the query, is assigned to variables in the program. There are two problems to overcome, however. The first is that the application program cannot be compiled when it has SQL queries within it since most programming language compilers cannot deal with SQL queries. This is usually handled by a pre-

6. American National Standards Institute, "The Data Language SQL," Document ANSI X3.135 (1986).

7. M. Jarke and J. Koch, "Query Optimizaiton in Database Systems," *ACM Computing Surveys* 16, no. 2 (June 1984): 111–152.

processor that converts each SQL query into a function call that calls a function defined in the DBMS. The details of the query are encoded in the parameters of the function call. Once the SQL queries are replaced by function calls, the program can be compiled normally by the compiler. The second problem is that the result of an SQL query is often a set of values, but program variables can accept only one value at a time. This is sometimes called the *impedance mismatch problem*. This is handled by having the DBMS return the result one value at a time. The application program uses a special function call to request the next value in the answer to a query.

The relational DBMS of today is rapidly replacing the older types. Most systems sold today are relational systems. Some of the most widely used relational systems include Oracle, Sybase, and DB2. Oracle runs on a variety of platforms from large mainframes and parallel multicomputers to small personal computers. Sybase is designed for a client server network of mainframes and workstations (see below). DB2 is designed to run on large IBM mainframe computers, parallel multicomputers, and workstations.

9.3.5   Object-Oriented Structure

While the relational DBMS offers many advantages, it is not ideally suited for all applications. In particular, applications whose data have complex structures that do not conveniently map to a set of tables may find a relational DBMS awkward to use. An example of such an application is computer-aided design and manufacturing, where the data needed to describe the design of a mechanical part or a VLSI chip can be highly complex.[8] Other examples include geographic information systems and multimedia systems.[9] To support the complex data structures required by these types of applications, and to better capture the semantics of these data and their manipulation, many researchers are exploring the use of object-oriented technology.

Object-oriented DBMSs are an evolution of the object-oriented programming paradigm that models an application as a set of objects and the interactions between those objects.[10] Since one object can reference other objects,

8. D. Spooner, D. Faatz, and M. Milicia, "Modeling Mechanical CAD Data with Data Abstraction and Object-Oriented Techniques" (proceedings of the IEEE International Conference on Data Engineering, Los Angeles, CA, 1986): 416–424.

9. R. Laurini and D. Thompson, *Fundamentals of Spatial Information Systems* (San Diego, CA: Academic Press, 1992); S. Christodoulakis, "Development of a Multimedia Informaiton System for an Office Environment" (proceedings of the Very Large Data Base (VLDB) International Conference, Singapore, 1984).

10. K. Dittrich, "Object-Oriented Database Systems: The Notion and the Issues" (proceedings of the International Workshop on Object-Oriented Database Systems, IEEE Computer Society Press, September 1986).

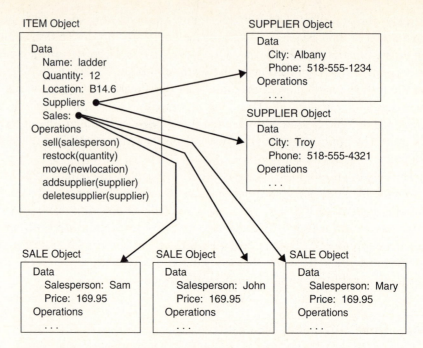

Figure 9.5 An object-oriented inventory database

arbitrarily complex data structures can be created. An object-oriented DBMS makes these objects persistent and provides a programming language interface that allows objects to be read and written to secondary storage by application programs written in an object-oriented programming language such as C++.[11] An object-oriented DBMS may also provide an SQL-like query language for retrieving objects, although these query languages are often very limited in scope since SQL was designed to work with relations, not objects.

In the simplest sense, an object is a collection of data values that describe some physical thing or abstract concept that exists in an application. The object may also contain a set of operations that define how the object is manipulated. An application program manipulates an object by invoking these operations. For example, if we were to redesign our inventory database as an object-oriented database, we might have ITEM objects, SUPPLIER objects, and SALE objects, as shown in Fig. 9.5. Relationships between the objects are often implemented by having one object directly reference an object it is related to, as shown in the figure.

11. B. Stroustrup, "The C++ Programming Language," 2nd ed. (Reading: MA: Addison-Wesley, 1991).

Some similarity is obvious between the data structures in Figs. 9.4 and 9.5. In fact, some people believe that the object-oriented DBMS is really just a special case of the network DBMS. There is also a debate in the database research community as to whether an object-oriented DBMS should be implemented as a stand-alone system or implemented on top of an existing relational DBMS to take advantage of the existing relational technology.[12] Time will tell which approach is the better one.

The object-oriented DBMS is just beginning to be commercially viable and has yet to take any significant market share. A few general-purpose object-oriented DBMSs are available commercially—for example, Object Store, Versant, and OpenODB—but these systems lack the robustness of relational systems. Other special-purpose object-oriented DBMSs are also commercially available, such as ST-Developer, which is designed specifically for design and manufacturing applications. It will be several years before the object-oriented DBMS establishes itself firmly in the commercial marketplace and becomes widely accepted, if it ever does.

9.4   Retrieving and Manipulating Data

From the discussion above, it is clear that one of the things that most significantly distinguishes between the different types of database systems is the type of query facility that is supported for retrieving and manipulating data. From the point of view of a distributed system, this is an important consideration. When a user or an application program issues a query requiring data from multiple nodes in the distributed system, the query must be broken into pieces and sent to the various nodes that contain the required data. Once each of these nodes retrieves the required data, the data must be collected and assembled into the final answer to the query. If this process can be done at a high abstract level using a declarative query language such as SQL, it is much easier to do than if it must be done at a lower more procedural level that requires generation of executable code to be processed by a DBMS in the distributed system. This is one of the main reasons why the relational model dominates the commercial market today. This ability to view query processing in a declarative rather than in a procedural way adds yet another level of data independence to distributed database systems. As long as the nodes of a distributed system can process SQL queries, it does not matter what changes

---

12. M. Atkinson et al., "The Object-Oriented Database System Manifesto" (proceedings of the First International Conference on Distributed and Object-Oriented Design, Kyoto, Japan, Elsevier Science Publishers, 1989); The Committee for Advanced DBMS Function, "Third-Generation Database System Manifesto," *ACM SIGMOD Record* 19, no. 3 (1990): 31–44.

are made to a particular node in the system. Other nodes can continue to send it SQL queries and expect to get the results of those queries in return.

Processing a query expressed in SQL involves several steps. First, it is necessary to parse and validate the query. Standard parsing techniques developed for compilers to parse programming languages are used to parse SQL queries. Validation of the query requires checking the names used in the SELECT, FROM, and WHERE clauses of the query to determine that the relations named in the FROM clause exist in the database, and that the attributes named in the SELECT and WHERE clauses are part of those relations. This validation is done using a data dictionary constructed from the schema for the database. Most relational DBMSs store this data dictionary as a set of relations. For example, one relation lists all the other relations in the database and a second relation lists all the attributes in those relations. By storing the data dictionary in this way, the DBMS is able to exploit existing functionality to manage the data dictionary, simplifying the overall design of the DBMS itself.

Once a query has been parsed and validated, the DBMS must generate a plan to compute the answer to the query. This is often done by making a list of all possible ways to process the query, computing an estimated cost for each way, and selecting the way that has the minimum estimated cost. For example, consider the following SQL query for our inventory database:

> SELECT ItemNames, Price
>
> FROM ITEM, SALES
>
> WHERE SALES.Item# = ITEM.Item# AND Salesperson = "Mary"

This query asks for the names and prices of the items sold by Mary. One way to compute the answer to this query is to look at the tuples in the ITEM relation one by one. For each of these tuples we search the SALES relation to see if there is a tuple in the SALES relation indicating that Mary sold the item. Another way to process the query is to look at the SALES tuples one by one. When a SALES tuple is found that lists Mary as the salesperson, we use the Item# in the tuple to search the ITEM relation for the ITEM tuple with this item number and extract the name of the item from this tuple. Other approaches for processing the query exist as well.

In particular, the index often plays an important role in efficiently processing queries. Conceptually, an index can be viewed as a table that defines a mapping between the value of an attribute in the column of a relation and the virtual addresses of the tuples in the relation that contain that value. Thus, for example, if there is an index on the Item# attribute of the SALES relation, this index would list each Item# value and the virtual address of the tuple containing that value. There are several data structures that can be used to construct indices for efficient search, but the B-Tree data structure is one of the most popular and efficient.[13]

Most relational DBMSs allow the creation of an index for any attribute of any relation. For example, if there is an index on the Salesperson attribute of the SALES relation, then this index can be used in the second plan above to quickly find the SALES tuples for Mary. If no such index exists, then the SALES relation must be searched in its entirety to find all tuples recording sales by Mary. In the first plan above, an index on the Item# attribute of the SALES relation would make it easier to find the tuples in the SALES relation for a particular item number. Similarly, an index on the Item# attribute of the ITEM relation will make it easier in the second plan to find the name of an item given its item number.

There are many ways to build an index for an attribute of a relation, but the most popular approach for a relational DBMS is to use a B-tree index.[14] A B-tree index has a tree structure that is very broad and not very deep (i.e., each node in the tree has many child nodes). It is based on information theory concepts that partition the ordered set of attribute values into blocks so that the probability that the desired attribute value is in a particular block is roughly the same for all the blocks at a given level of the B-Tree index. Each block forms a node in the B-Tree. Since the attribute values in a block (node) are ordered, searching the index requires starting at the root of the tree and following a path through the tree to a leaf node from one level of the partition to the next. Each node of the B-tree index along this path must be retrieved from secondary storage. Since the tree is shallow, not many nodes must be retrieved, so searching the index can be done efficiently with minimal secondary storage accesses.

While an index can improve performance of query processing, there are important tradeoffs to consider. An index requires space to store it and must be updated every time the database changes. If there are indices for many of the attributes of a relation, then every time a tuple is inserted into the relation or deleted from it, all these indices must be updated. This quickly becomes expensive if insertions and deletions are frequent operations. It is common to have an index for the primary key of a relation and possibly for a few of the other frequently used attributes in a relation, but it is not common to have an index on all attributes of a relation for these reasons.

Getting back to the processing of a query, we see that indices must be considered in generating the list of plans for processing a query. The data dictionary for the database usually indicates what indices exist for each relation to help in generating this list.

---

13. D. Comer, "The Ubiquitous B-Tree," *Computing Surveys* 11, no. 2 (June 1979): 121–138.

14. M. Stonebraker, "Relational Implementation Techniques," in M. Stonebraker, ed., *Readings in Database Systems,* 2nd ed. (San Mateo, CA: Morgan Kaufman Publishers, 1994), ch. 2.

Once the list of plans has been generated, the cost of processing the query using each of the plans is estimated. These estimates are based on a set of rules and database statistics, such as the sizes of the relations in the database and the sizes of the indices that exist. These statistics are usually maintained by the DBMS in the data dictionary. Estimating the cost of processing a query often involves computing estimates of the sizes of intermediate results. These estimated sizes are then used to predict the amount of CPU time and the number of secondary storage accesses that will be needed to retrieve this quantity of data from the database.

As an example, a rule might state that to estimate the size of the result of a query with a WHERE clause of the form

Attribute = value,

when an index exists for the attribute, divide the number of tuples in the relation by the size of the index. For example, suppose that the SALES relation contains an index on the Salesperson attribute and that this index has 50 entries corresponding to 50 different salespeople. Suppose also that the SALES relation has 10,000 tuples. The expected number of SALES tuples that satisfy the clause Salesperson = "Mary" is then 10,000/50 = 200 tuples. Clearly, this is a rough estimate with potentially large error, but it is a quick and easy way to compute the estimated number of tuples that satisfy the query clause. Experience using these techniques to estimate the cost of query processing in a relational DBMS indicates that they usually produce a poor estimate of the actual cost of processing a query. However, relative to the different plans, the costs are ordered correctly so that the correct plan is selected as the cheapest for processing the query.[15]

Other forms of optimization can also be used to improve the performance of query processing. For example, in the abstract sense, relations can be manipulated by selecting a subset of the rows, projected down to a subset of the columns, or joining two relations together by matching tuples in the two relations that share the same value in a specified column of both relations. Most queries can be answered by using a series of these selection, projection, and join operations. Processing a selection or a projection operation is more efficient than processing a join of two relations. If all selections and projections are done before any joins, then the sizes of the two relations that must be joined are as small as possible, making the join operation as efficient as possible.[16]

---

15. P. Selinger et al., "Access Path Selection in a Relational Database Management System," (proceedings of the ACM SIGMOD Internatinal Conference, Boston, MA, 1979): 23–34.

16. J. Smith and P. Chang, "Optimizing the Performance of a Relational Algebra Interface," *Communications of the ACM* 18, no. 10 (October 1975): 568–579.

Once the optimal plan for processing a query has been identified, the final step in query processing is the execution of that plan. Some DBMSs generate executable code to process the query while others use an interpreter to interpret an internal representation of the query.[17] The time required to generate code is often significantly less than the time saved by executing code rather than interpreting the query.

Note that the discussed optimization techniques are all static—that is, all the optimization is performed prior to the actual execution of the query. More recently, dynamic query optimization techniques, the optimization of the performance of the query as part of its actual computation, have been employed.[18] Based on the characteristics of the intermediate relations obtained in such optimization, a change in the planned execution strategy is possible.

9.5   The Concept of Database Views

Figure 9.2 illustrated the three levels in the architecture of a DBMS. Level 3 is the external level and consists of external schemas that define subsets of a database relevant to a particular group of application systems. The purpose of these external schemas is to simplify the database so that an application system need not be concerned with the parts of the database that it will not use.

The relational DBMS carries this idea one step further by allowing the users of a database to define their own subsets, called "views," of a database. A user can define as many views as desired and can use multiple views simultaneously in a query to simplify manipulation of the database. A view is a specification of a useful subset of a database expressed in a high-level query language such as SQL. For example, using SQL we can define a view of the inventory database that contains the names and prices of all items sold by Mary. Mary might create this view to make it easier for her to review her sales data. In SQL, this view would be defined as follows:

> CREATE VIEW MarysSales(ItemName, Price)
>
> AS SELECT ItemName, Price
>
> FROM ITEM, SALES

---

17. M. Astrahan et al., "System R: Relational Approach to Database Management System," *ACM Transactions on Database Systems* 1, no. 2 (June, 1976): 97–137; M. Stonebraker, E. Wong, P. Krebs, and G. Held, "The Design and Implementation of INGRES," *ACM Transactions on Database Systems* 1, no. 3 (September 1976): 189–222.

18. G. Graefe and K. Ward, "Dynamic Query Evaluation Plans," *ACM SIGMOD* (1989). F. Barlos and O. Frieder, "A Join Ordering Approach for Multicomputer Relational Databases with Highly Skewed Data," *HICSS–27* (January 1994): 420.

WHERE ITEM.Item# = SALES.Item# AND SalesPerson = 'Mary'

Conceptually, from the point of view of query processing, this view is just like having another relation in the database. It can be used in an SQL query just like any other relation. Physically, however, the view does not actually exist in secondary storage. Rather, when a query references the view, the data for the view are derived from the relations ITEM and SALE as part of processing the query. This process is sometimes called *view materialization*. The fact that a view is derived rather than being physically stored in the database is important because it means that the contents of the view is always based on the most up-to-date version of the database.

As an example, suppose that the following query is entered after the view above is defined:

> SELECT ItemName
>
> FROM MarysSales
>
> WHERE Price > 100

This query is asking for the names of all items sold by Mary for a price that is greater than $100. When the relational DBMS processes this query, it recognizes that MarysSales is a view and conceptually (although not necessary physically) modifies the query to the following:

> SELECT ItemName
>
> FROM ITEM, SALES
>
> WHERE ITEM.Item# = SALES.Item# AND SalesPerson = 'Mary'
> AND Price > 100

This modified query both materializes the view and retrieves the subset of the view that the original query requested. Suppose that Mary then sells several more items with a price greater than $100. If the query is run a second time after these sales, the new sales will be included in the new result of the query, since the view is materialized each time the query is run.

Views are primarily an enhancement to the user interface of a database. They provide no new functionality that is not already available in a DBMS. What they do provide is a simple way to develop "shortcuts" in expressing frequently asked queries. They also allow a user to simplify a database for an application that uses only a part of the database defined in an external schema. These benefits apply equally well in a centralized or distributed system. Views are also useful for security purposes, as is discussed below.

9.6   Data Integrity

The previous section focused on manipulating and retrieving data in a database. Equally important for a DBMS is the ability to maintain the integrity of the data it contains. If a company cannot trust a DBMS to maintain the integrity of data, then the usefulness of the DBMS is greatly diminished. Without this trust, the company cannot risk storing its critical data in a DBMS. As a result, most commercial DBMSs provide at least four types of services designed specifically to maintain the integrity of the data in a database: (1) enforcement of integrity constraints, (2) concurrency control, (3) backup and recovery, and (4) security enforcement.

9.6.1   Enforcement of Integrity Constraints

An *integrity constraint* is a specification of some semantic condition that must be maintained in a database for the database to remain valid. Examples of integrity constraints include the following: the quantity of an item in a warehouse must be nonnegative; all supplier numbers contained in the Supplier# attribute for tuples in the SUPPLIES relation must be valid supplier numbers for suppliers in the SUPPLIER relation; and all items in the ITEM relation must have unique item numbers. Ideally, it should be possible to specify integrity constraints such as these in the schema of a database when it is created and have the DBMS enforce them as the database is used, preventing any operations that would violate a constraint. This requires enforcement of the constraints during data entry to ensure that no incorrect values are entered into the database, as well as enforcement during all modifications to the database to ensure that no data item is changed to a value that violates an integrity constraint.

Most relational systems today allow some forms of integrity constraints to be specified and enforced. Uniqueness of primary keys and referential integrity in which a foreign key value used in one relation is constrained so that the same value must exist as a primary key in another relation are common examples. Most systems also allow constraints to be placed on the types of values stored in the attributes of relations. Some systems also enforce dependencies between relations so that when a tuple is deleted (created) in one relation a corresponding tuple must be deleted (created) in some other relation. For example, if you add a new item to the ITEM relation in the inventory database, you also need to add a new tuple to the SUPPLIES relation to specify who supplies the new item.

In the general case, integrity constraints are rules, and an integrity constraint manager for a DBMS is a rule processor. There is a substantial body of research that has been done on developing such general-purpose rule processors for database systems, but much of this work has yet to make it into commercial DBMSs.[19] Other related research areas include knowledge-based systems and deductive database systems.[20]

9.6.2   Concurrency Control

Consider the following situation. There is one ladder (item number 601) in a warehouse. Two customers walk into two different stores served by the warehouse and both ask to buy a ladder. A salesperson at each store accesses the database and determines that a ladder is available. Both stores then sell this ladder to their customers. Later, when they try to physically retrieve the ladder from the warehouse, one of the stores (whichever gets there second) will discover that the ladder they sold to a customer does not exist. Clearly, the company cannot effectively operate if this type of mistake is made frequently.

The problem here is caused by the fact that multiple people are using the database simultaneously, accessing and updating the same data in the database. If this concurrent activity is not carefully controlled, the integrity of the data in the database is corrupted, as seen in the example above. While in this case the problem can be solved with an apology and a refund to one of the customers, in other situations (for example, in a bank) such a problem could be much more serious and jeopardize the future of the company involved. This problem is known as the *concurrency control problem*, and it has been studied extensively.[21]

In our warehouse example, we said that the problem is caused by concurrent users of the database. This is only half the story, however. The reason that this type of concurrent activity can lead to problems such as the one above is that a typical interaction with the database may involve several steps and those steps may only be semantically correct if they are done without interference from other users using the database. For example, each salesperson might execute the following algorithm:

19. M. Stonebraker et al., "The POSTGRES Rules System," *IEEE Transactions on Software Engineering* 14, no. 7 (July 1988): 879–907.

20. E. Hanson, "Rule Condition Testing and Action Execution in Ariel" (Proceedings of the ACM SIGMOD International Conference, San Diego, June 1992); R. Ramakrishnan and J. Ullman, "Survey of Research in Deductive Database Systems," *Journal of Logic Programming* 23, no. 2 (May 1995): 125–149.

21. P. Bernstein, V. Hadzilacos, and N. Goodman, *Concurrency Control and Recovery in Database Systems* (Reading, MA: Addison-Wesley, 1988); A. J. Bernstein and P. M. Lewis, *Concurrency in Programming and Database Systems* (Boston, MA: Jones and Bartlett, 1993).

1.   Read the quantity of item 601 from the ITEM relation into variable Q

2.   If Q > 0 then

2.1   record the sale by creating a tuple in the SALES relation

2.2   Q := Q − 1

2.3   write Q into the ITEM relation as the new quantity of item 601

2.4   else

2.5   display a message saying the item 601 is out of stock

If the two salespersons both start the algorithm at approximately the same time, then it is possible for them to both execute step 1 before either executes step 2. The result is the problem above.

To prevent this type of problem, we must make a sequence of steps such as this one behave like one atomic operation so that once a salesperson begins execution of the first step in the algorithm all other salespersons are unable to begin the sequence until the first salesperson completes the sequence. If this can be guaranteed, then such problems cannot occur. This is the motivation behind the concept of a *transaction*—a set of operations performed against a database that takes the database from one consistent state to another. The algorithm above is an example of a transaction. If a DBMS can guarantee that all transactions are executed as atomic operations, then the concurrency control problem is solved.

The obvious solution is to have a DBMS execute only one transaction at a time; but this is not a practical solution. Most transactions operate on mutually exclusive parts of the database and can be executed concurrently without causing any problems. For performance reasons, it is necessary to let such transactions execute concurrently. It is often the case that only a small percentage of transactions conflict with one another by accessing the same data. Thus we must find a solution to the concurrency control problem that will allow transactions to be executed concurrently unless they conflict.

The solution that most commercial DBMSs use to solve this problem is known as *two-phase locking*.[22] It is derived from a formal theory of concurrent execution of transactions known as *serializability theory*.[23] If we assume that a database will remain consistent as long as all transactions are executed serially

22. K. Eswaran et al., "The Notions of Consistency and Predicate Locks in a Data Base System," *Communicaitons of the ACM* 19, no. 11 (November 1976).

23. J. Gray, R. Lorie, and G. Putzulo, "Granularity of Locks in a Shared Data" (proceedings of the International Conference on Very Large Data Bases, Boston, MA, September 1975).

one after the other, then we can prove that a database with concurrent transactions is consistent if we can show that its contents is the same as it would have been if the transactions had been executed serially. The theory goes on to develop the conditions that must be satisfied by a DBMS as it concurrently executes transactions to be able to guarantee this. These conditions can be met in several ways, one of which is two-phase locking.

In two-phase locking every transaction must obtain a *read lock* on an item in a database (e.g., a tuple in a relation) before it can read that item, and it must hold a *write lock* on an item before it can write that item. Many transactions can have read locks on the same database item, but only one transaction can hold a write lock on a particular item at a time, and if a write lock exists no read locks can exist simultaneously for that item (i.e., write locks are exclusive). As a transaction executes, it obtains the locks that it needs to perform its database reads and writes. If it attempts to lock an item and cannot get the lock because another transaction has a conflicting lock, then it is blocked and must wait for the transaction holding the conflicting lock to terminate. Once a transaction releases a lock, it cannot request any new locks. This explains the term two-phase locking. During the first phase, a transaction accumulates locks; during the second phase, the transaction gives up locks. If all transactions obey this two-phase requirement, then serializability theory tells us that the resulting database will be equivalent to the database that would have resulted from executing the transactions serially in some order.

Two-phase locking is a simple and efficient way to solve the concurrency control problem, but it is not without problems. In particular, because transactions are forced to wait while they hold locks, there is the possibility of deadlock in which a group of transactions are all waiting for one another and none will ever be able to complete. Thus, when two-phase locking is used, it is necessary to check for the presence of deadlock periodically.

Two-phase locking can also be used for concurrency control in distributed systems, but the implementation is more difficult. For example, suppose a transaction has pieces that are currently executing on several nodes of a network. One of the pieces is ready to release its first lock. How does it know whether the other pieces executing on the other nodes of the network have obtained all the locks they will need so that it can go ahead and release a lock? If it releases the lock and another piece of the transaction on another node later tries to obtain a lock, the two-phase requirement is violated and the consistency of the database is no longer guaranteed. The solution commonly used is called *strict two-phase locking*. In this case all the pieces of the transaction hold all locks until the very end. They then send messages to one another making sure that they are all done and ready to commit (terminate) the transaction. When these messages are received from all pieces of the transaction, each piece then releases its locks and terminates. Deadlock detection is also more complicated in a distributed system, but the standard deadlock detection algorithms can be generalized to handle this case as well.[24]

9.6.3   Backup and Recovery

Consider now a related but different problem. Suppose that a salesperson sells an item and is in the middle of processing this sale using the algorithm above. The quantity of the item in the warehouse is retrieved and a record of the sale written to the SALES relation. However, before the quantity is decremented and written back to the ITEM relation to complete the transaction, the salesperson's computer fails for some reason. The database is now inconsistent since the quantity of the item in the ITEM relation is one larger than it should be. The problem here is that a transaction, which is supposed to be an atomic operation, is in actual fact not atomic; only part of the transaction is executed against the database. To avoid this type of problem, a DBMS must guarantee that either all of a transaction is executed, or none of it is. The solution to this problem is to use a *backup and recovery* mechanism that will restore the database to a consistent state should a transaction abort in the middle.

A transaction can fail for many reasons. A hardware problem on the computer that is running the transaction may prevent the transaction from completing, the code that implements the transaction may have an error in it that causes it to abort, the DBMS itself may fail for some reason, or in a distributed system the communications between the computer executing the transaction and the DBMS may fail. In all these cases, the DBMS must be able to restore the database to a consistent state.

There are several approaches that can be used to provide a backup and recovery mechanism in a DBMS, and most of them are based on creating a log of database activity. Every operation that the DBMS performs is written in a log. This log includes the type of the operation, which transaction performed the operation, and, for updates, the original and the modified values of the tuple that is updated. Then, if a transaction fails to complete, this log can be used to undo any operations that the aborted transaction completed before it failed. This restores the database to the state it would be in if the transaction had never started execution.

---

24. R. Obermark, "Distributed Deadlock Detection Algorithms," *ACM Transactions on Database Systems* 7, no. 2 (June 1982): 187–208.

The backup and recovery manager in a DBMS is a complex piece of code. For example, care must be taken to ensure that the log is an accurate record of the operations applied to a database. If the log record is written before a database operation is done and a failure occurs before the actual operation is performed, the log will contain erroneous data. On the other hand, if the log record is written after a database operation is done, then a failure immediately after an operation can prevent the log record from being written. As another example, consider the complexity of dealing with a situation where the DBMS itself fails in the middle of executing the backup and recovery manager for some other failed transaction. In this case, once the DBMS is restarted, it must be able to correctly recover both the failed transaction and its own failure. In a distributed system, these problems are compounded by failures of the communications between the nodes of the distributed system. More details on backup and recovery mechanisms are provided in a survey by Verhofstadt.[25]

9.6.4   Security and Access Control

The final type of service that a DBMS provides to ensure the integrity of a database is security and access control. This includes not only preventing unauthorized users from accessing data but also preventing unauthorized users from modifying the database to either maliciously or accidentally corrupt it. Most commercial relational systems today allow at a minimum the ability to selectively control which users can access which relations of a database. This is done with the specification of *access rules* that define specific privileges that a user has to read and write tuples in the database. In some DBMSs a special database administrator is responsible for defining all access rules. In other DBMSs, a user that creates a relation is designated the owner of that relation and is responsible for defining the access rules for it to allow other users to read and write its tuples.

Access rules are usually stored in a special relation that is part of the data dictionary. A typical access rule contains the name of a relation to which the rule applies, the name of the user to whom the access rule grants privileges, and the type of access (i.e., read or read/write) that is granted. Many DBMSs carry this one step further and allow access rules to be defined for individual attributes in a relation.

This is sometimes called *content-independent access control* because it is defined over the objects in the database independent of their content. Often it is convenient to make an access decision based on the content of the data that are

---

25. J. Verhofstadt, "Recovery Techniques for Database Systems," *ACM Computing Surveys* 10, no. 2 (June 1978): 167–196.

accessed. This is called *content-dependent access control.* For example, we might want to restrict salespersons to read and write only their own tuples in the SALES relation. There are at least two ways that this can be done. The most popular way is to use database views.[26] We will illustrate this technique for a salesperson named Mary. Mary is given no access rules allowing her access to the SALES relation. Hence she can neither read nor write tuples in this relation directly. Instead, we create the following view:

> CREATE VIEW SalesForMary(Item#, Salesperson, Price)
>
> AS SELECT Item#, Salesperson, Price
>
> FROM SALES
>
> WHERE Salesperson = 'Mary'

Mary is given access rules that allow her to read and write tuples in this view. As a result, she indirectly can read and write those tuples of the SALES relation that are her own.

The alternate approach to using views to provide content-dependent access control is to use a mechanism called *query modification.* When query modification is used, rather than defining a view for a user to provide access to a subset of a relation, an access predicate is defined for the user that is automatically attached by the DBMS to all queries that the user generates for that relation. Using the same example as above, a predicate would be defined for Mary's queries of the SALES relation: Salesperson = 'Mary'. Then the DBMS automatically "ands" this predicate to the WHERE clause of any of Mary's queries that access the SALES relation. For example, if Mary enters the query

> SELECT Item#
>
> FROM SALES
>
> WHERE Price > 100

the DBMS automatically changes this query to the following before processing it:

> SELECT Item#
>
> FROM SALES
>
> WHERE Price > 100 AND Salesperson = 'Mary'

26. P. Griffiths and B. Wade, "An Authorization Mechanism for a Relational Database System," *ACM Transactions on Database Systems* 1, no. 3 (September 1976): 242–255.

As a result, when this query is processed, only tuples recording sales by Mary are retrieved.

Conceptually, there is little difference between view creation and query modification for enforcing access rules in a DBMS. They both involve modification of a query by adding extra clauses that restrict the query to a subset of the named relations. Since most relational DBMSs have a view mechanism anyway, most chose to use it for access control, rather than creating an additional mechanism to implement query modification.

The access controls discussed above are sometimes called *discretionary access controls* because they are defined at the discretion of the database administrator or owner of a relation, usually based on a need-to-know policy. An additional form of access control known as *mandatory access control* can also be defined. Mandatory access controls partition data into classification levels and assign users of the database similar levels. A user can access data in the database only if the user's level dominates the level of the data that is accessed. Otherwise the access is denied. Mandatory access controls such as this are often required for government database systems to protect military, financial, and other sensitive governmental data. The research community is still debating how well mandatory access controls apply to nonmilitary commercial applications. The U.S. government has published a series of documents that define a rating scheme to measure how well a DBMS meets the mandatory security requirements of the government.[27] Several commercial DBMS vendors have developed special versions of their products to meet the requirements established by this rating scheme. The highest, most secure ratings in this scheme are in general unattainable today due to the requirement for formal verification of the correctness of the security mechanisms.

9.7   Other Issues

So far in this chapter we have discussed DBMSs, the services they provide, and how those services are implemented. However, from the end-user's point of view, there are other issues that are often of more concern. One such issue is how to design a database to be managed by a DBMS. Another is how to deal with the fact that the real world is constantly changing and these changes must be captured in the database. A final issue is user interface tools that can simplify the use of a DBMS.

---

27. U.S. Department of Defense, *Trusted Computer System Evaluation Criteria* (The Orange Book), Report Number CSC-STD–001–83 (Washington: Government Printing Office, August 1983).

9.7.1   The Design Process

Almost any database is a model of some aspect of the real world. For example, our inventory database captures part of the real-world operation of the company that owns the database. When the decision is made to automate some real-world system with a database, this database must be designed as an accurate and complete model of the real world. Like any design project, designing a database is not an easy task. Typically, it begins by interviewing the various future users of the database to obtain descriptions of how they currently perform the tasks that the database is to automate. From these interviews it is possible to piece together a general description of the data that must be in the database and a sketch of the application code that will manipulate the database. It is perhaps obvious that the data requirements are needed to design the database, but the sketches of application code are also important because they define performance criteria for the database and indicate patterns of access that can be used to optimize the database design.

At this point, the real design process begins. A tool that is commonly used for database design is the *entity relationship model*.[28] This approach is based on modeling the real world using entities and relationships between those entities. For example, in our inventory example, entities would be things such as items in the warehouse, suppliers who supply items and records of sales. Relationships exist between items and sales records since the latter records the selling of an item. Relationships also exist between suppliers and items since suppliers supply items. Both entities and relationships can have attributes that define the details of an entity or relationship. For example, an item entity might have attributes such as item number, item name, item quantity, and so forth. The relationship between a supplier and an item might have attributes such as quantity (if it is important to record the quantity of an item supplied by a particular supplier) and price (if different suppliers supply the same item at different prices). Note that in both cases, the attribute defines a property of the relationship between an item and a supplier, not a property of just the item or just the supplier.

The entity relationship model includes a graphical notation for expressing the design of a database using the model. This notation is a useful tool for design since it allows a database designer to draw a picture of the database organization and then manipulate this picture to correct and improve the design. Entities are represented by boxes and relationships by diamonds with lines connecting the entities that are related. Attributes are written near the entity or

28. P. Chen, "The Entity-Relationship Model—Toward a Unified View of Data," *ACM Transactions on Database Systems* 1, no. 1 (March 1976): 9–36.

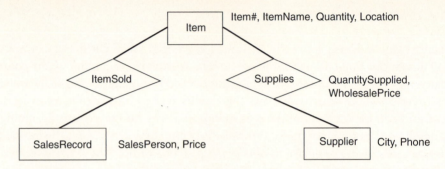

Figure 9.6   Entity relationship diagram for the inventory database

relationship they help define. Figure 9.6 illustrates an entity relationship diagram for our inventory database.

Once the design is complete, it must be translated into the schema definition language of the DBMS to be used. If this DBMS is relational, then the schema definition is done using CREATE TABLE commands in SQL. Each entity in the entity relationship diagram becomes a relation, where the attributes defined for the entity become the attributes of the relation. Each relationship also becomes a relation with foreign keys referencing tuples in the relations representing the entities contained in the relationship. For example, the Item, SalesRecord and Supplier entities in Fig. 9.6 become the ITEM, SALES and SUPPLIER relations in Fig. 9.1. Similarly, the Supplies relationship in Fig. 9.6 becomes the SUPPLIES relation in Fig. 9.1. Note that the ItemSold relationship in Fig. 9.6 does not occur as a separate relation in Fig. 9.1. Instead, it is merged into the SALES relation by including an Item# attribute in the SALES relation. This might be done, for example, to improve performance by eliminating the extra relation that would have been needed otherwise.

9.7.2   Schema Evolution

The real world is rarely static; things change all the time. A database that models some aspect of the real world must be able to change as well as to adapt to new situations and requirements. This is known as *schema evolution,* a process that allows a database to evolve through small changes to its content and structure without affecting the existing applications that use the database (unless they must take advantage of the new content or structure). This is another form of data independence. Schema evolution in the general sense is a hard problem to solve because new and old requirements can be contradictory and difficult to satisfy simultaneously for old applications and new. Yet rewriting and recompiling old applications to use a modified database can be expensive as well.

Many relational DBMSs support limited forms of schema evolution. New relations can be added to the database and sometimes new columns can be added to existing relations. Indices can be added to or deleted from a relation and integrity constraints and access rules added or removed. If more complex modifications are required, it is often necessary to dump the database to a set of files and then use these files to initialize a new database with the new structure.

In distributed systems, other types of schema evolution that are needed include migration of data from one node to another in the distributed system and the addition or deletion of copies of all or part of a database. Copies are used both to improve reliability of the system and performance by storing data close to where it is needed to reduce communications overhead. Hence, when the distributed system is tuned to improve performance, such changes are likely.

9.7.3   User Interface Tools

Many commercial DBMSs contain a variety of user interface tools to simplify the use of the system. One of the most common tools is a report generator that makes it easy to generate printed reports from the data in a database. Using a graphical interface or a simple report formatting language, the content and format of the report are defined as well as the data queries necessary to compute the values to be included for each field in the report. For example, in our inventory database, a daily sales report might be produced each night summarizing the sales for the day. The data for this report would be taken mostly from the SALES relation in the database.

Another common tool is a forms package for generating graphical forms on the user's screen to be used for entering data into the database. Most of these forms packages also provide integrity checking on the values entered for each field in a form so that only valid data are entered into the database. In our inventory database, we might have a form for processing a sale. A salesperson would fill out the form on the computer screen as the sale is made and the data in this form would be used to produce the record of the sale in the SALES relation of the inventory database.

Other user interface tools that are common include graphing tools for generating plots and charts from the data in a database and high-level query interfaces that allow users to enter queries in a limited natural language style and then translate the query to SQL for processing. In general, the user interface is one of the least developed areas for DBMSs. Research is needed to expand the functionality of user interface tools to simplify the use of DBMSs and make them more widely usable by the general public.

9.8   Current and Future Trends

Database management is a developing field within the computer science research community. Much has been accomplished to reach the state described above, but much work remains to make systems more flexible and easier to use, to improve performance, and to facilitate the development of commercially viable distributed systems. In this section, we provide a brief overview of three potentially important trends in the development of database systems.

9.8.1   Client-Server Architectures

As we have seen, centralized database systems are commonplace today but distributed database systems are not. That is not to say that distributed systems do not exist, because they certainly do (airline reservation systems being a notable example); but the existing systems are largely special purpose rather than general purpose. The difficulties of handling distributed query processing, concurrency control, and backup and recovery in the general case limits the commercial viability of general-purpose distributed systems today. Instead a compromise between centralized and distributed systems, often called *client-server systems,* is becoming popular.

In the simplest sense, a client-server system is a distributed system in which the nodes of the network are partitioned into server nodes and client nodes. The server nodes each contain a database system. The client nodes run user application programs and other query tools. When a query is executed at one of the client nodes, a message is sent through the network from the client node to a server node that contains the requested data. The data are retrieved by the server node using the DBMS at that node and sent back to the client node.

In this simple case, which is the most common case today, the servers are individual nodes with centralized database systems that operate independently of the other nodes of the network. In the more general case, the servers may be distributed themselves, leading to all the problems of distributed database systems within the server. The DBMS for a server, whether centralized or distributed, processes queries from client nodes as if they were entered by a user at the server directly. A small front-end to the DBMS at the server handles the communications with client nodes but behaves like a local user from the point of view of the DBMS at the server. If we assume the simplest case where the server is a single centralized DBMS, then this DBMS need not deal with the problems of distributed query processing, concurrency control, and backup and recovery. The advantage in this case is that many users from many different locations in a network can all share a database more or less transparently. All that is needed on a client node is a small DBMS interface that passes all DBMS requests through the network to the appropriate server.

The client-server approach has several disadvantages when compared to a truly distributed DBMS, however. First, even if there are multiple server nodes on a network, a query from a client node must be restricted to a single server since the servers operate independently of one another. Hence, true distributed query processing across multiple servers does not exist, and there is no synchronization between the servers. Second, because there is no synchronization between the servers, replication of data between servers is restricted, with a resulting reduction in reliability.

Nevertheless, the advantages of client-server systems over strictly centralized systems can be significant for organizations whose computing requirements are best supported by a network of personal computers or workstations and for organizations that frequently need to expand their computing resources by acquiring new computers. In these situations, all the computers have access to the databases at the server nodes from anywhere on the network. Many commercial database systems support a client-server mode of operation. One of the first systems to do this was Sybase, but other systems have since been released in client-server versions.

9.8.2   Multimedia Databases

The proliferation of personal computers and workstations with sophisticated graphical interfaces has created great interest in the use of multimedia applications—applications that integrate text, graphics, audio, video, and other media into a single application. Multimedia is becoming popular for a wide variety of uses, ranging from educational and vocational training to business and marketing to entertainment. As multimedia systems become more sophisticated, it becomes necessary to use database technology to manage the data that are part of the system. This creates many challenges for traditional forms of database technology that were designed to handle textual data. The database systems must now handle bit strings of arbitrary size representing such things as graphical images, audio passages, and video clips. The systems must be able to locate and retrieve these data at speeds sufficient to support real-time audio and video and to synchronize the simultaneous playback of multiple media at once.

Object-oriented database technology is considered promising as a solution to the problems of storing data representing a wide variety of media. Experimental multimedia projects have shown that object-oriented systems can outperform relational systems for many types of multimedia applications.[29] However, research in this area is only beginning. As the interest in multimedia grows, one should expect the research in multimedia database systems to grow as well.

9.8.3   Knowledge Bases

The logical evolutionary path for database management systems is toward systems that incorporate and exploit more of the semantics of the data in the database. For example, semantic integrity constraints that define more precisely valid states for the data in a database and valid operations that manipulate these data greatly enhance the accuracy and dependability of the database. Rules that allow new data to be derived from existing data simplify the process of query specification from the user's point of view. General-purpose rule systems that are part of a DBMS can be used to implement such things as query processing and optimization, integrity enforcement, security and access control, and concurrency control, simplifying the overall implementation of the DBMS and allowing the operation of the DBMS to be tailored more easily to a particular organization's operating policies.[30]

Systems that incorporate additional semantics of the data they manage in the form of constraints and rules are called *knowledge based systems*. When the rules are used to trigger actions in the DBMS based on the results of prior actions, the systems are sometimes called *active systems*. Knowledge-based and active systems are receiving a great deal of attention from the research community.[31] Few if any general-purpose systems exist today, but many experimental systems are under development in research organizations. It is clear that database systems are evolving in this direction.

29. D. Woelk, W. Luther, and W. Kim, "Multimedia Applications and Database Requirements" (proceedings of the IEEE Office Automation Symposium, IEEE Computer Society Press, Los Alamitos, CA, April 1987).

30. M. Stonebraker and G. Kemnitz, "The POSTGRES Next-Generation Database Management System," *Communications of the ACM* 34, no. 10 (October 1991): 78–92.

31. L. Kerschberg, ed., "Expert Database Systems" (proceedings of the First International Workshop on Expert Database Systems, Kiawah Island, South Carolina, October 1984) Benjamin/Cummings, 1986; L. Kerschberg, ed., "Expert Database Systems," (proceedings of the Second International Conference on Expert Database Systems, Charleston, South Carolina, April 1986), Benjamin/Cummings, 1987.

9.9   Information Retrieval

A problem that is related to database management is information retrieval. There are several important differences between database management and information retrieval, however. The most important is that information retrieval focuses on storing and retrieving unstructured data (e.g., text), as opposed to the structured data in a database system (e.g., records). This has important impacts on the way data are stored, indexed, and queried in an information retrieval system. Since information retrieval systems are designed to handle unstructured data, they are better able to manage multimedia data that includes text, graphics, video, and audio.

We will not discuss information retrieval in detail here. A discussion of related issues on this topic can be found in Chapter 12.

9.10   Summary and Comments

While database technology has advanced to the point where centralized database systems and even simple client-server database systems are commonplace, there are many technical problems that must be overcome before truly distributed general purpose database systems become practical. One of the most fundamental problems that must be solved is efficient handling of heterogeneous data and data structures when database systems of different types are combined to form a distributed system. When data are moved from one node to another as part of query processing, their structure must be changed to match the structure of the target database system. Queries written by the user in a high-level query language such as SQL must be decomposed into subqueries for processing by the database systems at the various nodes of the distributed system. If these systems are not all relational, then generating these subqueries is more difficult. In addition, since most common security enforcement mechanisms depend to at least some degree on the query processing mechanism in a system, this added complexity has important implications for security enforcement in distributed systems.

Enforcement of data integrity is also significantly more complex in a distributed system. Integrity constraints may have to be enforced for data that are distributed across several nodes of the network. An update at any one of these nodes can violate a global integrity constraint involving data at several nodes. Even more complex is concurrency control in a distributed system. As discussed above, the simple two-phase locking scheme no longer works and strict two-phase locking must be used. Deadlock detection, which is necessary any time two-phase locking is used, becomes more difficult and less efficient.

Backup and recovery are more complicated in distributed systems because of the potential for communications failures. This potential adds a degree of uncertainty to all aspects of data management. The extreme case is a network failure that partitions the network so that the nodes in each partition are able to continue operation but coordination between partitions is prevented. Reconciling the database when communications are restored may then be difficult, especially if the database is replicated so that it contains multiple copies of a particular data item.

While these problems are significant, there is substantial research underway to develop robust and efficient solutions to them. The theoretical results that have been obtained to date must be migrated into experimental systems for testing and evaluation. This is starting to happen. The arrival of general-purpose distributed database systems in the commercial marketplace will not be far behind.

9.11   Problems

1. You have been hired by a large university to design a database that includes academic data about the university. Some of the information in this database will be related to students, faculty, departments, courses, grades, and transcripts.

    (a) Develop an entity relationship diagram for this database. Use your knowledge about the organization of a typical university to provide the details needed to complete the design. (b) Convert the entities and the relationships in your diagram into a set of relations that implement the university database. (c) Assume that the university has several branch campuses located in other cities and a distributed network of computers that link the campuses. How would you distribute the database between the computers at each campus? On what do you base your decisions? Make any assumptions that you feel are necessary and state what they are and why they are needed.

2. Assume that the inventory database in Fig. 9.1 is implemented as a distributed database. The warehouse has a computer that contains the Inventory relation, the company headquarters has a computer that contains the Supplier and Supplies relations, and there are three stores that share a computer that contains the Sales relation.

    (a) Suppose that someone at the company headquarters enters the following SQL query:

    SELECT Item#, ItemName, Quantity

    FROM ITEM, SALES

    WHERE SalesPerson = "Mary" AND Price > 100.00

            AND SALES.Item# = ITEM.Item#

The query processor for the distributed database system must take this query and break it into pieces to be executed at the individual nodes containing the data requested by the query. We will assume that the results of these query pieces are then sent to the warehouse computer where the final processing is done. Use SQL syntax to show the query pieces to be executed by each node as this query is processed. Describe the final processing that must be done by the warehouse computer to compute the final answer to the query once the results of all the query pieces have been moved to the warehouse computer. (b) Suppose that someone at one of the stores enters the following SQL query:

SELECT Supplier#, Phone

FROM SUPPLIER, SUPPLIES, ITEM, SALES

WHERE SalesPerson = "John" AND

Quantity = 0 AND

SALES.Item# = ITEM.Item# AND

SUPPLIES.Item# = SALES.Item# AND

SUPPLIER.Supplier# = SUPPLIES.Supplier#

The query processor for the distributed database system must take this query and break it into pieces to be executed at the individual nodes containing the data requested by the query. We will assume that the results of these query pieces are then sent to the store's computer where the final processing is done. Use SQL syntax to show the query pieces to be executed by each node as the query is processed. Describe the final processing that must be done by the store's computer to compute the final answer to the query once the results of all the query pieces have been moved to the store's computer.

3. Consider two transactions, T1 and T2. Transaction T1 executes the following sequence of operations against a database: *read(x), read(y), write(x), write(y), write(z)*, where *x*, *y*, and *z* are data items in the database. Transaction T2 executes the following sequence of operations against the same database: *read(z), write(z), read(x), write(x)*.

   (a) If these two transactions are allowed to execute concurrently, they can interfere with one another. In other words, the final state of the database after these two transactions execute may not be equivalent to the state of the database if the two transactions were executed serially (in either order). Explain what can go wrong when these two transactions are allowed to execute concurrently. (b) Two-phase locking can be used to control these two transactions so that if they try to execute concurrently, they are prevented from interfering with one another and the problems from part (a) do not occur. Explain how two-phase locking prevents these problems. (c) Suppose now that transactions T1 and T2 are executed against a distributed database with data items *x*, *y*, and *z* each at different nodes in the distributed system. If we assume that each node implements its own two-phase locking algorithm independently of the other nodes, then the problems in part (a) may again occur. Explain how this can happen. (d) Strict two-phase locking must be used in distributed systems to prevent concurrently executing transactions from interfering with one another. Explain why strict two-phase locking prevents the problems from part (a) when normal two-phase locking does not. How much communication between the nodes of the distributed system is required to implement strict two-phase locking?

4. Remember that the schema of a database contains a description of the data in the database and its structure. As a result, a DBMS must consult the schema frequently when processing queries. An interesting question for the designer of a distributed DBMS is where to store the schema. There are several options, each with its advantages and disadvantages.

(a) One option is to store the complete schema at one node of the distributed system and require all other nodes to consult that single copy of the schema. List several advantages and disadvantages of this approach. (b) Another option is to allow each node in the distributed system to contain the schema for the part of the database stored at that node. List several advantages and disadvantages of this approach. (c) A third option is to replicate the full schema at all nodes in the distributed system. List several advantages and disadvantages of this approach. (d) Can you think of other approaches that can be used to store the schema of a distributed database? What are the advantages and disadvantages of your approach(es)?

Chapter 10

Interfacing Systems, Protocols, and Standards

The tasks of a data communication system include delivery of information that is correct, in proper sequential order, and understandable to the recipient.

Dictionaries define "protocols" as being a set of rules and ceremonies by which diplomats and heads of state communicate. The rules of diplomatic protocol ensure that communications are completely and correctly understood by both parties. In data communications, protocols perform a similar function, and their use is almost as complex as the use of diplomatic protocols.

John E. McNamara[1]

10.1 Chapter Objectives

In any exchange of information it is important that the participants clearly understand what is intended. This requires far more than just conveying the text of a message. As an example, the phrase "clear the runway" spoken by an aircraft control tower operator to clear the runway of vehicles so a plane can land, if misunderstood by a snowplow operator, can lead to disastrous results. World history is full of conflicts that started because of messages that in the formal language sense were correct in syntax and semantics, but which were misinterpreted or misunderstood by the recipients. In our experience with computer systems, there are a correspondingly large number of examples in which messages were received correctly by a computer but misunderstood with unfortunate consequences.

1. John E. McNamara, *Technical Aspects of Data Communications*, 3rd ed. (Bedford, Mass.: Digital Equipment Corporation, 1988).

Effectively interconnecting the different components of a distributed computer system is a complicated and challenging problem. This is true whether the components already exist, or the system is new and being designed from a "top down" approach. In fact, the interfacing of "foreign systems" may well be the area in which there is the most serious lack of understanding today. It is a complex and fundamental problem that will not go away in the foreseeable future. By the term "foreign systems" we imply different hardware, systems software, applications software, or all three. As has been noted, the objective is the ability to connect in a meaningful fashion any two arbitrary information systems. The terms "open world" and "open systems" refer to that objective and environment.

This chapter will focus on the issues involved in interfacing foreign systems—from pragmatic ones such as what we can do today, through the impact of economic, social and governmental trends, to theoretical questions such as the limit of what it is reasonable to expect from standards. At the theoretical end of the spectrum, we do not have a framework that will tell us in general what the necessary and sufficient conditions are for it to be possible to interface two arbitrary systems, nor do we have a sound basis for establishing standards. Whether solutions suggested by a more complete theoretical understanding would be viable is an open question. From a complexity theory viewpoint, the computations might be too time consuming. There is also the possibility that the answers to some issues of interest might be noncomputable.

It is important that readers understand the importance of protocols and standards. It is also important that they have some picture of our abilities in these areas today, including the limitations on those abilities. Providing perspective involves current practice, state-of-the-art technology, political and economic realities, and the consequences of the limitations of our knowledge in these areas. Our emphasis is on the overall picture. To use an analogy we invoked earlier, we are interested in the forest as a whole. At the same time, there are included examples of trees in the forest and a great many references to specific details. However, in this text, we do not wish to get so involved with the details that we lose sight of the overall picture. This is very easy to do in a field in which there are an overwhelming number of rapidly changing approaches and details.

10.2 Protocols for Distributed Systems

We shall use the term "transport" to indicate moving or transporting a message between two points. Protocols and standards are essential in the transport of messages. However, in the context of distributed information systems, protocols and standards are more of an information system issue than a data communications issue. They are concerned with far more than just transporting messages between systems. A good parallel can be found in the U.S. mail system. The post office transports an envelope that you mail and its contents between two points. Your message is contained in the envelope. What that message means to the recipient is of no concern to the post office. The post office system addresses the pure transport problem. If the message is in a language that you do not understand, or is concerned with areas unfamiliar to you so that you do not understand the message, that is your problem. To mail a letter, you must follow certain transport protocols. If you follow those protocols, you have every reason to believe that the letter will arrive. Whether the contents of the letter will be understood is a different matter.

We cannot have distributed computer systems that address only the transport problem of messages. We must ensure that messages are meaningful to the recipients. Applications, if they are to work together, need a common understanding at the level of both data and information. Succinctly, the various applications must be able to communicate with one another in a meaningful fashion. Each must be able to do so in the context of its application. Since applications that have an interest in a common set of data may be quite different, establishing a satisfactory set of protocols can be difficult.

Zimmerman, Lorin, and others have pointed out that establishing protocols and standards is perhaps the central issue of distributed computers.[2] Their orientation is toward filling the needs of distributed applications, not just transport. We prefer the term distributed information systems rather than distributed applications, but we will use the terms synonymously. Of course there are many other issues, but satisfactory protocols and standards appear to be a necessary condition for distributed information systems to function in an integrated fashion. There is much written today about "communications protocols" that implies that protocols are an issue in communications. The context is communications in the classical communications or transport sense. Let it be clearly established that for computers the primary problem is interfacing at the information system level. As we have pointed out, protocols are needed that are concerned with the transport of data, but transport is the simple part of the problem. Meaning, along with the ability to make use of received data at the application level, is essential and the more difficult part. We need protocols and standards that will facilitate the latter.

2. H. Zimmermann, "On Protocol Engineering" (Information Processing 83: Proceedings of IFIP Ninth Computer Congress, North Holland, 1983); Harold Lorin, *Aspects of Distributed Computer Systems*, 2nd ed. (New York: Wiley, 1988), ch. 6.

10.3 Layered Protocols

The discussion above implies that there should be protocols that apply to the transport of data and also protocols that apply to the exchange of information between applications. This suggests that a layered structure should be considered. The reader is undoubtedly familiar with and has used layered protocols for there are many examples in real life:

> In letters there are protocols for formatting a letter: the form of the address, the salutation, the order in which things are presented, the closing statement, the procedure for submitting the letter to the post office, etc.

> In many organizations it is understood that communications are to go through channels (e.g., from boss to boss up the chain of command). This set of protocols is particularly rigid in the military where the rules pertaining to endorsing, commenting on, forwarding, etc., are clearly defined.

> There are protocols to be followed in conducting meetings. Many readers will be familiar with Robert's Rules of Order for the conduct of meetings.

> There are protocols that are to be used in addressing surface mail and protocols for addressing electronic mail. Just try reversing the order or levels in an electronic mail address; you know that the message will bounce back to you.

It is convenient to consider protocols in a layered structure, such as that shown in Fig. 10.1. For the time being, we shall put at the bottom level those protocols and standards that have to do with the transporting of physical messages. We shall call this the physical transport level and designate it as level 1. At the top we shall put the applications that the information system users are interested in. We shall call this the information system level and designate it as level N.

At each level there will be a set of protocols that apply. A message will be received at a given level, acted upon using that level's protocols, and passed on to the next level. For example, the interpretation and action that is taken on a portion of an E-mail address depends on the level. Looking at diplomatic parallel, if you are an ambassador, you have one set of protocols to apply, and if you are the secretary of state, you have another set of protocols. The reason we have included the notation (n), $(n-1)$, $(n-k)$ is that applying the protocols at a given level, n, may depend not only on knowledge of adjacent levels but also on knowledge that resides several levels away. Succinctly, applying or implementing the protocols at a level n:

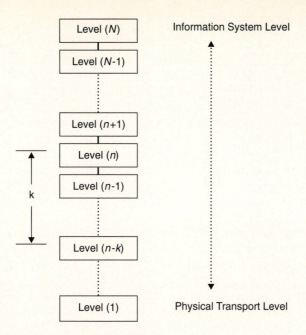

Figure 10.1   A protocol level structure

1. May require only knowledge of the protocols and actions at the levels (n), $(n-1)$ and $(n+1)$. We shall refer to this as the "neighbors only" case.

2. On the other hand, knowledge of activities and the protocols at level $(n-k)$ or $(n+k)$, where k may have multiple values greater than 1, may also be required.

Figure 10.1 presents a protocol level system ranging from a source of physical messages to the information systems that are to use the data or information in the messages from those sources. In reality, our challenge is to connect information systems so that they can share data and work together. This is a two-way street. The real situation is more like Fig. 10.2. Through the application of a series of protocols, the original information is transformed to a physical message and transported to another computer system. The recipient system acts upon that information. After computation is complete, a reply message may be constructed. Through the application of *similar* inverse actions, the results of

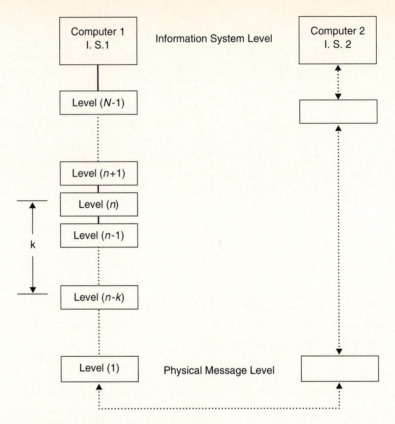

Figure 10.2 A protocol level structure

the computation are transformed to the information needed by the other information system and transported to it. The term "similar" was selected with care. In our general model:

1. There is no real requirement that the number of levels be the same on the two sides of Fig. 10.2.

2. There is no real requirement that the protocols at a given level on the two sides be the same.

3. The things that must be equivalent on the two sides are the bottom layers and correspondingly the top layers. In other words:

   At the physical transport level the same standards must apply.

   To applications, the two systems must appear as one consistent system.

In designing systems, simplicity is a great advantage. Standardization is often a component of simplicity. Upon these grounds restricting k to 1 in the above model is a tremendous advantage. Each level would have well-understood operational rules that depend only on its neighbors. The only actions relevant to what it does will be those at the interfaces to its neighbors. Furthermore, if there is a standard set of levels and rules (or protocols) applicable to all such models, that would be a tremendous advantage in design. In other words, the number of levels is fixed and the same. The protocols at any level are the same. At any level, one is concerned only with immediate neighbors. From the point of view of simplicity of concept, this is an ideal situation. There are two questions, however, that we might well raise:

1. Is such a model realistic in the real world? Does the model correspond to the way that the world operates?

2. Will a set of standards that fulfills all requirements be acceptably simple and lead to cost-effective systems, or will it be so complex that implementation becomes difficult, and result in some cases in inefficient information systems?

Let us address the first question. Is a model including the "neighbors only" restriction realistic? In the following example, we limit ourselves to information flowing within government diplomatic channels. In our diplomatic parallel, the implication is that an ambassador must operate only with information that is obtained from people working for him, and from his immediate boss, the secretary of state. He needs to know nothing about how the president operates, or the world situation, except for what the secretary of state tells him. He is to follow the protocols at his level, and those protocols are not dependent on other levels. Given information to transfer to the president, he will not formulate it in a way matched to that particular individual. Such action would require changing protocols when the president (or application) changed. Regardless of what he knows, he will not contact other than his neighbors in the protocol hierarchy. This is in some respects an ideal system, but is it realistic? It is very likely that such a system will work most of the time. As a matter of fact, to a large degree, it does. However, it would be very foolish to rule out situations in which it will not work satisfactorily. Special envoys who circumvent many layers of protocol, etc., would be prohibited. Sources of information within the administration, with whom the ambassador had particularly good personal interfaces, could not be directly utilized.

What does this have to do with distributed computing? More and more, computerized systems are interacting with each other and are playing an important role in decision making. In some cases, computers make the decision.

In other cases, computers supply information to humans and the humans make the decision. Often in the latter case, the implications of the computer results are so strong, that in effect the computer is making the decision. Humans have been working on evolving protocols and modes of operation since the dawn of history. It most cases, humans leave the door open for bypassing rigid protocols as necessary. They utilize the "neighbors only" structure but when necessary go outside of that structure. Computer information is key to decision making today and will be even more so tomorrow. Can we really expect to design automated information systems with no alternative to the rigidity of multilevel, neighbors only, fixed protocols? Would it not be better to recognize at the very beginning that the $(n-k)$ model is more applicable in many situations? Many of our information systems mimic those of nonautomated human systems. We should learn from that human experience. In addition, it may be totally unrealistic to think that automated information systems, considering their evolution and that they often involve distributed heterogeneous development efforts, will become entirely rigid in structure and standardized.

Consider the second question. Will a set of standard levels and protocols that are all things to all applications prove to be efficient?[3] Let us be clear; the authors firmly believe in standards and protocols. However, steps that generalize can often lead to the necessity of covering many cases, and processing the many cases to select what is proper. Furthermore, a situation may arise that is not covered by any of the alternatives in the existing standards set. The processing can be time consuming. Potentially, each of the levels in Figs. 10.1 and 10.2 can have many alternatives or branches. You may encounter situations in which it may not be desirable to consider all of those alternatives. You may want to selectively apply protocols and standards, or perhaps have your own standards and protocols. Today the performance of packet-switched systems is to a large degree limited by software and the processing of protocols. People are beginning to worry about the complexities and overhead in the ATM and Signaling System 7 protocols that are under development. Another example is that the standards for picture processing are quite different in the medical imaging and television fields.[4] It would be nice to have a general package of standards that covers all pictures, but would that be cost effective? The applications are quite different. It is not clear that in all situations we shall be able to afford the overhead of general purpose completely standardized systems.

3. Jonathan Grudin, "The Case Against User Interface Consistency," *Communications ACM* 32, no. 10 (October 1989): 1164.

4. "ACR-NEMA Digital Imaging and Communications," ACR/NEMA Standards Publication No. 300–1988, © National Electrical Manufacturers Association; E. C. Jordon, ed., *Reference Data for Engineers: Radio, Electronics, Computer, and Communications*, 7th ed. (Indianapolis, Ind.: Howard Sams, 1985), ch. 35.

Rigid standards and protocols are attractive when it comes to simplifying system design at high levels. When applicable, they can greatly expedite implementation and performance. They can potentially provide the glue that holds the system together. Ideally, they might make a general heterogeneous system appear as one system. On the other hand, there are situations in which they do not appear to be so attractive. This possibility is often overlooked in the literature focused on particular standards proposals and systems. The standards and protocols under discussion are often viewed as covering the general case and providing general solutions. It is implied, or stated, that the system should be applied in all cases. We believe that it is important that the reader realize that this is not necessarily the case. We shall discuss this further after we introduce the OSI conceptual model.

10.4 OSI Conceptual Model

What is widely known as "The Open System Interconnection Model," or the "OSI Reference Model," can be viewed as a special case of Figs. 10.1 and 10.2. It closely corresponds to the ideal "neighbors only" case discussed in the previous sections. Figure 10.3 presents the seven layers of the OSI reference model. The functional roles of the layers are indicated in what follows. Additional details can be found in Stallings and Lorin.[5] It should be noted that the services provided by the layers discussed below are not necessarily unique to a specific layer. For example, error correction and flow control may be addressed at several layers. Also, it is significant that within a given layer there may be multiple protocols and the protocol invoked will depend upon the application and the circumstances. These factors are partially responsible for the complexity issue discussed earlier.

Physical layer: This layer is concerned with interfacing or connecting to physical devices and transmitting unconstrained and unstructured bit streams over physical media. This includes making mechanical connections to the proper points, making those connections at the proper voltage, etc. Examples of standards and protocols at this level are RS–232-C; RS–4499/422/423; and parts of X.21.

Data link layer: This layer ensures that a message sent over a physical link will arrive without error. It organizes and sends blocks of data with the necessary structure to provide for data synchronization, the control of the

5. William Stallings, *Handbook of Computer-Communications Standard,* vol. 1, *The Open Systems Interconnection (OSI) Model and OSI-Related Standards* (New York: Macmillan, 1987); Harold Lorin, *Aspects of Distributed Computer Systems,* 2nd ed. (New York: Wiley, 1988), ch. 7.

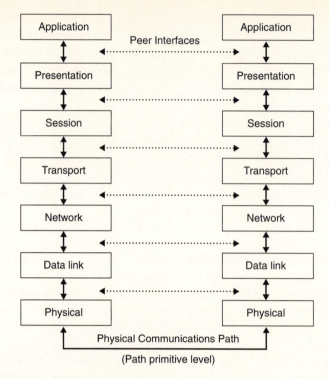

Figure 10.3   OSI Reference Model

flow of data associated with a single message, error control, etc. These types of functions are not necessarily unique to the data link layer and may in part be performed at other layers.

Network layer: This layer is concerned with the switching and associated transmission within a network. In the terminology that we have used, it focuses on integrating the switching components within a network. The network layer is responsible for establishing, maintaining, and terminating connections.

Transport layer: In a sense, this layer is the user interface to transport facilities at the lower levels. Those facilities may be concerned with one or more networks which may have properties that differ widely. An objective of this layer is to interface to and utilize the facilities of those networks in an efficient manner. In other words, it should ensure the reliable transfer of data between end points. The details of the networks that may be used should be transparent to higher levels. It may be concerned with end-to-end recovery and flow control. If error problems get by lower levels, they should be corrected here. Both flow control and error correction may be treated quite differently in networks, and this level is to provide the integration between the networks. In brief, all functions relating to transport per se are within the transport layer or lower layers in the hierarchy.

Session layer: This layer provides the control mechanism to ensure communication between two entities or processes. It provides the structure within which the dialogue between the two entities takes place. It establishes, manages, and terminates connections (sessions) between cooperating applications. It may establish checkpoints on data to permit retransmission if data failures occur in the dialogue.

Presentation layer: This layer is concerned with the syntactic aspects of the exchange of data between entities. Its purpose is to resolve differences in format and data representation. It defines the syntax used between application entities and provides for the selection and subsequent modification (translation or interfacing) of the representations used. Semantic considerations are left to the application layer.

Application layer: The functional responsibilities of the application level are the least clearly defined of the seven layers of the OSI reference model. Some utility type services are mentioned in the literature, among them file transfer, electronic mail, and synchronization of applications. In a sense, the application layer is intended to serve as a bridge between the actual applications and the OSI environment including some services of common interest. The focus is on issues that may be considered relevant to communications transport issues.

The reference model does not deal with implementation issues at the various levels. Rather it specifies in broad terms what functionally is expected at each level. Its objective is to provide a framework within which various standards groups can develop standards. Making those detailed standards consistent and compatible with each other is left to those individual groups. Standards setting bodies, discussed later in this chapter, try to integrate these efforts.

There is a peripheral aspect of the lack of implementation detail that can be important to information system designers. The implementation of one manufacturer may fit within the functional framework of the OSI model but fail to satisfactorily operate with the products of another manufacturer. In such situations, both manufacturers are likely to advertise that they meet the OSI standard. If both solutions fall within the OSI level guidelines, strictly speaking the advertisements may be correct. Being correct in that sense, however, will not help the information system designer, who may have two systems that cannot be interconnected. Nevertheless, the OSI reference model is an excellent idea. Where it is viable with respect to available products and cost performance considerations it should be followed.

Section 10.3 presented a general perspective on layered protocols. In doing so, the stage was set for a corresponding discussion, *in that context*, of the OSI model. It is important that we understand not only the role of this model, but also the danger in believing that it is ideal and applicable to all circumstances.

1. The OSI reference model appears to be a relatively loose structure, with a lot of potential functional overlap between layers. For example, error detection and correction are addressed at several levels. This may be a logical necessity and is not inherently bad. However, it does mitigate against the concept that the individual "adjacent only" layers can be neatly and cleanly separated functionally. Are they really totally independent?

2. Intentionally, and for good reason, the functions at a given level are not discussed in detail, nor is specific implementation of a level discussed. (Implicit reasons will be discussed in a later section on standards.) However, as noted earlier, this means that two systems that adhere to the model may not be able to communicate.

3. If the mode of operation is always to go down the chain and back up, can we afford the overhead in all cases?

4. The control of access to data or functions does not seem to be mentioned. Presumably, any such requirement is thrown back to the individual applications. Access control, however, should in many situations be separated from applications just as database management systems are separated from applications. It is arguable that access control is a function that transcends both specific applications and a database management system. For example, as noted elsewhere, access control my be a function of location and exercised by the communications network. Consequently, it would appear appropriate to consider access control in establishing network protocols and models.

5. In view of the above, it would appear that general information system utilities are needed and should be available in the model. In other words, there is need for utilities that would be useful to the information system designer and that are somewhat similar to the utilities provided those working in operating systems. Both areas are concerned with large-scale resource and allocation problems.

6. It almost appears as if everything that is not in the lower six layers has been pushed into the application layer. The need to expand the application layer is recognized in some circles but little real progress has been made.[6] Certainly if communication in the broad sense is considered primarily an information systems problem, serious consideration should be given to dividing the application layer into at least three or four layers. For example, the language translation often required when going between systems, and the interfacing of databases, are general problems that should not be assigned to each application but covered by different layers in the OSI model. It would be reasonable to place those new layers below that for specific applications and above the remaining layers of the current ISO model.

Figure 10.4 is a modification of the OSI reference model. It makes no attempt to describe in detail how the information system level should be divided into separate levels. (Macomber in his report does make some specific suggestions.) Figure 10.4 is presented with the hope that it will get the reader thinking about the more general problem in terms of information systems. It is a result of the following convictions:

1. Any general model should include the information system level(s). That is, the model must recognize where the users are and that they are the ones to whom we must interface. Users may be people, specific processes, or specific applications.

2. A model should include data services that are available to applications at the information system level. The implication is that one or more of the information system levels should address this issue.

3. It is likely that some of the data services needed at the information system level can be better performed if integrated into the communications transport network. If so, they should be included in a model that is proposed as a communications model.

4. It will be increasingly difficult to separate issues involving communications, computers, and distributed heterogeneous information systems.

Figure 10.4 can be viewed as a logical model that may or may not be totally related to the physical world. Because it is basically the OSI model with upper levels added to the information system level, the discussion of earlier pages is

6. H. Zimmerman and R. Shuey, private discussion at IFIP83, Ninth World Computer Conference, 1983, Paris, France; Ted Macomber, "The Upper Layers of the OSI Reference Model" (unpublished paper, Dept. of Computer Science, Rensselaer Polytechnic Institute, Report 89–21, September 1989).

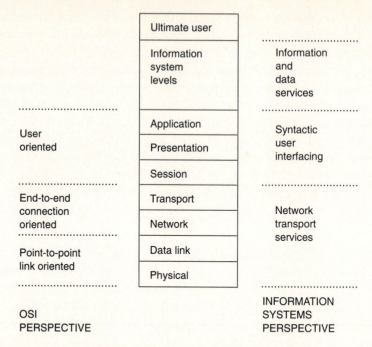

Figure 10.4   Possible modification of OSI reference model

still applicable. To the degree that things like security, database functions, memory mapping and access control become functions performed within a network, it may be difficult to apply. Of course we could argue that any function that involves the execution of programming and logic should be considered a node function, even if that function is performed within the network. This would not appear to be a good paradigm, however. We would then have nodes that are internal to the network. Extreme examples might be a network that sends messages to an individual regardless of location, or sends messages to a location that depended upon their content or intended use. As indicated earlier, we prefer a viewpoint that assigns workstation activities to nodes. There will be further discussion of this in a later chapter.

It is clear that although most discussions of the OSI reference model are in terms of a communications network, within a multiprogrammed computer system there are the same interfacing problems. A multiprogramming system can be running virtual systems or applications that are quite different. There is a need to establish communications between the various processes. With the introduction of multiprocessor systems, the similarity with computer networks is even stronger. Succinctly, today all computer systems have communications networks internal and external to what might be considered a computer.

The important message of this section is to apply the concepts of the OSI model where appropriate. If cost effective, it can lead to a great deal of simplification in design. At the same time, it is important to recognize the limitations of that model. Let us now turn to examples of alternatives that are not as globally well-organized and complete as the OSI model.

10.5 Some Interfacing Alternatives

System designers have been interfacing foreign information systems for some time. When confronted with specific needs, designers have devised special-purpose (i.e., designed just for that need or application) methods of accomplishing the desired interfacing. These interfacing techniques have included facilities to do direct translation between the two foreign worlds, translation that goes through a common language or database, and the simulation of one world in terms of the other. We call these mechanisms interfacers. Lorin calls them adapters.[7] In what follows, we assume that communications in the data transport sense are not the major problem. We are much more concerned with interfacing methods that make the data in one system available to another system in a way that they have meaning and are useful. We consequently follow an information system perspective.

Figure 10.5 shows six information systems, or in a more limited scope six application programs, that are running on different hardware or in a multiprogrammed system. The systems, or programs, may be quite different and often independently developed. Perhaps the only thing that they have in common is the need to share data. The question is, how do we interface these systems? This is really the protocol problem. We assume for purposes of discussion that the data transport problem is solved (i.e., we can get an arbitrary data stream from one system to another.).

One solution to this interfacing problem is for the designer responsible for interfacing the kth system with the jth system to build a special-purpose interface. There may be two interfaces required, one from k to j and one from j to k. This is of course often done. For example, AmiPro, the word processing system used in writing this book, has a great many "input filters" that will accept or produce text files of other word processing systems. This is an effective system. One of the authors has many old text files prepared under the Multimate word processing system. Those files can be read by AmiPro using the

---

7. Lorin, *Aspects of Distributed Computer Systems* 2nd ed. (New York: Wiley, 1988).

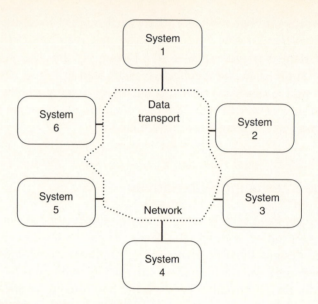

Figure 10.5   Interfacing foreign systems

Multimate input filter and the operation produces an AmiPro file. There is no need to store Multimate archival files in a different format. They can be read with the current system. The same type of interfacing could be present in a group in which the individual workers used different word processing systems and wanted to exchange text files over a LAN. (However, many of the commercial filters available today do not effectively exchange document files containing graphics, pictures, or equations.) Word processing is an area in which for ten years there has been an effort to develop a word processing exchange standard. The common commercial practice still is to build filters. This fact is an illustration of the difficulty of defining and implementing standards.

Building interfaces along the lines above has one serious drawback. In the case of our six systems, if all systems are to be able to accept files from each of the other five "foreign" systems, then (6) × (5) or 30 filters would be required. For n systems $(n)(n-1)$ filters would be needed and this number grows rapidly as n increases.

Clearly it is desirable to standardize the way data are handled by applications and processed in file and database systems. The objective is to make it easier to interface systems. For example, if each application utilizing a database manager uses a compatible relational database system, and all interactions are at the SQL level, then the problem is much simpler. Compatible implies compatibility both at a database management system level and with respect to data structures, data dictionaries, etc. The previous chapter discussed some of the problems associated with meeting these objectives. Both the information system designer and the computer analyst should be aware of these problems. Often the information system requirements, specifications, and design, if judiciously done, can greatly minimize interfacing problems. This fact makes it important that the computer analyst, and the information system designer, work closely together at the early stage of a project.

There are of course other possible solutions. Regardless of what they do internally, all systems could agree to provide a standard output filter. In other words, each system will provide an output filter that meets an agreed protocol or format. The early data interchange effort and .DIF files developed primarily for interfacing data from foreign spreadsheets are examples of this.[8] The work on data exchange standards for various application areas such as engineering product data and electronic publishing data falls in this area. It is not clear how successful these efforts will be. One factor is that there is very little reason why large companies such as Microsoft should make it too easy for foreign systems to couple into their products. Thus the individual manufacturers may be more interested in data exchange among their own products than with the products of others. Such issues will be discussed later.

There are other examples that we would like to describe. They are in part generalizations of the earlier examples in this section. In the example in which $(n)(n-1)$ interfaces were required, it may not be reasonable for each system to internally provide its own interfaces to other systems. It may be more cost effective to have a central point perform the necessary interfacing and translation. Figure 10.6 shows such an arrangement. Each system transfers data to the central system using its own formats, commands, etc. The central system assigns the work to the appropriate systems and translates the data and commands into that used by the target systems. This type of arrangement was used in the "Designer's Workbench" to interface the subsystems of electronic design software.[9] The application packages were running on different hardware and at different locations. The different subsystems were independently developed, but the overall design of electronic equipment required the integrated use of all subsystems. Designers using a specific system had only to learn to communicate with the central (hub) system. They did not need to know the details of the other systems.

8. "DIF Technical Specifications," (Software Arts Products Corp., 1983), DIF Clearinghouse, P.O. Box 638, Newton Lower Falls, MA 02162.

9. L. A. O'Neil, "Designer's Workbench—Philosophy," *BSTJ* 59, no. 9 (November 1980): 1757; P. H. McDonald and T. J. Thompson, "The Designer's Workbench—The Programmer Environment," *BSTJ* 59, no. 9 (November 1980): 1793; J. R. Breiland and R. A. Friedenson, "Designer's Workbench—The User Environment," *BSTJ* 59, no. 9 (November 1980): 1767; T. J. Thompson, "The Designer's Workbench—The Production Environment," *BSTJ* 59, no. 9 (November 1980): 1811.

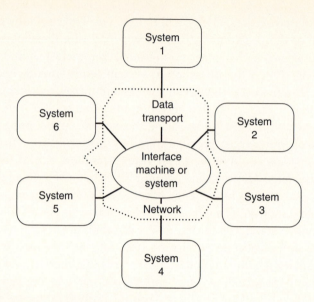

Figure 10.6   A centralized interface

Figure 10.7 depicts another alternative often used to interface the data in design databases. It is important to keep two factors in mind here. The first is that many of the older systems, like those in the Designer's Workbench, were independently developed and did not necessarily use a common database management system. The second is that even today, with much of the applications work being distributed, there is a great variety of applications system software in use. (The term *applications system software* implies spreadsheets, database managers, word processors, simulators, etc., which distinguishes it from software written for specific applications.) After the original independent applications work is done, the users often find that they want to use the components as an integrated system. In Fig. 10.7 the databases of the individual systems are translated or restructured into what is referred to as a *neutral database*. The restructuring can be done by the individual systems or, as in Fig. 10.6, by a central system. The neutral database is usually located at a central point, however. It should be noted that in this case the number of interfaces required is $2n$.

An analogy can be drawn between many of these systems and Esperanto, a language that was intended as a universal language but also as a neutral language into which all languages could be translated.[10] Thus a person would

10. *American Heritage Dictionary for Windows* (Cambridge, Mass.: Wordstar International, 1993).

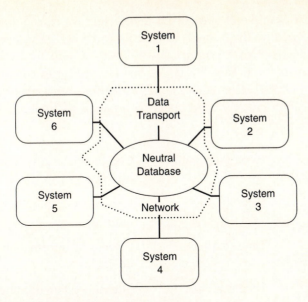

Figure 10.7   A neutral database system

only need to be able to translate from his or her native tongue to Esperanto to be able to have access to written material in any language. The assumption was that Esperanto served in effect as a neutral database. The Esperanto movement has not been popular or successful. The reasons are both technical and psychological, but basically there were not a significant number of people who would accept the idea. This experience has some relevance in the area of information systems and computers. In the long run, what is done will depend upon acceptance by users.

The factor of $2n$ in the preceding example can be reduced to n by a pipelining technique. The reduction to n filters is achieved by forming a logical ring and always translating the source in a clockwise or counterclockwise manner, depending on how the translation ring is set up. In effect calculations are made step by step until the desired point on the ring is reached. This approach may require a large amount of computation and is subject to the accumulation of errors from each step. Since perfect translators are extremely rare, the approach usually results in poor translations. In summary, although double the number of interfaces are required for the common interface approach, as compared to the logical ring approach, the common interface approach is preferred. For a specific interaction, only two translations are required. Given the need for only two translations (instead of the possible $n-1$ or the average case $(n-1)/2$), the quality of the translation is likely to be much better, and the processing time much lower than in the ring-structured case.

As the last example of specialized interfacing, we consider an operating system developed by the General Electric Research and Development Center (GE CRD), which serves the entire General Electric Company. In the late 1960s a decision was made to install a large-scale GE 600 series computer as a replacement for GE 200 series equipment. At that time, other major components of GE were using three different operating systems that operated on GE 600 series machines:

GECOS	Batch processing	Commercial equipment business offering
	Time sharing	Commercial equipment business offering
Mark II	Time sharing	Offered by Information Service Business
Deskside	Time sharing	Internal system used by some GE military departments

The goal was that the CRD system would provide a capability to work with computer programs from these four sources (systems) as well as a platform upon which programs could be developed that could later be transferred to company components using those systems. Additional goals were also formulated:

> The application software systems available under the four systems could be run unchanged. The intention was to use the standard documentation for those systems (e.g., the FORTRAN compilers and associated documentation). This would make available to the research staff all of the resources of GECOS batch and time sharing, Mark II, and Deskside.

> An application prepared by any research staff member should be able to utilize the resources of all four systems.

> In addition to providing computing for the physical scientists at CRD, the computing facility should provide the tools needed by the computer scientists.

These goals presented the designers with a formidable interfacing problem. Transparency was required up to the applications program level. These goals were met by developing an operating system based on the hardware of a military version of the 600 computer to which had been added four base registers.

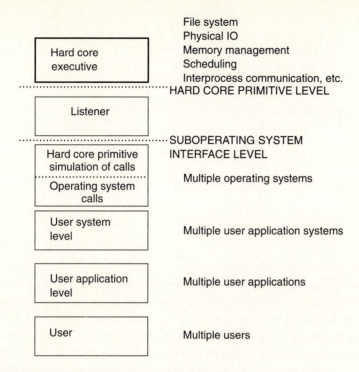

Figure 10.8   Basic concepts of the GE CRD operating system

The general structure of the operating system is shown in Fig. 10.8.[11] The development and implementation were under the immediate direction of Robin H. Kerr and the team consisted of selected people from the computer science staff and from the computing center.[12] The impact of earlier work on the Atlas, Dartmouth's 600, DAD, and Multics systems was significant. The operating system developed served CRD for approximately 15 years.

In Fig. 10.8, everything shown below the suboperating system interface level is associated with a particular suboperating system or virtual machine. There are consequently many parallel systems, only one of which is shown. Figure 10.9 illustrates this point and shows some of the virtual systems. The listener is the one process that is always in the system. It spawns other processes as they are needed and passes on to them the parameters that they

11. R. L. Shuey, "A Perspective on Operating Systems" (keynote address 1970 Stanford Computer Forum, GECRD Information Sciences Laboratory Report 70-C206, June 1970).

12. A. J. Bernstein, G. D. Detlefsen, and R. H. Kerr, "Process Control and Communications" (proceedings of the Second Symposium on Operating Systems Principles, ACM, Princeton University, October 1969).

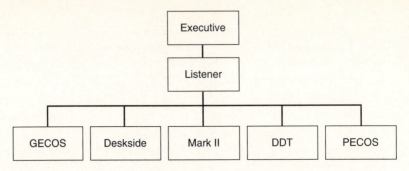

Figure 10.9   A sample of production software on the CRD operating system

need. The general operation is that up to the multiple operating system level, a specific virtual system behaves as its physical counterpart. At the multiple operating system level, the operating system calls of the corresponding virtual system are simulated in terms of the 50 or so primitives of the hard core system and then passed on to the hard core executive.

Figure 10.9 shows five of the 40 to 50 virtual systems that existed in normal operation. Once signed onto a virtual system, the user interface and capabilities were identical to those that would be experienced in using the corresponding real dedicated system. For example, a card deck that ran on a standard commercial system under GECOS would run on the CRD system by adding one card. That card invoked the virtual GECOS system. If terminal users asked for Mark II, they got a virtual Mark II that was identical from their perspective to the commercial time sharing offering. The DDT subsystem provided sophisticated debugging tools, and other subsystems could be run under it. This was a great aid to system development. PECOS was a system in which programs could be written in the command languages of the other virtual systems. Clearly with such a system it is possible to run several versions of a virtual system at the same time. This was done with GECOS, where the business functions would usually use the old tested version and the technical staff might run on the new version to utilize the new features there in.

In many circumstances, the interfacing of information systems and applications is easier if they are running under a common operating system. This is another alternative. The UNIX operating system originated in a computer system research group at Bell Telephone Laboratories as a system for that group's use. However, the main thrust soon became an attempt to evolve it into a portable operating system that would operate on many platforms. In the communications industry this has been fairly successful. UNIX is often the operating system used in all of the computers that make up a large electronic switch. As the reader probably knows, there is a current effort to make UNIX available more broadly on many different computers in the computer industry. However, whether there will ever be a standard operating system throughout the industry as a whole is an open question. It is unlikely in the near future.

Why are these examples relevant to the subject of this book? In each case the designers faced the problem of interfacing heterogeneous systems. It is true that the systems often were existing systems with a cadre of users and associated software, documentation, and applications. However, considering the distributed nature of information system development, this may often be the case in the future. The solutions selected were relatively straightforward and simple. Would a designer today, facing a similar problem, follow an alternative along lines similar to those discussed, or elect to strictly follow the OSI standard? That should depend upon the circumstances, which is the point that we are trying to make.

10.6 Standards

A prescribed set of rules, conditions, or requirements concerning definition of terms; classification of components; specification of materials, performance, or operations; delineation of procedures; or measurement of quantity and quality in describing materials, products, systems, services, or practices.[13]

(from 1979 National Policy on Standards
for the United States [NSPA79]

The communications industry has long recognized the importance of industry-wide standards. This was probably due to the nature of communications, and also in part to the fact that it was a noncompetitive industry. This was not a common viewpoint in the computer industry, because of the isolated nature of initial systems and a supplier's desire to monopolize or "lock in" customers. Much of the thrust for standards has come from the users and computer user groups.

In the distributed computer and information system era, standards are a necessity. At the same time, it has been very difficult to develop an integrated view of standards that involves both the computer and communications sectors of business. Today, the need for standards is recognized in both sectors. The time is coming when the marketplace will be dominated by products that

13. William Stallings, *Handbook of Computer-Communications Standard,* vol. 1, *The Open Systems Interconnection (OSI) Model and OSI-Related Standards* (New York: Macmillan, 1987).

meet in some sense commonly agreed upon standards. The result is unlikely to provide the ease of integration that the users would like, but it will represent a significant continuous movement in the right direction. Whether that movement will be faster, or slower, than the increase in user expectations is an interesting question.

On the plus side, widely accepted standards can accomplish the following:

> Permit components from multiple sources to operate together in an integrated system (e.g., machine tools, computers, instruments, communications networks).

> Encourage mass production of key items (e.g., ISDN interfacing chips, communications modems, byte and word-oriented memory, SQL databases, encrypting chips).

> Foster cost-effective integrated systems (e.g., airline communications and reservation systems, order entry systems coupled to manufacturing, interfaced banking systems).

> If properly chosen, can expedite technological developments (e.g., the digitization of the national network, development of color TV).

> Foster the establishment of common tools (FORTRAN, COBOL, C, C++).

> Function as a basis for the interchange of "information" (Internet, fax).

At the same time, pragmatically there are disadvantages:

> Waiting for standards can hold up progress (e.g., broadband ISDN).

> Frozen standards can limit technological progress (e.g., COBOL, the DS n multiplexing hierarchy, NTS TV and the introduction of digital TV).

> A wrong standard can create serious problems (e.g., some would put the ADA programming language in this category).

There are also limitations on our ability to introduce new meaningful standards. These might be viewed more broadly as limits on our ability to create new standards.

In some areas, we lack the knowledge needed to create new standards. Lasting standards must anticipate the future and not put constraints on the use of new technology. We cannot predict the future well enough.

The establishment of a standard usually requires that a diverse group reach a common agreement. There are technical, commercial, political, and international political issues that often make this extremely difficult.

Pragmatically there are three classes of standards:

1. *Voluntary:*

   Most of the familiar standards fall into this category. The ipso facto standardization of PC software to three or four operating systems is an example. The OSI reference model, Hayes modems, SQL standards, etc., are all voluntary.

2. *Regulatory:*

   Many communications standards fall into this category. Examples include the assignment of radio frequencies and stability requirements, the use of channels, the services that can be offered by the telephone industry, the specification of the form in which TV signals will be sent, the inclusion of closed-caption capabilities in new TV sets, etc. Meeting these standards is required by law.

   The assignment of licenses and channels by the government can mean a lot to some politicians. One almost has to play the game with the politicians to be successful.

   Few computer standards are regulatory. The limits set on electromagnetic radiation is an exception.

3. *Regulatory use of voluntary standards:*

   The government will often require that government purchases be limited to products and services that meet a selected set of voluntary standards. Examples are COBOL, ISDN compatible communications equipment, TCP, and ADA.

   The same type of imposed standards are common within business firms, but they lack the authority of the government. For example, some major firms require that all purchased communications equipment meets ISDN standards.

In addition, the communications industry is subject to mandatory tariffs that regulate the services that are permitted and the prices. Some of these are imposed by the federal government, some by the states, and some by cities.

10.6.1 Standards Organizations Related to the United States

The CCITT

The CCITT (Comité Consultatif Internationale Telegraphique et Téléphonique) is a committee of the International Telecommunications Union (ITU), which at present is a United Nations treaty organization. Its charter is "to study and issue recommendations on technical, operating, and tariff questions relating to telegraphy and telephone." A CCITT objective is to "standardize, to the extent necessary, techniques and operations in telecommunications to achieve end-to-end compatibility of international telecommunications connections, regardless of the countries of origin." CCITT members are governments. The U.S. representation is the responsibility of the Department of State.

The CCITT is organized into 15 study groups. There are three areas of activity related to OSI matters: (1) data communications, (2) telematic services, and (3) ISDN. Work in these three areas involves six study groups (i.e., Groups: I, VII, VIII, XI, XVII, and XVIII). The approval of standards is on four-year cycles (i.e., approval takes at least four years). Roughly speaking, CCITT has been involved with the three lower levels of the OSI model, although the technical head often has wider interests.

International Organization For Standardization (ISO)

ISO is a nontreaty, voluntary, international organization whose members are designated standards bodies of the participating nations and nonvoting observer organizations. ISO was founded in 1946 and has issued more than 5000 standards. Although a nongovernmental organization, 70 percent of ISO member bodies are governmental standards institutions or organizations incorporated by public laws. The U.S. member body is the American National Standards Institute (ANSI).

OSI matters are handled by Technical Committee 97, which is divided into subcommittees (SC) and working groups (WG). For example, SC 6 is concerned primarily with levels 1–4 of the Reference Model and consists of five working groups. SC 21 focuses more on the overall picture and contains the following working groups: WG 1 (OSI architecture), WG 2 (computer graphics), WG 3 (database), WG 4 (OSI management), WG 5 (specific application services and protocols), and WG 6 (session, presentation, common application service elements, and upper layer architecture).

Other Standards Organizations in Communications

American National Standards Institute (ANSI): A nonprofit, nongovernmental organization composed of manufacturers, users, communications carriers, and other interested organizations. It serves as a national clearinghouse for voluntary standards. It is a U.S. designated member of ISO.

National Institute of Standards and Technology (formerly the National Bureau of Standards)

Federal Telecommunications Standards Committee (FTSC)

Defense Communications Agency (DCA)

Electronics Industries Association (EIA)

Institute of Electrical and Electronic Engineers (IEEE)

European Computer Manufacturers Association (ECMA)

Standards Related Organizations

Manufacturing Automation Protocol (MAP)

Technical and Office Protocols (TOP)

Corporation for Open Systems (COS)

U.S. Government OSI User's Committee

The Frame Relay Forum

The ATM Forum

10.7 Data Exchange Standards

As discussed above, standards play an important role in distributed systems in the area of exchange of data between systems. Data exchange is needed any time that two or more systems pass data back and forth, and the data are structured differently in each system. In these cases, it is not sufficient to simply send the data through a communications channel from one system to another, since the receiving system has no way to interpret the data that it receives. Rather, the data must be transformed in some way so that the receiving system is able to interpret and use the data that it receives. This transformation may involve converting the data into the format used by the receiving system, or adding some additional information to the data so that it can be interpreted successfully at the receiving end. Standards play a role in either case.

The key to successful data exchange is to arrive at a mutually agreed upon semantic model for the data to be exchanged. This semantic model represents the basis for the transformation of data as they are moved between systems. The role of standards in data exchange is largely to define these semantic models. If a data exchange problem is restricted to a small enough problem domain, then one semantic model may be sufficient, and the standard is simply a specification of this model. Each system that intends to exchange data based on the standard must provide mapping functions between the standard semantic model and the internal database used by that system. It is usually the responsibility of the system implementers to provide these mapping functions.

This approach to data exchange is illustrated in Fig. 10.10, which shows two systems exchanging data. The mapping functions for a system use the semantic model specification in the standard and the proprietary schema for the internal database used by the system to control the transformation of data. One of the mapping functions is an "import" function that takes data conforming to the standard semantic model and transforms it into the form required by the internal system database. The other function is an "export" function that takes data from the internal system database and transforms it to

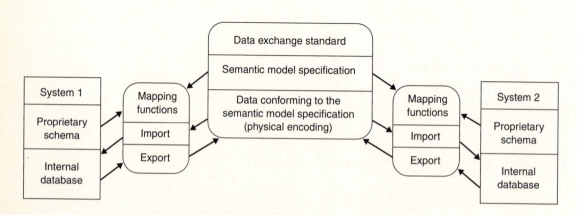

Figure 10.10   Using a data exchange standard

conform with the semantic model defined by the data exchange standard. Data are then exchanged between two systems using the export function of one system and the import function of the other. (Note the similarity between this figure and Fig. 10.7, which shows a neutral database system.) In many ways, a semantic model in a data exchange standard is like a neutral database.

An example of a data exchange standard that follows this approach is the Initial Graphics Exchange Specification (IGES), which is an international standard for the exchange of two-dimensional and three-dimensional graphical data.[14] The standard includes a data model that describes how points, lines, curves, etc., are to be specified. Graphics systems supporting IGES provide mappings from these standard representations to the internal representations that they use. IGES has been used successfully for many years in computer-aided design and manufacturing applications to exchange engineering drawings between systems.

If a data exchange problem domain is large and complex, a single semantic model that encompasses the entire problem domain may be too cumbersome for practical use. In this case, the data exchange approach outlined above is too restrictive, and a better approach is to include a schema definition language as part of the data exchange standard. Systems that wish to exchange data use this schema definition language to specify a semantic model for just that data from the larger problem domain that they intend to exchange. The data exchange standard may, in addition, use this schema definition language to specify semantic models for commonly used parts of the problem domain. Once the schema definition language is used to define an appropriate semantic model, data exchange between the systems proceeds as described above.

An example of an international data exchange standard that follows this approach is the STEP standard for the exchange of engineering product data.[15] Product data in this case includes far more than the graphical data found in engineering drawings such as those handled by IGES. Product data includes detailed geometry and tolerances, material properties, configuration data, manufacturing process specifications, etc. The STEP standard includes a schema definition language named EXPRESS for specifying the detailed product data models.[16] It then uses the EXPRESS language to define libraries of common semantic models for a variety of different engineering design and manufacturing application domains.

14. B. Smith, G. Rinaudot, T. Wright, and K. Reed, "Initial Graphics Exchange Specification," National Technical Information Service (NTIS) order number PB 88–235452 (1988).

15. "Industrial Automation Systems—Product Data Representation and Exchange. Part 1: Overview and Fundamental Principles," ISO International Standard 10303–1, Geneva, 1994.

16. D. Schenck and P. Wilson, *Information Modeling the EXPRESS Way* (Oxford: Oxford University Press, 1994).

In addition to a semantic model, a data exchange standard often includes two other components: a physical encoding and an application program interface. The first is a specification for a physical encoding of data instances that conform to the semantic model in the data exchange standard. This specification often takes the form of a file format. While the semantic model describes the data structures that are valid in a particular standard, it does not specify how data instances conforming to the semantic model are represented as bit strings. To use a data exchange standard such as that shown in Fig. 10.10, data from one system must be transformed to the semantic model defined by the standard and then encoded as a string of bits to be sent through a network to another system. The receiving system must be able to interpret the bit strings that it receives to construct data instances in the semantic model of the data exchange standard. Only after this is done is it possible for the system to apply its import function to transform those data instances into the form required by the internal database of the receiving system. Thus the physical encoding specification is a necessary part of the data exchange standard, since there would otherwise be no way to map the logical data structures in the semantic model to physical representations (bit strings) that can be physically exchanged between systems in a meaningful way.

The final component in a data exchange standard is an application program interface (API) specification. The purpose of this interface is to provide programmers, particularly the programmers who develop the import and export functions for a system, with the ability to read and write data instances represented using the physical encoding specified as part of the standard. The API is usually a library of functions callable from a programming language. These functions interrogate and update data instances stored using the physical encoding for the standard. As a result, the API represents the primitives from which all import and export operations are built.

In the paragraphs above, the use of data exchange in computer-aided engineering is used for examples. This is one area where successful international data exchange standards exist today. However, data exchange is needed and used in many other areas as well. A simple example of this is a heterogeneous distributed database system. In such a system the individual databases are of different types (e.g., relational and object-oriented). Data cannot be moved directly from one system to another as part of query processing because it is represented differently in the two systems. Data exchange software that transforms the data as they are moved between systems is needed to overcome this problem. DeMichiel provides a good discussion of some of the issues that must be considered.[17] Another area where data exchange standards exist is document processing. SGML is a data exchange standard for docu-

17. L. DeMichiel, "Resolving Database Incompatibility: An Approach to Performing Relational Operations over Mismatched Domains," *IEEE Transactions on Knowledge and Data Engineering* 1, no. 4 (December 1989): 485–493.

ments that allows the contents of a document, with figures, footnotes, and chapter and section structures, to be exchanged between word processors and document processing systems.[18] In the future, we can expect even more sophisticated data exchange standards that will simplify the process of moving data between systems. As discussed throughout this book, however, sharing data between systems is, in general, a difficult task, and no data exchange standard can remove all of the complexity from this task.

10.8 Data and Information in the World at Large

All of us would like our computer-based information systems to have access to the data and information that are available in the world at large. At the same time, we would like to ensure that there are proper controls over the access to information. This chapter is concerned with protocols and standards. Consequently, we shall focus on issues related to information in the world at large that are particularly pertinent to these two subjects.

10.8.1 Security and Encryption

Protocols and standards relating to the communications between computers have already been discussed. Two areas that have not been discussed are encryption and security.[19] Encryption technology is well in hand. It is applicable to both the transport and storage of messages. Technology exists that, to any degree desired, will ensure that the contents of a message can only be deciphered by a computer or a person with the key or code book. Those for whom the system is being designed need only to reach a decision based upon their requirements (security) and cost performance tradeoffs. There will be performance factors that involve technical issues such as throughput as well as constraints on the intended user community. There will also be a monetary cost associated with encryption. In brief, subject to possible legal constraints on the choices, it is up to the users for whom the information system is being built to decide what is required.

---

18. "Information Processing: Text and Office Systems: Standard Generalized Markup Language (SGML)," ISO International Standard 8879, Geneva, 1986.

19. C. E. Shannon, "Communication Theory of Secrecy Systems," *BSTJ* 28 (October 1949): 659–715; Dorothy E. Denning, *Cryptography and Data Security* (Reading, Mass.: Addison-Wesley, 1982); Dorothy E. Denning, "The Clipper Encryption System," *American Scientist* 81 (July–August 1993): 319; C. Fritzner et al., "Experimental Secure Distributed Information System," *Electrical Communications (Alcatel)* 62, no. 3/4 (1988): 31; R. Ganesan and R. Sandhu, eds., "Introduction to Special Section on Securing Cyberspace," *Communications of the ACM* 37, no. 11 (November 1994): 28; D. Stevenson, N. Hillery, and G. Byrd, "Secure Communications in ATM Networks," *Communications of the ACM* 38, no. 2 (February 1995): 39.

Encryption that is implemented in software or special purpose hardware can be both expensive and, with respect to performance, time consuming. In this context special purpose hardware refers to hardware built from standard components and chips (e.g., chips not specifically designed for encryption). To mitigate this fact, VLSI chips designed specifically for encryption are being produced. Concurrently in the United States there is work on standardizing encryption techniques and chips for use in communications. The government intention is to specify a chip and system that will provide the user with privacy but will simultaneously permit (with proper judicial authorization of course) governmental authorities to decipher messages. This is similar to the regulations concerning the wiretapping of phone lines. However, the proposal has led to regulatory and political controversy. Details can be found in the references cited. The argument on one side is that the government needs such authority to control the use of communications systems by criminals and for national security reasons. The other side maintains that privacy must be preserved and that the ability of the government to control improper access is questionable. In any event, if designers wish to implement an encryption scheme, internal to a distributed computer system that does not utilize communications systems that come under regulation and mandatory standards, they can do what they want. This of course means that neither radio nor common carrier services can be used. What the resolution of this controversy will be was not known at the time this book was prepared.

Security and access control are things that should be addressed at all levels of a distributed system. For example, as noted earlier, it would in many cases be possible to cut off access to data at a network level. Access may also be cut off at the memory system hardware level. The latter has a parallel in the library: you can keep a person out of a library rather than attempting to control what he looks at in the catalog or on the shelves. There will be further discussion of such factors in later chapters. The relevance here is that to handle encryption and security in a generally consistent way requires protocols and standards.

10.8.2 Computerized Databases for Well-Structured Data

There are a great many computerized databases in the world today. Many of these are commercial databases or databases that are open to the public at no charge. Any respectable library has network on-line access to its catalogs and often to its abstracts. Many journals are today available on optical disks and first-rate libraries have a great deal of material in this form. As telecommunications improves, these too could be accessible over the network. This capability is potentially a great boon to the research community, providing worldwide data at the fingertips of users. For average citizens, whether on-line access for most of the material they would like, will be cost competitive with alternatives is an open question. For example, they are unlikely to use the network to access an encyclopedia if it can be purchased for a few dollars on an optical disk. One of the authors of this book has a CD-ROM World Atlas for which he paid six dollars; he would thus be extremely reluctant to pay the communications charges associated with accessing similar information over a network.

Data that are in machine-readable form are either currently available or potentially can be made available in the future. There will be problems associated with deciding what should be put into databases and made available. For example, some researchers gather a tremendous amount of experimental data, often recorded and stored in computerized systems. How much of it should be made available and in what form? The current practice is for researchers to write papers that summarize their work and the specific data included. Such papers are likely to end up in one or more databases along with abstracts, etc. There are today thousands of databases that are available to the public. These include legal databases, a variety of medical databases, chemical abstracts, reservation systems, and library systems. In most of these cases storing the data, if one is willing to pay for the cost, is not a problem. Organizing data so that they can be located, and abstracting important features, is a much more serious problem than just storage. In other words, storing data in a structure along with retrieval methods that will retrieve meaningful information is the challenge.

It is easy to put pictures, plots, figures, etc. into a computer. Given state-of-the-art technology, any existing document can be put into machine readable form. In addition, increasingly a larger fraction of the new data and information being created are in machine-readable form. For example, some of the figures in this book came from references and were scanned into the computer. They were then made a part of the word processing files for this book. The other figures were generated by the authors on a computer. They were created as part of the computer files. At this point, for purposes of discussion, we must make a distinction between normal text and such figures. The standards and protocol problems associated with the latter are more difficult than those associated with normal text. This is illustrated by our earlier remarks indicating how easy it is to transfer text between different commercial word processing systems and how difficult it may be if the material contains graphics. In this section we emphasize text. The next section discusses graphics and pictures.

To a large degree, the databases that are available do not follow any standard set of protocols and standards. They have been designed to interact with people and as requested provide interactive terminal sessions, reports in printed form, reports as files, etc. In other words, each system has defined its own internal database structures, protocols, standards, etc. Consider a problem in which it is necessary to interact with many of the available databases, for example, databases that describe the properties of materials in different areas (e.g., mechanical, chemical, medical). The present resources and practices are fine as long as a human is interacting with the individual systems. He or she can provide the interface to the different databases. However, expecting that a computer system can interact with a group of databases, and process the data from those sources in a meaningful way, is a different matter. Many of problems encountered in doing this are discussed in Chapter 9 on Database Management Concepts or the earlier parts of this chapter. It was pointed out earlier that there is not a single comprehensive solution to this problem. We should continue to push for good protocols and standards, and hope that, whatever our success, it will simplify our problems with new databases. We might even be able to restructure some old databases, or at least provide "filters." However, there are a lot of computer readable data available in the world today. Additional data are being added at a rapid rate. Our computer systems are not well connected to the data in the world at large in a meaningful way. It is inescapable, that at least in the foreseeable future, we shall have to use "alternate methods" along the lines discussed in Section 10.5.

Today there is much discussion of the "information highway." It should be clear that our real problem is not associated with this term in the transport sense. To a large degree, the inherent capacity exists in the common carrier system of today. With the introduction of ISDN and other advances, the transport facilities should be able to keep up with demand. It is, in the authors' view, unfortunate that the politicians appear to stress the information highway rather than the more fundamental issues of protocols, standards, and interfacing that underlie the opportunity.

There are incompatibilities between some system features and services that people expect. In a sense, you cannot have it both ways. A good example involves medical records. It would be nice if, when you are traveling, your medical records would be available in an emergency on-line to authorized medical personnel. At the same time, you might want to keep your medical records private. Pragmatically these two concepts are incompatible. The first requirement of necessity makes personal information potentially available to too many people. There are always a few people who do not adhere to the expected standard of behavior and there would be leaks.

Today there are people who make a business out of investigating other people from workstations by accessing legal and financial databases over the network. In fact many of them offer such services to others. Unfortunately, it is to be expected that a certain number of professional investigators seeking such information will not feel constrained by existing laws. There is little that you can keep private. In the United States we have yet to face up to the issue of privacy versus the availability of data.

10.8.3 An Example of Computerized Technical Databases and Metadata

The fact that data are available in machine-readable form does not ensure that the corresponding information is. Most data are much more complex in character than say a telephone directory or a stockmarket report. Text, pictures, and sounds, for example, can convey a lot of information that is not easily reduced to numerical or formal logical representation. How would you describe the information of music or pictures? How would you retrieve it? It is somewhat easier for most of us to visualize information that can be represented numerically, and consequently for illustrious purposes in what follows we consider technical numerical data.

There are many ways of recording and presenting technical numerical data and their proper interpretation can be very complicated. We are all familiar with the term *multimedia.* If we are considering technical numerical data, we must also consider the many ways in which information can be described or presented. There are many ways, for example, in which visual information can be presented and stored. In addition, the proper interpretation of the data may depend upon metadata—the data about the data.

Much information, indeed even that necessary to minimally understand the numeric values of technical information, is contained in metadata. In some cases, metadata can exceed in volume (bytes) the numerical values themselves by a factor of 10 to 100. Furthermore, if a database is being built from extracts from printed records (technical books or journals) much of the metadata will be implicit rather than explicit in character, being embodied in the associated text, footnotes, or choice of typeface, or in the arrangement of tables or graphs, etc. All of these metadata, explicit or implicit, must themselves be retrieved, manipulated, and displayed in an effective computerized information system.

The metadata concept will perhaps be more clear with reference to a representative technical information system—namely, one relating to the properties of engineering materials such as those that might be used for the design of aircraft, turbines, bridges, electronic devices, etc.[20] The American Society for

---

20. H. Krockel and J. H. Westbrook, "Computerized Materials Information Systems," Philosophical Transactions of the Royal Society, A322 (1987): 373–91.

Table 10.1   Principal Metadata Parameters for Materials Property Data

Data Source	**Units**
Database	Unit classes
Exhibit ID	Standard units
Exhibit type	Valid/units conversions
Data set	**Characterization of Data and Data Values**
Materials	Source format
Names	Class
Designations	Reliability
Equivalent designations	Data quality
Descriptors	**Statistical Descriptors**
Properties (dependent variables)	Data value descriptors
Names	Descriptors of population of data values
Synonyms	**Test Descriptors**
Allowed values	Specimen description
Units	Test conditions
Independent Variables	Date and time of test
Names	Laboratory operator
Synonyms	**Footnotes**
Allowed values	**References**
Units	

Testing Materials (ASTM) has recently published a manual on building databases for this field.[21] For a particular property value to be understood, a host of metadata must be associated with it. Some of these are summarized in Table 10.1. Note that although the user (application) may be concerned with a single numerical value such as the strength of a given material, in order to interpret and know what that number means the metadata are required. Assurance of

---

21. C. H. Newton, ed., *Manual on the Building of Materials Databases,* ASTM MNL 19 (Philadelphia: American Society for Testing Materials, 1993); see pages 4–6, 34–44 for discussion of standardization issues.

completeness of the metadata and standardization of the terminology is essential to establish the internal integrity of the database, to facilitate the compatibility of databases intended to work together, to serve diverse users with different backgrounds and different intended applications, and to establish an audit trail when the source or history of any individual data value is required. These matters are fully discussed by Westbrook and Grattidge.[22]

Another issue is that not all of the needed data are in the form of written text or single numbers. For example, graphs, nomographs, tables, and pictures, are forms in which technical numerical data with a great deal of information will be found. These often comprise the information that engineers need to put into their workstations to solve a problem. There are neither standards nor protocols that cover this area. It is easy to copy a curve, table, or a nomograph into a computer as a picture by raster scanning to generate a bit map. Such a bit map, however, does not permit the information contained therein to be searched or manipulated. More sophisticated capture techniques have been developed that are successful in this regard, at least for tables and Cartesian plots, but some human intervention is still required.[23] Generally speaking, there are not yet standards or protocols that address the computerization of printed data. Lacking formal agreement (a protocol) and the standards for graphs and nomograms, the human provides the interface between the data source and the machine. As noted, there is work on mechanizing the interpretation of this type of data, but it is not an easy problem, and we are a long way from a mechanized solution.

True understanding of the significance and reliability of individual numbers represented by tables, and graphs and other pictorial presentations, depends upon the answers to many questions. For example: Under what conditions were the experimental data obtained? Who performed the work? What assumptions were made? If others have different numbers for the same thing, how is the difference to be resolved? Whom do I believe? How would a computer system seeking the data I want answer these questions? Would the computer system know enough to consider the records and professional reputation of the people involved? Would it know enough to start seeking additional data that might be relevant to reaching a decision? These are not trivial questions. Today a design engineer or scientist familiar with the field answers

22. J. H. Westbrook and W. Grattidge, *The Role of Metadata in the Design and Operation of a Materials Database*, vol. 2, edited by J. S. Glazman and J. G. Kaufman, ASTM STP 1106 (Philadelphia: American Society for Testing Materials, 1991), pp. 84–102.

23. W. Grattidge, "Capture of Published Materials Data," in J. S. Glazman and J. R. Rumble, Jr., eds., *Computerization and Networking of Materials Databases*, ASTM STP 1017 (Philadelphia: American Society for Testing Materials, 1989), pp. 151–74.

them. In fact, he or she may spend more time answering questions like this, and deciding what to put into a workstation, than computing. If so, *we are not going to speed up the overall design process by just speeding up computing. We must address the issues of protocols, standards, and information storage and retrieval in the context of both data and metadata.*

Let's look at an important example: It is perfectly clear, that an aircraft company with a good interface between the world's data on materials, and its internal computers doing engineering design, would have a tremendous advantage in design cycle compared to competitors lacking that capability. In addition, better technology along these lines represents a business opportunity for those providing information system hardware and software.

As pointed out earlier, although computers are today involved in collecting, analyzing, and storing almost all experimental data, the information therein may not be readily available. People still publish graphs, pictures, etc. Rarely is all of the raw source data or metadata available to the readers of a publication. Even if it were, they might not be able to interpret it. Consequently, the problems discussed in this section are relevant to old data and also data that will be generated and collected in the future.

It is obvious that there are similar issues in other areas, be it economics, law, medicine, or politics. And in some areas the issues are much more difficult. At least in technological fields, there are reasonably well understood core physical and mathematical laws that underlie what we observe. That is not necessarily true in other areas.

Consider the legal profession and databases to assist lawyers. It is easy to computerize the text of what is contained in court records and decisions. This has been done by the two major companies in the United States offering legal reference books and computer retrieval services. There are a vast number of relationships between the various decisions that have been reached in the courts. The hard task is building the indexes and retrieval system that can access databases and extract information from them. The interpretation and creation of those relationships may have to be made in the presence of what appear to be, and in fact are, logically inconsistent facts. The major task is in creating a meaningful database. That is the task that represents the major cost of those providing computerized legal databases. It involves professional, knowledgeable people. That is really the service that the lawyer pays for.

The real point of this section is that there are serious problems, and at the same time opportunities, in building better bridges between the world of data and our computer systems. In the sense in which we have used these terms, the issues involve protocols, standards, metadata, and meaning. Because we are dealing primarily with the transfer of data and information between systems, they are also very much intertwined with database technology, as discussed in Chapter 9.

10.9 Summary and Comments

Establishing protocols and standards is a central issue in the development of distributed information systems. It is a difficult task. At any one time, they will not be able to provide the level of integration that we would like, but we must use what is available. We must develop and introduce standards in a rational fashion and as rapidly as we can. At the same time, we must be realists. Given a problem to solve, a system to design and implement, and the challenge of integrating it with other systems, we must be aware of all the alternatives to reaching the desired objective.

This chapter may be viewed by some people as not supporting the work on existing standards. That view would be a misinterpretation of the perspective we are trying to present. It is important that we not expect too much of standards and protocols. We must understand their limits. We must be prepared to step outside of the structures implied by those standards when dictated by performance and economic considerations. This is a view often not recognized in textbooks and academic courses. It is certainly desirable that students have an understanding of ideal solutions, for such solutions may provide the yardsticks by which we can measure current technology and opportunities for research. At the same time, we are preparing students for the real world and they should realize the limitations of idealized cases.

It takes years to introduce protocols and standards. The tendency is to rush out and proclaim that the new ideas have solved our problems. They usually have not. How long ago was it that the OSI reference model was proclaimed as the solution to our communications protocol problems? We should recognize that standards may represent a desirable step forward, but that they have their limitations. In fact, it is unsettling to realize that maybe the level of interfacing and transparency that we would like is unattainable. In this chapter, our main goal has been to put things in perspective.

We must recognize that serious scaling problems often arise when an attempt is made to apply initial concepts to very large scale and complex problems. This is not a criticism of preliminary work in standards. Preliminary standards that apply to part of the overall problem are usually a necessary first step. We should simply recognize that scaling is a problem, and our programs should incorporate this perspective. In the information age, we must be prepared for very large distributed systems on the scale of the telephone system.

In closing this chapter we want reemphasize some things that have been explicitly or implicitly stated:

Standards and protocols are essential in distributed information systems. Improvements in these areas could have a large impact on our ability to design systems.

Work in standards and protocols is difficult. They are nasty problem areas. Few people in the academic community are interested. The payoff in terms of the measurements placed on an academic person are not clear. The risks are too high. Consequently, there is little basic research in these areas.

There are basic research issues associated with standards and protocols. They are tough issues, and the national payoff could be very large. Support on a national scale should be given more serious consideration. Fortunately, there has been some recognition at the national level. The funding by the National Science Foundation of the Center for Telecommunications Research at Columbia University is an example.

Lastly, we must keep things in perspective. Don't expect too much. Take what you can get. Be prepared to look at all alternatives.

10.10   Problems

Note: You should not spend more than 2 hours on any single problem given below.

1. The protocol models of Figs. 10.1 and 10.2 permit the action at a level n to be influenced by conditions at the level $(n-k)$. Consider a computer system or programming problem in which you might consider this to be desirable. You may pick a real-life example that you have encountered, or make up an example.

    In not more than two pages prepare a critique of the example that you have picked. Indicate what you consider to be the pros and the cons of using the $(n-k)$ model compared to the alternatives.

2. Consider Fig. 10.2. The two sides do not have to have identical structures nor do they have to have identical protocols at the various levels. In not more than two pages prepare a critique of the advantages and disadvantages of requiring that the level structure and protocols on the two sides be the same. This should be in the context of information systems and computers.

3. Consider the information system and application levels of Fig. 10.4. In not more than two pages describe (a) the number of levels that you would recommend and (b) the functions that you would place in each of your recommended layers.

4. Figure 10.5 introduced the concept of interfacers or adapters. Give three examples, including a brief description at a conceptual level, of where you believe this approach has been applied.

5. In not more than two pages discuss the major factors that you believe are holding up the development of interfacing standards.

6. There are many databases that can be accessed from data networks. Assume that you have a problem in which you wish to use data in four of the available databases. Make it a real problem if you can.

   Your task will be to write a report that involves data from all four databases. There will be some numerical computation involved. You are to use data from the databases without retyping or redrawing it. What problems would you expect to encounter in meeting your objectives? How would you get around those problems?

Chapter 11

Data Classification
and Distribution

classify: (1) To arrange or organize according to class or category. (2) To designate (a document, for example) as confidential, secret, or top secret.

The American Heritage Dictionary[1]

11.1 Introduction

It is important to understand the flow of data and information in any computer system. The ability to share data under proper and authorized conditions is the key feature of a distributed system. The intended uses of those data are key factors in answering a variety of questions:

Where data should be located?

Who should have access to data?

How should data be protected?

How important is it that data always be available?

Upon what time scale must data be available?

Can one afford the possibility of data being lost?

Who should be able to modify data?

Who owns a specific subset of the overall data?

There is not a single answer to any of these questions, which encompass the totality of data. Instead these issues must be addressed for subsets of the totality of data. Analysis in these terms can have a profound impact on the overall

---

1. American Heritage Dictionary for Windows, Wordstar International, 1993, Cambridge, Mass.

architecture and performance of an information system. In earlier chapters we introduced data concepts that are important in taking such an approach. After a brief review of some of the important factors, we present an integrated view of data classification and distribution.

Chapter 4 discussed at a requirements level many of the things that system designers must be prepared to provide if required by an application. Although the implications of those requirements are not discussed in detail, in the case of a given application, it is clear that specifying requirements that are not needed is a foolish thing to do. The price that might be paid in performance and cost could be unacceptable. For example, encrypting all data in a system, including that which should be accessible to everyone, would be costly with respect to performance, implementation effort, and operational expense. Requiring real time response when it would never be used is another example. Including mechanisms to update data, when data are static and will never be changed would be poor design. The point is that pragmatically we cannot afford to treat all data the same when it comes to system design and architecture.

Chapter 5 reviewed from a computer system and operating system perspective where technology is today, and by implication additional capabilities that are needed in order to meet the requirements of the heterogeneous systems of tomorrow. As mentioned above, it is not necessary, or desirable, to invoke those capabilities under all circumstances and in all applications. What should be provided in a specific case will depend upon the purpose of the information system, the nature of the data, and the uses that will be made of the data. For example, if numerous ports are required to switch data consisting of an occasional very short message among a very large number of ports, it would be foolish to utilize a crossbar switch, with its relatively long set-up time or cost.

Chapter 9 reviewed some of the database management system concepts that are relevant to meeting information system requirements. Again, it is clear that all features and data should not be made available to all users. The very concept of a view is a restriction on the data available to users. Another example is that facilities for rapid recovery and restart in an on-line transaction processing system can be expensive and can even degrade performance. If the application is such that the time to restructure a database from journal tapes is acceptable, reliance on journal tapes may provide a better solution than procedures requiring duplication at a higher level of memory (than tape) or even redundant computing equipment to provide fail-safe performance. As the discussion in Chapter 9 indicated, in the database management area scientists and engineers face real challenges in providing satisfactory distributed database management systems.

Chapter 10 addressed the problems of interfacing the components of heterogeneous information systems and the need for standards. Protocols and standards do not provide a general purpose cost-effective solution to all problems and it is doubtful that they ever will. At least for the present, when faced

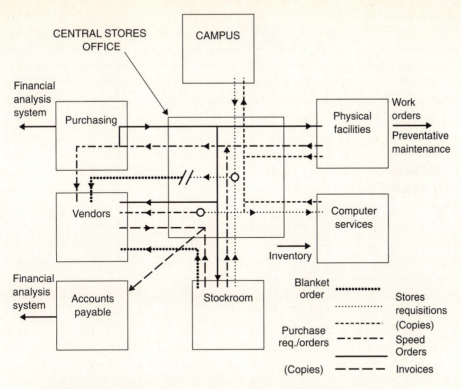

Figure 11.1   Simplified paper flow diagram of central stores. *Source:*
Albert J. Bunshaft, "A View of Administrative Information Flow and
Usage" (report submitted to Rensselaer Polytechnic Institute,
September 1, 1983).

with designing a system, we shall have to analyze the tradeoffs and alternatives and reach decisions as to how specific foreign systems will be interfaced. Those choices will depend upon the data and what they will be used for.

It is clear that in this environment for information systems we cannot treat all data the same. The present chapter focuses on what can be done in the area of categorizing data to make the architectural and database management challenges referred to in earlier chapters more tractable. Data classification is needed to adequately solve today's problems. Beyond this, we should clearly understand that even if the challenges in operating systems, architecture, database management, and interfacing have been addressed, we must still face the necessity of categorizing or classifying data. The key to categorizing data is understanding the flow and use of data in an existing or planned information system.

Figures 11.1 and 11.2 illustrate this point. Both figures are taken from a report by Albert J. Bunshaft that was prepared in 1983 at Rensselaer Polytechnic

INFO. \ DEPT.	Physical Facilities Systems						Financial Systems			Academic Systems		
	Prop. Mgmnt.	Space Mgmnt.	Prev. Maint.	Inventory	White prints	Work orders	Purchase orders	RPI Payroll	Accounting System	Student Accounts	Student Records	Alumni Systems
Purchasing	M			R		R	(M)		M			
Scheduling			(M)	R	R	(M)	M					
Accounts payable				R		M	M		M			
Receiving/ Cen. Stores				(M)	R	M	M		R			
Risk Mgmnt.	R	R	R	R	R	R	R					
Prop. Mgmnt.	(M)	R	R	R	R	R	R					
Housing	R	M	R	R	R	R	R		R	M	M	
Security/ Safety	R	R	R	R	R	R	R				R	
Registrar		R		R	R	R	R		R	M	(M)	M
Bursar				R		R	R	R	M	(M)	M	
Admissions				R		R	R			M	M	
Medical				R		R	R				R	
Payroll				R		R	R	(M)	M	M		
Personel				R		R	R	M				
Academic campus	R	R		R	R	R	R		R		R	
Research accounting	R	R		R	R	R	R	M	M	R	R	
Dean of students				R	R	R	R	R	R	R	R	R
Planning	R	(M)		R	(M)	R	R					
Shops		R	M	R	R	M	R					
Comptroller	R			R		R	M	M	(M)	M		
Cashier				R		R	R	M	M	R		
Alumni development				R		R	R				R	(M)

R → Read only → Initiate transaction inquiry
M → Modify → Selective information modification
(M) → Control → System controller

Figure 11.2   Information usage matrix. *Source:* Albert J. Bunshaft, "A View of Administrative Information Flow and Usage" (report submitted to Rensselaer Polytechnic Institute, September 1, 1983).

Institute.[2] The study focused on the administrative information systems that existed at that time. RPI was selected both because it was something that RPI students could relate to and because it represented typical activity in the information field. We shall not discuss the figures in detail but rather provide them as examples of data flow and the sharing of data. Figure 11.1 indicates the information flow relevant to the operation of the Central Stores and Receiving Department. That department maintained an inventory from which other RPI departments could obtain standard supplies. The diagram was prepared as part of a program to automate more of the information handling involved.

Figure 11.2 takes a broader look at the administrative functions of the campus as a whole and indicates the relationship between various types of data and the departments that must share information. Not only is there a need for multiple departments to access specific data, but there are cases in which multiple departments need to update that data. It should be noted that the users are specified as departments or groups of people. There is no reason to believe that in a situation like this, all people in a group should be given equal access to data. For example, it may be desirable for only a few people in payroll to have access to all of the payroll records.

11.2   An Atomic Level Model

Many organizations have an immense amount of data. The Social Security system, including Medicare, is a prominent example, as are organizations involved in medical diagnostic imaging and manufacturing. For example, aircraft turbines have thousands of parts, each one with its engineering and manufacturing history recorded by serial number. The minute details of the operational history of nuclear reactors serve a crucial function in power plant operation. In libraries where both the amount of data and the number of users can be immense, there are databases being created that will contain thousands of terabytes of data.[3]

Given that there are areas where terabytes of data are being collected every day, it is important to recognize that there are users that access those data under widely varying conditions. (When we speak of users in this sense, we imply either people or machines.) Considering the quantity of data and the

2. Albert J. Bunshaft, "A View of Administrative Information Flow and Usage" (report submitted to Rensselaer Polytechnic Institute, September 1, 1983).

3. Robert Pool, "Turning an Info-Glut Into a Library," *Science* 266 (October 7, 1994): 20.

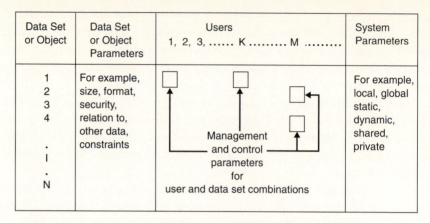

Data Set or Object	Data Set or Object Parameters	Users 1, 2, 3, …… K ……… M ………	System Parameters
1 2 3 4 . I . N	For example, size, format, security, relation to, other data, constraints	Management and control parameters for user and data set combinations	For example, local, global static, dynamic, shared, private

Figure 11.3 Data requirements matrix. *Source:* Richard Shuey and Gio Wiederhold, "Data Engineering and Information Systems," *Computer Magazine* 19, no. 1 (January 1986): 19. Reprinted with permission of IEEE.

number of users, the dimensionality of the overall problem is staggering. Perhaps the best way to comprehend the dimensionality, the number of parameters involved, and the quantity of design and control data implied is to approach the problem from the absolute bottom. What would be the complexity of the problem if we were to control data at a microscopic level?

Let's consider small sets of data, which we shall refer to as data sets, data atoms or objects. We illustrate this in terms of the data requirements matrix shown in Fig. 11.3.

The first column entries identify a data set that may consist of one data object or even one datum in a database. In what follows we shall use the term data set to denote all of these.

Entities in the second column describe the parameters of the individual data sets important in managing and controlling the data set.

The third group of columns is divided into users, where the term user implies a single person or a class of individuals, a location, a computer applications program, or any combination of these. The entries for a specific data set and user combination indicate the control parameters desired by the user, and also which of the corresponding services can be provided or allowed within other constraints that must be imposed by the overall system. At this point it may be necessary to resolve any differences that arise between user desires and global constraints in the second column.

A row entry in the fourth column considers all user entries in that row and summarizes the system parameters applicable to the data set represented by that row. By system parameters, we imply those aspects of the data sets and their use that may be important to the computer system designer and system architect. At this stage it may be necessary to resolve inconsistencies in system parameters that result from conflicts between the desires of individual users.

Let us be more specific. In Fig. 11.3 the controls on a data set or object are represented by a small square box in column 3. The figure shows that user 1 has access to data set 1 under conditions that are specified in the corresponding box. User K also has access to data set 1, but the control conditions might be quite different. In a similar fashion, user M has access to data sets 2 and 4, but the control conditions may be different for those two data sets. We may thus have individual and possibly unique control characteristics for each combination of a data set and a user of that data set.

Taken as a whole, the matrix is a method of assembling the data that are important in establishing the necessary controls and creating a design for the overall system. Examples in the latter category include where data should be assigned in a memory hierarchy, where data should be located physically, and whether strict concurrency control is required for the elements of a data set. After the resolution of conflicts and constraints, the control parameters for the use of a particular data set by a specific user should reside in the corresponding box in column 3. A more detailed and expanded set of the examples shown in Fig. 11.3 is given below:

Data set or object parameters: Size of data set, data formats, standard and protocol information, security level, relation to other data sets, general global constraints on use.

User parameters: Single or class (set) of individual users, locations, computers, application programs, service to be requested, etc.

Management and control parameters: Access rights, time of response needed and allocated, proposed use of data, whether the data are working or archival data, etc.

System parameters: Local or global data, shared or individual data, static or dynamic data, time scales required, etc.

For illustrative purposes here, we have given emphasis to the management and control parameters in column 3. However, as noted earlier and as we shall see in later sections and chapters, many of the parameters in columns 2 and 4 are important in architectural design. Taken as a whole, the details in the matrix have a large impact on which data should be where and under what conditions.

Let us assume that we have a very large number of data atoms in what we call the maximum complexity case. Referring still to Fig. 11.3, we wish to consider how things scale as the numbers get large. Let

N = the number of data objects or atoms.

P_d = number of data parameter categories for the dth data atom. To the degree that the number of relations between data atoms can be a function of the number of data atoms, P_d may increase as N increases.

M = number of users.

P_m = number of user parameter categories for the mth user.

Forgetting about the possible increase in P_d as a function of N due to the number of possible relations between data atoms, the number of potential entries in a box in the third column of Fig. 11.3 is equal to

$$\text{Number of potential entries in a specific box} = (P_d)(P_m) \qquad (11.1)$$

As there are $(N)(M)$ possible boxes, the total number of potential entries are given by

$$\text{Number of potential entries} = [(N)(M)][(P_d)(P_m)]. \qquad (11.2)$$

The important thing is the growth in the number of users and data atoms. If the data atoms are small, the control data for a data atom could well exceed the data contained in that data atom.

The possible growth of P_d with N, which was ignored in the last paragraph, can be troublesome. It is primarily a database question. In network database terminology, the number of relationships, links, or rings can grow rapidly. In relational terminology, if the number of data objects and their interrelationships become very large, which is analogous to complex relationships in a network database, the required relations and the number of foreign key links between them can become very large. This significantly increases the complexity of the data management task. Basically, under these circumstance, the problem does not scale.

On the other hand, the relationships of the data in an information system are usually not that complex and are more or less under control. If they were not, current database management systems would not provide acceptable performance. In effect, the nature of the applications are such that only a small part of the potential complexity is relevant. The applications themselves are in effect categorizing the relationships between the data elements into the subsets (nonexclusive) that are relevant and important.

The basic reason that we must categorize data is that we cannot cope with the potentially large number of data management and control entities in column 3 of Fig. 11.3. For a large system, the only alternative is to assign data elements and users to categories and apply the same rules to all the elements within a given category. The reduced number of possibilities that result from categorization is more manageable. Both techniques simplify design and make reasonable performance possible.

There is nothing unique about this approach nor is it presented as the only possible way to address the problem. However, it is clear that if we plan to design and control a large database at a truly atomic level of control, we are being unrealistic. There is no way that this will be possible. The amount of "data control" information would be unmanageable and the impact on system performance unacceptable. We must therefore consider data in units that are larger chunks or subsets, and we must be willing to treat all data in a given subset the same. Concurrently, we must be willing to categorize users and treat all users in a specific category the same. Then the model of Fig. 11.3 is concerned with relatively large data sets and groups of users. The problem is more tractable. There is no choice but to consider categories of users and of data. A purpose of the model is to emphasize this fact by reducing the alternative to an absurdity. At the same time, if the data are placed in sets (subsets), and the users placed in categories, the model provides a good indication of what we must be prepared to do.

It is necessary to stress two additional points:

1. It should be clear that a specific atom of data can be assigned to several sets (or subsets). In other words, there can be a many-to-many relationship between data atoms and data sets.

2. Even after aggregating data into categories and classes, we cannot expect to deal with the numbers involved in a large and complex database by hand. Whatever we are able to do in partitioning and aggregating data will be limited by the available automated design tools. The need for an adequate design discipline, and the absolute necessity of automated design tools is clear.

11.3   The Categorization of Data

In many respects the ideal situation would be to consider the requirement for data and the control of data at the lowest possible atomic level, as illustrated in Fig. 11.3. That would give us a superb level of control and permit us to allocate computer resources in a truly detailed fashion. However, as has been pointed out, considering the size of the databases that we must deal with, this is unreasonable. The bookkeeping data (i.e., the data necessary for microscopic control and design) could well exceed the useful data, and the impact on overall performance would be unacceptable. Thus we are confronted with the problem of collecting data atoms into sets where the members of a set have identical or acceptably similar control or system properties. What is meant by similar will depend upon the tradeoffs and circumstances. Let us turn now to alternatives for performing that classification and subsetting.

There are of course many approaches to the partitioning of data. Unfortunately, partitioning methods that appear near optimum in one set of circumstances may be poorly matched to other areas of application or to different circumstances. With shared data, the requirements and usage patterns of different users may vary widely. For example, good response is required by some users and not by others. What is viewed as static data by one application may be dynamic data to another. The creation of views that define the data that can be seen by a user was discussed in Chapter 9. The creation of a view in a sense involves the creation of a data set or subset.

Given the above situation, what is a reasonable set of criteria for the classification of data? What are the criteria that will prove to be important in the design and operation of distributed information systems? The specific categories suggested in what follows are somewhat arbitrary but we believe them to be useful. What we are looking for are pragmatic categories that will lead to simplified design and higher performance. They are not necessarily independent or orthogonal. As noted earlier, a given object can be categorized in many ways and can therefore belong to many categories. Furthermore, the boundary between two categories may not be any more precise than the boundary between, for example, fast and slow animals.

11.3.1 Categories of Data Sets Based on Latency and Transfer Rate

Latency and transfer rate are important parameters in system design. As discussed in Chapter 3, it is assumed that we are considering computer systems in which there are memory hierarchies. In that context, it is convenient to think in terms of five sets of parameters and correspondingly five categories:

1. *Operational:* The data required for the internal operation of a computer. Examples would include data associated with microcode, the storage of display data, and the instructions in a RISC computer.

2. *Working:* The data required by a "processing" or "logic" unit on an instruction-by-instruction basis. Examples would include the data being used by a vector processor, in a relational database currently being processed by a CPU (or in the case of a database machine by the active CPUs), and in a program loop.

3. *Active:* The data required by a computer on a process, partial problem, or problem basis. Examples would include the data associated with the design of a VLSI chip or with the design of a particular turbine blade or of the overall turbine, the data associated with corporate stocks in a specific area, the data in a spreadsheet that you are working with.

4. *Reference:* The data required when in the normal course of work the problem changes as well as the data you expect to need in the near future. Examples would include the data on the parts of a design for a VLSI chip that you are going to work on tomorrow, data associated with the current value of all stocks on the New York Stock exchange, files on the current financial status of a corporation, the records of students currently enrolled at a university.

5. *Archival:* The data that you have no short-term need for and perhaps never intend to use. However, there is some reason to believe that although the probability is small, you may need the data at a future date. Examples would include your tax records or correspondence of five years ago, or the records associated with manufacturing a steam turbine 30 years ago.

The importance of these categories is that in each area there are vastly different requirements with regard to the following factors:

1. Latency

2. Bandwidth

3. Communication network alternatives

4. Access control

5. Maintenance of data integrity

Latency, bandwidth, and communication network alternatives are usually the most important of these five areas. The differences in requirements in each category imply that their goals can be met by different devices, networks, system software, etc. The cost of the different alternatives may vary by orders of magnitude. For example, working data sets require fast access and should be in fast memory, or if that is not possible because of size, paged into fast memory from disc (e.g., disc cache). Fast memory is expensive. At the other extreme, archival data might just as well be put in the cheapest memory at the bottom of the memory hierarchy. There is usually ample time to retrieve it.

The classification of data sets provides the primary reasons that a memory hierarchy is required in order to obtain high performance. There are other reasons for distributing data, but performance alone dictates the use of a memory hierarchy. The design of an appropriate memory structure is dependent on estimates of the data set sizes in the indicated categories and their anticipated use. As discussed in Chapter 3, the one-level store concept (virtual memory) should be utilized to provide for the automatic migration of data sets between the different levels in the hierarchy.

It is clear that the categorization discussed here also has relevance to the physical location of data in a distributed system. It also has relevance to the design of information systems. Although most of the discussion of these issues is in Chapters 9, 12, and 13, we give one example here.

Assume that you are working with an information system at a location A, and that the program you are running must operate on relational tables at both A and at distant location B. During the time the program is running, the working data set consists of a subset of data at A and another subset of data at B. As discussed in Chapter 9, this can lead to serious performance problems. Those problems could have been avoided if the data were all on the computer system at location A. That alternative might have been something that the computer system architect could have selected. It is more likely, however, that the decision will be dependent on the design of the overall information system. The point is that the overall design must involve both computer system and information system tradeoffs and both viewpoints must be represented. The classification categories being considered are particularly relevant to the design.

11.3.2 Categories of Data Sets Based on Logical Domains

It is often convenient to classify data on the basis of *logical domains*. Implicit in our use of this term is the concept of the two domains of users who need the data:

1. *Local:* Of relevance to a user or a specific restricted group of users.

2. *Global:* Of relevance to more than one user or more than a restricted group of users.

The word *logical* implies that neither the physical location of the users nor the data are determining considerations. For example, a good deal of personal family information can be viewed as local to a family even though the family may be located at many different locations. The implication is that such information should only be accessible by those within the family. Where the data are located in principle is not important—for example, they might be on a remote time-sharing computer and accessed by family members all over the world. Another example would be a driver's license number. The number belongs to one individual but its use is more global, and there might be many others, from diverse groups, who might have a need to access the data.

At the same time, it should be realized that logically local information will often serve a group of users who are at the same location. As far as the mail system is concerned, the precise location of a home, the side of the street, etc., is local information that only the local post office needs to know. Similarly, the database that specifies in a factory stacker crane system the cubical in which a part is located is of interest only to the stacker crane controller. The relevance of these types of considerations is that the users who define a logically local category, and their location, may be a significant factor in determining where, for system performance reasons, data should be physically located. It is also clear that these considerations may impact on the design of a system to meet requirements such as security.

11.3.3 Categories of Data Sets Based on Temporal Properties

One of the most significant ways of categorizing data has to do with whether a data set is fixed or changes with time. Three categories must be considered:

1. *Static:* Data are fixed and do not vary with time. Examples would include library books and journal articles, court records, and engineering drawings for products that have already been manufactured. Provision will often be required for adding data to this category and the relevant static databases—for example, when books are added to a library.

2. *Pseudostatic:* Data are unlikely to change during the interval of time of interest. Examples would include a computerized English dictionary or a company's organization chart. For design purposes these data can often be considered as static. However, provisions must be made for updating the data—for example, when the meaning of a word or a company's organization changes.

3. *Dynamic:* Data are likely to change at any time. Examples would include bank accounts, a stock market database, and the status of machines in a factory.

The data in these categories can clearly be treated differently from a system design standpoint. In the static category, data are only read and never modified. They can be duplicated and located at many different locations. Concurrency problems never arise. The options for distributing machine-readable data are many, varying from electronic or optical disks to magnetic tapes. For example, many journals are now distributed on optical disks, with specific articles accessed from computer terminals and selectively printed out by the user.

The pseudostatic category is somewhat fuzzy and lies between the extremes of static and dynamic data. Concurrency problems do not exist in the normal sense, although occasional or periodic updates are required. Good examples are the core records of chemical abstracts, legal databases, and libraries. Although these would be considered static, those parts of the overall database that are concerned with indexing, information retrieval, and often meaning are not. For example, the importance of a court case and the decisions associated with it may be dependent upon changes in the law, the decisions of higher courts, or the outcome of later cases. This illustrates that there may be a relationship between static and pseudostatic data that in some respects operates in two directions. From a system design standpoint, it may be that the retrieval mechanism for static data should change with time. In the legal area, a previously important case may become a case of little importance that is rarely examined in detail. Thus, it may no longer be necessary to have an efficient mechanism for locating and retrieving it. In brief, the retrieval and information extracting parts of a system dealing with static data may be both pseudostatic and in some cases even dynamic. Nevertheless, pseudostatic data in the short term can usually be considered as static data.

The dynamic category is the one that from a system design standpoint presents most of the problems. The environment is highly interactive—that is, there are interactions between programs, processes, people, etc., and changes in the (dynamic) data as a result of those interactions. (If this were not the case, the data could be categorized as static or pseudostatic.) Communications delays and concurrency considerations can be serious problems and have a tremendous impact on design alternatives and performance. Examples would include information systems that are committing finite resources such as inventory, people's time, etc., and scientific computations in which two processes are accessing and modifying the same data.

It is clear that when categorizing data in terms of their temporal properties, it is important to identify the proper category. Static data should be so categorized and treated accordingly. Only dynamic data should be placed in the dynamic category and so treated.

11.3.4 Categories of Data Sets Based on Access Control or Security

In the area of security we must consider users (both people and computer processes) and data.

The users: Governments and corporations have long classified their employees into levels of clearance that define the documents that they will be permitted to see. In information systems we face similar problems with the additional constraint that, although users may be able to read a data item, they may not be permitted to modify it. (Again, we use the term *user* to refer to a human or a computer program.) An additional requirement often placed on obtaining classified data is that users, regardless of their level of clearance, must establish a need to know. This would be a useful feature to include in the access control mechanism in some information systems, but it is administratively difficult to establish. If algorithms to establish need to know could be implemented, they might mitigate the need, in some cases, to go to an atomic level of control (discussed earlier). In other words, are some of the access control entries in the boxes of Fig. 11.3 computable dynamically, and if so how?

The data: Having categorized the users, there is need to categorize the data. The result should be that users in a given category will be allowed access only to specific categories of data.

Unfortunately, access controls may not be as effective as they appear on the surface. Salary records are an example. Suppose that a person, or a computer process, is denied access to the salary information on specific individuals but is allowed to ask statistical questions of the salary database. There are people who have a real need for statistical data but no real need or authorization for detailed data. Clever statistical questions may provide the information necessary to determine the salary of a specific individual. In other words, security may depend not only on access controls but also on the use that a user intends to make of the data. Such access is particularly difficult to control.

11.3.5 Categories of Data Sets Based on Organizational Affiliation

Categorization by organization affiliation is very similar to categorization by logical domains, as discussed earlier. In fact, such categorization could be viewed as a special case of that earlier viewpoint and in that sense serve as an example of the nonorthogonality of the categorization schemes we are reviewing. In any event, if you look at any business you will probably see an organizational structure that is formed by groups in clearly defined domains:

Engineering

Manufacturing

Finance

Marketing

Personnel

Information Systems

11.3.6 Categories of Data Sets Based on Location of Use

Considering propagation delays and other constraints that are imposed by communications systems, the location of real users and where data are used can be very important in the design of systems. From a system performance standpoint, it is often desirable to locate data where it is going to be used.

Administrative and management personnel may require that data for which they are responsible be located where they are. This is not a requirement based on computer system performance. It is more likely to be a question of management style and personalities.

Location of use and data can also have a large impact on security, reliability, and availability requirements. For example, at the highest levels of security, you can locate the data and users at the same point, prohibit communications outside the facility, and install a fence around the facility. This is done in the military and intelligence areas. On the other hand, if the users are really dispersed, perhaps for reliability and availability, the data categorization will evolve in another direction.

11.3.7 The Importance and Pragmatics of Categorization

It is clear that, depending on the category or categories in which data can be placed, there are vastly different needs with regard to such things as latency, bandwidth, communications network alternatives, access control, and the maintenance of data integrity. Latency, bandwidth, and network properties (including location of nodes) have a direct and large impact on performance throughput. Access and integrity considerations can have a significant but less direct impact on performance. If we can pick appropriate categories, we can both simplify design and improve performance. Let's consider an example.

The location in a warehouse of specific items of stock can be categorized as local data, dynamic data, etc. The data are best kept in the database of one of the warehouse computers. The typical information relevant to the location of specific items in a stacker crane are best kept in the memory associated with the control computer of that stacker crane. At the same time, there is derived information such as the number of specific items stored in a warehouse that are of general interest and should be categorized as global. The numbers of items in stock are of interest to those in manufacturing, production scheduling, sales, marketing, finance, etc., and the people and computers associated with these functions may well be at remote locations.

The complexity of the interrelationships between data items in the information systems associated with societal activities far exceeds that normally found in scientific computing. Our emphasis on examples from societal applications is to stress that fact to the reader.

11.4   An Enterprise Viewpoint—The Road to Data Location

11.4.1 The Necessity of an Enterprise Viewpoint

Our discussion to date has been largely oriented toward data categorization focused on system optimization issues. This is certainly one way of viewing the location of data, but it is hardly adequate.

We are really interested in a view of the "enterprise" as a whole and the flow of data within that enterprise. The term *enterprise* implies an information and data perspective that considers the entire organization, whether it is a business, a branch of civil government, a military unit, etc. We need to understand for the entire enterprise: What information is needed? Where is it needed and under what circumstances and conditions? That knowledge is necessary to obtain the design requirements (design input data). The following factors are among those that impact on such an analysis:

The applications and users that need specific data.

Time requirements for specific data.

Access constraints as a function of use and user. These are often primarily established to maintain the correctness and integrity of data. There is another aspect that is often overlooked—namely, security. It may be important to prevent unauthorized access to data.

The pattern of references made to the data.

The location of changes made to the data.

The role the data plays in the decision-making process.

The need for currency in the data across all users.

The need for consistency of data.

The need to recreate lost data or information on an acceptable time scale.

The interaction level between different clusters of data.

The detailed access control required for clusters of data.

The level of system robustness, or fail-soft capability, required and the implications thereof to specific data.

The opinions of management and administrative personnel with respect to the location and control of data and associated computer systems.

Many of these areas are in part covered in the data requirements matrix discussed earlier, but we need to derive them from actual needs within the enterprise being considered.

As discussed earlier, it is clear that in a large system the partitioning of data will be required both for performance and for the reasons implied above. The dimensionality of partitioning decisions is significant, and there will be uncertainties in the information upon which those decisions should be based. It will be necessary to deal with both data and metadata. There is great merit in an enterprise viewpoint. However, as discussed earlier, there is some question as to whether things really scale. Some believe that this sets a limit on centralized systems and, by implication, on distributed systems unless the coupling is very loose. To a large degree, however, the heterogeneous distributed systems that we are emphasizing are essentially loose coupled systems. The reasons for this have been discussed earlier and include the heterogeneous nature of many of the hardware and software components utilized, as well as the heterogeneous nature of the development of many information systems.

Given the current state of the art, we cannot expect to have an entirely satisfactory design methodology. Adequate optimization methods do not exist. Succinctly: (1) We do not today have a design methodology that is satisfactory and (2) we do not have the automated tools that are required to handle the detailed data inherent in building large heterogeneous distributed systems.

11.4.2 Suggested Methodology for Design Decisions

Under the circumstances, our best strategy is to gather the available facts and proceed from there using our best judgment in making the necessary design decisions. The first thing to be done is to determine the location and flow of data within the enterprise. In so far as mechanization may lead to some modification of that flow, this may be an iterative task. This will permit us to start categorizing data so that they correspond to the location and flow of data within the enterprise. The purpose is to try to get information that enables us to do the following:

Make judgments concerning the control of data.

Decide where data should be located: (1) in a logical memory hierarchy; (2) in a physical memory hierarchy; or (3) with regard to physical spatial (geographic) location.

Following the methods implied in earlier sections of this chapter, a procedure for gathering relevant data has been used in some businesses and other sectors of the economy.

It can be effective with respect to current information systems and computer files.

It can be instructive with respect to what we intend to do in the future.

It has not been applied to all of the factors we have discussed. The complexity is too great for current design methodology and tools.

It has nevertheless been very useful. Works by Lorin, Shuey and Wieder-hold, and Bunshaft are again relevant.[4]

The basic steps can be summarized briefly:

1. Partition enterprise data as best you can. Utilize as many of the parameters that we have discussed as possible.

2. Form a matrix similar to the data requirements matrix presented in this chapter; consider the partitions of data (clusters of data) as one dimension.

3. Let the users (human, department, program) be another dimension.

4. Describe on a partition or matrix cell basis as many of the requirements as you can.

5. In light of what you now know, iterate what you have done if it appears that would be useful.

6. Apply the insight that you have gained to system specifications and architectural design.

Figure 11.4 shows the type of matrix that results. (One of the authors of this book has seen a similar matrix, created for a medium-sized business, which covered the walls of a large classroom.) The X's in the figure indicate that a given business function has an interest in and a need for data element *n*. There has been no attempt to indicate who owns the data element, who can have access, for what purpose the data element can be used, etc. These are refinements that are often added.

Figure 11.4 is in a simplified form. In reality, each business function has many components that can be broken down into more detail. However, if one attempts to put all of the available details in a matrix like Fig. 11.4, the complexity is similar to the discussion associated with Fig. 11.3 and soon becomes intractable. Nevertheless, the more limited analysis is a good step forward and provides a tie between data elements and function. The details within a specific function can be added later if desired.

The indicated procedure provides useful information in an organized fashion that can be used in design. However, the burden of design rests primarily on the ingenuity of the designer—which is not a satisfactory state of affairs. There is little formal methodology that can help the designer. At least for the

---

4. Harold Lorin, *Aspects of Distributed Computer Systems,* 2nd ed. (New York: Wiley, 1988); Shuey and Wiederhold, "Data Engineering and Information Systems," 19; Bunshaft, "A View of Administrative Information Flow and Usage."

Business Function	Data areas / elements										
	1	2	3	4	5	6	....	...	x	...	n
Marketing			X							X	
Engineering			X		X	X					
Manufacturing			X			X					
Sales									X		
Finance	X		X								
Personnel	X									X	
Information systems	X										
Research and development						X					
Legal		X	X		X	X	X				
Patent					X	X					
Public relations											

Note: The "X" indicates that the business function has a need for the data element.

Figure 11.4   An example of a business data analysis/data flow matrix.

foreseeable future, good designers are unlikely to be replaced by computers. However, regardless of what is done, we want to categorize data and users into the largest groups that make sense.

11.4.3 Some Rules of Thumb

In the absence of an adequate methodology, rule-of-thumb practices are often used once the available information has been gathered. They can be helpful, although as always there are exceptions. Some examples are given here:

Insist on reasonable requirements.

Work with the users.

Separate static and dynamic requirements.

Subset as much as possible.

Partition and locate static data.

Partition and locate dynamic data.

Provide capability for dynamic relocation.

Give emphasis to consistency, integrity, etc.

Assume that there will be no backup system other than that which is a part of the design.

Assume that communications costs, both dollars and performance, can be significant.

This is not a formal design procedure, nor does it point to existing "publicly available" tools that will really help the designer. Much is left to the ingenuity and overall capability of the designer. That is just the way things are today.

One of the main issues is the location of data in a distributed system. We have indicated how to gather much of the information needed in deciding this question, and we have referred to many of the tradeoff issues. However, we have not really discussed the main issue of data location, except when it has been convenient in discussing other issues to give a few examples.

The location of data is particularly crucial in designing information systems, in which the overall system is distributed and the properties of the communications network are important. This topic will be addressed in the next two chapters.

11.5   Summary and Comments

In an information system, it is important to understand the flow of data in the organizations being served. This flow plays a key role in many design decisions. To the degree that the information system serves an entire organization, the perspective must be that of the entire enterprise.

In a large distributed information system, it is not possible to either treat all data alike or individually at an atomic level. It is necessary to categorize data elements into groups with respect to latency and transfer rate requirements, logical domains, temporal characteristics, access control requirements, organizational relationships, location, etc. The elements of a given group then can be stored and processed using identical methods. In like manner, the users, be they people or processes in a computer, should be categorized into groups. In both cases, specific elements can be assigned to multiple categories.

The categorization of data and people is important in deciding upon memory structures and where the different computers and types and levels of storage equipment in a distributed memory hierarchy should be located, etc.

There does not exist a satisfactory architectural design discipline applicable to distributed memory in a large distributed system, but there are systematic ways to go about gathering the facts that are needed. Simulation can help in gaining insight to some of the design tradeoffs. However, in large measure, the success of a design is largely dependent upon the creativity and competence of the principal designers.

11.6   Problems

The following problems are focused on a first cut of data analysis in the administrative area. One should not spend more than four hours on any problem. You should submit what you have been able to accomplish during that time interval. It is recognized that it will be necessary for you to make assumptions.

1. (a) Consider a typical university department and the flow of administrative information within that department. The objective is to take the initial steps toward a first cut of an information system architecture for that department. You will have to make assumptions as to the interfaces with other university activities. (b) Prepare a diagram similar to the matrix in Fig. 11.4. Put in the boxes of the matrix constraints such as read, write, dynamic, etc. (c) Prepare a first cut architectural design for an information system to serve the department.

2. For a small business, real or imaginary, prepare an analysis as outlined in problem 1 above.

3. Consider a university as a whole. Pick one area of information systems. For example, information services to help students (excluding computers for solving problems and research) could be selected and specific categories might include registration, evaluating potential employers, signing up for interviews, changing courses, finding out about social activities, etc.

    Prepare an analysis as outlined in the statement of problem 1.

4. Prepare a similar analysis for the entire university selected in problem 3.

Chapter 12

Distributed Memory, Memory Hierarchies, Directories, and Data Retrieval

Caching in distributed systems: *When a resource (for example, a file or a name table) is accessed by a client, copies of some or all of the data values representing the resource are likely to be transferred to the client environment. The term caching refers to a mechanism, implemented by software in the client computer, for the retention in the client's environment of a copy of the data values for subsequent reuse, avoiding the need to request them again when the same resource is accessed subsequently. Since the storage available for caching in a client's environment is likely to be more limited than that available to the relevant resource manager, only a fraction of the data held by the resource manager can be retained in the client environment. The usefulness of caching therefore depends upon the hypothesis of locality in the pattern of references to data values—that data values from resources that have been accessed in the recent past are likely to be accessed again in the immediate future.*

George Coulouris, Jean Dollimore, and Tim Kindberg[1]

12.1 Introduction

In this chapter, we focus on the location of data in a widely distributed system. To do so, we must also consider memory systems. We have previously discussed memory systems and memory hierarchies for single systems or for

---

1. George Coulouris, Jean Dollimore, and Tim Kindberg, *Distributed Systems, Concepts and Design*, 2nd ed. (Reading, Mass.: Addison-Wesley, 1994), p. 46.

multiprocessor systems. The above excerpt is a good summary of the situation in that environment. It is necessary to refine and expand that concept so that it is applicable to the heterogeneous spatially distributed world that we are now considering.

1. As discussed earlier, we must consider a multilevel memory hierarchy in which caching may exist between various levels in the hierarchy.

    The components of that hierarchy may be at spatial locations that are separated by large distances.

    At any one level in the hierarchy, there may be many components at different locations.

    In effect, there may be a complex network of memory locations, and many sub-hierarchies in the overall hierarchy.

2. We must include the possibility that hardware will be utilized in reaching caching decisions and taking action (similar to what was done in the Atlas, IBM 367, GE 645, and SDS 940).

3. With prior knowledge of expected use, we may elect to preload caches and even tie down selected data in those caches. (This use of the term is well within the concept. For example, food and supplies are "cached" by explorers and travelers.)

4. We must consider environments that are much broader than a single computer system. For example, an environment may be a department, a campus, etc., and our actions taken to support all relevant computers in that environment. (In effect there may be a hierarchy of environments.)

5. As will be considered in more detail in the next chapter, it may be desirable to selectively place data management and storage within the communications network rather than at the nodes. (In effect, data management and storage are special "data service" functions.)

6. The focus will be on loosely coupled systems.

As we did earlier in this book, we shall make a distinction between data and information. The processors and users of information, be they humans or computers, are vitally interested in obtaining and retrieving both data and information from memory systems. The retrieval may be from parts of a distributed system at remote locations. The user may be interested in raw data, or information, or a combination of the two. In any event, communications system capabilities, and limitations, may have a large impact on the design of the overall memory system. It is important to consider information and data retrieval issues in this context.

Shared data provide the common threads that define the relationships among the components of a distributed system. As more and more computers and information systems are interconnected, the numbers and possible complexity grow. It is to be expected that this growth will continue. System models, analysis methods, and design concepts should be viable in that environment. Consequently, scaling factors will be important. We should always ask ourselves, will the model and techniques under consideration scale? In many respects, because there are fewer interactions between components, loosely coupled systems scale more satisfactorily than tightly coupled systems. In the extreme, loosely coupled systems can be expected to scale linearly.

12.2   Memory Hierarchies

It is to be expected that there will continue to be large differences in the cost of different types of memory. At the same time, the amount of data to be stored is increasing rapidly. To store large amounts of data economically, we need memory hierarchies. Unfortunately, although at the lower levels in a hierarchy the cost may be orders of magnitude less, the performance is correspondingly lower.

Well thought-out memory hierarchies must perform certain functions:

1. Provide the massive data storage that is required.

2. Given a hierarchy, reduce cost without reducing the performance of large memories. To accomplish this, it is necessary to make memory at all levels appear to be faster than it is both with regard to access time and transfer rate. The limitations of communications networks may impact on both access time and transfer rate.

3. Distribute data throughout a distributed computer system. In a distributed system, the memory at most levels, including parts of various hierarchies, may be distributed.

In Chapter 3, items (1) and (2) were discussed in the context of a single computer system. Our concern is distributed systems, and in such systems data are distributed. In this chapter, we focus on memory hierarchies and the location of data in a distributed environment. As noted, communications and network issues are important in that context, and some are considered. However, many of the important issues related to networks will be deferred to the next chapter.

The general hardware situation is shown in Fig. 12.1. In a distributed system, although it is not shown, there may be at any one level components at different locations. Consequently, the architecture is really more of a tree or

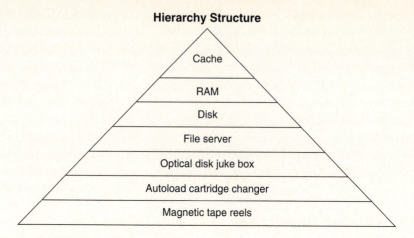

Typical memory costs (1994)

RAM
 ~50 nanosecond access time
 ~$40/MB

Magnetic Tape Cartridge
 ~50 GB loader (10 cartridges), $6,000
 ~$0.1/MB for loader
 ~$0.015/MB for tape
 ~15 seconds for new cartridge
 ~1 MB/sec transfer rate

Figure 12.1   A hierarchical data storage system

network structure than is indicated in the figure. Typical memory hardware costs during the fall of 1994 are also shown in the figure.

The rate at which data in machine-readable form are being collected is staggering. Much of the information is pictorial. Until recently the costs of storing pictures on photographic film were much smaller than digitizing a picture and storing it in machine-readable form. This is no longer necessarily the case. In addition, if the information is originally in digitized form, converting it to an analog picture on photographic film results in an information loss. Medical images from computer-aided tomography, magnetic resonance imaging, and ultrasound, as well as satellite pictures, are examples. Lastly, the processing of pictorial images can be much more sophisticated and involve many more parameters than processing by photographic means. In summary, it is clear that we are at a threshold where now, or in the near future, a large fraction of the pictorial information associated with information systems will be acquired, stored, and processed in digital form by computer.

Although memory costs particularly at the lower levels continue to drop rapidly, regardless of projected memory costs, data compression to reduce storage requirements can play an important role. As discussed in Chapter 6, it is believed that the redundancy of most pictorial information is very large. At the same time, the performance of specific high-performance compression techniques will be very application dependent. Nevertheless, there is a large potential payoff to be realized by improving compression methods. In addition, improved compression of data will reduce communications bandwidth requirements and cost.

Another area of memory and storage that becomes more complex with distributed systems is providing backup for data. For static data, this is obviously not a problem, except for the cost of duplicating memory. For pseudostatic data, providing backup is also not difficult. However, for dynamic data the situation is much more complex as concurrency control can be of major importance. Regardless of the temporal properties of the data, as the databases themselves can be extremely large, backup procedures must be based upon physical storage of comparable complexity and size. At what levels data should be duplicated, and at how many places, are design issues.

The magnitude of storage requirements is illustrated by the following examples:

The California Department of Water Resources has 500,000 photographic slides that they intend to put into a digitized database for use statewide. Each slide contains 3 to 4 megabytes of data for a current total of roughly 2 terabytes. To meet the objective, a physical storage system is needed as well as a computer system that will make it possible to retrieve the desired information and pictures.

In 1990, it was estimated that a 200-bed hospital generates approximately one terabyte of image data each year (i.e., X-ray tomography, magnetic resonance images, and sonic scans). There is every reason to believe that medical requirements for data storage will increase.

Earth-orbiting satellites generate in excess of one terabyte of data per day. Much of this is of interest to people in the earth sciences who are distributed throughout the country and world. It is also relevant to farming and industries related to ecology.

There is an international program underway to provide instant access to information from maps, about species, habitats, inventories of plant and animal genetics, etc. One hundred countries are involved and the intention is to preserve species diversity. There is a formal international treaty establishing this program. Initial plans are for a centralized database rather than integrating a large number of independent databases.[2]

2. Richard Stone, "Proposed Global Network for Ecology Data Stirs Debate," *Science* 266 (November 18, 1994): 1155.

Many of these large databases are primarily library systems, which means that they contain primarily static or pseudostatic data. Almost all library systems have many users (people or computers) and these users are increasingly at different locations. Today, perhaps the best example of a complex, distributed library system is the World Wide Web. Even though library systems are devoid of many of the problems associated with dynamic data, there are important areas that must be addressed:

> The determination of a reasonable structure for the memory hierarchy serving a library system is one such area. The architectural design alternatives and tradeoffs should include levels of physical memory, the location of memory, communications tradeoffs, etc. At stake are both system performance and system cost.

> Techniques that will make it possible to find the data are required. This is a nontrivial issue. A large library full of shelved books in no known order, and for which there is no catalog (card or computerized) would be of little use. The rate at which data are being gathered is so great that the cataloging and information retrieval functions need to be mechanized. It can no longer be done by human beings. Usability is at stake.

The Internet has in the communications sense made databases and computers accessible worldwide to millions of users. There are both opportunities and problems in melding this into an adequate scalable library system. To address such issues, at the time this chapter was written, the National Science Foundation was funding six programs, each involving a lead university and industrial partners.[3] The focuses of the individual programs indicate the broad applicability of the core technology: digital video with math and science emphasis (Carnegie Mellon University); environmental information (University of California/Berkeley); multimedia for space science (University of Michigan); geographical information (University of California/Santa Barbara); virtual libraries (Stanford University); and engineering and science journals (University of Illinois). The schools involved are some of the major universities in computer science and engineering.

12.3   Location of Data

In a spatially distributed system, memory will be located at many organizational levels and often at physically remote locations. Thus at a particular level of memory, factors such as response time and bandwidth will be important in

---

3. Robert Pool, "Turning an Info-Glut into a Library," *Science* 266 (October 7, 1994): 20.

both the local environment and the more remote global areas with which there may be interaction. Given this environment, how do you decide what should be where?

Communications considerations will certainly be of great importance. Although most of the issues related to where data and physical memory should be located are discussed in Chapter 13, it is worth summarizing some important factors here.

Consider a large distributed system. Depending upon where the elements of physical storage are located, there can be substantial differences in certain factors:

Costs

System performance

Reliability

Applications utilizing the memory

Except at the lower levels of the memory hierarchy where a significant economy of scale exists, the cost of memory itself may not be an important factor in locating memory. On the other hand, the location of memory can have a significant impact on communications costs. Thus location can impact on total system cost.

The impact of memory location on system performance is often far more important than cost considerations. The delays experienced in communications networks can be significant and limit performance—to a moderate degree in library systems and to a crucial degree in systems that are storing dynamic data and in which concurrency control is important.

We must assume that hardware will fail, as will communications systems. Both equipment and software are subject to errors. Furthermore, on a wider scale, a fire or a natural catastrophe such as an earthquake can make equipment unavailable or even destroy it. Under these circumstances, it is unacceptable to have the only copy of critical data stored at one location, or its accessibility subject to one point of power or communications failure. Consequently, reliability and availability requirements can have a large impact on where memory hardware should be located.

Memory location design decisions associated with cost, performance, and reliability are dependent upon the applications and the users, both of which may change with time. In fact, it is almost certain that they will change with time, sometimes in just a matter of hours, and not always in a predictable manner. Examples can be cited over a wide range: banking activity varies in different time zones as the day progresses; airline reservations and seat assignments change as an aircraft moves from city to city; stock market activity operates as a function of local time; tactical military situations are affected by database access that depends on where the action is. It is thus desirable to provide a means of shifting, as a function of time, the location of specific data in a network of distributed computers. We cannot of course rapidly move storage equipment, but if we wish to have the above capability, it does influence what memory equipment should be used and where it should be installed. The goal is to move data so that response time and communications costs are reduced. The former is usually by far the most important.

When should we move a process to memory and when should we do the reverse? When should we move a database close to the expected use? Most server experience is on local area networks. We are now asking much broader questions. Where should a multiplicity of servers, which may contain functionally related data, be located? Most applications today are optimized for the local environment. As the origin of the load changes, it would be desirable to move the data dynamically. The implication is that the location from which a particular service (or a partial service) is provided may shift dynamically.

It is possible that, considering all the tradeoffs, it may be desirable to install memory in a system for the sole purpose of providing the capability of dynamically shifting data. This may well mean that at any one time there may be unused memory. However, the cost of the additional memory could well be justified by increased performance.

We have raised a good many issues that are important in deciding where memory should be located. Unfortunately, there does not exist a design methodology that will answer the related synthesis and design questions. The usual procedure is to assume a model and through simulation of alternatives within that model to develop a sense of the tradeoffs. We are in no way criticizing that approach. It is a tough problem, and this is often the best that can be done.

12.4   Directories

12.4.1   Introduction

In what follows, we use the terms *files* and *objects* interchangeably. We also assume that, although not emphasized, directories can refer to the location of people, machines, memory, etc. There are similarities between directories and network control in voice networks and data networks. After all, people in a sense are computers, and data exchange by voice can be considered a special case of data exchange by messages.

We do not discuss directory issues in computer systems in detail. Our objective is to present some of the key issues and to provide perspective. There are good discussions of directory issues for computers in Coulouris, Dollimore, and Kindberg and in Lorin.[4] Our discussion in this chapter is focused on storage. At the same time, in Chapter 6, it was emphasized that the general communications model and concepts are applicable to communications, data storage, and information retrieval. In a real sense, directories are applicable to all three areas and in many cases integration over the three areas is necessary. The discussion that follows is in that context.

It has been suggested that the concepts and models of distributed systems should "scale" or be applicable to very large systems. Searching for a person or a file by using a broadcast system, or a linear search, does not scale. The discussion that follows neither considers, nor is applicable to, broadcast systems or linear searches. They are excluded with full knowledge that such methods are often a fallback substitute for directories. Examples in the PC world are utilities that will search for a lost file.

12.4.2   Generalities

A mechanism is needed to tell where a particular file or data object is. It should be clear that the directory function—i.e., determining where an object is located—is quite different from fetching or obtaining the actual object. For example, the file allocation table on the disk of a personal computer indicates where the file is located on the physical disk, not what the file contains. In other words, the input to a directory is the specification (e.g., the name) of what you want, and the output is where the desired object is located. A directory maps what you want to where it is. Locating a data object in a distributed heterogeneous computer system is not a simple matter.

The directory function should not be a part of the application program. Many different application programs utilize the same data and should utilize the same directory. Directory services are general-purpose utilities or service functions. To be more specific, we consider a directory to be a "data service" function and data services are discussed in more detail in Chapter 13.

Files, and the directories indicating where those files are, do not have to be located at the same place. Furthermore, directories may be distributed and hierarchical in nature. In a personal computer, the directory indicating the physical location of a file on the disk is usually located on that disk. On the other hand, if the file is in a disk cache in main memory, there is also an associative

4. Coulouris, Dollimore, and Kindberg; *Distributed System Concepts and Design;* Harold Lorin, *Aspects of Distributed Computer Systems,* 2nd ed. (New York: Wiley, 1988).

translation table in main memory pointing to the "cached" location in main memory. As a matter of fact, the entire directory itself may be in a cache.

If the users of a computer in a distributed system ask for a file, they either have to know which computer has the file, or they need some other unique name for the file and access to a directory server that will indicate where the file is. At the same time, the file in a distributed system might be moved from place to place. In other words, in the terminology of the last chapter, the directory information may be pseudostatic or even dynamic. A parallel in the telephone industry is to be found in cellular phone systems. The physical location of a phone is not known, or if known it may be changing dynamically. It may be necessary for the network to search for the location. We might call this a directory search. It is pretty clear that there is little difference between such systems for portable phones and for portable computers. In a real sense, the directory function is a part of the communications network, not any one node or combination of nodes. As we shall discuss, there are other data service functions that are better viewed as network functions rather than node functions.

This latter point introduces a new issue. Finding the location of a data object is a directory function; contacting or retrieving that object is a different function. In a single computer, the operating system performs the retrieval function. In a file server–oriented system, the file server will if necessary perform the function (i.e., if the file is not already in the local system). In a peer-to-peer system, the situation is more complex.

There is again a parallel in the common carrier telephone network. An example will illustrate similarities to examples of data communications in computer networks. When you look up the name of a person in a telephone directory, the directory indicates the relevant telephone number. As indicated above with the cellular phone case, it may be necessary for the communications network to perform a "search" to determine the location. That in itself does not connect you to the person. When you or your computer dial the number, or the communications network performs an equivalent operation for the user, the network control function takes over. It sets up the necessary communications paths and connects you. As pointed out in Chapter 7, the communications and computer resources to locate and establish the path are usually much smaller than those necessary to transfer the desired data.

There will be many requests on a directory system, each one different and from different environments. The directory function cannot be optimized for all. An objective must be to handle the majority of requests efficiently. With some exceptions, as in most computer systems, we must focus on average performance.

Such examples clearly illustrate how complex the directory function can be. The functions of a directory and network control are two distinct entities. In some systems they are not totally independent and they do interact. In other words, the directory function may be coupled to the network control function.

Let us now summarize some of the facts and issues focused more on distributed information systems.

Directories will often be at locations different than the data to which they refer.

Directories may be in a hierarchical structure and related.

The directory mechanism or the location of a file may or may not be transparent to the user.

It should not be required that the user know where the file is. In this sense, the location should be transparent to the user.

It should be possible for the user (e.g., the application designer) to find out where the data are located and to make use of those facts. If a location is dynamically changed by the system, the user may only be able to learn the relevant algorithms.

Depending upon the directory system used, directory entries may include much of the access control information shown in Fig. 11.3, and they may provide some control over the access to data.

Because directories and data objects may be in different locations, directory services cannot include the control of synchronization.

The above discussion has been in the context of files and simple objects. As noted in Chapter 9, object-oriented databases have become an area of active research and initial products are available. Great emphasis is being given to object-oriented design in general.[5] A software object can have many components and become very complex. In a distributed system, it could in principle contain information or data from many different physical sites and locations. (A parallel would be a network structured database in which the data items making up a linked list were located at different physical locations.) Consequently, there will be a directory function associated with locating the components of an object. Discussion of this complexity is beyond the scope of this book except to note that it is a viable subject for research.

5. Grady Booch, *Object Oriented Design with Applications* (Redwood City: Benjamin/Cummings, 1991).

12.4.3   Some Alternative Directory Systems

The discussion in this section is applicable to directories in the usual sense. The alternatives discussed are not necessarily orthogonal. In addition, because of the nature of hierarchical directory structures, several alternatives may be utilized in a hierarchy.

Master control directory: Consider a specific subsystem—for example, the disk drive on a personal computer. There is usually one master control directory (file allocation table) on that disk drive that maps a file name to a file location. Actually, in Microsoft DOS there are two, but one serves only as a backup. All directory information is in that one directory. A master control directory may contain information on access control and other file attributes, and in an overall system there may be more than one (e.g., one each for clearly defined disjoint areas). For example, there may be a master control directory for each personal computer, as has been the case of the computers used in preparing this book. On the other hand, there may be a master control directory that contains entries for all of the files in the overall system. For a large heterogeneous system, the latter approach does not scale very well. It was used initially in computer network address directories and then discarded as the networks grew.

Directory server: This is usually a single computer functioning as a directory server and having no other function. The server in all likelihood contains the master directory for the overall system. However, there is nothing in the concept that prevents the server from providing the directory service for disjoint and independent systems.

Modern Centrex and network service offered by common carriers (see Chapter 7) can provide a customer with a virtual network that is largely under customer control. The customer's directory may be located in a central office switch as a separate directory, perhaps associated with a particular remote switching partition.

Fully replicated directories: In this case duplicate copies of a directory are stored at multiple locations. In a dynamic environment there may be the usual concurrency control problems.

Local directories: This type of directory contains information on data stored locally. Usually, although not always, the implication is that this is the only location of directory information for the local system.

Point of control directories: In this case, the directory function is located at the point at which access control is exercised. This in effect is done with the hard disk on a personal computer. There is much merit in this type of directory from a security standpoint. If the directory includes access control criteria, the data are protected where they are located (assuming that the directory cannot be circumvented by a knowledgeable user).

The methods discussed above describe strategies that are largely pure strategies. Just as there are many reasons for locating data at different points, there are many reasons for locating directory information at many points. One of the factors of greatest importance is scaling. In the context of a very large system, the pure strategies considered above do not scale well.

A solution to the scaling problem is to go to a hierarchical system, in which at each level there are directories concerned with the domains at that level. The post office has done this for years in the area of addresses: street, city, state, etc., in effect define different domains. It is a little curious that it took Arpanet/Internet as long as it did to develop a well structured domain address system.

Utilizing mixed directories is often a reasonable thing to do for other reasons. For example, a system may have local directories, local duplicate directories from other places, and a master directory that contains all directory information. Most directory requests will likely be for information from directories that are now on the local system. Consequently, most requests will be served rapidly at a local level. When necessary, the request will default to the master directory. In the extreme case, if the desired information is not in the master directory, it may be necessary to perform a system search.

Before concluding this section, there are several observations that are worth noting:

The backup of directory structures is extremely important. Considering the amount of information in computer systems today, the loss of all directory information would be almost as serious as the loss of the information. The reconstruction of directories from examining the content of the files may not be viable.

Maintaining coherency and consistency in a directory structure can be a real problem. As systems become larger, and there are more interrelated directories, it will become more challenging.

Directory information may be cached at sites of use. Keeping a cached directory structure updated requires thoughtful system design.

Standards are playing a role in the area of access control. The X.500 standard (supported by CCITT and ISO), although primarily a directory service for addresses, does consider such things as what data at an address (or user) should be made available to the network.

In our discussion in this section, we have often made a parallel between memory directories and those for voice communications. This was done to provide a simple explanation and examples of the concepts. It should be clear that the complexity and scale of the requirements for directories in distributed computer systems far exceed those in current voice systems.

12.5   Comments on Access Control

At the atomic level discussed in Chapter 11 (and shown in Fig. 11.3), access control can be detailed and complicated. Consequently, it is usually applied on the basis of categories of people and of data. In this section we consider the alternatives with respect to the location of access control. It should be noted that access control may or may not be associated with directories. Directories have a primary function of providing the physical and in some cases logical location of data. Access control ensures that only authorized users have access to the data and under approved conditions (e.g., read only). These two functions are quite different and do not have to be performed at the same location.

Access control can be exercised at many different points in a distributed memory system. Some of the alternatives are as follows:

As a function of the application program. In this case the person responsible for the application program is responsible for controlling access to the data that are needed to execute it. This may be fine if the programmer is also responsible for the data. However, if the program references data supplied by others, the supplier may be interested in controlling access. In general, this is not an attractive approach in systems that share a lot of data.

As a function of the database management system. This is probably the most common way to exercise access control. In a distributed system, however, with distributed and interlocking databases, the state of the art is not satisfactory.

At the point where the data are physically. This is in principle an appealing alternative. The control is where the data are. You would never run a conventional library any other way. Unfortunately, current memory hardware is not configured to provide this capability. Memory hardware just does not have the access control sophistication and capability of database management systems.

As a function of the communications network. This is attractive because the communication network has the potential of preventing a user (or intruder) at one location from even initiating action with other specified ports. In principle the network knows the location of a port. Cutting off all outside communication is an extreme example of this, but at the highest levels of security this is often done. It is also possible to specify on a port basis, as well as on a user on that port basis, etc., the type of access that will be granted. A simple example is the feature on some PBXs that a user is able from the national network to dial into the local system, provide the necessary password, and request access. The PBX will then dial the place where the user is supposed to be (for example the user's home), and if conditions are satisfactory, provide the requested connection. In brief, in addition to normal passwords, the user must be at a specified location.

The above alternatives have different pluses and minuses, and they are practical and effective in different circumstances. Consequently, serious consideration should be given to utilizing a combination of methods. For example, utilize the access control in database management systems, but do not entirely rely on that. Shut people off at the communications network where that is possible. Above all, do not permit more access than is required.

12.6   Information Retrieval

12.6.1   Introduction

In this chapter, we have discussed how to locate a file or data object in a memory system providing you know precisely what it is you are looking for. In the California Department of Water Resources database containing the 500,000 photographic slides mentioned in Section 12.2, it is equivalent to finding where a single slide (or its corresponding digitized representation) is located, providing the slide identification key (e.g., its number) is known. Similarly, if you can identify a book in a library, the card catalog (e.g., directory) will tell you the location of the book. That is often not the problem facing the user, however. The user wants the pictures or documents that meet certain conditions. In our slide example this would mean pictures of a certain location, pictures that show certain environmental problems, pictures that show specific crops, etc. To put it another way, the user is interested in information, or in data that are relevant to the desired information. This is the information retrieval problem.

Information retrieval is the dissemination or retrieval of data and information in response to a user's query. In that sense, information retrieval is similar to related services in a database management (DBM) system and its associated query capabilities. Unfortunately, the intent of many questions that people (or systems) would like to ask extends beyond the present capabilities of current DBMs and the structure of their associated databases. Consequently, information retrieval can be considered a much broader field than what is commonly understood to be that of database management, and a field in its own right.

In earlier chapters we discussed the difficulty of getting data or information from published articles or books into engineering calculations (see Section 10.8 for example). Putting tables, curves, pictures, nomograms, etc., into a computer is not the problem. In fact many of the pictures and graphs in this book were scanned into a computer system. At least at the present state of the art for engineering and other calculations numbers are needed. As noted, selecting the most relevant numbers from what is available involves both data and metadata. Accomplishing this is an unsolved information retrieval problem, but one that we do not intend to revisit at this time.

Data that are well structured and adequately handled by the retrieval capabilities of existing database management systems can be processed satisfactorily, as discussed in Chapter 9. In what follows, we focus primarily on text and numbers in written documents, which are often much less structured than the examples in Chapter 9. This is a domain in which many important applications fall. An understanding of available technology is relevant to the design of distributed information systems.

12.6.2   Textual Data in Documents

In the context of this book, we are concerned with all forms of documental textual data. Consequently, we briefly overview the classical field of information retrieval. For further details, interested readers are referred to texts by Salton and McGill.[6]

Several characteristics differentiate information retrieval and traditional database applications. The first and foremost is the type of data stored. Traditional databases typically contain structured data. That is, databases in general, and relational databases in particular, are predominantly used for business-oriented applications in which the data are highly structured and precise, as shown in our working example in Chapter 9. Information retrieval data, however, are often documents, and they are, in comparison to such rela-

6. Gerald Salton and Michael J. McGill, *Introduction to Modern Information Retrieval* (New York: McGraw-Hill, 1983); Gerald Salton, *Automatic Text Processing: The Transformation, Analysis, and Retrieval of Information by Computer* (Reading, Mass.: Addison-Wesley, 1989).

tional data, unstructured. Clearly, it is easier to process structured data than unstructured data. The example that follows considers text retrieval from documents.

Complicating the query processing of documents is the lack of precision typically associated with database information retrieval. For example, consider queries of the form, "Find all documents that discuss the Middle East peace talks." Clearly, any document that uses the phrase "Middle East peace talks" would be applicable, but so would any document that discusses meetings between Jordan and Israel. These additional documents are indeed relevant, but they fail to use the exact words in the given query and hence complicate the retrieval process.

So how should a user issue a query so that all the relevant documents are retrieved? That is an open issue. There are those who believe that the approach of choice should be based on natural language processing (NLP). The problem with this approach is that NLP is not a mature technology, it is difficult to implement, and it generally is compute intensive.

Other accepted approaches include Boolean retrieval and weighted Boolean retrieval. In a system employing Boolean retrieval, keywords are "AND'ed" or "OR'ed" together. A document containing all (in the case of "AND") or one (in the case of "OR"), of the keywords is retrieved. Some systems include a TAND (threshold AND) operator, in which a document is retrieved if the number of keywords found in the document equals or exceeds a given threshold. If weights signifying the importance of each keyword are included, then it is said that the system employs a weighted Boolean approach. Although most metrics demonstrate that NLP provides better retrieval accuracy than both Boolean and weighted Boolean querying, because of their simplicity in implementations and efficiency in terms of computation time, most commercial systems implement some variant of Boolean retrieval.

Another notable difference is the volume of data associated with the various databases. With the continued developments in optical storage, scanners, and communications technologies, worldwide data are becoming globally online. Thus, whereas 100 GB relational databases are considered large, such magnitudes of data in the information retrieval domain are common. The question is how you can get at what you want when it is present in the raw data. Consider the following examples.

1. There are two major firms that provide law books to the legal profession. The law books are being supplemented by, and will ultimately probably be superseded by, computerized database systems. The firms are evolving from publishers of books to providing database service either from a central point or on optical discs to be run on workstations in the lawyer's office. The major contribution of those

firms supplying books and access to computerized databases is in abstracting and building the information retrieval systems that let the lawyers find the information that they need efficiently. Lawyers do not want a large unstructured library containing the text of court decisions. In the context of their current investigations, they want a summary of what those decisions mean and the most relevant text of court decisions. The important thing to note is that the cost of legal services of this type is not in printing the books or buying the computer hardware. The cost is in building an "abstracting and information retrieval" system.

2. It was noted in Section 12.2 that satellite systems are generating terabytes of data per day. This is a retrieval problem like in (1) above, but with orders of magnitude more data. The data are also largely pictorial. There is no way that humans, without substantial help from computer systems, can do the indexing, cataloging, and abstracting that is necessary if an effective information retrieval system is to be built. In effect a satisfactory system must supply a retrieval mechanism including a cataloging system, associated abstracts, and access to selected raw data. It is likely that a satisfactory system will for the immediate future focus on communicating with the retrieval system utilizing text.

3. Retrieval in terms of "give me something like this picture or these sounds" would be desirable. In specific areas, such systems exist today. For example, there are systems for voice and fingerprint recognition and retrieval. However, these fall into the pattern recognition or artificial intelligence area and are not further discussed in this book. We should not underestimate the importance of developing more general systems along these lines, however.

12.6.3   Document Retrieval Quality and Access Methods

There are predominantly two metrics that evaluate the accuracy of information retrieval systems—namely, precision and recall. Precision and recall are defined as follows: Let Z be the set of all documents within the entire document collection that are relevant to a given query. Let Y be the set of documents retrieved in response to the given query. Finally, let X be the intersection of Y and Z, representing those documents that are retrieved and are indeed relevant. Then, precision is defined as X/Y and recall is defined as X/Z. Note that in the general case, Z is not precisely known, and hence, recall is commonly only an approximation.

We have thus far discussed the differentiating characteristics between databases and information retrieval and we have reviewed metrics aimed at evaluating the quality of the retrieved documents. What remains to be discussed are the access methods used to retrieve the documents. As with most applications in computer science, the access methods commonly employed face the tradeoff of time and space. Furthermore, the larger the overhead attributed to the access structure (space), typically, the greater is the burden to maintain the structure.

We begin by reviewing the two extremes: full access support—namely, complete indexing—and no access support—namely, full text scanning. Full text scanning involves scanning all the documents and matching the requested keywords against the individual documents. Because this method involves accessing the entire collection, hardware support in the form of filters is often needed. More recent hardware support includes efforts by those listed in recent references.[7]

Keyword and phrase indexing implies the creation of inverted files where keywords or phrases are listed along with pointers to the documents that contain them. Indexing is the fastest access method but suffers from significant storage overhead. Reported percentages of storage overhead resulting from indexing have been as high as 300 percent, however overheads of roughly 50 to 70 percent of the volume of the stored documents are more common approximations.[8] We should not be alarmed by high storage overhead rates, for the additional cost may be a small price to pay for substantially higher performance.

Note that the addition or deletion of a document is accomplished easily in a full text system—namely, by just adding or removing a document from the collection. However, in an indexed based approach, the addition or removal of a document requires the updating of all the indices associated with all the keywords or phrases found in the document.

Two compromise solutions exist. Word signatures or signature files yield roughly a 10 percent overhead. In signature file processing, each document is represented by a document signature—a fixed length string of ones and zeros, one bit for each keyword in the document collection. A one in bit position j of a document signature implies that keyword j is found within the corresponding document. A document is selected as relevant if the bits within its signature that correspond to the keywords supplied in the query are set to one. Hashing and compression techniques are commonly used to reduce the size of the document signature files. However, for our introductory purposes, the processing is roughly equivalent.

7. L. A. Hollaar, "Special-Purpose Hardware for Text Searching: Past Experience, Future Potential," *Information Processing and Management* 27, no. 4 (1991): 328; V. Mak, K. C. Lee, and O. Frieder, "Exploiting Parallelism in Pattern Matching: An Information Retrieval Application," *ACM TOIS* 9, no. 1 (1991): 52; D. Lee, "Altep—A Cellular Processor for High-Speed Pattern Matching," *New Generation Computing* (1986): 225.

8. R. L. Haskin, "Special-Purpose Processors for Text Retrieval," *IEEE Data Engineering* (1981): 16.

The final access method that we will overview is clustering. Clustering, as the name implies, clusters or groups related documents. Using a set of attributes or expected user profiles, documents are grouped together based on a hypothesis claiming that documents sharing similar values for a set of attributes are likely to be related to the same queries.

For each cluster, a "typical cluster document," known as the cluster centroid or simply centroid, is created to represent the cluster in the retrieval process. When a query is issued, a search of the set of cluster centroids is made. If a centroid is deemed relevant to a query, then all the documents belonging to the cluster represented by the selected centroid are retrieved. Algorithms exist that yield a diversity of clusters, including overlapping, nonoverlapping, or hierarchical partitions of the document collection.

Finally, recent efforts have focused on the integration of text with relational database technology. Prior efforts added functionality by modifying the relational database management system to support text processing. Today, several efforts are adhering to accepted SQL standards, hoping to capitalize on all of the corresponding advantages associated with standardization (see Chapters 9 and 10). These efforts focus on using SQL unchanged to support integrated text and relational database processing.[9] Experimentation has shown that the additional overhead incurred is not prohibitive (approximately an additional 40 percent of the size of the stored document collection as compared to strict information retrieval systems), but the performance improvement and functionality gained particularly on certain queries merit further investigation of the approach. It is still premature to speculate on the success of such efforts although at least one major parallel database system vendor is seriously considering it.

12.6.4   Generalities and Observations

We must be prepared to deal with very large heterogeneous computer systems. The environment will present problems that lie outside of our current experience. The computer systems that are currently on the Internet comprise a large heterogeneous system. Experience gained on the Internet may well provide insight into the future.

There will often be a collection of many very large databases that must be considered. We must think in terms of terabytes of data per database. The contents of those databases may or may not be related. In other words, the com-

9. R. Fidel, *Database Design for Information Retrieval: A Conceptual Approach* (New York: Wiley, 1987); D. Grossman, D. Holms, O. Frieder, "A Parallel DBMS Approach to IR" (proceedings of NIST's TREC–3, 1994).

ponents of an object, in the "object-oriented sense," may encompass multiple databases. There will be multiple users in very large numbers. A significant number may well be accessing the same categories of data, or more specifically, related data objects.

A query usually asks for information, not a mass of data. It would not be realistic, in response to a query, to plan on transferring hundreds of terabytes of raw data to a workstation. Systems are needed that will transfer relevant information, data, and metadata. In very large databases, linear search of data to extract the information that is desired is not viable. For example, the search of relational tables, or document files, that contain large amounts of core data is unrealistic.

Systems similar to keyword search, probably the most popular technique today, are unlikely to be satisfactory in the long run. Cataloging based upon "significant properties" is essential. Because of the shortcomings of keyword related techniques, current on-line systems provide only rudimentary information retrieval.

Cataloging in the long run needs to be mechanized. We cannot afford, in a significant number of very large databases, the human abstraction evident in some present on-line systems (e.g., Westlaw's legal system, Chemical Abstracts). Just from scaling considerations, there is a real challenge in the mechanization of abstraction. Mechanization is probably a necessary condition in many application areas.

Sophisticated information retrieval gets into the areas of pattern recognition, knowledge engineering and artificial intelligence. These fields are beyond the scope of this book except to acknowledge their relevance and importance.

Efficient information retrieval is a keystone in the information world that we are entering. Mosaic, World Wide Web, gophers, etc., are interesting in this regard. For those using these facilities today, the problem is not as much access to the nodes of the worldwide network as locating the information that is desired. In the long run, systems of this type will find widespread use only if there are adequate cataloging and information retrieval tools available. Developing those tools is a challenging task. Considering the heterogeneous nature of information systems, and the difficulty of establishing firm standards, it is not clear how soon that goal can be met.

12.7   Summary and Comments

In reviewing the major points in the chapter, it is important to remember the following in regard to very large distributed information systems:

Categorization of users and data is essential.

Data will be located in multiple hierarchies of memory devices.

Memory will be distributed spatially.

The properties of communications networks will be very important. These properties will have a major impact on the distribution of storage and computing components.

Directories will in many cases be distributed.

Access control will often be distributed.

We must seriously consider cataloging and information retrieval methods. Inadequate methods in these areas can seriously limit performance.

Present methods are inadequate for the size and nature of the databases that are being created.

The mechanization of cataloging, abstracting, and indexing is almost essential.

Knowledge engineering and artificial intelligence can play a significant role. In the long run, techniques in these fields will be needed to realize a quantum jump in performance.

There is no satisfactory overall design methodology for the design of generalized information retrieval systems. Those that do exist, do not really scale. One can gather the available facts, evaluate the tradeoffs, and make design decisions. Those decisions will be judgment calls. Going about things systematically can be a big help in your work.

There do not exist satisfactory automated tools to help in the above process. The number of parameters and level of detailed data involved will require automation. In studying such systems, simulation is often the best tool that we have today. Standards are playing a role. The X.500 standard (supported by CCITT and ISO), although primarily a directory service for addresses, does consider such things as what at a specific address should be made available to the network.

Dynamic restructuring of catalogs, memory, databases, and information retrieval systems is desirable. A structure or architecture that provides near optimum performance is dependent upon the application and the pattern of use. If either of these changes, the details of the architecture should be able to change accordingly.

A small example of this is database design. Regardless of the effort put into the initial design, the pattern of use cannot be accurately predicted. As use evolves, it is usually necessary to fine-tune or restructure the database. The pattern of use of a distributed system may change in a matter of hours or even minutes.

12.8   Problems

1. What are the main factors in deciding where data should be placed? Are some factors more important than others? What are the main constraints? Are these application dependent?

2. Under what circumstances would you move data to functions rather than functions to data?

3. In the context of this chapter, should dynamic relocation of data be possible? If so, for what functions and when?

4. How important are scaling considerations? Why?

5. For the problems that you were assigned in Section 11.6, prepare a summary of the following: (a) Indicate the locations at which you would install memory. Specify the memory type and quantity. (b) What directory structures would you use, and where would you place them? (c) What access control methods would you recommend, and where would you place them? (d) What would you recommend doing in the area of information retrieval services?

Chapter 13

Communications Networks as Providers of Data/Information Services

We're taking the lead in creating a world where smart networks connect to smart devices, giving people easy access to each other and to the advanced information services that will enrich the way they live, work and play.

Robert E. Allen, CEO, AT&T[1]

13.1 Introduction

It is no longer possible to cleanly separate computing and communications. This has been a theme of this entire book. As a corollary to that premise, it no longer makes sense to consider classical "computing" and "network" activities as mutually exclusive functions.

This chapter will review the issues involved and make a strong case for including computing and database functions within the communications network. The issue to be raised is that of providing data services selectively at both nodes and within a network.[2] Circumstances will dictate where, for a particular application, a specific service should be provided.

The format here differs from earlier chapters:

1. We summarize the network transport services that are available today in the components that make up the national network. We then consider where we stand today with respect to more general

1. Robert E. Allen, *AT&T 1994 Annual Report,* February 9, 1995.

2. Richard Shuey and Gio Wiederhold, "Data Engineering and Information Systems," *Computer* 19, no. 1 (January 1986): 18; Ophir Frieder and Richard Shuey, "Communication Needs in a Data Engineering World," *Computer Networks & ISDN Systems* 25 (1992): 259–273.

services. This is important for several reasons. There are many services that are available today "over the network"—i.e., utilizing the national transport network. Those services are a step toward a more distributed world. Both the associated networks, and the services offered, are evolving. What is the path that they will follow? Will they end up structured as we envision, or will environmental and other conditions lead to a different endpoint? In any event, today's facilities are a stepping stone to tomorrow.

2. We then discuss many of the reasons why we believe the option should exist to place data services in the network. Examples and reasons have been mentioned earlier in the text. In this chapter we endeavor to bring the reasons together in a more coherent fashion.

3. We try to put all of the preceding together, largely by way of examples.

4. Many of the design issues that have been raised in the book are discussed. The issues are reviewed, and the limitations on our knowledge and the state of the art discussed. Some useful practices are summarized.

13.2   Where We Are Today in Communications

Our focus in this section will be largely on communications transport. Furthermore, because of our interest in spatially separated systems, the emphasis will be on the national network. In the term national network, we include both the common carriers and the added-value carriers. The latter will be discussed in terms of the Internet. In closing, there will be brief discussion of some of the most significant issues in communications.

13.2.1   The Campus Environment

As in previous chapters, by campus environment we imply a community that covers a limited spatial area: a college campus, a business at one location, an office complex, Capitol Hill in Washington, etc. All fall within our concept of a campus environment. The options and requirements for data communications within such an environment are far different than in the national network. For example, inside the campus, it is not necessary to conform to national network standards. It is relatively inexpensive to install your own cable (wires), data switches, and a data network that does not conform to national network practices. Consequently, there has been a great deal of data communications innovation in the campus environment. The national network does not have a corresponding opportunity for rapid innovation for reasons discussed in Chapter 8.

In campus environments, we can find today a variety of data switches, wireless systems, cabling plants, networks, etc. For example, there are standard Ethernets, T-based Ethernets, token systems, ATM switches, etc. In many cases, these systems are not easily coupled to the national network. We do not intend to examine campus environments in detail for several reasons.

> We have commented on many of the techniques being utilized. That discussion has established many of the basic techniques and principles.

> There is no unifying integrating force except to the degree that some issues are being forced because of the desire to communicate over a wider area. An example is, communications with other campuses and the world.

> Our interest is largely in distributed heterogeneous systems that cover large spatial areas and many sectors of society. These are becoming much more important in our society. From a communications standpoint, the common carriers, and the added value carriers, provide a more realistic perspective than campus networks. They are a better arena in which to discuss the status and the opportunities of widely distributed systems.

13.2.2   Common Carriers

The components of the overall national network are often classified as follows: (1) local (a town or area served by a central office); (2) wide area (an area code that may contain many towns and central offices); (3) long lines (calls made from New York to Chicago); and (4) international (calls from Washington to London). We have added one more communications category, "campus," which from the common carriers' standpoint would usually be viewed as station equipment. We do not consider a campus environment to be a part of the national network.

The national network and the common carriers provide the data highway system used in almost all "off-campus" communications systems. Radio systems such as cellular systems use the common carriers to communicate between their transmitter/receiver hubs. In effect, the carriers provide the highways for use by others. There is competition in many areas between common carriers. There are radio systems in some of the large cities that compete with the local telephone carriers, there are satellite systems that compete with the long lines carriers (although as noted earlier the satellite systems have delays that in many cases are unsatisfactory), MCI competes with AT&T in long lines, etc. The important thing is to realize the central role of the communications industry and the national network.

It is also important to realize, as discussed earlier, the role of tariffs, laws, and regulations. Through interconnect charges, various groups are compelled to subsidize other groups. The services that one can provide are regulated—for example, just as this is being written, it appears that telephone companies may be permitted to provide cable television. A consequence of regulation is that in considering development of new services the carriers must consider the opportunities provided by technology in the context of what they might legally be permitted to do.

What are the technologies in use today? In transmission, outside of the local area, fiber optics are almost universal. Within the local area, fiber is used between distribution points, although there is also copper. Radio systems are also coming into use locally. In areas of very low population density, satellite systems are often used (e.g., in parts of Canada, Alaska).

In switching, the predominant technique for voice circuits is our old friend time slot interchange used in conjunction with space diversity switching. In the data area, supplemental Bus, Frame Relay,[3] and ATM switches and services are in use. (We have not discussed frame relay earlier. Frame relay employs a connection oriented virtual circuit utilizing variable length packets. It is likely to lose out to ATM).

ISDN is still the main thrust of the common carriers and is likely to be the highway vehicle. This means that many of the services being discussed can be integrated with the core of ISDN. As noted earlier, the ATM switching developments grew out of the ISDN program. The option exists to use ISDN standards and equipment within a campus environment. ISDN basic and primary service in the near future may be provided to the user at a network node of the national network.[4]

We have noted that the common carriers will attempt to the degree that they are permitted to broaden their business base. For example, advertisement in the Yellow Pages is a significant business for some of them. The latitude that they have today in business is determined by regulation.

There is a tendency in computer circles to underestimate the role of the common carriers and the communications industry. They are providing the information highway for some of the largest systems today. Chan, Jeanes, and Shastry[5] review one such system used by the airlines in the context of the

---

3. Uyless Black, *Frame Relay Networks: Specifications and Implementations* (New York: McGraw-Hill, 1994).

4. David Frankel, "ISDN Reaches the Market," *IEEE Spectrum* 32, no. 6 (June 1995): 20.

5. Alfred Chan, David Jeanes, and Bal Shastry, "DPN–100: a blend of power and performance," *Telesis*, no. 95 (December 1992): 55.

Northern Telcom DPN–100 Switch that is used.[6] The airline system at that time served 460 airlines in 187 countries and 31,000 travel-related offices, and it was connected to 120,000 terminals or printers. It was involved in 36 billion transactions and data transfers per year. In this and other private or public networks, at the time the article was written, nearly 5000 DPN–100 switches were deployed. A more general picture of the role of the communications industry and the common carriers in the development of the "information highway" is contained in a special issue of Telesis that provides an integrated perspective on the roles of ISDN, ATM, fiber optics, etc.[7] These *Telesis* articles can be easily read by computer scientists with the background provided by this book.

13.2.3   Internet and Added-Value Carriers

The added-value carriers utilize common carrier facilities and services, add features, and market their expanded service. This was briefly discussed in earlier chapters. In this section, as an example of common carrier supported services, we review some of the features of the Internet. The reason for focusing on the Internet is that it is the state-of-the-art. In many respects what follows is a summary of things discussed earlier in the book, and therefore specific detailed references are not repeated. The discussion will focus on data and information retrieval with an emphasis on library systems.

The Internet was not subject during its development to the regulatory constraints of the communications industry, and it was financed primarily by the government. It uses common carrier leased long lines facilities, has its own data switches, and uses wide and local area common carrier services. It is in the process of going commercial.[8] It utilizes and runs over the common carrier communications highway system.

In its initial phases, Internet evolved from Arpanet, which was used largely for electronic mail (E-mail), file transfer, and access to remote computers. Access to it was initially limited to selected universities and research institutions. As the successor to Arpanet, the Internet has been made available to a wider community of users. Bridges have been established between the Internet and other added-value carriers. For the last several years, Internet use has been growing at a rapid rate.

---

6. David Jeanes and David Drynan, "Global data networking with DPN–100," *Telesis,* no. 93: 37.

7. John Bourne and Ian Cunningham, "Implementing the Information Highway," *Telesis,* special issue, no. 98 (May 1994): 4. (The other articles in this issue are excellent but not listed separately here.)

8. Andrew Lawler, "NSF Hands Over the Internet," *Science* 267 (March 17, 1995): 1584.

Internet has introduced the world to electronic mail (E-mail). The use of E-mail today is widespread. Often business cards, personal and business stationary, letters to the editor, and advertisements include E-mail addresses, thus encouraging additional use of this means of communicating. The role of E-mail in society is well established, although the increased use of "voice mailboxes" in the telephone network is in some respects a competitor.

With the introduction of Gophers, Archie, World Wide Web, etc., the Internet has opened the door to a vast amount of data, including pictorial information. What is available is what the various users have elected to make available. In similar fashion, you can duplicate on paper and distribute any data you want, but in the case of the Internet, the distribution is much easier than distributing printed copies. It is significant that to date the Internet has been largely at no cost to the users and the originators of data. At the same time, commercial use and services are being introduced. Exactly what advertisers will be willing to pay, or what services customers will pay for, are not clear. In addition, there are current discussions at a governmental level of the control of material on the network both with respect to inappropriate content and security.

In earlier chapters, we discussed the information retrieval problem. In the opinion of many, the Internet has opened the door to a world of data, but it has not provided a reasonable information retrieval mechanism. There is a serious cataloging and retrieval problem along the lines discussed in Chapter 12. To quote Clifford Stoll, author of *The Cuckoo's Egg:*[9]

Q. What's wrong with having all this information at your fingertips?

A. The information highway is being sold to us as delivering information, but what it's really delivering is data. Numbers, bits, bytes, but damned little information. Unlike data, information has utility, timeliness, accuracy, a pedigree. Information I can trust. But the data coming across American On-line, or CompuServe, or whatever, nobody stands behind it.

In his recent book Stoll discusses his reservations more broadly.[10] If we are to turn the door that has been opened to the world of data and information to useful purposes, it would be well to understand the reservations, limitations, and potential utility of what lies on the other side of that door.

9. Matthew L. Wald, "A Disillusioned Devotee Says the Internet Is Wearing No Clothes," *New York Times,* April 30, 1995.

10. Clifford Stoll, *Silicon Snake Oil: Second Thoughts on the Information Highway* (New York: Doubleday, 1995).

There are thousands of computerized databases in existence today. Some of the commercial ones, and some sponsored by the government, have been successful. The lack of a communications network has never really been a limitation. The limitations and costs, as noted earlier, are in creating the database and turning raw data into information. The cost of raw computing and communications are secondary factors. To a first approximation, the core data highway already exists. Politically focusing on the information highway without proper qualification serves no purpose and detracts from the real problem areas.

13.2.4 Issues

In closing this section of where we are today in communication transport, it is worthwhile to consider the nature of some of the issues that we either face or will face in the near future. Issues related to more general data services and information system architecture are discussed in later sections.

There are serious questions regarding what the total traffic on the national network will be. It is true that the Internet and data traffic are growing at a very high rate, but it is also true that the sum is relatively small when compared to the total traffic. What are the components of potential computer associated traffic, for example as related to specific services, that people will be willing to pay for? What is the total computer related traffic that people will pay for? To a first approximation, if the total computer associated traffic is projected to grow so that it is similar to the present day total traffic, it is to be expected that the cost associated with it will be similar to that of today's national network. What will be the role of alternatives such as ROM disks, cassettes, etc.?

It is to be expected that an important part of future traffic may be multimedia. There are problems in merging and synchronizing the components of such traffic. It is hoped that ATM can provide a basis for this, but as we have seen there may be problems with the evolution of all pervasive ATM.

Somewhat relative to the above is the question as to whether it is reasonable to expect one all-purpose switching method. This must today be considered an open question.

Regulation will continue to be an issue. In some areas regulation appears to be necessary. In other areas, regulation can seriously constrain facilities and services. The decisions regarding regulation are often more driven by political considerations than by technology, service opportunities, or public demand.

The merging of communications and computer technology is almost essential. Will cultural considerations of those associated with the technical professions but involved in different business environments foster or inhibit this?

Many of these issues, because of the need to merge computer and communications technology, carry over to the computer area.

13.3   Information Systems, Nodes, and Networks

We now turn to a consideration of networks and their broader functions in the context of the information systems that they may serve. Our primary interest is in computer systems having the following characteristics:

The information systems involved are potentially far more than information retrieval or library systems.

There may be a multiplicity of on-line users.

There may be a significant amount of dynamic and pseudo static data involved.

The working computers involved may be dispersed over a wide spatial area (e.g., communications delays may be important).

Figure 13.1 shows the functional structure of a typical information system that might well be in one computer or involve many distributed computers. The functions and applications performed would be the same in both cases. There are systems or programs that are doing the work that the users request. The user application programs require data as input and provide data as output. We refer to services that provide data to the applications, and accept data from the applications, as data services. Storage, retrieval, access control, communications, etc., are all data services. They are similar to utility functions, operating system calls, database operations, etc. Many utility functions and most database functions can be considered as data service operations.

There is no reason that general data service functions should be the responsibility of application programs any more than database management functions should be put into application programs.

We wish to make a clear distinction between the function of doing the computations requested by the user and the function of providing data services for those computations. At the same time, we recognize that such a division may not be precise and the boundary between the two types of functions may be fuzzy. Our justification is that such a distinction is a paradigm that clarifies our analysis of systems. We wish to take this viewpoint in the context of heterogeneous distributed systems and databases. To do so, it is necessary to consider the role of communications networks in such an environment.

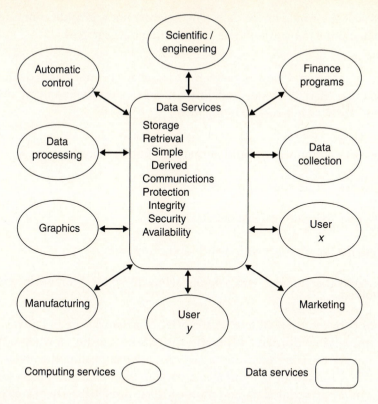

Figure 13.1   A functional structure of an information system

13.3.1   Distinction of Nodes and Networks

A distributed computer system can be viewed as a combination of nodes and networks. We wish to categorize these as two separate entities:

Nodes at which computers are located. The computers at a node can be of many sizes and have a normal complement of memories, etc. Node computers, from the user's standpoint, do the work. Node computers do the computation that is of interest to the user. A user's computation may involve the use of many node computers.

The network to which the nodes are connected. The network provides the means by which nodes can effectively and economically exchange data and information. This does not preclude the network from doing more than just the transport of data. The network may include computers for managing the transport of data or providing data services.

Taking a more general view of networks as a means of connecting devices and systems other than the nodes as defined above, we can define many different levels and kinds of networks, among them:

Networks within what would normally be called a single computer

Networks within a multiprocessor

Networks that perform just data transport

Networks that interact with distributed computers

Networks that interact with heterogeneous distributed computer systems

The lines between these different categories of networks are not always clear. For example, a computer with many processors can be viewed as having nodes that are the computers and a network interconnecting the nodes. A hypercube multiprocessor computer is a combination of many processors embedded in a particular data communications transport network structure. Even a personal computer with a mathematical accelerator can be viewed as having two nodes and a network (probably a bus). In these terms, the conclusion is that networks fit into a hierarchy that is similar to, in many respects related to, and often integrated with the hierarchies of computers and storage.

What kind of networks do we want to consider? Clearly our core interests are heterogeneous distributed information systems and their related distributed computer systems, where the spatial dimensions are large and the consequences of communications delays may be significant. Furthermore, we assume that there may be a large number of users and computers. In other words, we want to consider very large systems in terms of concepts and models that will scale. This, as has been pointed out earlier, is the general case.

Under these conditions, our focus will be on the higher levels of the network hierarchy. By higher levels we imply the national network and we will work down from there. It should be noted that this notation is conceptually the reverse of the common notation for computer memory, where the higher levels of memory refer to that close to the CPU. We use this somewhat confusing notation to be consistent with that used in the computer and communications industries. The reader should be alert to our usage in what follows.

13.3.2   Computation and Data Services

As inferred in the previous section, although the distinction may not be sharp, we consider that *computations* and *data services* are two different types of operations.

Computations are generally associated with node computers. Examples are scientific and engineering computing, commercial computing, data collection, automatic control, and single library systems. Computations perform the operations specified by the application algorithms and programs. It should be noted that in general, programs are separate from, and independent of, the data or data objects upon which they operate.

Data services are involved with making data available to the computational processes within node computers. Examples are storage, retrieval (simple or derived), communications, data protection (integrity, security), protocol conversion, data access control, and data availability. It is clear that data services may be performed within a single computer. Interprocess communications and I/O are examples. For more general nodes that contain multiple computers, more sophisticated data services may be performed. The preprocessors of super-computers are an example.

Nodes themselves may have internal networks, which leads to the conclusion that we must deal with a hierarchy of networks and a hierarchy of data services.

13.3.3   What Should Networks Provide?

Figure 13.2 shows data services being performed at nodes, within the network, or both. Figure 13.3 places this in the context of a hierarchical system and the national network. At issue is whether *networks should provide only data transport,* or whether there are *data services that should be performed in the network* as well. Our view is that design and operational options should be available that will permit data services within the network. The location of a specific data service should not be viewed as an exclusive node or network issue. Rather, the circumstances should determine whether a specific data service should be provided (1) at a node or nodes, (2) in the network, or (3) at both the nodes and in the network.

In some cases, the network will be the most efficient place and reduce duplication (protocol conversion where protocol is used in the broad sense, global directories, etc.). On the other hand, it may be desirable to locate other directories—for example, static directories, both at nodes and within the network.

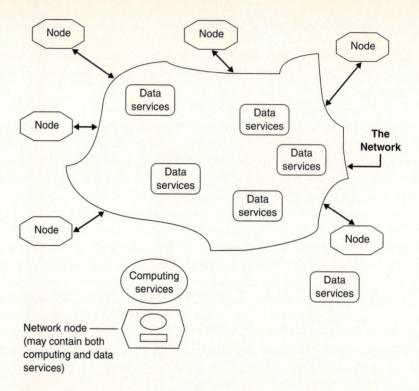

Figure 13.2 A functional structure of a distributed information system

There is a fundamental reason for locating some services in the network. The network may have more knowledge of resource and performance issues than any node on the network. An example is network traffic and loading within the common carrier system. Database reference statistics are another example. Consequently, within the network may be a more suitable place to perform certain services than at nodes. A node may not have the needed information, and it may be an artificial crutch for the network to gather and distribute information for nodes to render services better performed within the network. For example, depending on the time of day or the use, the network may decide to move a service to a different physical location. This involves reconfiguring data service resources (which has a parallel in reconfiguring a communications transport network, depending on the use).

It could be argued that the network could order that a specific data service function be moved from one external node (e.g., computer) to another. That in itself would be a data service function performed by the network. This however begs the philosophical question of whether there are data services that are

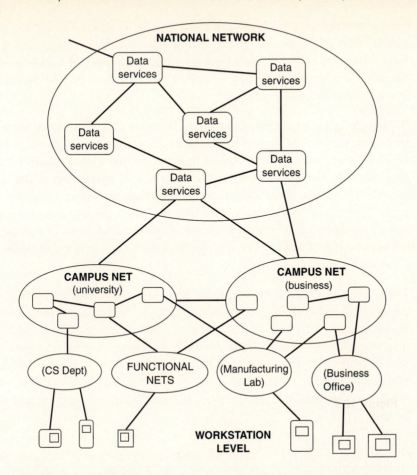

Figure 13.3 Distributed information system in the national network hierarchy

basically more network services than node services. Global directories are an example. The paradigms that one uses are important.

Let us consider several examples that illustrate some of the issues involved.

Would it be better to assign all responsibility for protocol and language translation to computers attached to network nodes, or to provide this as a network service? We have already discussed this in earlier sections where, for example, neutral databases to interface foreign database systems are performing data service functions.

Should the hub of a star network be at a node location? The location of a hub is often selected to minimize spatial effects such as delays, and maximize other factors. A hub may or may not be collocated with a node as we are using the term. It may be that a data service would be best performed at a hub at a nonnode location.

Switching is a clear example of this. Common carrier national network switching centers are located to maximize network performance and reliability. Not all switches are located in areas where a good deal of traffic originates. In satellite systems, some switching is performed in the satellite, and clearly that is at a different location than the nodes using the network. This break will be even more evident when the user asks for a person or computer rather than a phone number or address. It will be the network, with its knowledge, that will locate the recipient and make the connection.

There is some of this at the "campus" level today, and to a lesser degree in the national network. A much simpler example can be found in voice mail boxes, systems that also illustrate a data service that may be provided at many levels. You may have a personal phone answering machine and recorder on your desk, you may have the service provided by a PBX, or you may have the service provided by the national network. Are voice mail boxes in principle different from correspondence and picture mail boxes?

The bandwidth internal to a network generally exceeds that available at its ports. This may be important. If a data service requires very broad bandwidths, just from data transport considerations, it may be best performed within the network.

Consider the bus switches and the DV–1 discussed in Section 7.7. The servers internal to the switch are on an internal 40 MB/s internal bus. Servers external to the switch would be on a 2.5 Mb/s port. (It is worth noting that more modern switches have much broader bandwidth internal buses and ports.) Would you rather have servers on an internal bus or a port? This may be particularly important if the servers are to interact with each other.

In general the bandwidth available within a network will be significantly wider than at the ports to that network. Therefore the issue raised by reference to the DV–1 is equally valid in a large network. It is likely that servers that are internal to the network will have access to broader bandwidth channels than those servers that are attached to network ports. The server concept developed with emphasis on "a" server. In principle there may be many servers, which may find it necessary to interact with each other at very high data rates.

The basic concept is that networks can provide far more than data transport. They can provide data services far beyond those visualized by the present common carriers and the operators of campus networks. There is need to be creative in thinking of and classifying data services. Only after this has been done can location issues be addressed.

It is a real challenge to develop analysis and models that will let us decide in a rational way what data services should be in the network and which should be at nodes. It is recognized that specific types of data service may be performed at both nodes and within the network. Directories are a good example. Decisions as to what should be provided where will be very dependent upon the environment and upon the application.

13.4   Information Retrieval in the Network?

Information retrieval plays a central role in a great deal of computation and decision making. Specific aspects of information retrieval have been discussed in earlier chapters. One may well ask if networks could not play more of a role in information retrieval than just data transport. Directories are acceptable in networks. Should there be more general data services that are associated with information retrieval for working computers at nodes?

We referred earlier to some of the challenges in extracting information as distinct from locating and obtaining data. We noted that work on library systems is beginning to address some of the challenges and opportunities.[11] There is recognition on the part of many people working in the field that a centralized monolithic system would be unlikely to scale and consequently would be unworkable. The authors believe that this assessment is correct. One reaction to this situation is to place responsibility for information retrieval on the application programs. This is not necessarily a good thing to do for reasons that have been referred to earlier. The similarity to database management operations, in which everyone understands that the core manipulative mechanisms should be part of the data management system, not the application programs, is clear. We need general mechanisms, independent of specific applications, to perform the retrieval function. Those mechanisms must be consistent with distributed databases and distributed computers accessing those databases.

Researchers in the area have introduced agents, mediators, etc., whose function is to find the required information.[12] In some cases, these are active search mechanisms. As has been discussed earlier, active search mechanisms

11. "Digital Libraries," Special Issue of the *Communications of the ACM* 38, no. 4 (April 1995). (Individual articles are not listed in the references.)

12. Doug Riecken, "Intelligent Agents," Guest editor's introduction to special issue of the *Communications of the ACM* 37, no. 7 (July 1994): 18.

have their limitations in many situations when compared to creating catalogs and abstracts. An alternative is to use agents and mediators to create catalogs and abstracts. Clearly these are not mutually exclusive alternatives. For example, we may well use catalogs and abstracts in high-use areas, and active agents and mediators to search for data in low-use areas. Experience will determine the utility of these alternatives, which in a specific case may change with time. The agents and mediators can be expected to modify the detailed retrieval mechanisms. The situation can be viewed as being pseudo-static.

Wiederhold has been addressing the information retrieval problem for some time. The recent papers from his group are well referenced.[13] There is recognition that a hierarchy of mediators is required and that mediators can provide general service functions to many applications. There are formal suggestions for implementation. The important question raised here is the inclusion, as appropriate, of such functions in the network. Communication and memory location constraints, and tradeoffs, can have a substantial impact on performance. Consequently, inclusion of mediator services as an integral part of the network could have a substantial payoff in performance.

13.5   Putting It Together—An Example

the·sis *A proposition that is maintained by argument.*[14]

The thesis of this text has been that the key to distributed systems lies in the ability to interchange data between the elements that constitute a distributed information system. The most severe case involves dynamic or changing data that are accessed by many users (or processes) under circumstances in which communications delays are important. Our focus has been on this most severe case where the elements constituting the information system are heterogeneous in nature. We have adopted this stance for two principal reasons.

First, it represents the most general case. If we understand the most general case, we understand the special cases. Unfortunately, it cannot be said that we fully understand the general case. A full understanding is beyond the state of the art and of necessity, emphasis has been given to understanding the issues and parameters that are important. Understanding those issues is a necessary step towards the development of a full understanding. It also provides

13. Gio Wiederhold, "Mediators in the Architecture of Future Information Systems," *IEEE Computer* (March 1992): 89; Gio Wiederhold, "Interoperation, Mediation, and Ontologies" (paper presented at the International Symposium on Fifth Generation Computer Systems 1994, Workshop on Heterogeneous Cooperative Knowledge-Bases, December 15–16, 1994); Gio Wiederhold, "Digital Libraries, Value, and Productivity," *Communications of the ACM* 38, no. 4 (April 1995): 85.

14. From the *American Heritage Dictionary for Windows*, Wordstar International, 1993.

valuable information and a sense of the tradeoffs involved in reaching the design decisions that we must make today.

Second, societal information systems increasingly involve heterogeneous systems that often have dynamic components. Although those dynamic components may be small, in some applications they can be very important. In other applications, the dynamic component may interact with pseudo-static components.

In Chapter 3, memory hierarchies were introduced, because of the mismatch between logic speed and the speed of memory and the large variation of both memory cost and performance for different types of memory. The concepts of one-level stores and caches were an important part of the discussion. Further details of memory hierarchies were discussed in Chapters 5, 9, and 12. In the meantime, it became clear that hierarchies in other areas are also important in distributed computing. The properties of communications systems discussed in Chapters 3, 7, 8, and 13 imply hierarchies of communications networks. The database management, interfacing, and data location discussions of Chapters 9, 10, and 11 imply hierarchies in those areas. Our discussion in this chapter implies a hierarchy of data services. Thus it is a central point of large heterogeneous systems that many of their properties, associated issues, and architectural alternatives will be hierarchical in nature.

Key to our discussion has been the issue of what data should be where. To illustrate this point, Fig. 13.4 presents a restricted view of Fig. 13.2 with slightly different notation. Included are some communications paths that will

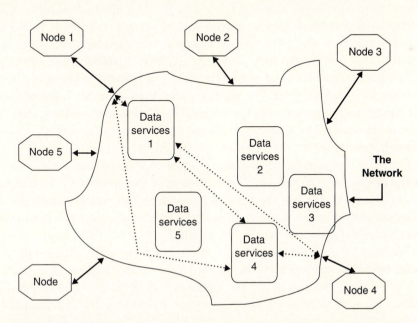

Figure 13.4   A functional structure of a distributed information system

be discussed. It is assumed that a "data service" element may perform several data service functions as illustrated in Fig. 13.1 and that data storage hardware associated with such an element may have the hierarchical nature shown in Fig. 12.1. It is clear from earlier discussions that storage may be distributed and hierarchical in nature. We assume that there will be dynamic movement of data, including caching, within the network. We further assume in Fig. 13.4 that the geometry shown and implied distances are important. Although for simplicity the figure shows direct dotted communication paths, the communications paths may in fact be hierarchical and pass through many data service centers. Simple examples are the routing of long-distance telephone calls through many switching centers, and packets of data passing through Internet switches. The assumption is that closeness in the figure implies substantially smaller delays. Thus it is assumed that the propagation and other communication delays for communications between node 1 and data service center 1 are substantially less than those between node 1 and data service center 4.

Let us assume that there is a data set, A, which we know will be used by node 1 and other nodes including node 4. (Although this paragraph is written in terms of data use, we also include data services that may be included at that location.) It is also known that most of its use will be from node 1. Clearly, if system performance is the issue (we are ruling out other factors that might determine location), data set A should be located at data service center 1. However, if the usage changes dramatically—for example, so that node 4 becomes the predominant user—locating data set A at node 1 will no longer be optimum. Data set A should be moved to data service center 4. If such a shift of load is anticipated in advance—for example, because use is a function of the time of day—a move can be planned in advance. If shifts in use are unpredictable, dynamic caching of secondary store (e.g., moving the data to storage at data service center 4) can be used. Clearly, there may be multiple caches, and concurrency control can be a factor. The objective of shifting data is to fine-tune the overall system so that overall performance is improved. As noted earlier, the design of the information systems being used may have a profound impact upon the parameters, and if performance is inadequate, it may be necessary to consider modifying the structure of the information systems. It should also be noted that we have not considered the many parameters discussed in earlier chapters, such as security and reliability, which can impact upon where data services should be provided.

We have taken a simple example. In many respects the above example is trivial, but at the same time, there is a certain amount of realism to it. There are different time zones and usage can shift spatially with time of day. Even in a campus network, homework assignments may dramatically shift use patterns in that an entire group—for example, the freshman in a single dorm—may be accessing the same database to do a problem. The problem is not just dynamic data. It may also involve multiaccess to static or pseudo-static data. Being able to move data within a distributed hierarchy of physical storage can be important. Above all, the reader should remember that we have only considered a few of the parameters discussed earlier. The example, however, illustrates data services and physical storage that are network-oriented.

13.6   Summary and Comments

In this section, we review many of the issues raised in earlier chapters of this book. The difference is that the discussion is now in the context of networks, data services, and overall information systems. From the earlier discussion, readers should have formulated their own opinions and evaluation of issues. Thinking about the issues and related questions, they will very likely develop a perspective assessment in the context of overall distributed systems. At the same time, they should recognize that there may not be adequate, definitive answers to many important questions. The state of the art and our knowledge are inadequate. Even if a general answer exists to a specific question, the answer is likely to depend on the applications and environment and on other circumstances. The issues and questions discussed in what follows are not necessarily independent or orthogonal.

What should be the role of a network? We have seen examples of data services that should be performed in the communications network. The computing associated with the control of a network is one example. What have come to be known as file servers are a second example. Clearly, we should not think of networks just in terms of data transport.

However, we do not have a clear general picture and set of formal guidelines that indicate what level of data services should be provided within a network. Furthermore, it is to be expected that specific data services should be provided both in and outside the network. Access control to data and access to systems at nodes are examples. Under the circumstances, we can only address the opportunities to include data services within the network on a case-by-case basis.

The situation is not as bad as may be implied here. It is known that the location of data services should be dependent upon the application and environment. We can hope for a design methodology that will provide the alternatives and guidance in making selections among those alternatives. We do not have a satisfactory methodology, but what we have provides a good deal of insight into the tradeoffs among alternatives. That is a great help.

There are "state of mind," "attitude," or "viewpoint" factors and guidelines that can be important. Basically they are at a paradigm level. We should make certain assumptions: (1) that networks should provide data services; (2) that we should actively seek data services that might be provided within networks. Do not be too swayed by where they have been performed historically. The trend is to move services to networks; (3) that data services should be distributed as appropriate among the workstations attached to nodes of the network and to data servers that are internal to the network. (Duplication of data services is often appropriate.)

Is there a difference between a "server" on the network and a "server" that is part of the network? With regard to type of function, there may not be a difference. With regard to what can be specifically done, there may be a substantial difference. An example is the ability to shut off access at the level of the communications network. This cannot be done at workstation nodes for one does not usually have control of what is attached at nodes. Access control should be exercised at many levels of the information system hierarchy.

When should a data service be at a node? When should it be considered part of the network? The location of a specific data service is very dependent upon the application. There is no general answer to this question. It may well be that the service should be provided both within the network and at workstation nodes.

Are there facts concerning the use of data that the network will know and a "server" at a node will not know? If so, are those facts relevant to performance and cost? In some areas, the network will know far more than the nodes. For example, the network knows what the traffic is and may know what data are being accessed and from what nodes. No node will know these facts unless they are supplied by the network. This is one of the reasons that data services should be made part of the network. The network can uniquely provide some services. This is not just a performance and cost issue. At the same time, it should be recognized that there may also be an impact on performance and cost.

Are there functions that from a pure cost standpoint are better done in the network? There are things that from a pure cost standpoint may be better done in the network. These things may also impact on performance. Distributing directory functions is an example.

Can concurrency control and maintenance of data integrity be simplified by performing certain functions in the network? Yes. For example, a point within the network central to the nodes utilizing the data may not be near any one node. Placing selected storage and database managers at that central point of the network might be an advantage.

What part, if any, of the directory hierarchy might be better placed in the network? Certainly global directory information should be given some consideration.

Can placing key functions in the network make design and performance problems more tractable? There may well be a large impact on performance. Exercising such an option may also simplify design.

Does the detailed design of information system requirements impact on the associated computer system? The answer here is a resounding yes. It may be that the information system requirements cannot be met by any computer system architecture that is cost effective. Furthermore, it may not be possible to meet requirements at any cost. For example, the specification of where data are to be located, without considering computer and communication system tradeoffs, can be disastrous.

Information system requirements and architecture (from the users' viewpoint) must be coordinated and integrated with the architecture of the computer system (from the system designers' viewpoint). The architecture of the computer system provides the basis for meeting the information system requirements. Information system requirements and design, and computer and communication system design, must be integrated. This often means iteration between the two professional sectors. Multidisciplinary project teams are desirable.

13.7   Problems

1. (a) Review the problem statements of problems 1–3 of Section 12.8. If you have answered the questions in those problems, review your answers. (b) Consider the problems given in Section 11.6. You have presumably done one or more of those problems. Review those problems that you have done. (c) There is the design option of distributing data both within the communications network and at equipment attached to the nodes of the network. For those problems that you addressed in Section 11.6, make an analysis of where you would recommend locating data and indicate the reasons for your decisions.

2. This problem can be assigned either as a problem to be addressed in writing or as a problem in which the students are prepared for discussion in class, including writing their views on the blackboard.

    (a) Why are we not further along in implementing Distributed Systems? There are many applications in which what we would like to do, and we believe should be attainable, is apparently beyond our grasp. It is pertinent to ask why this is so. There are of course both technical reasons and other factors. With respect to technology, is the inadequacy due to a lack of development effort or to a lack of our fundamental understanding or both? For example, with regard to standards there appears to be an insufficient effort to develop specific standards, but there is also insufficient knowledge to permit us to develop the needed standards. Does the often necessary requirement of upward compatibility constrain our freedom of action? In the nontechnical areas, what are the business and financial constraints? Are the lack of funds to support development or to purchase capital equipment a limitation?

(b) Prepare a matrix listing areas that you feel limit the deployment of distributed systems and relate those factors to potential limitations in technology, business, or any other circumstances that you wish to consider. (The issue is one that can lead to interesting class discussion.) The following is a suggested format.

Factors	*Limitation*	*Is Knowledge a Limitation?*
Standards		
Application software		
Capital investment		
Skilled professionals		

Chapter 14

Outstanding Problems and Research Opportunities

One of the first things a research institution needs is a technical or scientific objective. Only by having some reasonably well-defined goals can researchers make those choices which they face at every turn as to which one of several possible lines to follow. This statement does no violence to the classical concept that true research is without restraint and follows the intellectual curiosity of the researcher. Anyone who has ever done scientific research knows how many interesting paths are continually opening to view in the maze of undiscovered knowledge. Only with a compass can unilateral progress be assured. And without progress of which to be proud there is discouragement and loss of vitality.

Ralph Bown[1]
Vice President, Research,
Bell Telephone Laboratories

14.1 Introduction

The article from which the above is quoted had a profound effect upon one of the authors of this book. It clearly states that we must really think about and plan scientific and engineering research, be it on an institutional or an individual basis. Further more, it clearly indicates that what was arguably the premier industrial research and development laboratory of this century was motivated by the real-world problem of improving electrical communications. For those

---

1. Ralph Bown, "Vitality of a Research Institution and How to Maintain It," (paper presented at the Sixth Annual Conference on the Administration of Research, Georgia Institute of Technology, September 8–10, 1952, BSTJ Bell Telephone System Monograph 2207).

of us developing information science, there exists the wider objective of improving mechanized information processing in the broad sense. That objective encompasses work from basic research to implementation, and it includes academic programs essential to the development of the professionals necessary to bring this about.

Much of this book has been devoted to the alternatives that we face in designing distributed systems. In this chapter, we consider in more general terms selectivity in professional work. The ability to select a good path to follow extends into all areas of human activity. Of specific concern to us, however, are the engineering, research, and educational communities involved in the technology of distributed systems. There is a good deal of interaction and integration among these three areas. In the fast-moving field of information systems (e.g., computers and communications) there is little point in trying to establish clean boundaries between the three communities.

Outstanding organizations and people rarely just stumble into important areas of work. In some cases intuition is the deciding factor. More often there is a conscious effort on the part of the leaders of the organization, or the individuals involved, to selectively pick important areas to work on. Methodology, to be discussed in this chapter can help in reaching "selection" decisions in a rational way. The philosophy is applicable at both an organization and at an individual level. However, this is a book primarily for professional people. Consequently, the emphasis is on the individual and the impact that such methods may have on the personal development of professional people. In part this posture is taken in the belief that the thoughtful leaders of institutions usually build their careers on the early development of a thoughtful discipline for their own professional lives.

Problem solving in general is much easier than problem defining. Engineering education generally emphasizes problem solving. Many students like problem solving because they just turn the crank and out comes the answer. Unfortunately neither engineering design nor research fit this model. One must first define what the problem really is. Problem definition is a first step to design. Much of this book has been aimed at problem definition. This chapter reviews a methodology for being selective in engineering and scientific work with emphasis on distributed information systems. We use the term information systems in the broadest sense.

In what follows, we place a great deal of emphasis on the terms "significant" and "significant work." How do we determine whether work is significant or not? Of course if we wait decades it is usually clear. But, how do we reach a short-term assessment? A good measure is the judgment of peers, with one qualification. The circle of peers should not be too small. Too often the workers in a small field lack the perspective to judge their work in a broader context, and it is that broader context that we are concerned with, that tells us what is important.

14.2   Environment and Motivation for Work

Engineering: The application of scientific and mathematical principles to practical ends such as the design, manufacture, and operation of efficient and economical structures, machines, processes, and systems.[2]

The profession in which a knowledge of the mathematical and natural sciences gained by study, experience, and practice is applied with judgment to develop ways to utilize, economically, the materials and forces of nature for the benefit of mankind.[3]

In some circles there is a continuing debate as to whether computer science is science or engineering. In some cases, the split between "science" and "engineering" is associated with that between computer hardware and computer software. In either case, the level of integration required between the two is substantial and is in fact largely responsible for the introduction of the term *computer architecture,* which implies that integration. It seems that the debate serves little purpose. In either case, as we shall see, most of the work is related to filling the needs or aspirations of the real world. There are different categories of work, research, applied research, development, design, implementation, deployment, etc. All of these categories come under the umbrella of engineering and also fall in the domain of people practicing computer science. In what follows, we make no distinction between computer science and computer engineering. In keeping with the tenet of this book, we include both under the category of information science and engineering.

It may appear that we are evading a discussion and recognition of "pure" science for the sake of science. Perhaps the best examples of pure science are in some fields of mathematics. We recognize the importance of such fields just as we recognize the importance of the arts. We do not believe, however, that there is a significant amount of work in the information system or computer science area that falls in this category. This will become evident in what follows.

---

2. *The American Heritage Dictionary,* 3rd ed. (Novato, CA: WordStar International, 1993).

3. Engineers' Council for Professional Development, *Annual Reports,* (31st: 1962–63; 32nd: 1963–64).

14.2.1 Filling Societal Needs and Expectations with Significant Work

It is clear that society justifies its support of information systems work because of the potential societal impact of such work. This is true whether the activity under consideration is educational, research, development, or the implementation and operation of information systems. This environment has led to the expansion of joint industrial and academic research efforts in the field.[4] The potential payoff may be in the present or in the future. Consider two examples. Most information systems work on business systems is directed to short-term payoffs. Basic research and university education are examples of anticipated long-term payoff. Regardless of whether the work is short or long term, or whether the work is considered to be basic or applied, to a very large degree the justification for support (from a societal standpoint) is anticipated payoff.

As indicated above, the significance of specific work to society is a primary measure of its importance. However, it may take a long time for that significance to become clear. The people who did the work may no longer be around. There are immediate intuitive shorter-term measures that are usually used. One such measure is an evaluation of the importance or significance of the proposed or actual work. Your coworkers, your peers, your bosses, and society in general are always making such judgments. All of us make such evaluations of the work of others, and if we are smart, of our own work.

One measure of the significance of work is the reaction of a wide peer group and in particular the leaders of that group. Does their individual reaction fit into one or more of the following patterns?

I expected it.

I wish I had done that.

That is really interesting.

So what?

A fundamental result. Now we shall be able to do _____

That proves something that I thought might be true for a long time.

The results change or add paradigms in the field.

---

4. Walter Massey, "Research and Industry: Forging New Ties for the Twenty-First Century" (Keynote Address, March 8, 1995, Seventeenth Annual Conference, Industrial Liaison Program College of Engineering, University of California, Berkeley).

We all know which of these responses indicate significant work and which do not. In the next section, we discuss significant work in computer science, for we believe that there is much to be learned from examining the reasoning and motivation behind past significant work in our field.

14.3   Significant Work in Information Systems/Computer Science and Selectivity

The truly outstanding work in engineering and science is performed by people who continuously evaluate the importance of their work. If the area in which they are working ceases to be an important area in which significant work is possible, they will shift to a new area that is important. In a technical field moving as rapidly as computer technology, few outstanding people remain in the same narrow field for long. They move to the leading edge where the excitement and opportunity are greatest.

As pointed out earlier, almost all of the truly significant work in the information field is in areas that are perceived to be associated with real-world problems. This observation is important because it provides a criterion that can be applied in selecting a course of action. We should always ask, why might this work be significant or important? Furthermore, that question should be answered in the context of real-world opportunities and impact.

14.3.1   Examples of Work in the Information Systems Field

Think of the research leading up to the significant events listed below. Each of the accomplishments listed is recognized as being a major contribution to computer science and engineering. In each case, the work was motivated by a very real perceived need, the satisfaction of which would be a significant contribution. The examples were need driven in the sense that a solution would have a substantial impact on real-world problems that were being faced at the time the work was undertaken.

Computability and the Turing machine

The stored program concept

One-level store concept

Microprogramming

Communications theory

Application-independent generalized database management systems

The theory of encryption and secrecy systems

The transistor

The magnetic disk

Complexity theory

Fiber optics for communications

Fortran

Why were these areas of research selected and what was the motivation of the individuals doing the work?

Alan Turing's work that led to the Turing machine and the stored-program concept was aimed at understanding what a person (called a computer in his original paper) could compute. Specifically, what could the operators of the then existing mechanical calculators compute if they were given adequate instructions? What were the limits on their ability?

The one-level store concept that led to virtual memories and caches developed from the need to circumvent the size limitations of core memory and take advantage of the much larger memory available on magnetic drums. This of course was the first step toward the hierarchical and virtual memories of today.

Microprogramming was developed to expand the instruction set of computers without expanding the instruction execution hardware that at that time was very expensive. In a sense, the RISC processors of today are a further step in this direction, at a different architectural level and with slightly different goals.

Communications theory was developed to better understand the fundamental processes of communications in order to improve communications systems. The theory resulted in combining in a general model many of the earlier practices and providing a theoretical basis for many of those practices. It then led to entirely new fields.

As noted in Chapter 9, the first application-independent database management systems were developed to solve manufacturing and business problems.

The work on solid state devices that led to the transistor was aimed at circumventing the limitations of vacuum tube diodes and later amplifiers.

Magnetic disk files were developed to avoid the limitations of magnetic tape systems. Magnetic tape systems had earlier been developed to mitigate the problems with paper tape and punch cards. Work in these areas fostered a great deal of work in magnetic materials.

Magnetic core storage was developed to circumvent the shortcomings of cathode ray tube storage systems.

Work on computational complexity was initiated because it was clear that how the complexity of calculations would scale was an important issue in the use of computers.

The development of fiber optics resulted from a long research program to circumvent the limitations of copper wire, coaxial cable, wave guides, and radio relay systems.

Fortran was developed to provide a more cost-effective means of writing computer programs involving algebraic formulas.

The point is that everyone admires such world-class work, much of it of Nobel Prize or Turing Award quality. There are always "interesting" problems that can be worked on, but the outstanding scientists pick interesting problems that are also significant. They always know why what they are doing is important. In computer science, most significant problems are related to the real world. Each of the accomplishments listed above was related to perceived needs or challenges in the real world. Picking an important problem, or defining a problem, is often more difficult than solving the problem once it has been selected.

14.3.2   The Selectivity Challenge

Good research is dependent on finding a good problem.

John S. Mayo, President, AT&T Bell Laboratories[5]

Selectivity is important in both research and engineering. However, an engineering task is often associated with a particular application. Consequently, specific engineering problems are frequently presented in terms of a set of requirements, and selectivity focuses on methods of addressing those requirements. The available technical alternatives can often be related to areas of more general and less constrained research. In a sense, pragmatic design alternatives are based upon a subset of research results and knowledge. We are examining distributed information systems broadly, and in this context consider selectivity in research as a vehicle for selectivity in systems architecture.

Our conception of what we believe information systems are capable of doing extends far beyond what is in place today. Most people believe that computer systems will play an increasing role in our every day lives. Assuming that the long-term goal is to benefit society, it seems appropriate to consider questions like the following:

What are the future opportunities to apply information systems to the benefit of humankind?

What are the dangers?

What are the safeguards that are needed and should be required?

What are the real problems that we face in pushing the "applications" frontier of information technology? In the economic and societal area? In technology? In the political area?

Where do we need research results to do what we believe can and should be done with computer and communication systems?

Pragmatically, what are the opportunities for really significant work? In answering that question we should evaluate both the impact of a program, if successful, and the probability of success. There is little point in working in an area in which results would be important, but in light of current knowledge and technology unattainable. Simply put, the objective should be to determine what is worth doing that there is a fighting chance of accomplishing.

5. "Telecommunications in the Third Millennium" (paper presented at the Industrial Liaison Program Fifteenth Annual Conference, College of Engineering, University of California Berkeley, March 11, 1993).

Unfortunately, a necessary assumption to the above objective is the ability to determine what the likelihood of success is. This, however, is often more of an educated guess than a factual assessment. The danger is that speculating that a problem is simply "too difficult" or "beyond current technology" may prevent a researcher from working on a possible attainable breakthrough. However, underestimating the difficulty of the problem is likely to result in the researcher simply spinning his or her wheels without yielding any tangible results.

14.4   Methodology

14.4.1   Establishing Technical Areas of Opportunity

Think about areas where information technology should and could have a large impact. In effect, formulate need and requirements goals. We all intuitively have ideas on this. Write down a list of areas where you would expect information technology could make a big difference. Figure 14.1 shows the

Education
Manufacturing
Entertainment
Medicine
       Diagnostics
       Pharmacy
       Health records
       Imaging
       Hospital operations
       Research
       Statistical records and analysis
Legal profession
Law enforcement
Sports
Marketing
Sales
Military
Insurance
Office work
Post office
Communications
Legislative bodies
Libraries

Figure 14.1   Examples of Areas Where Advanced Information Technology Could Have a Large Impact

start of such a list. It is by no means complete, but it is included for illustrative purposes.

We wish to consider the following questions. Of the areas shown, where will the big payoffs be to society? What technology will be needed to get there? Is there any chance of developing the technology today? Is there any chance of obtaining research results today that will make it possible to develop the needed technology tomorrow?

Establish areas of information technology where you believe specific research results are needed to further the attainment of general societal goals in the areas shown in Fig. 14.1. Give emphasis to those areas of technology in which results would be viewed as significant. The objective is to use these areas of information technology as the basis for developing plans and programs. Make this as complete a list as you can. The list can be screened later. In fact, in deriving the list of technological areas from societal needs, one stage of screening has already been invoked. Figure 14.2 shows what a small part of a list of technological areas might look like.

There are three qualifications that should be placed on the procedure discussed so far.

1. It is not intended that the subareas listed be orthogonal or independent. Nor is it intended that they be orthogonal with the subareas that may appear under other major areas. Databases, for example, will appear in many places. The reason for their inclusion in many areas is that many of the issues considered will be sensitive to the application area, such as in database technology for communications systems.

2. We started with societal needs. It may be desirable to impose another screen associated with the needs of a more restricted group. For example, if associated with a business, a university, or a specific segment of government, the general societal needs can be screened and transformed to the needs of that segment. For example, starting with business needs the technological needs can be derived.

3. Clearly a particular individual may wish to take a more restricted view than we are here. That is understandable. We encourage the reader to make up such a list associated with his or her immediate environment and interests. Ask in the case of each item on your list why it is important. Now, to place your items in perspective with the broader field, widen your list to cover other related areas. Compare the items on your original list with those on the expanded list. It is

<u>**Communications**</u>

Transmission
        Satellite
        Fiber optics
        Radio
        Infrared
Switching systems
        Hardware
                IC based
                Optics based
        Software
        Distributed operating systems
        Call processing
        Feature processing
        Database management
                Hardware
                Software
        Architecture
Compression
Multimedia integration
Modulation / location
Networks
        Architecture
                Inside multiprocessor
                Local area
                Regional
                National
                International
Traffic studies
Multimedia
Network data services
Propagation
Video text
Picture processing
Cryptography
Security
Standards

Figure 14.2   Technical Area Example

only through making such comparisons that people decide to shift from a field that is no longer important to a new area of more significance and opportunity. Examples are the shift of physicists from atomic physics to nuclear physics, of communication engineers from classical signal processing to digital techniques and switching, of computer scientists to knowledge engineering and databases, etc. In fact the shift of work, both academic and research, at leading universities usually follows such an analysis.

14.4.2   Screening

In most cases, a complete list of areas of technical opportunity as discussed in Section 14.4.1 is much larger than any one individual or organization can focus on. A procedure is needed that will select from that larger list those areas that are most significant, have potential for obtaining significant results, and will have an impact on the community that is involved. It is suggested that this be accomplished by utilizing a series of "screens" that will screen out or eliminate those areas and projects that are of lesser importance to the individuals and institutions that are involved. In brief, put the areas through a series of screens to establish their importance to you or your organization. The specific screens will depend on the environment and circumstances such as the organization to which the component or individual doing the analysis belongs. The screens should involve factors such as organizational or professional needs, academic stature, competitive impact, new markets, efficiency, likelihood that results are attainable, and promising R&D areas today. Figure 14.3 shows a generic set of screens.

There are many organizations and people who can initiate a screening analysis as suggested above. It is clear that the details of the screening process will be different for these different groups. In the last analysis, the significance should be in terms of the impact on the group, be it an individual or an organization. In addition, as mentioned earlier, solvability is important. Do not try to solve a problem before the core technology and knowledge are in place, unless you can create it. The work on compiler theory at the General Electric Research Laboratory was initiated after those involved concluded that although a theory of operating systems might be more important, developing a theory for compilers was much more tractable.[6]

It is also important to consider the resources that are available in an environment. Experimental work in high energy particle physics and chemistry requires a source of high energy particles. One would be ill advised to try to work in that field in an environment that lacked the necessary particle acceler-

---

6. P. M. Lewis, D. J. Rosenkrantz, and R. E. Stearns, *Compiler Design Theory* (Reading, MA: Addison-Wesley, 1976).

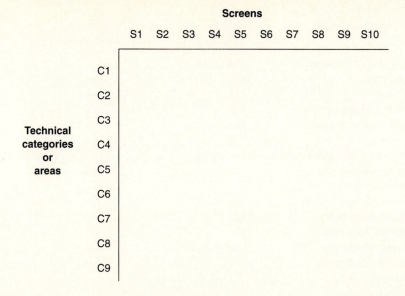

Figure 14.3   Area analysis and screening

ators. In fact, because of the necessity of a high order of computer technology for the control of experiments and the collection and analysis of data, computer resources are a must. Consequently, every major accelerator center today has leading-edge computer facilities.

Figure 14.4 gives an example of two-level screening from approximately ten years ago. The authors make no pretense that it is complete or accurate. The point is that one learns a lot making up such charts.

In summary: Put technical areas through a series of screens to establish their importance. The specific screens will depend on circumstances, such as the organization to which the component or individual doing the analysis belongs. The screens should involve factors such as the following:

Organizational or professional needs

Impact on academic stature, competitive posture, new markets, the organization, efficiency, etc.

Promising R&D areas where there is a reasonable chance that significant results could be obtainable

Likelihood that results are attainable

Technical Categories	Important Need Area	Research Opportunity
Fault Tolerant Systems	Yes, critical	Yes
Hardware	Yes	Yes
Software	Yes	Yes
Hardware/software	Yes	Yes
Distributed architecture	Yes	Yes
Architecture	Yes	Yes
Distributed information systems	Yes, critical	Hard, great opportunity
For special functions	Yes	Yes
Real-time control		
Communication systems	Yes, critical	Yes
Database machines	Yes	Yes
General multiprocessors	Yes	?
Integrated networks	Yes, critical	Yes
Artificial Intelligence	Yes	Spotty
Theorem proving		
Game playing		
Knowledge engineering	Yes	Yes
Problem domain databases	Critical	Yes, likely main problem
Inference methods	Yes	Yes
Machine architecture	Needed for quantum step	Yes, hard, critical
Real applications	Small domain opportunity	Opportune time for
Natural languages	Very important	Yes, hard
Robotics	Very important	Yes
Speech recognition	Very important	Yes, hard
Fuzzy sets/logic	Yes	Yes
Neural nets	Yes	Be careful
Human Factors	Yes, key to future use	Critical quantum step
Professional interfaces	Yes, key to future use	Critical quantum step
Ultimate user interfaces	Yes, key to future use	Critical quantum step
Multimedia systems	Yes	Yes

Figure 14.4   Examples of technical areas

Promising areas in the individual's environment

Available resources

Support potentially assignable

Available staff with required expertise

R&D in which an individual has a personal interest

Because of dependencies between screens, iteration between them may be required.

14.4.3   Generic Examples of Screens

For illustrative purposes in this section, we suggest possible screens in several areas of activity. The focus is on industry and universities.

Figure 14.5 presents an example of a reasonable set of screens for an industrial research and development activity. It is not the only set and frankly could well have more layers. It does portray the concept, however. Figure 14.6 presents the same material in a different form.

One starts by determining the technical needs of the organization or corporation. This can be done by screening the full set of technological categories down to those that are important to the corporation.

The next screen determines if those needs can be filled from existing sources. We should always make use of needed technology that is available from any source. There may be important economic factors that we do not elect to discuss here.

The screen that follows is to select those technologies that are so important to the organization that the business must be considered a participant in the technology. For example, if company components are participating in

---

Start with technical categories, and then filter them through screens of:

Corporate use needs (components must use technology)

Sources of technology (government labs, universities, internal work, etc.)

Corporate core needs (components must be a part of technology)

Technology competitive status (lag, equal, lead, etc.)

Technology competitive opportunities

Promising R&D areas

Promsing R&D areas matched to resources

Impact on organization as a whole

Proposed program

Figure 14.5   Example of industrial screens

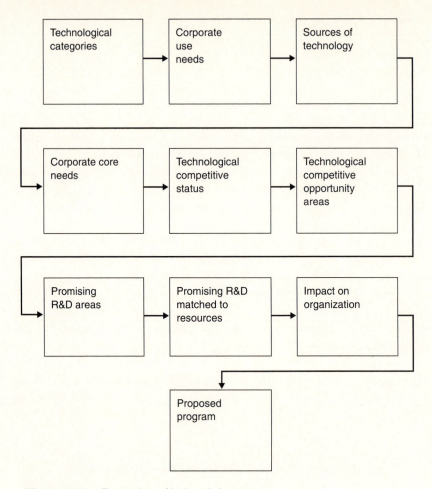

Figure 14.6   Examples of industrial screens

materials research, a satisfactory interface to external research groups in that area is much more viable than if the company is considered to be an outsider. It is also often true that to effectively use outside technology it is necessary to have internal competence. The latter is certainly true in the area of computer technology.

The next screen determines whether the organization lags, equals, or leads its competitors in the technologies that remain after the preceding screen. The screen that follows determines whether improving the company's technological competence in specific areas would enhance its competitive position. Corporations are basically interested in results that will make them more competitive. If so, the next screen examines promising R&D areas within the above constraint. The promising R&D areas are screened for those that are matched to existing resources or resources that can be added if merited. An analysis of cost versus projected payoff may be a factor here.

It is also necessary to consider the impact that a program would have on the organization as a whole. From the viewpoint of management that is important, not just the impact on specific components of the organization. Because of the pervasiveness of computer technology this is an important consideration in our area. In light of the above screening, it is then time to propose a program. An overall program may well include shifting resources from program areas that no longer are as important as that being proposed.

It should be recognized that such an analysis involves a great deal of uncertainty and intuition. There are uncertainties both in estimating the probability of success of a proposed R&D program, and the impact that success of the program might have on the business. General Electric's creation of man-made diamonds, and Bell Laboratories' introduction of fiber optics communications are examples where a long-term investment in research had a major impact on the industries.

We next turn to academia and suggest parameters that should be considered in that environment. The figures focus on parameters at the levels of:

Ideal faculty research level (Fig. 14.7)

Pragmatic faculty research level (Fig. 14.8)

Student level of research (Fig. 14.9)

Course level of a department (Fig. 14.10)

The technology of distributed information systems is in a real sense a multidisciplinary field. By that we mean that it involves the integration of the fine-grained (sub) disciplines of computer science and computer engineering (including communications). The items listed in the preceding figures often involve many of those subdisciplines and, as noted earlier, they may share those subdisciplines. Consequently the figures do not adequately represent the relationships or interactions between the listed items. This is the type of situation that network databases, and more generally object-oriented technology, address. Certainly if we were creating a large database to contain such data, serious consideration should be given to an object-oriented approach and a database management system. In the context of this book, however, the current method of presentation in the figures is likely more understandable to the reader.

Societal needs

Important need areas requiring additional technology

Technical requirement categories

R&D opportunities

Synergism with educational program and objectives

R&D opportunities at university

Areas with potential for funding

Areas with potential for quick and many publications

Areas with potential for nucleated staff and program

Proposed program plan

> *Does the environment at most universities foster this type of analysis, or are the priorities quite different?*
>
> *The priorities are often quite different unfortunately, in particular for the junior faculty.*
>
> *Those few universities fortunate enough to have research establishments that are funded on a lump-sum basis may be able to follow this discipline.*

Figure 14.7   Parameters academic level (What the ideal faculty research level should be)

Areas with potential for funding

Areas with potential for quick and many publications

Technical categories

Important need areas requiring additional technology

R&D opportunities

R&D opportunities at university

Areas with potential for nucleated staff and program

Synergism with educational program and objectives

Proposed program plan

> *This is probably more representative of the priorities at most universities, particularly with respect to junior faculty.*
>
> *Outstanding senior faculty may well be in a position to follow the discipline outlined in Fig. 14.7.*

Figure 14.8   Parameters academic level (pragmatic faculty research level)

Important need areas requiring additional technology

Technical categories

R&D opportunities

R&D opportunities at university

Ph.D. research or M.S. project opportunities at university

Individual Ph.D. research or M.S. project opportunities at university

Opportunities of interest to the individual

Possible university advisors

Proposed Ph.D. research or M.S. project topic and plan

> *Is this the procedure followed by most students?*

> *Pragmatically, is this an option that is left open to them?*

Figure 14.9   Parameters academic environment (student level-research)

Societal needs

Target area of society

Need areas that will require professional people in fields

Need areas falling within the domain of the department

Need areas not covered by other departments in university

Educational synergism within the department and the university as a whole

Joint programs established with other departments

Synergism with research programs

Possible courses

Resource constraints

Proposed program

Staff requirements

    What staff is available?
    What staff is needed?
    What staff is convertible?
    What staff needs to be recruited?

Iteration required

Proposed program or courses

Figure 14.10   Parameters academic level (course level-department/academic area)

14.5   Application of Methodology to Distributed Information System Technology

Figure 14.11 shows the start of a set of screens for the distributed information system field. It is not intended to be complete. It is intended to indicate a framework within which readers can formulate their own thinking. Most of the entries are left blank and the figure is referred to in the problem section.

There is of course literature that can provide background information for applying the suggested methodology to an organization, or to professional

Technical Categories	Important Need Area	Research Opportunity	....
Distributed information systems	Critical	Yes, hard, essential	
Trade off analysis	Yes	Yes	
Functional	Yes	Yes	
Spatial	Yes	Yes	
Psychological	Yes	Yes	
Conditions for integration	Critical opportunity	Yes, hard, opportunity	
Existing techniques	Good starting point	First step	
Distributed databases	Critical	Yes, hard, opportunity	
Interfacing foreign information systems	Critical	Yes, very hard, critical	
Existing techniques	Need to understand	First step, probably	
Real-world experience	Need to understand	First step	
Problem definition	Critical	Hard, essential	
Theory	Need, will come later	Hard, essential	
Educational information systems	Tremendous opportunity	Tremendous opportunity	
Memory hierarchies	....	....	
....	....	....	
Location of parts			
Data services in network	....	....	
Needs for data services	....	....	
When in network	....	....	
Object-oriented systems	....	....	
Implementation issues	....	....	
Complexity	....	....	
Scaling	....	....	
Humanlike decision making	....	....	
Formal logic	....	....	
Other theoretical models	....	....	

Figure 14.11   Start of screening for distributed information systems

career planning. Geppert, Mervis, and Weingarten discuss the relevance of societal needs to selectivity in research, including the increasing trend to consider that a factor in funding.[7] Hartmanis and Lin is concerned with the status
of computer technology including comments on research opportunities.[8] The
papers by Brassard and by Zadeh are included because they question the applicability of the current paradigms of theoretical computer science to better
understanding of much of the world's information processing.[9] Theoretical
computer science could well seek to supplement its existing paradigms and
models with concepts better matched to world experience. The book edited by
Baumgartner and Payr focuses on "cognitive science."[10] It includes contribu-
tions by Allen Newell, Herbert Simon, Joseph Weizenbaum, Robert Wilensky,
Terry Winograd, and Lotfi Zadeh, all of whom are eminent in the field of computer science.

14.6   Summary and Comments

The procedure and methodology suggested in the chapter provides the
following:

A systematic way of evaluating what is important and significant.

A methodology that has been used in both industrial and academic environments with considerable success.

A discipline that can be utilized at both an organizational and individual
level.

A methodology applicable to the development of both research and educational programs; if applied, it can assist in formulating a plan for your own
professional work.

7. Linda Geppert, "Industrial R&D: the new priorities," *IEEE Spectrum* 31, no. 9 (September 1994):
30; Jeffrey Mervis, "Asking Science to Measure Up," *Science* 267 (January 6, 1995): 20; Fred
Weingarten, "Government Funding and Computer Research Priorities," *ACM Computing Surveys*
27, no. 1 (March 1995): 49.

8. Juris Hartmanis and Herbert Lin, eds., *Computing The Future—A Broader Agenda For Computer
Science and Engineering* (Washington, D.C.: National Academy Press, 1992).

9. Gilles Brassard, "Time for Another Paradigm Shift," *ACM Computing Surveys* 27, no. 1 (March
1995): 19; Lotfi Zadeh, "The Albatross of Classical Logic," in *Speaking Minds* (Princeton: Princeton
University Press, 1995), 300.

10. Peter Baumgartner and Sabine Payr, *Speaking Minds—Interviews with Twenty Eminent Cognitive
Scientists* (Princeton: Princeton University Press, 1995).

In more general terms, we as professional people face the following challenges:

We should understand needs, requirements, and opportunities in the application of information systems.

Quality research and academic programs are driven both by what is important to society and technological opportunities.

The motivational objective should be to do significant, not superficial, science and engineering.

The educational motivation should be to develop professionals who can play key roles in filling society's future needs.

Problem solving is easy; problem definition is hard. We should focus on techniques that will teach problem defining—the essence of research, development and design.

The world is full of complex problems that do not have the simple models that we would like. This is particularly true in the area of heterogeneous distributed information systems. Our professional discipline and programs must be attuned to this situation.

We must be willing to seek, with care, new paradigms and models that are better matched to our problems and challenges than those that are popular.

In the long run, there is the possibility that systems with an extremely large number of computing components, organized architecturally quite different than the systems we are accustomed to, will supplement today's and tomorrow's computers. The speculative ideas being considered include quantum effect computing elements, holographic and other optical systems, chemical systems, and DNA-like systems. Some of these areas are discussed in a short paper by James Glanz.[11]

14.7   Problems

There are many levels of screening implied by Figs. 14.3–14.10. In Fig. 14.11 only two levels of screening are portrayed. The purpose of this set of problems is to prepare more detailed charts along the lines of Figs. 14.1–14.2.

1. As a student in an academic program, prepare a chart along the lines of Fig. 14.11 that covers a significant number of levels as indicated in Fig. 14.9.

11. James Glanz, "Computer Scientists Rethink Their Discipline's Foundations," *Science* 269, no. 5229 (September 8, 1995): 1363.

2. There is much importance attached to the student evaluation of specific courses. This is an important input to the academic staff and administration. Consider your academic department or field of study. Prepare an analysis along the lines of Fig. 14.1 that covers the screening areas outlined in Fig. 14.10.

3. Consider the field of heterogeneous distributed information systems. Prepare a chart similar to Fig. 14.1 that covers the entire field. The major headings should cover the entire field. Pick two major areas (headings) of particular interest to you and expand the details along the lines of Fig. 14.4. By expand we mean add appropriate columns and include your assessment in the cells of the new columns.

4. For your particular area of commercial activity, prepare a detailed chart corresponding to Figs. 14.3 and 14.5.

5. The possibility of utilizing an object-oriented approach in addressing significant research areas and planning programs has been mentioned in the text. Assume that you have been confronted with this problem along the lines of the problems given above. Assume that the entire field of heterogeneous distributed information systems is to be covered and a corresponding database is to be created. It is intended that the database be applicable to group planning, individual planning, and academic course planning.

   Write a short paper, not more than 20 single-spaced pages, that examines alternative database management systems that might be used. Recommend a specific database management system and indicate your reasons for making the selection.

Glossary

The definitions that follow are in the context of usage in this book.

Access Control: The functional part of a computer hardware/software system that decides whether a user has been authorized to read or write a particular data item. More generally, those parts of an information system that control the access to data, software, or hardware.

ACM (Association for Computing Machinery): A professional society for computing professionals that sponsors many conferences and publishes a variety of journals and magazines on all aspects of computing.

AD Converter: A device or mechanism for taking samples of an analog signal, such as voice, and converting those sample values to binary numbers. The process is known as analog to digital conversion.

Added-Value Common Carrier: A provider of communications services that utilize common carriers for communications transport and offer additional features. America On-Line and the Internet are examples.

Added-Value Services: In the communications industry, services that extend beyond data transport.

AFIPS (American Federation for Information Processing Systems): An early professional society in the United States that sponsored conferences and published journals in the area of computing and information systems. It is no longer active and has been replaced by the International Federation for Information Processing (IFIP).

Agents: A term used in information retrieval systems for processes that seek out information for the user. The process is an "agent" for the user. The term generally implies finding, in a network of computers, the information that is desired.

Analog to Digital Converter: (see **AD converter**)

ANSI (American National Standards Institute): An organization in the United States that coordinates standards activities in the country in technical areas such as computing and communications.

Applications Systems Software: A software system designed to solve a class of problems. Examples are spreadsheets, word processors, and database managers. We use the term to distinguish such software from system software, such as an operating system, and applications software, directed to solving a specific application.

Archie: The term refers to a computer(s) on the Internet that is a server to help the user find a particular file or directory.

Architecture: The overall requirements of an information system and the merging of application, hardware, and software considerations into a coordinated and integrated view. The design of an appropriate structure involves both computer and communications technology.

Associative Memory: Memory in which a word is retrieved by its partial contents. For example, retrieving a word based on a virtual address in which other parts of the retrieved word contain the physical address of the data that are sought. In this application the associative memory is used to rapidly map a virtual address into a physical address. The term originally applied to hardware implementations but the function can be accomplished by either hardware or software. The term content addressable memory is sometimes used for a hardware implementation.

377

ASTM (American Society for Testing Materials): An organization that plays a major role in setting standards for defining the properties of materials.

Asynchronous Transfer Mode (ATM): A specific switching and transmission method that is based upon fixed-length virtual packet switching. ATM was developed by CCITT for broadband ISDN.

ATM: (see **Asynchronous Transfer Mode**)

Attribute: The name of a column in a relation.

B-tree: An indexing technique commonly used in database systems that efficiently allows data to be retrieved, both randomly based on its primary key values and sequentially in primary key order. A B-tree is an m-way tree, where m is usually large so that the tree is wide and shallow.

Backup and Recovery: The functional part of a database system that is responsible for saving a consistent state of the database, so that, following a failure of some kind that corrupts the database, the database can be restored. The term is applicable to computer systems more broadly where it may mean restoring the state of the computer system, or even a calculation, to what it was prior to an interruption or failure.

Bandwidth: The range of frequencies occupied by a time-varying function. For example, an A.M. radio station may occupy a bandwidth of 10 KHz.

Baseband: Signals that are limited to a band of frequencies around the origin— for example, from 0 to W. Actually, because of the symmetry of real signals around the origin, the limitation is from $-W$ to $+W$.

Basic ISDN Service: A common carrier communications service that provides on one telephone line (or its equivalent) two digitized channels of 64 Kb/s and one channel of 16 Kb/s. In common practice, one 64Kb/s channel will be used for digitized voice and the other for computer data. The 16 Kb/s channel is used in part for control and in part for low-speed computer data.

Bit: A unit of information. Also used to indicate one symbol (i.e., a 0 or a 1) in a binary string. Thus transfer rates may be given in bits per second. (See also **Information**)

Broadband: Signals that occupy a band of frequencies offset from the origin. For example, limited to a band from $(W_0 - W)$ to $(W_0 + W)$ where W_0 is larger than W. As a matter of fact, W_0 is usually much larger than W. Good examples are an AM radio station and the frequency used by a cellular radio connected to a portable computer.

Broadband ISDN Service: ISDN data services that may go up to hundreds of Mb/s.

Bus: An electrical connection between devices that, for communications purposes, is shared by the devices. The sharing is usually accomplished through time multiplexing the different communications channels.

Bus Switching: A switching mechanism utilizing a bus to which all ports (data sources) are connected. The switching is accomplished by assigning specific, common time slots to the two communicating parties. Clearly this technique can be extended to communicating groups (e.g., multiparty or conference telephone calls).

Cache: There are two meanings. The most common in computers is an implementation that duplicates selected data from a slow memory in a faster memory, so that it can be retrieved when needed from the faster memory. Selection of data is usually based upon use. Changes in data in the faster memory are usually automatically copied to the slower memory. A second meaning is to store (cache) data, in advance of its anticipated use, at a given location. (See also **One-Level Store**)

Campus: An area or environment like a university laboratory or factory, or a cluster of government buildings. The importance is that a campus defines an environment that in many respects is free standing with respect to communication and computer requirements and capability. The term is used to distinguish it from local, metropolitan, wide area, and national areas that are more common classifications in the communications industry.

Capacity Theorem: The theorem (originated by C. E. Shannon) that states that the maximum information, C (in bits per second), that can be sent over a communication channel, of bandwidth W and signal to noise ration (S/N), is given by the formula $C=W\text{Log}_2[1+(S/N)]$.

Carrier-Based Signals: Baseband signals (i.e., signals occupying a frequency range around the origin) that have been moved up to a higher frequency by modulating with a carrier. Radio and television are examples. The importance in the national common carrier network is that all communications, with the exception of local loops, utilize carrier-based signals.

CCITT (Committee Consultif Internationale Telephonique et Telegraphique): A committee of the International Telecommunications Union (ITU).

Central Office: An electronic switch in the common carrier communications system (telephone system) to which home and business communications have a direct connection. Central office facilities are owned by the common carriers and located on their property.

Centrex: A common carrier central office service that is similar to that provided by a PBX. In older Centrex systems, the switching was provided at a central office.

In newer systems, there is the option of having the switching done by a remote switching partition on the customer's site but controlled by the central office switch.

Channel: The pathway assigned to communications between nodes or devices connected to a network. The term pathway is used in a liberal sense. A channel may be defined by frequency assignment, time assignment, carrier waveforms, physical propagation path, etc., or any combination thereof. In the simple case, a channel is designated by assigning areas in frequency-time space along with specified physical paths. In a complex case, it may also involve assigning degrees of freedom in frequency-time space. (See also **Degrees of Freedom**)

Circuit Switching: The establishment of a communications path (or circuit) for the exclusive use of the parties involved for the duration of the call (or session). The normal switching of telephone calls is an example.

CODASYL (Conference on Data Systems Languages): The Database Task Group of this committee presented a report in 1971 that defined the original network data model and support languages.

Common Carriers: Those businesses that provide communications transport and related services, as distinct from the manufacturers of communications equipment. Common carriers can be businesses, as in the United States, or branches of the government, as in some other countries.

Computations: Operations specified by application algorithms and programs. Computations are generally performed at network nodes. Computations do the users' work. It should be noted that programs are in general separate from and independent of the data or data objects upon which they operate. Data services, as distinct from computations, make the required data available for computations.

Computing Services: (see **Computations**)

Concurrency Control: The functional part of a computer system that regulates time access (from multiple users) to shared data. Concurrency control ensures that no two users are allowed to access the same data at times, and in a way, that would corrupt the database or the applications using the database.

Covering Architecture: An architecture that provides all of the capability that might be required. A covering architecture can be viewed as a superset of a group of more specialized architectures designed to provide more restricted application oriented capability. The more specialized architectures represent special cases of the covering architecture.

Crossbar Switch: A switch in which a unique physical path is established between the input and output lines. Examples are relays and semiconductor switching elements that connect the input and output lines.

Cursor: A mark (or symbol) on a display (or screen) that establishes the interaction point between the user and the data presented.

DA Converters: A device or mechanism for taking digital signals or numbers and converting them to analog signals such as voice. The process is known as digital to analog conversion.

Data: Raw facts, numbers, text, etc., as distinguished from information that implies a higher order of abstraction.

Database: The data managed by a database management system. The word is sometimes used more broadly to mean any collection of data.

Database Management System: A software system designed to efficiently store large quantities of structured data in secondary storage, retrieve that data on demand, and control how the data are accessed and shared by possibly many concurrently executing user processes.

Data Computation: A process that is performed on data. The data may be from sources other than the computers performing the computations. (See also **Computations**)

Data Engineering: The analysis and design of information systems based primarily upon data considerations. In other words, the design focuses on making data available, as needed, by the various components that make up the overall system.

Data Independence: The separation of the physical implementation of a data structure in a database management system from the logical view of the data as seen by user processes. This allows changes to be made to the physical implementation without adversely affecting the operation of user processes.

Data Services: Services that make data available to the computational processes within node computers. Data services may be performed either in node computers or the communications network, or both. Where data services should be performed depends on the applications and environments.

Data Transport: The physical movement of data between two points. An example is the movement (or transport) of the symbol string representing a program between two computers.

Degrees of Freedom: Having defined a signal space or communications channel, the number of degrees of freedom that are available for assigning data values within that space. In other words, the number of degrees of freedom that are available for message information. This number may be considerably smaller than the dimensions occupied by a signal. For example, the FM signal transmitted by a radio station occupies a large bandwidth (or channel), and a correspondingly large number of sample points (or dimensions). However, those sample points are not independent. The number of independent sample points (or degrees of freedom) is related to the bandwidth of the audio signal, not the bandwidth of the transmitted signal. The coding scheme shown in Fig. 6.19 is another example. It occupies three dimensions, but there is only one message degree of freedom (i.e., a zero or a one).

Detection: Extracting the data or information from a modulated signal—for example, extracting the audio signal from the actual electromagnetic high frequency signal received from a radio station.

Die: In semiconductors, a term synonymous with the *chip*. An example is a chip that contains an Intel 486 processor.

Digit: A term used almost exclusively to indicate a single value of 0 or 1. Thus a digital communications channel implies a channel that utilizes strings of 0's and 1's.

Digital to Analog Converter: (see **DA Converters**)

Dimensions: The maximum number of independent sample points that can be assigned to an arbitrary signal occupying a specified bandwidth for a specified period of time. The number of dimensions of a baseband signal equals $2TW$, where W is the bandwidth and T the time. For broadband signals the value is $4TW$. (See also **Quadrature Components**)

Dynamic Redundancy: The term implies the dynamic replacement of a faulty component by a spare component.

Economy of Scale: A theory stating large numbers or large equipment are often cheaper (per unit of performance) than small quantities or small equipment. For example, buying 100 units is generally cheaper on a per-unit cost basis than buying a single unit. To a large degree, and except in special cases, the economy of scale once realized in large computers no longer exists.

Entity-Relationship Model: A database design technique in which everything is modeled as things (entities) and the associations (relationships) between them. Both entities and relationships have descriptive properties called attributes. Diagrams in which entities are shown in boxes, and relationships in diamonds with lines to the associated entities, are commonly used for recording the details of a database design.

Entropy: The average information per symbol (or sample point of an analog signal) that can be associated with messages (or computer words) that are constrained to a given set of statistics. As with thermodynamic entropy, the maximum is when the probabilities are independent and equal.

Ethernet: A packet oriented network consisting of a common cable shared by a number of nodes (stations). Various algorithms are used to control conflicts of access and the collisions of packets.

Export: To convert a data file (or database) from one system (or environment) into a format (or structure) that is acceptable to a foreign system, and then exporting (transporting) it to the foreign systems (or environment).

Extended Memory: In IBM compatible 286, 386, and 486 personal computers, the memory above the normal 1 megabyte of memory. In some older mainframe computer systems, a level of memory larger and usually slower than that associated with the CPU.

Factory Control: A computer-based information system designed to control the processes and logistics associated with the real-time operation of a factory.

Fail-Soft System: A system in which the failure of parts of the system do not make the system inoperative. Instead, the system will continue to operate but with reduced capability.

Fault Tolerance: The normal operation of a system despite the failure of components. (Obviously, this will be true for only a limited number of component failures.)

Feature Size: The smallest linear dimension of a lithographic and etched image that can be reliably created on a semiconductor chip. This determines the minimum size of logic and memory elements.

Fiber Optic(s): The use of glass fibers as the transmission media in communications systems. For transmission in such a system, the data are shifted up in frequency to light frequencies, thus explaining the term optics.

Field: A specific area in a computer record or in communications a group of time slots associated with a particular category of data. In communications, a field is generally associated with a particular channel.

Foreign key: Attributes in a relational database in which the primary key values for the tuples of one relation are used in a second relation, so that the tuples in the second relation can refer to the tuples in the first relation. The attributes in the second relation containing primary key values from the first relation are called foreign key attributes.

Foreign System: An information or computer system that has different properties than the local system under consideration. For example, the hardware and software or the standards adhered to may be different.

Fourier Series: The representation of a periodic function as an infinite series of sine and cosine functions.

Frame Relay: A data service that employs a connection-oriented virtual circuit utilizing variable length packets.

Generalized Fourier Series: The representation of a function by an infinite series expansion in terms of orthogonal functions.

Gopher: A menu-driven hierarchical system that makes it easy to access many of the Internet's services.

Grosch's Law: A theory that quadrupling the computational power of a computer only doubles the cost. Historically applied to mainframe computers. Not applicable today. (See also **Economy of Scale**)

Hardwired Connection: A permanent physical connection between components or systems.

Hertz (Hz): A unit of measure equal to one cycle per second. For example, the electric power system in the United States operates at 60 cycles per second, or 60 Hz. The normal metric system units of KHz, MHz, GHz, etc., are used.

Heterogeneous System: A system composed of dissimilar hardware, software, or architecture.

Hierarchical Database: A database organization in which data are organized into record types, and the record types are arranged in a hierarchy to represent the relationships between the record types.

Holding Time: The time that a circuit switched channel is exclusively assigned to a telephone conversation or computer session.

Homogeneous System: A system composed of similar hardware, software, and architecture.

Hybrid Switch: A communications switch that utilizes several switching methods—for example, a switch that utilizes time slot interchange for voice and bus switching for data.

Hypermedia Link: All of the forms of information (e.g., voice, data, pictorial) are linked together providing the user with easy integrated access to all.

Hz: (see **Hertz**)

Import: The importing (transporting) of a data file (or database) from a foreign system, and then converting it into a format (or structure) that is acceptable to the local system (or environment).

In-Band Signaling: Sending network control information in the same channel (path) that is used to convey the message.

Index: A table that maps the value of an attribute to the address of the record (or row in a relation) that contains it.

Information: A higher level of abstraction than raw data (bits) and specifically related to the uncertainty of that abstraction. For a given message (or computer word), i, the information in bits is given by $-\log_2(p_i)$, where (p_i) is the probability of message i. The average information in an infinitely long sequence of messages is given by the expectation taken over all possible messages (i.e., entropy).

Information System: A mechanized information processing system utilizing electronic computer, communications, or control equipment.

Information Theory: A theory associated with the communication and processing of information.

Integrity Control: A functional part of a database system that is responsible for maintaining the semantic constraints on the content of a database. At one extreme, this includes checking that individual data values are of the correct type. At the other extreme, this includes verifying that complex application-specific semantic constraints are maintained when data are entered into the database and updated.

Interface: The term is used to describe a system that makes it possible to connect two components of an information system together in a meaningful fashion. Interfacing involves both hardware and software standards and practices. In this book, emphasis is given to the nonphysical protocols, standards, etc., that are involved.

Internet: The government-sponsored interconnected computer networks that grew out of Arpanet, as well as other interconnected networks.

Inverted File: A file that is indexed on many data attributes.

ISDN: (Integrated Digital Services Network) The communications architecture and set of standards, supported internationally by common carriers and standards organizations, aimed at providing generalized data transport. It is anticipated that the transport capability will be utilized for many different forms of data and communications—for example, both digitized voice and computer data.

ISDN Service: (see **Primary, Basic,** and **Broadband ISDN Service**)

ISO: The International Organization for Standardization.

Join: A set of records formed by merging those records from two sets of records that meet a common stated criteria.

Journal Files: Files that record computer activity and can be used to reconstruct a database in the event of system failure.

Jukebox: A storage device containing many reels of magnetic tape, magnetic cassettes, or optical discs. Upon demand, the individual storage elements are mechanically loaded into a reader attached to a computer.

Key: A data item, or group of data items, used to identify and locate a record. In effect, the individual records in an index file provide a mapping from the elements that identify the desired records to the physical locations of those records.

Knowledge-Based System: An extension of a database system that incorporates additional semantics for the data it manages in the form of constraints and rules. A knowledge-based system typically contains an inference engine to process the rules that it contains to validate the semantic correctness of the database and to derive new data from the database.

Latency: The time between a request for data, or the communication of data, and the start of the actual transfer of data.

For example, the time that it takes to find the correct location on a disk in order to start a data transfer.

Library: A collection of documents, data, pictures, information, etc., that is used in the read-only mode and accessed by a variety of users.

Linear File System: A database organization in which data are organized into record types that are stored sequentially in a file. This is the simplest type of database organization.

Lithography: In semiconductor manufacturing, a printing process that transfers a picture to a chip. The chip image is generally much smaller than the original.

Local Loop: The communications lines between a central office and user network nodes. For example, the wires between the central office and a person's home.

Long Lines: The transmissions facilities (e.g., cables, repeaters, etc.) that provide communications transport between widely separated switching facilities in common carrier networks.

Loosely Coupled Systems: Systems that process data on their own and only exchange final results.

Many-to-Many Relationship: A common type of relationship between two types of data in a database, in which one data item of the first type can be related to many data items of the second type, and one data item of the second type can be related to many data items of the first type.

Mb (Million Bits): A unit of measure having the normal metric system unit extensions of Kb, Gb, Tb, etc.

MB (Million Bytes): A unit of measure having the normal metric system unit extensions of KB, GB, TB, etc.

Mb/s (Million of Megabits per Second): A unit of measure usually associated with a transfer rate or communications channel rate. The normal metric system unit extensions of Kb/s, Gb/s, Tb/s, etc., are used.

MB/s (Million of Megabytes per Second): A unit of measure usually associated with a transfer rate or communications channel rate. The normal metric system unit extensions of KB/s, GB/s, TB/s, etc., are used.

Mediators: (see **Agents**)

Member Record Type: A set type in a network database establishes a one-to-many relationship between two record types, so that a single record of the first record type can be related to many records of the second type. The second (many) type is called the member record type for the set.

Metadata: Data about data; data that transcend the information contained in a given collection of data but are necessary to properly interpret the data.

Modulation: A method by which a signal is transferred to a communications channel—for example, amplitude modulation (AM radio) or frequency modulation (FM radio).

Multiplexing: A method by which individual channels are created and transferred to other channels. An example is time division multiplexing on the bus of a microcomputer.

Multiprocessor System: A system that combines a multiplicity of similar processors into a single computer.

National Network: Generally, all of the interconnected common carriers and their networks.

Navigational Style Query Processing: A form of query processing in which a program is written that traverses a data structure to locate the desired data. The alternative is declarative query processing in which a description of the desired data is written and the database system determines how to locate that data.

Network: A communications system that provides the means by which computers external to the network can effectively and economically exchange data and information. This does not preclude the network from doing more than just the transport of data. A network may include computers for managing the transport of data and providing data services.

Network Database System: A database organization in which data are organized into record types that are organized into a graph or network structure that establishes one-to-many relationships between the record types.

Node: A connection point to, or a port on, a communications network.

Node Computer: A computer that is external to a communications network but connected to the network.

Noncontention Switches: Communications switches in which the signals from different sources do not interfere with each other.

Non-Uniform Memory Access (NUMA): A system in which all memory units are directly accessible by all processors in spite of being physically partitioned across the nodes. Local memory units, however, require less time to access than remote units.

NPL (Natural Language Processing): A system that retrieves information based upon textual analysis.

Object-Oriented Database System: A database organization in which data are organized into object types that are related through an inheritance hierarchy. Objects contain attributes and methods that manipulate the objects. The attribute of one object can reference another object so that complex relationships between objects can be modeled easily.

One-Level Store: A storage system in which the user perceives and interacts with one address space, usually interacting at the level of the fastest memory, when in fact the actual physical memory is spread throughout a hierarchy. Furthermore, the response realized

approaches that of the fastest memory. The concept originated with the Manchester University computer group and the Atlas computer. It is the basis for virtual memories, caches, etc.

One-to-Many Relationship: A common type of relationship between two types of data in a database in which one data item of the first type can be related to many data items of the second type. For example, a tree data structure is composed of one-to-many relationships between parent and child nodes in the tree.

Open Architecture: An architecture that permits foreign systems to interact in a meaningful way.

Open System: An environment that permits foreign systems to interact in a meaningful way.

Open System Interconnection (OSI) Reference Model: A specific seven-layer model whose protocols interface with different computers and information systems.

Open World: An environment that permits foreign systems to interact in a meaningful way.

Orthonormal Set: A set of functions in which the individual members are orthogonal to each other. Orthogonal implies that the integral over the function space of the product of two different members of the set is zero. Over the same space, the integral of the square of a member of the set is 1.

OSI Model: (see **Open System Interconnection Reference Model**)

Out-of-Band Signaling: A network in which the control information is sent over a different channel than the message information.

Owner Record Type: A set type in a network database establishes a one-to-many relationship between two record types, so that a single record of the first record type can be related to many records of the second type. The first (one) type is called the owner record type for the set type.

PABX (Private Branch Exchange): A privately owned switch for voice, or data, or both. For example, a university may have a voice data PABX that provides telephone and some data communication services on the campus.

Packet: A short segment of a longer message.

Packet Switching: A switching system in which originally a destination address was added to each packet and the packets were individually routed through a network. Also refers to Ethernet, which is a contention packet switched system in which packets are resent if interfered with. A virtual packet switched network assigns a common routing to all packets of a message.

Page: A subdivision of a computer file. (See also **Page Box**)

Page Box: A hardware associative memory that maps the higher order bits in a virtual address to a physical address in high-speed memory. The higher order bits define a page consisting of all of the words that contain those bits in their address. The page box concept had its origins in the one-level store of the Atlas Computer.

Paradigm: A set of assumptions, or a model, relevant to processes and beliefs.

PBX: (see **PABX**)

Peer-to-Peer System: A computer system in which, from a control standpoint, the individual computers are equivalent.

Primary ISDN Service: A common carrier communications service that provides on one telephone line (or its equivalent) 23 digitized channels of 64 Kb/s and one channel of 64 Kb/s. The use of the 23 64 Kb/s channels is at the customer's discretion and they can be combined, for example, into one wideband channel. The single 64Kb/s channel is used for network control. This ser-

vice is generally described as 23B + D. The European standard is 30B + D. In both cases, B is a customer digitized channel and D is a network control or signaling channel.

Primary Key: A subset of the fields (attributes) in a data record (tuple) whose values uniquely identify that record (tuple). The primary key is commonly used to build indices to allow data to be located more quickly, given the primary key value.

Projection: In a relational database, a new relation that is created by removing from the original relation all columns that are not given as projection parameters.

Propagation Delays: Delays due to the time that it takes for a signal to pass through the propagation media—for example, the time that it takes a signal to pass from a ground station to a communications satellite.

Protocol: A set of rules for establishing effective communications.

Quadrature Components: The two components of any broadband signal. The first represents a baseband signal modulated on a sine wave carrier at the center frequency of the band; the second represents a baseband signal modulated on a cosine carrier.

Quadrature Detection: Detection that separates the quadrature components of a broadband signal. (See also **Quadrature Components**)

Quantization: A representation of the amplitude of a sample point of an analog signal by that value of a predetermined set of values that is closest to the amplitude. This usually means replacing the analog value by a binary string whose length determines the number of values in the predetermined set.

Quantization Noise: The difference between the original and quantized signal. This corresponds to the round-off error in a binary representation.

Query: A request to retrieve or modify data in a database. Every database system uses some language in which queries are expressed. One such language is SQL.

RAID (Redundant Arrays of Inexpensive Disks): A bank of on line hard disks connected in a sophisticated way to increase the total storage, transfer rate, and reliability, and at the same time reduce the access time.

RAM (Random Access Memory): Utilizing solely electronic circuits, a byte (word) can be directly retrieved from (written into) a physical location in memory. The access times to randomly selected physical locations are equal. This distinguishes RAM from memory systems such as disks in which the access time is a function of physical location.

Raster: A process that generates a picture line by line as in a normal television set. In other words, the picture is painted one horizontal line at a time.

Redundancy: That portion of a message (or computer file) that is dependent (perhaps statistically) upon the remainder of the message and therefore contains no information. With proper coding, the message can be compressed and the redundancy removed.

Relation: A table of data in a relational database. The rows of the table are called *tuples* and the columns are called *attributes.* Some subset of the attributes form the primary key for the relation.

Relational Database System: A database organization in which data are organized into record types and each record type is stored as a table called a *relation.*

Remote Switching Partition: The switching mechanism in a switch is partitioned and part of it moved to a remote point. The control is retained at the main switch.

Remote Concentrators: Equipment that combines a number of user communications channels into a broader bandwidth channel, so that they can be sent to a remote site for switching. In like fashion, the equipment can be used in the reverse direction from switch to user.

Repeater: A device that reduces the effect of noise in the communications channel; the signal is requantized prior to transmitting it to the next relay station.

Sampling Theorem: The theorem that establishes that a bandlimited baseband signal can be represented by sample values spaced at intervals of 1/(twice the bandwidth).

Scale: The number of components, size, or alternatives of a system. In a sense, the term relates to complexity, which often grows much more rapidly than the size of a system. If the size is increased by a factor n, and the complexity increases exponentially with n, it is said that the system does not scale with size. On the other hand, an increase of complexity of n would usually be acceptable. Another way of viewing it is that if all or a significant number of possible permutations and combinations must be dealt with, a system will not scale with size.

Schema: The description of a particular database, including the names and types of the individual data items, how these data items are organized into data structures, how these data structures are mapped to physical storage, and how the users view and manipulate the data structures.

Schema Evolution: The process of change that the contents and structures in the database must undergo to meet the new requirements.

Semantic Model: A model for data that attempts to capture the semantic meaning of the data with various language constraints.

Set Type: The creation of a one-to-many relationship between two record types in a network database. A set type is usually implemented as a linked list, in which the header of the list is a record from the first record type (called the owner record type), and the remaining nodes in the list are records from the second record type (called the member record type).

Setup Time: The time that it takes to establish a channel (or path) through a switch or a communications network.

Shannon Capacity Theorem: (see **Capacity Theorem**)

Shared Memory Paradigm: The sharing that occurs among all nodes in a computer system.

SIGMOD (Special Interest Group on Management of Data): An ACM group of researchers and practitioners interested in general issues of database and knowledge based systems.

Signal: A function of time representing data or information. An example is speech.

Signaling: In the communications industry, the data used to control a network. An example is Signaling System 7, the control system used in ISDN networks and much of today's national and international networks.

Signal Processing: The technology of processing signals.

Signals Around Origin: Functions of time that are confined to a symmetrical frequency region around zero frequency.

Signature File Processing: A procedure that represents a document by a document signature, a fixed length string of ones and zeros, one bit for each keyword in the document.

Societal Systems: Information systems that serve society broadly, as distinct from those in the scientific area. Examples of societal systems are found in education, business, government, entertainment, and the legal system.

Source-Path Routing: A process during which a message route is generated at the source node and each node along the path parses its portion of the route.

SQL: A query language for relational database systems that is a national and international standard. Queries in SQL have the general form: SELECT [attribute names] FROM [relation names] WHERE [predicate]. The result of the query includes the attribute values for the attributes in the SELECT clause from tuples in the relations listed in the FROM clause that satisfy the predicate in the WHERE clause.

Static Redundancy: In database management systems, the introduction of permanent, redundant components to mask out possible failures—e.g., triple modular redundancy.

Strong Consistency: Rigid, lock-step, synchronized execution of all executing sites within a distributed computing architecture.

Switch: This term is used in two senses. First, in earlier chapters, it refers to the elements that make up a logical circuit. More commonly, it is used to refer to the specialized electronic circuits and computers that switch communications channels. In other words, in the latter case, the switch establishes a path between two of its ports over which data can be sent.

Switching Partition: The actual mechanism that does the switching can be partitioned into parts. Those parts are referred to as switching partitions. (See also **Switch; Remote Switching Partition**)

Synchronous: Synchronization in time is implied. The term is used in several senses. It is used in discussing frequency division multiplexing and switching to indicate the necessity of keeping time slots synchronized. It is later used in referring to multiplexing channels to higher frequencies and applicable detection systems. Lastly, it is used in the discussion of keeping energy from one communications channel out of other channels. The maintenance of synchronized timing is important in all these cases, although accuracy requirements vary widely with the application.

Synchronous Detection: Detection that requires time synchronization of the detector with the received signal (usually the carrier of the received signal).

Syntactic Model: A model based upon syntax.

Tightly Coupled Systems: Computer systems that interact at a detailed internal level with each other. In other words, their internal processes can interact.

Time Slot: In this book the term is synonymous with a sample time of an analog signal, or a digit in a binary sequence.

Time Slot Interchange: A particular method of switching. The value of a sample of an incoming message is stored in memory and placed on the required outgoing line (or channel) at an appropriate time.

Traffic: The number of messages passing through a communications network, or the associated message statistics.

Transaction: A logical sequence of queries or operations that perform some logical function against a database. Since transactions represent semantically complete operations, they are used for both concurrency control and for backup and recovery.

Transfer Rate: The rate at which bits or bytes are transferred between two points.

Transparency: The concept is that users see only their local environment, although in fact they have access to an entire distributed system. Their access is in terms of what they are accustomed to in their local environment. The fact that they may be remotely performing operations in other environments is transparent to them. (See also **Open Systems** and **Open World**)

Transport: To physically move or transport bit streams or messages.

Trunk: A communications channel between switching centers that is shared by a number of user channels or access lines.

Tuple: A row of a relation in a relational database.

Twisted Pair: A pair of relatively small insulated wires that are twisted around each other to minimize inductive effects and interference (with other wires). Twisted pair are widely used in the telephone industry.

Two-Phase Locking: A technique used in many commercial database systems to implement concurrency control. The technique requires that a user process obtain a lock on any data item that it is about to read or write. If all concurrently executing user processes operate in two phases, where the first phase obtains needed locks and the second phase releases those locks, it can be shown that the final state of the database is equivalent to the state that would have been achieved if the user processes executed one at a time in some order.

Type: A category of a variable that is determined by the type of data stored in it.

Uncertainty Principle: The theory that the product of the "uncertainty in time" and the "uncertainty in bandwidth" is approximately 1.

Uniform Memory Access (UMA): A system in which all memory is centrally located and is equidistant in terms of access.

View: A logical subset of a database tailored to the requirements of a particular user or group of users. The view may omit some data, combine data in different ways, or even do simple changes of type for data items. Views are particularly important in relational database systems to both simplify the use of the database as well as provide a form of access control.

Virtual Circuits: Communications circuits and paths that share physical resources. As long as virtual circuits do not statistically compete for a shared resource, performance can appear to the user to be that of circuit switching. The concept implies that once established the paths are fixed for the duration of the call or session.

Virtual Memory: To the user, a memory address space that may in size far exceed that of physical memory. It may even exceed that physical address space of the lowest level of memory in a memory hierarchy, or of memory attached to a network. The mapping from virtual address space to physical address space is the responsibility of the operating, file, and communications systems that are involved. (See also **One-Level Store**)

Weak Consistency: Collective agreement at predetermined execution points within a computation that crosses multiple sites within a distributed computing architecture.

World Wide Web: An information retrieval system available on the Internet. It is a hypertext oriented system with hierarchical links to related data.

Index